Scheduling Theory and Algorithms for Sustainable Manufacturing

Scheduling Theory and Algorithms for Sustainable Manufacturing

Guest Editors

Alexandre Dolgui
David Lemoine
María I. Restrepo
Frank Werner

Basel • Beijing • Wuhan • Barcelona • Belgrade • Novi Sad • Cluj • Manchester

Guest Editors

Alexandre Dolgui
Department of Automation,
Production and
Computer Sciences
IMT Atlantique, LS2N-CNRS
Nantes
France

David Lemoine
Department of Automation,
Production and
Computer Sciences
IMT Atlantique
Nantes
France

María I. Restrepo
Department of Automation,
Production and
Computer Sciences
IMT Atlantique
Nantes
France

Frank Werner
Faculty of Mathematics
Otto-von-Guericke University
Magdeburg
Germany

Editorial Office
MDPI AG
Grosspeteranlage 5
4052 Basel, Switzerland

This is a reprint of the Special Issue, published open access by the journal *Algorithms* (ISSN 1999-4893), freely accessible at: www.mdpi.com/journal/algorithms/special_issues/7C92M715OY.

For citation purposes, cite each article independently as indicated on the article page online and using the guide below:

Lastname, A.A.; Lastname, B.B. Article Title. *Journal Name* **Year**, *Volume Number*, Page Range.

ISBN 978-3-7258-3164-7 (Hbk)
ISBN 978-3-7258-3163-0 (PDF)
https://doi.org/10.3390/books978-3-7258-3163-0

© 2025 by the authors. Articles in this book are Open Access and distributed under the Creative Commons Attribution (CC BY) license. The book as a whole is distributed by MDPI under the terms and conditions of the Creative Commons Attribution-NonCommercial-NoDerivs (CC BY-NC-ND) license (https://creativecommons.org/licenses/by-nc-nd/4.0/).

Contents

About the Editors vii

Preface ix

Alexandre Dolgui, David Lemoine, María I. Restrepo and Frank Werner
Special Issue on Scheduling Theory and Algorithms for Sustainable Manufacturing
Reprinted from: *Algorithms* **2025**, *18*, 15, https://doi.org/10.3390/a18010015 1

Vladimir Modrak, Ranjitharamasamy Sudhakarapandian, Arunmozhi Balamurugan and Zuzana Soltysova
A Review on Reinforcement Learning in Production Scheduling: An Inferential Perspective
Reprinted from: *Algorithms* **2024**, *17*, 343, https://doi.org/10.3390/a17080343 5

Yong Han Kim, Wei Ye, Ritbik Kumar, Finn Bail, Julia Dvorak and Yanchao Tan et al.
Unlocking the Potential of Remanufacturing Through Machine Learning and Data-Driven Models—A Survey
Reprinted from: *Algorithms* **2024**, *17*, 562, https://doi.org/10.3390/a17120562 28

Patricio Sáez, Carlos Herrera and Victor Parada
Reducing Nervousness in Master Production Planning: A Systematic Approach Incorporating Product-Driven Strategies
Reprinted from: *Algorithms* **2023**, *16*, 386, https://doi.org/10.3390/a16080386 54

Manli Dai and Zhongyi Jiang
Multiprocessor Fair Scheduling Based on an Improved Slime Mold Algorithm
Reprinted from: *Algorithms* **2023**, *16*, 473, https://doi.org/10.3390/a16100473 70

Khwansiri Ninpan, Shuzhang Huang, Francesco Vitillo, Mohamad Ali Assaad, Lies Benmiloud Bechet and Robert Plana
Mitigating Co-Activity Conflicts and Resource Overallocation in Construction Projects: A Modular Heuristic Scheduling Approach with Primavera P6 EPPM Integration
Reprinted from: *Algorithms* **2024**, *17*, 230, https://doi.org/10.3390/a17060230 85

João A. M. Santos, Miguel S. E. Martins, Rui M. Pinto and Susana M. Vieira
Towards Sustainable Inventory Management: A Many-Objective Approach to Stock Optimization in Multi-Storage Supply Chains
Reprinted from: *Algorithms* **2024**, *17*, 271, https://doi.org/10.3390/a17060271 96

Guilherme Zanlorenzi, Anderson Luis Szejka and Osiris Canciglieri Junior
Multi-Criteria Decision Support System for Automatically Selecting Photovoltaic Sets to Maximise Micro Solar Generation
Reprinted from: *Algorithms* **2024**, *17*, 274, https://doi.org/10.3390/a17070274 117

Vladimir Kats and Eugene Levner
Maximizing the Average Environmental Benefit of a Fleet of Drones under a Periodic Schedule of Tasks
Reprinted from: *Algorithms* **2024**, *17*, 283, https://doi.org/10.3390/a17070283 137

Luis Tarazona-Torres, Ciro Amaya, Alvaro Paipilla, Camilo Gomez and David Alvarez-Martinez
The Parallel Machine Scheduling Problem with Different Speeds and Release Times in the Ore Hauling Operation
Reprinted from: *Algorithms* **2024**, *17*, 348, https://doi.org/10.3390/a17080348 156

Yumin He, Alexandre Dolgui and Milton Smith
An Algorithm for Part Input Sequencing of Flexible Manufacturing Systems with Machine Disruption
Reprinted from: *Algorithms* **2024**, *17*, 470, https://doi.org/10.3390/a17100470 . . . . **174**

Oludolapo Akanni Olanrewaju, Fabio Luiz Peres Krykhtine and Felix Mora-Camino
Minimum-Energy Scheduling of Flexible Job-Shop Through Optimization and Comprehensive Heuristic
Reprinted from: *Algorithms* **2024**, *17*, 520, https://doi.org/10.3390/a17110520 . . . . **186**

About the Editors

Alexandre Dolgui

Alexandre Dolgui studied automated systems for information processing and management from 1978 to 1983 at the Minsk Radioengineering Institute (Belarus) and graduated with a distinction. He received a Ph.D. degree in Engineering Cybernetics and Production System Management in 1990 from the Engineering Cybernetics Institute of the National Academy of Sciences of Belarus and defended his habilitation thesis in 2000 from the Technological University of Compiègne, France. He is an IISE Fellow, Distinguished Professor, and the Head of the Automation, Production and Computer Sciences Department at the IMT Atlantique, Nantes campus, France. His research focuses on manufacturing line designs, production planning, and supply chain optimization. His main results are based on exact mathematical programming methods and their intelligent coupling with heuristics and metaheuristics algorithms, robust optimization, and risk and resilience analysis. He is the co-author of 5 books, the co-editor of 32 books or conference proceedings, and the author of over 335 peer-reviewed journal papers. He is an Area Editor of *Computers & Industrial Engineering*, past Associate Editor of the *International Journal of Systems Science*, *IEEE Transactions on Industrial Informatics*, and *Omega*. He is a Member of the Editorial Board of 24 journals, including the *International Journal of Production Economics*. He is an Active Fellow of the European Academy for Industrial Management, Member of the Board of the International Foundation for Production Research, former Chair of IFAC TC 5.2 Manufacturing Modelling for Management and Control (2011–2017, and is currently a vice-chair), and Member of IFIP WG 5.7 Advances in Production Management Systems, IEEE System Council Analytics and Risk Technical Committee. He has received several scientific awards and recognitions for his outstanding achievements. He is the Editor-in-Chief of the *International Journal of Production Research (IJPR)*.

David Lemoine

David Lemoine is a full professor at IMT Atlantique, Nantes campus, France, in the Automation, Production, and Computer Sciences department and is a member of the Modelis team from the LS2N French laboratory (UMR CNRS 6004). He received a Ph.D. in Computer Science (2008) from Blaise Pascal University (France) and defended his habilitation thesis (2020) at Nantes University (France). His research focuses on decision-making integration in production planning (Lot-sizing models), particularly by incorporating financial criteria and considering maintenance decisions to enhance the robustness of production plans. He co-leads the transversal theme "Industry and Enterprise of the Future" within the LS2N laboratory and the ORIGIN Working Group, which is shared between two CNRS Research Groups. He also chaired the organizing committee of MIM 2022 on management and control in the era of Industry 4.0., as well as the APMS 2021 conference on Artificial Intelligence for Sustainable and Resilient Production Systems.

María I. Restrepo

Maria Isabel Restrepo is an Associate Professor in the Department of Automation, Production and Computer Science at IMT Atlantique, Nantes campus, France. Her current research interests are the use of decomposition methods to solve scheduling and routing problems under uncertainty and preferences. She was awarded French national Young Researcher funding (ANR JCJC) for the project "HOPES: Home service operations planning with employees' preferences and uncertainty" (2022–2026).

She received an MSc degree in Industrial Engineering (2010) from Universidad de los Andes (Colombia) and a PhD degree in Applied Mathematics (2015) from École Polytechnique Montréal (Canada). Before her current job, she was an Assistant Professor at Université Catholique de l'Ouest and a Postdoctoral Researcher at the Interuniversity Research Centre on Enterprise Networks, Logistics and Transportation (CIRRELT), and at the National Institute for Research in Digital Science and Technology (INRIA).

Frank Werner

Frank Werner studied mathematics from 1975 to 1980 and graduated from the Technical University of Magdeburg (Germany) with distinction. He received a Ph.D. degree (with summa cum laude) in Mathematics in 1984 and defended his habilitation thesis in 1989. From this time on, he worked at the Faculty of Mathematics at the Otto-von-Guericke University Magdeburg in Germany, and since 1998, has has been an Extraordinary Professor. In 1992, he received a grant from the Alexander von Humboldt Foundation. He has been a manager of several research projects supported by the German Research Society (DFG) and the European Union (INTAS). Since 2019, he has been the Editor-in-Chief of the journal *Algorithms*. He is also an Associate Editor of *The International Journal of Production Research* (since 2012) and *The Journal of Scheduling* (since 2014), as well a member of the Editorial/Advisory boards of 19 other international journals. He has been a Guest Editor of Special Issues in ten international journals and has served as a member of the Program committee of more than 160 international conferences. Frank Werner is an author/editor of 17 books, including the textbooks *Mathematics of Economics and Business* and *A Refresher Course in Mathematics*. In addition, he has co-edited four proceedings volumes of the SIMULTECH conferences and published more than 300 journal and conference papers, including in *The International Journal of Production Research, Computers & Operations Research, The Journal of Scheduling, Applied Mathematical Modelling*, and *The European Journal of Operational Research*. He has received Best Paper Awards from *The International Journal of Production Research* (2016) and *IISE Transactions* (2021). His main research subjects are scheduling, discrete optimization, graph theory, and mathematical problems in operations research.

Preface

This is the printed edition of a Special Issue that was published in the journal *Algorithms*. The Special Issue is based on selected best papers at the IFAC conference MIM 2022 in the track on planning and scheduling in relation to sustainability and resilience issues. In addition to the Editorial, this reprint contains eleven research papers focusing on optimization models and algorithms of production systems from sustainability and resilience perspectives. Among the subjects addressed in this reprint, one can mention advanced models and algorithms to optimize energy consumption, environmental benefits, and resilience; demonstrations of how to reduce the cost of installing photovoltaic systems; and investigations of how to organize sustainable inventory management.

Finally, we extend our gratitude to all the people who have contributed to the success of this Special Issue, including, but not limited to, the authors from nine different countries, numerous reviewers from all over the world, and the staff of *Algorithms*. We hope that the readers of this Special Issue find many stimulating ideas for their own future research in this challenging field of scheduling and planning algorithms in relation to sustainable manufacturing, which plays an important role in daily life.

Alexandre Dolgui, David Lemoine, María I. Restrepo, and Frank Werner
Guest Editors

Editorial

Special Issue on Scheduling Theory and Algorithms for Sustainable Manufacturing

Alexandre Dolgui [1,*], David Lemoine [1], María I. Restrepo [1] and Frank Werner [2]

[1] IMT Atlantique, LS2N-CNRS, 44307 Nantes, France; david.lemoine@imt-atlantique.fr (D.L.); maria-isabel.restrepo-ruiz@imt-atlantique.fr (M.I.R.)
[2] Faculty of Mathematics, Otto-von-Guericke-University, 309106 Magdeburg, Germany; frank.werner@mathematik.uni-magdeburg.de
* Correspondence: alexandre.dolgui@imt-atlantique.fr

Received: 24 December 2024
Accepted: 24 December 2024
Published: 3 January 2025

Citation: Dolgui, A.; Lemoine, D.; Restrepo, M.I.; Werner, F. Special Issue on Scheduling Theory and Algorithms for Sustainable Manufacturing. *Algorithms* **2025**, *18*, 15. https://doi.org/10.3390/a18010015

Copyright: © 2025 by the authors. Licensee MDPI, Basel, Switzerland. This article is an open access article distributed under the terms and conditions of the Creative Commons Attribution (CC BY) license (https://creativecommons.org/licenses/by/4.0/).

The following Special Issue was initiated at the 10th IFAC triennial conference MIM 2022 (https://hub.imt-atlantique.fr/mim2022/ accessed on 24 December 2024) on Manufacturing Modelling, Management and Control, held in Nantes, France. The authors of the most outstanding papers on the topics of decision aid, combinatorial optimization, and scheduling from the corresponding sessions of the conference were invited to submit extended versions to the present Special Issue. A special focus was placed on how the scheduling theory and algorithms can help to solve complex combinatorial optimization problems in manufacturing from sustainability and related perspectives.

Following their presentation at the conference and selection by the session chairs and members of the program committee, as mentioned above, a select group of authors were invited to submit an extended and improved version of their work to this Special Issue. However, the Special Issue was also open to papers that were not presented at the conference if they fell within the scope of the issue and were in relation or complementary to the papers selected at the conference.

The motivation of this Special Issue was to present state-of-the art mathematical models and algorithms providing efficient solutions for practical planning and scheduling issues in digital, sustainable, and human-centric manufacturing and logistics [1]. At present, the production and logistics systems for goods and services are faced with both production cost optimization and scarcity of resources, including energy [2]; such systems are becoming increasingly digitalized [3]. Scheduling and algorithms play a central role and offer the possibility to reduce production waste, manage efficiently, and limit the consumption of material resources and energy [4].

An increasing number of scholars are focussing their efforts on applying sustainability criteria when solving planning and scheduling problems in modern digital production environments [5,6]. Artificial intelligence techniques are often used, taking into account a large amount of available data and the complexity of the problem that needs to be solved. To address this issue, multi-objective optimization approaches have been developed.

The majority of studies on the planning and scheduling of production systems and their logistics from sustainability perspectives focus on economic issues and the minimization of electricity consumption and/or carbon emissions. These factors represent the economic and environmental parts of sustainability. Some researchers also integrate social responsibility issues into their work [6].

Various models and algorithms have been developed for planning and scheduling sustainable production systems, with various parameters, objective functions, constraints, model types, and optimization methods employed. Energy consumption and greenhouse gas emissions are the most studied factors of sustainability in the current planning and scheduling approaches [7].

The objective of this Special Issue was to complement the existing literature with the most recent research findings and to extend the scope of possible applications and techniques used in the planning and scheduling of production systems and logistics in the digital and AI era.

After a rigorous peer review process in accordance with the high standards of the journal, the following two reviews and nine research papers were selected for publication in this Special Issue:

"A Review on Reinforcement Learning in Production Scheduling: An Inferential Perspective" by Vladimir Modrak, Ranjitharamasamy Sudhakarapandian, Arunmozhi Balamurugan, and Zuzana Soltysova presents a systematic review of production scheduling based on reinforcement learning techniques covering the period between 1996 and 2024. This review provides new insights into the use of reinforcement learning in production scheduling and outlines future challenges to be addressed by practitioners and members of the academic community.

In the review "Unlocking the Potential of Remanufacturing Through Machine Learning and Data-Driven Models—A Survey" by Yong Han Kim, Wei Ye, Ritbik Kumar, Finn Bail, Julia Dvorak, Yanchao Tan, Marvin Carl May, Qing Chang, Ragu Athinarayanan, Gisela Lanza, John W. Sutherland, Xingyu Li and Chandra Nath, the authors examine the integration of artificial intelligence and data-driven and machine learning technologies into remanufacturing processes to improve both operational efficiency and sustainability. A comprehensive review of existing knowledge and algorithms is presented and the possibilities to use these techniques in the circular economy are discussed.

"Reducing Nervousness in Master Production Planning: A Systematic Approach Incorporating Product-Driven Strategies", presented by Patricio Sáez, Carlos Herrera, and Victor Parada, addresses the widely recognized issue of nervousness in master production schedules. Taking into account variations in demand, production schedules change and create instability in the system. The findings presented in this article suggest a product-driven system to complement master production scheduling techniques with intelligent agents to reduce nervousness without significantly increasing production costs.

Manli Dai and Zhongyi Jiang, in their article "Multiprocessor Fair Scheduling Based on an Improved Slime Mold Algorithm", propose an improvement to the "Slime Mold Algorithm" optimization method along three axes: the definition of a better initial population (based on reverse learning of Bernoulli mapping), an improved mutation strategy, and an optimized boundary-check mechanism. This enhancement allows for faster convergence of the algorithm. Experiments on test functions are conducted to demonstrate the performance and robustness of the approach, which is then applied to the multiprocessor fair scheduling problem to reduce the average execution time on each processor.

In the article "Mitigating Co-Activity Conflicts and Resource Overallocation in Construction Projects: A Modular Heuristic Scheduling Approach with Primavera P6 EPPM Integration" by Khwansiri Ninpan, Shuzhang Huang, Francesco Vitillo, Mohamad Ali Assaad, Lies Benmiloud Bechet and Robert Plana, a heuristic approach for managing complex construction projects is presented, integrating Primavera P6 EPPM and Synchro 4D. The approach enables proactive conflict detection and the resolution of spatial conflicts during concurrent tasks, in addition to resource verification prior to task initiation, thereby ensuring the generation of feasible and conflict-free construction schedules. This approach integrates seamlessly with existing industry tools.

In the article "Towards Sustainable Inventory Management: A Many-Objective Approach to Stock Optimization in Multi-Storage Supply Chains" by João A. M. Santos, Miguel

S. E. Martins, Rui M. Pinto, and Susana M. Vieira, the authors consider the issue of sustainable supply chain management consisting of the optimization of inventory levels in storage facilities, minimizing holding costs, energy consumption, and shortage risk concurrently and thus integrating sustainability considerations into inventory management.

The next article, "Multi-Criteria Decision Support System for Automatically Selecting Photovoltaic Sets to Maximise Micro Solar Generation", by Guilherme Zanlorenzi, Anderson Luis Szejka, and Osiris Canciglieri Junior takes into account technological advancements that have made solar energy more accessible. The authors propose a multi-criteria decision support system to select the most suitable photovoltaic systems for microgrids, using the AHP and TOPSIS methods. When tested in real-world conditions, the system provided solutions with efficient yields and high internal rates of return. The authors of this article establish a methodological framework and a practical decision tool to enhance the feasibility of solar projects and improve their accessibility.

Vladimir Kats and Eugene Levner, in their article "Maximizing the Average Environmental Benefit of a Fleet of Drones under a Periodic Schedule of Tasks", present a new, environmentally oriented problem aimed at determining the optimal number of vehicles that maximizes the average profit of a fleet of drones. The authors model the problem as an infinite periodic graph and reduce it to a special type of parametric assignment problem. They develop a method that allows the problem to be solved to optimality for larger fleets of drones than any previously known exact algorithm.

In the article "The Parallel Machine Scheduling Problem with Different Speeds and Release Times in the Ore Hauling Operation" by Luis Tarazona-Torres, Ciro Amaya, Alvaro Paipilla, Camilo Gomez, and David Alvarez-Martinez, the authors present an approach to determine the minimum amount of hauling equipment required to meet an ore transport target. The authors model the problem as a parallel machine scheduling problem with different speeds and release times, with the objective of minimizing both the completion time and the costs associated with the equipment used. The approach helps decision-makers ensure that loading and hauling equipment are utilized to their fullest potential while adhering to budgetary constraints and operational schedules.

Yumin He, Alexandre Dolgui, and Milton Smith in their article "An Algorithm for Part Input Sequencing of Flexible Manufacturing Systems with Machine Disruption" explore the management of disruptions in flexible manufacturing systems (FMSs), with a particular emphasis on part input sequencing. Disruptions, such as machine breakdowns, are unpredictable and can significantly impact supply chains and production processes. An efficient algorithm is proposed to make part input sequencing in an FMS under machine failure conditions and is subsequently tested through simulations. Lastly, managerial implications and further research directions are provided.

In the paper "Minimum-Energy Scheduling of Flexible Job-Shop Through Optimization and Comprehensive Heuristic" by Oludolapo Akanni Olanrewaju, Fabio Luiz Peres Krykhtine, and Felix Mora-Camino, the authors consider a flexible job-shop scheduling problem in high energy-consuming flexible production plants. The primary objective of the study is to generate energy-efficient schedules with acceptable production delays for each job. The authors develop an ad hoc heuristic as the computational complexity of the problem increases with the requirement to generate efficient schedules in a dynamic environment.

It is our hope that this carefully curated selection of papers will be of interest to readers of the journal *Algorithms* and useful for all members of our community.

Conflicts of Interest: The guest editors declare no conflict of interest.

References

1. Luo, D.; Thevenin, S.; Dolgui, A. A state-of-the-art on production planning in Industry 4.0. *Int. J. Prod. Res.* **2022**, *61*, 6602–6632. [CrossRef]
2. Dolgui, A.; Ivanov, D.; Brintrup, A.; Chen, W.; Shen (Jerry), B.; Paul, S.K. Design and management of energy-efficient and energy-resilient supply chains. *Int. J. Prod. Res.* **2024**, *62*, 8921–8923. [CrossRef]
3. Tiwari, M.K.; Bidanda, B.; Geunes, J.; Fernandes, K.; Dolgui, A. Supply chain digitisation and management. *Int. J. Prod. Res.* **2024**, *62*, 2918–2926. [CrossRef]
4. Wen, X.; Sun, Y.; Ma, H.L.; Chung, S.H. Green smart manufacturing: Energy-efficient robotic job shop scheduling models. *Int. J. Prod. Res.* **2022**, *61*, 5791–5805. [CrossRef]
5. Akbar, M.; Irohara, T. Scheduling for sustainable manufacturing: A review. *J. Clean. Prod.* **2018**, *205*, 866–883. [CrossRef]
6. Zhang, C.; Juraschek, M.; Herrmann, C. Deep reinforcement learning-based dynamic scheduling for resilient and sustainable manufacturing: A systematic review. *J. Manuf. Syst.* **2024**, *77*, 962–989. [CrossRef]
7. Jabeur, M.H.; Mahjoub, S.; Toublanc, C.; Cariou, V. Optimizing integrated lot sizing and production scheduling in flexible flow line systems with energy scheme: A two level approach based on reinforcement learning. *Comput. Ind. Eng.* **2024**, *190*, 110095. [CrossRef]

Disclaimer/Publisher's Note: The statements, opinions and data contained in all publications are solely those of the individual author(s) and contributor(s) and not of MDPI and/or the editor(s). MDPI and/or the editor(s) disclaim responsibility for any injury to people or property resulting from any ideas, methods, instructions or products referred to in the content.

Review

A Review on Reinforcement Learning in Production Scheduling: An Inferential Perspective

Vladimir Modrak [1,*], Ranjitharamasamy Sudhakarapandian [2], Arunmozhi Balamurugan [2] and Zuzana Soltysova [1]

[1] Faculty of Manufacturing Technologies, Technical University of Kosice, 080 01 Prešov, Slovakia; zuzana.soltysova@tuke.sk
[2] School of Mechanical Engineering, Vellore Institute of Technology, Vellore 632014, Tamil Nadu, India; sudhakarapandian.r@vit.ac.in (R.S.); arunmozhi.b@vit.ac.in (A.B.)
* Correspondence: vladimir.modrak@tuke.sk

Abstract: In this study, a systematic review on production scheduling based on reinforcement learning (RL) techniques using especially bibliometric analysis has been carried out. The aim of this work is, among other things, to point out the growing interest in this domain and to outline the influence of RL as a type of machine learning on production scheduling. To achieve this, the paper explores production scheduling using RL by investigating the descriptive metadata of pertinent publications contained in Scopus, ScienceDirect, and Google Scholar databases. The study focuses on a wide spectrum of publications spanning the years between 1996 and 2024. The findings of this study can serve as new insights for future research endeavors in the realm of production scheduling using RL techniques.

Keywords: bibliometric analysis; production scheduling; reinforcement learning

Citation: Modrak, V.; Sudhakarapandian, R.; Balamurugan, A.; Soltysova, Z. A Review on Reinforcement Learning in Production Scheduling: An Inferential Perspective. *Algorithms* **2024**, *17*, 343.
https://doi.org/10.3390/a17080343

Academic Editors: Alexandre Dolgui, David Lemoine, María I. Restrepo and Frank Werner

Received: 6 June 2024
Revised: 28 July 2024
Accepted: 2 August 2024
Published: 7 August 2024

Copyright: © 2024 by the authors. Licensee MDPI, Basel, Switzerland. This article is an open access article distributed under the terms and conditions of the Creative Commons Attribution (CC BY) license (https://creativecommons.org/licenses/by/4.0/).

1. Introduction

Production scheduling is considered as one of the most critical elements of manufacturing management in aligning production activities with business objectives, in ensuring a smooth flow of goods resources, and in supporting company's ability to remain competitive in the marketplace. Scheduling algorithms play an important role in enhancing production efficiency and effectiveness, and therefore have long been a subject of extensive research in various interdisciplinary domains, such as industrial engineering, automation, and management science [1]. The production scheduling tasks can be solved using three main types of step-by-step procedures such as exact algorithms, heuristic algorithms, and meta-heuristic algorithms [2,3]. Although an exact algorithm can theoretically guarantee the optimum solution, the NP-hardness of major problems makes them impossible to address effectively and efficiently [4]. Heuristics use a set of rules to create scheduling solutions quickly and effectively without consideration of global optimization. Furthermore, the creation of rules is heavily reliant on a thorough comprehension of the particulars of the situation [5–8]. Whereas meta-heuristics can produce good scheduling solutions in a reasonable amount of computing time, the way search operators create them significantly depends on the specific situation at hand [9–13]. In addition, the iterative search process poses challenges in terms of time consumption and applicability in real-time scenarios when dealing with large-scale problems. Scheduling approaches based on reinforcement learning (RL) have proven to be a useful tool in this regard. Reinforcement learning is a subfield within the broader domain of machine learning. RL is considered one of the most perspective approaches for robust cooperative scheduling, which allows production managers to interact with a complex manufacturing environment, learn from previous experience, and select optimal decisions. It involves the process of an agent autonomously selecting and executing actions to accomplish a given task. The agent learns via experience and aims to maximize the rewards it receives in certain scenarios. The primary goal of RL is to optimize the cumulative reward obtained by an agent through the evaluation and selection of actions within a dynamic environment [14–20]. The most current development in artificial intelligence technology has allowed successful application of RL in sequential decision-making problems with multiple objectives which are usable for robot scheduling and control [21,22]. The research on production scheduling using RL since 1998 has been evolving as advancing optimization techniques compared to metaheuristics. RL significantly improves the computational efficiency of addressing scheduling problems. Numerous research articles of RL on production scheduling have been undertaken since its inception in 1996, establishing a substantial and valuable foundation (see few of them, e.g., [23–27]), but only two recent review papers [28,29] paid attention to this subject. However, both the papers published in 2021 were focused on different perspectives of RL-based scheduling algorithms than presented in this paper. In other words, the content of the proposed paper is in a disjunctive and complementary relation to the two mentioned studies.

The research question of this paper is multi-faceted including multiple features of this domain that require separate answers. The main features that this paper will address are: What are the main emerging research areas in the field? Which related topics are being covered in production scheduling based on RL? What are typical implementation domains within RL applied to production scheduling?

Its novelty lies in providing the additional analyses and assessments regarding RL in production scheduling. It encompasses, e.g., the citation trend for RL on production scheduling, the most influential authors in this domain, the most relevant sources in the field, comparison of deterministic types of scheduling methods and uncertain types of scheduling methods.

2. Materials and Methods

The bibliometric approach employed here, as the main research method, presents a quantitative instrument for monitoring and representing scientific progress by examining and visualizing scientific information. The growing acceptance of bibliometric methods in several academic disciplines indicates that their use brings expected effects [30–33]. The present investigation of RL-based production scheduling is conducted utilizing the procedure comprising of five coherent phases, as depicted in Figure 1.

Moreover, this research follows an inferential approach, where the sample of population is explored to determine its characteristics [34,35]. Moreover, the inferential concept of scientific representation proposed by Suárez [36] was applied here to formulate research outputs. Its essence is to employ alternative reasoning to reach results that differ from the isomorphic view of scientific representation in the sense that empirical knowledge plays an important role in inductive reasoning [37,38].

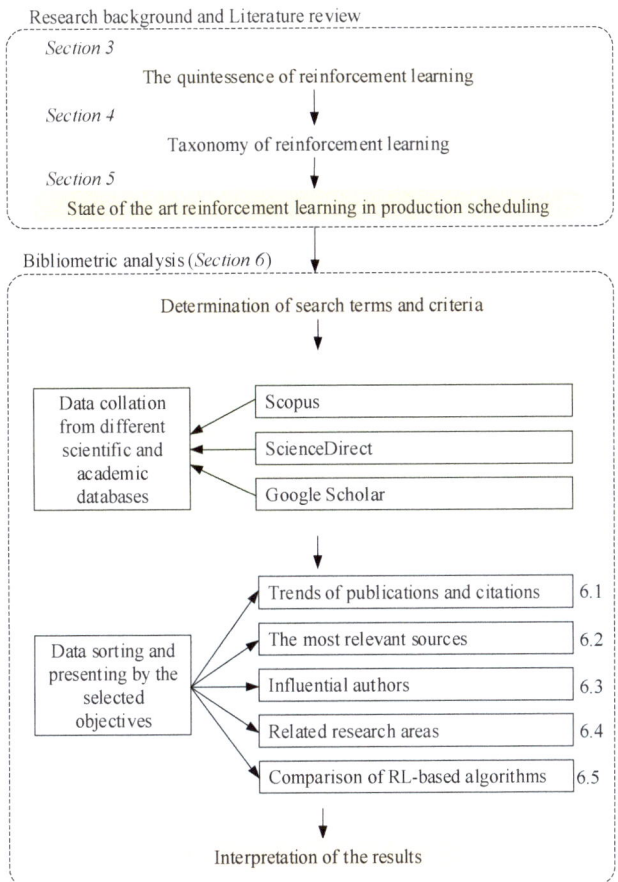

Figure 1. Research methodology framework.

3. The Quintessence of Reinforcement Learning

Artificial Intelligence (AI) has become an integral and significant aspect of our daily life as we approach the conclusion of this decade. Artificial Intelligence has been present for the past seven decades but has gained significant momentum in the recent three decades, leading to extensive research in this field [39]. AI refers to various techniques that allow computers to acquire knowledge and make choices by analyzing data. Out of these techniques, machine learning (ML) has made significant advancements in the past two decades, transitioning from a mere curiosity in laboratories to a widely used practical technology in commercial applications. In AI, ML has become the preferred approach for creating functional software in areas such as computer vision, natural language processing, speech recognition, robot control, and various other applications [40].

Many AI developers now acknowledge that, in several cases, it is more convenient to train a system by demonstrating ideal input-output behavior rather than manually programming it to anticipate the desired response for every potential input. ML has significantly impacted various areas of computer science and sectors that deal with data-driven problems. It includes consumer services, diagnosing defects in intricate systems, and managing logistics chains. ML approaches have had diverse effects on several empirical sciences, such as biology, cosmology, and social science. These approaches have been used creatively to examine vast experimental data [41].

Three major ML paradigms are supervised learning, unsupervised learning, and reinforcement learning [15]. Supervised learning entails the process of training a model using a dataset that has been labeled, meaning that each input is associated with its corresponding accurate output. The objective is to acquire knowledge about a transformation from given inputs to corresponding outputs, which can then be utilized to make accurate forecasts on novel, unobserved data. Unsupervised learning involves the identification of concealed patterns or inherent structures in unlabeled input data. The model aims to acquire knowledge about the fundamental distribution or grouping of the data without explicit instructions on the desired outcome [28]. RL is centered around teaching an agent to make numerous choices by engaging with an environment and receiving rewards or punishments as feedback. The agent acquires the ability to optimize its activities to maximize the total rewards it receives over a period [42].

Due to its dynamic and adaptive methodology, RL is highly effective for addressing problems in the manufacturing systems and robotics research domain [22,28]. RL is distinct from supervised learning, where a model is trained on a predetermined dataset, and unsupervised learning, where the model discovers concealed patterns within data. In reinforcement learning, an agent is educated to make a series of decisions by engaging with an environment. The agent's objective is to acquire a strategy, sometimes known as a policy, that optimizes the total rewards obtained over time [43].

RL is a decision-making process influenced by behavioral psychology. It involves an agent learning to achieve a goal by acting and receiving feedback from the environment through rewards or penalties. This trial-and-error method is akin to how humans and animals learn from their environment. The critical components of RL are the agent, the environment, actions, states, and rewards. The agent observes the environment, takes actions, and receives rewards, which are used to guide future actions [14]. RL is particularly effective in tasks with uncertain outcomes, such as playing games, controlling robots, and managing resources. In these situations, the agent must balance exploration (trying new actions) and exploitation (using established actions that lead to significant rewards) to develop an optimal policy efficiently [42].

The mathematical framework of RL is commonly represented using Markov Decision Processes (MDPs), which offer a systematic approach to modeling decision-making problems, including both random and agent-controlled outcomes. Solving an MDP entails determining a policy that prescribes the optimal action to be taken in each stage, aiming to maximize the predicted cumulative rewards in the future. The recent progress in deep learning has dramatically improved the capacities of RL [15,16]. The combination of deep neural networks and RL algorithms has resulted in the emergence of deep reinforcement learning (DRL), which has demonstrated exceptional achievements in intricate situations. Prominent instances include AlphaGo, developed by Google, which triumphed over human champions in the game of Go, as well as diverse implementations in autonomous driving, where DRL algorithms acquire the ability to navigate intricate and ever-changing surroundings successfully. Reinforcement learning remains a dynamic and swiftly advancing domain in machine learning, where ongoing research constantly pushes the limits of what artificial agents can accomplish. As we delve into the complexities of RL, we discover fresh opportunities for intelligent systems that possess the ability to acquire knowledge and adjust their behavior in real-time. RL paves the way for a future where computers can seamlessly cooperate with people and function autonomously in more advanced manners [42].

4. Taxonomy of Reinforcement Learning Algorithms

Sutton and Barto [42] emphasize the crucial role of the three essential components in the RL process:

- A policy determines the actions to be taken in each environmental state.
- A reward signal categorizes these actions as beneficial or detrimental based on the immediate outcome of transitioning between states.

- A value function assesses the long-term effectiveness of actions by considering not only a state's immediate reward but also the anticipated future rewards.

The primary objective of the agent is to optimize the cumulative reward. Consequently, the reward signal is the foundation for modifying the policy and the value function. In specific RL systems, an additional component known as a model of the environment exists, which is optional. It replicates the behaviour of the climate or enables more comprehensive assumptions about the behaviour of the environment. Models are utilized for strategic planning, which involves making decisions based on anticipation of future scenarios before their actual occurrence [24]. Model-based methods are used to handle reinforcement learning problems by utilizing models and planning, in contrast to more straightforward model-free methods. They exhibit apparent trial-and-error learning behaviour and are considered the reverse of planning [26,27]. RL processes can be represented and analysed using a mathematical framework called MDP. The stochastic mathematical model can be formalized using a 5-tuple (s, a, p, r, γ), in which the first symbol 's' represents the finite collection of all possible environment states, while s_t—is the state at a specific time 't'. Letter 'a' represents the set of all possible actions, while the action taken at time 't' is marked as a_t. Symbol 'p' refers to the transition probabilities matrix, which defines the conditional probability of transitioning to a new state 's', with a reward 'r', given the current state 's', and action 'a' (for all states and actions) [44]. Figure 2 shows the RL of the production scheduling cycle.

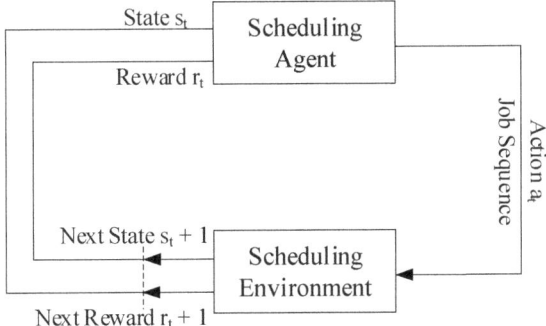

Figure 2. RL production scheduling cycle.

The learning methodologies of RL algorithms or agents can be classified into two distinct categories, model-based and model free. Model-based RL is often known as indirect learning. The agent uses a predictive model to learn the control policy from the environment through a limited number of interactions. The agent then applies this model to subsequent episodes to obtain rewards [15]. Model-free RL, or direct learning, refers to learning where an agent learns to make decisions without explicitly building a model of the environment. The agent acquires knowledge of the control policy through experiential learning from the environment, employing trial and error methods to optimize rewards without relying on any pre-existing model. This approach showcases the adaptability of RL algorithms, allowing them to learn and evolve in dynamic environments [45].

As there are many different RL algorithms, it is sensible to understand the difference among them. For this purpose, classification systems have been established to categorize them by different criteria. For instance, ALMahamid and Grolinger [46] proposed to categorize RL algorithms based on the environment type. RL algorithms can also be classified from the perspective of policy: on-policy vs. off-policy learning [47,48]. RL are mostly classified according to their learning approaches [15,45]. With this regard, updated classification of RL algorithms from the perspective of learning approaches used is provided in Figure 3.

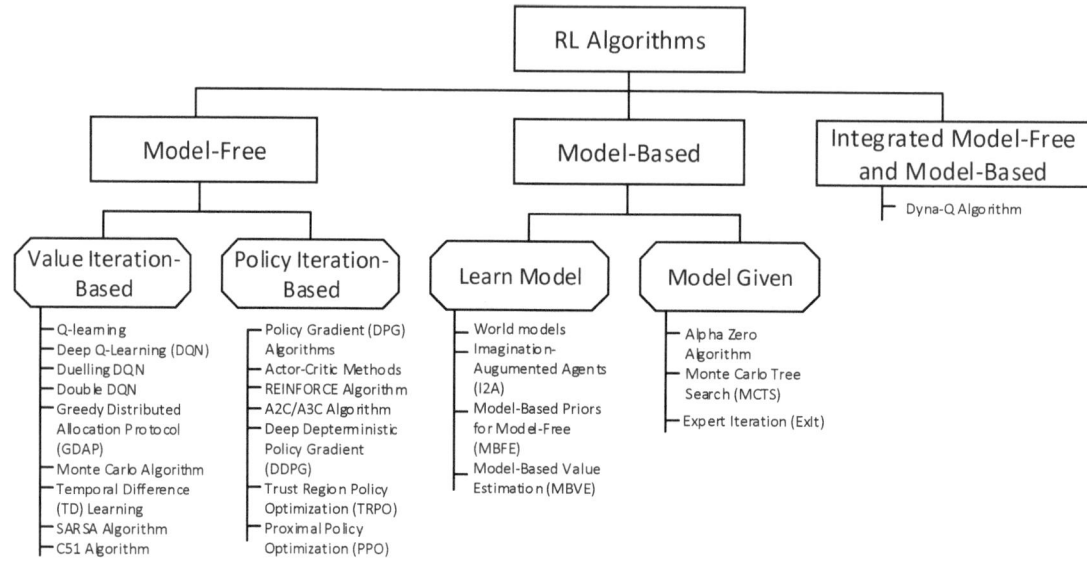

Figure 3. Classification of RL algorithms.

5. State of the Art of Reinforcement Learning in Production Scheduling

Deterministic scheduling encompasses organizing and planning tasks under fixed parameters and known constraints. Its goal is to optimize production efficiency and minimize turnaround times. A comprehensive work [49] explores fundamental principles and advanced techniques in deterministic scheduling, providing insights into various algorithms and their applications. Pinedo's work [50] thoroughly reviews deterministic scheduling theory, algorithms, and practical systems, highlighting their significance in manufacturing and service operations. Flowshop scheduling involves sequencing operations on multiple machines in a fixed order to minimize makespan or total completion time. Allahverdi [51] discusses various flowshop scheduling problems, including setups, and reviews algorithms and approaches to address them. Panwalkar and Smith [52] provide a seminal survey of classic and contemporary research on flowshop scheduling, covering both exact and heuristic methods.

Reinforcement learning (RL) techniques have gained popularity, affirming the interest in agent-based models. Previous studies have primarily focused on using RL to solve job-shop scheduling challenges. The manufacturing sector faces challenges such as customer satisfaction, system degradation, sustainability, inventory, and efficiency, impacting plant sustainability and profitability. Industry 4.0 and smart manufacturing offer solutions for optimized operations and high quality products. Paraschos et al. [53] integrate RL with lean green manufacturing to create a sustainable production environment, reducing environmental impact through minimized material consumption and lifecycle extension via pull production, predictive maintenance, and circular economy practices. Rigorous experimental analysis validates its effectiveness in enhancing sustainability and material reuse.

Recently, significant progress has been made in using RL to tackle several combinatorial optimization problems, including production scheduling, Vehicle Routing Problem, and Traveling Salesman Problem [54–59]. In RL, a production scheduling task can be viewed as an environment in which an agent operates, developing a policy through offline training by interacting with this environment. This approach offers a novel way to address scheduling challenges, requiring stringent real time constraints, such as dynamic job shop scheduling problems [22,60–64].

In production scheduling problems, value based RL algorithms are commonly used, including Q-learning, temporal difference TD(λ) algorithm, SARSA, ARL, informed Q-learning, dual Q-learning, approximate Q-learning, gradient descent TD(λ) algorithm, revenue sharing, Q-III learning, relational RL, relaxed SMART, and TD(λ)-learning. In Deep Reinforcement Learning (DRL), many value-based approaches are employed, such as DQN (Deep Q-Learning Networks), loosely-coupled DRL, multiclass DQN, and the Q-network algorithm [43,44,65–73].

Qu et al. [25] applied multi-agent approximation Q-learning, demonstrating its effectiveness through numerical experiments in static and dynamic environments and various flow shop scenarios. The goal was to create and implement an efficient manufacturing schedule considering realistic interactions between labor skills and adaptive machinery. Luo [74] uses the DRL method to address dynamic flexible job shop scheduling, focusing on scenarios to reduce tardiness. Luo et al. [75] first employed 'hierarchical multi-agent proximal policy optimization' (HMAPPO) for the constantly changing partial-no-wait multi-objective flexible job shop problem (MOFJSP) with new job insertions and machine breakdowns.

Machine deterioration during production, increases operational expenses and causes workflow disruptions, necessitating costly corrective maintenance. Preventive maintenance prolongs machine life but entails downtime and costs. The study [76] addresses these challenges by optimizing production and maintenance schedules in multi-machine systems, introducing knowledge enhanced Reinforcement Learning to enhance RL effectiveness in guiding production decisions and fostering machine collaboration. Comparative evaluations in deterministic and stochastic scenarios highlight the algorithm's ability to maximize business rewards and prevent failures.

According to Wang et al. [54], the production scheduling process involves manufacturing various items using a hybrid production pattern incorporating the multi-agent Deep Reinforcement Learning (MADRL) model. Popper et al. [60] proposed MADRL to optimize flexible production plants considering factors like efficiency and environmental targets. Du et al. [77] used the Deep Q-Network (DQN) method to address the flexible task shop scheduling problem (FJSP) amid changing processing rates, setup time, idle time, and task transportation. This approach integrates state indicators and actions to enhance the DQN component's efficiency. Additionally, it includes a problem driven exploratory data analysis (EDA) component to improve data exploration.

Li et al. [78] used a Deep Reinforcement Learning (DRL) method to solve the discrete flexible job shop problem with inter tool reusability (DFJSP-ITR), addressing the multi-objective optimization problem of minimizing combined makespan and total energy consumption. The proposed solution includes few generic state characteristics, a genetic programming based action space, and a reward function. Zhou et al. [79] proposed using online scheduling strategies based on RL with composite reward functions to improve industrial systems effectiveness and robustness. The work [18] utilized an advanced DRL algorithm to optimize production scheduling in complex job shops, highlighting benefits like enhanced adaptability, global visibility, and optimization. Some authors have focused on developing various DRL algorithms capable of formulating complex strategies for production scheduling. For instance, Luo et al. [26] created an online rescheduling framework for the dynamic multi-objective flexible job shop scheduling problem, enabling minimization of total tardiness or maximization of machine usage rate. Zhou et al. [27] used the deep Q-learning technique to address dynamic scheduling in intelligent manufacturing. Another dynamic scheduling method using deep RL is proposed in [80], employing proximal policy optimization to determine the ideal scheduling policy. Wang and Usher [81] examined using the reinforcement Q-learning algorithm for agent based production scheduling. The integration of RL with production scheduling signifies a major advancement in optimizing manufacturing processes. As research and technology continue to evolve, it promises even greater efficiency and adaptability in the industry. Delving into bibliometric data can provide valuable insights into research trends, influential works, and key contributors in this rapidly developing field.

Industry 4.0 and Smart Industry lead contemporary manufacturing and production. Industry 4.0 integrates advanced technologies like the Internet of Things (IoT), Artificial Intelligence (AI), Big Data, and Cyber-Physical Systems to create highly automated and networked production environments. The concept of intelligent industry emphasizes real-time data analytics, predictive maintenance, and adaptable manufacturing processes to improve efficiency, flexibility, and production [27]. Implementing RL algorithms is crucial in these paradigms, facilitating machine learning and future prediction through interactions in the production environment. This enhances scheduling, resource allocation, and quality control, enabling firms to achieve high automation and precision in decision-making, leading to more resilient and responsive modern manufacturing [54]. Table 1 illustrates the contribution of RL algorithms to production scheduling

Table 1. Contributions of reinforcement learning on production scheduling.

Scheduling Type	Reward	Contribution
Category: Environment		
Complex Job Shop [18]	Penalties	Advanced DRL algorithm optimizing production scheduling, highlighting adaptability, visibility, and optimization.
Flow Shop [25]	Finished order vs. overdue penalty	Efficient manufacturing schedule considering labour skills and adaptive machinery.
Flexible Job Shop [74]	Tardiness/machine utilization rate; energy cost; late products	Online rescheduling minimizing tardiness or maximizing machine usage. MARL method optimizing for efficiency and environmental targets.
Job Shop [54]	Penalties	DQN technique for minimizing task completion time in dynamic scheduling. MADRL optimizing system-level performance considering workpiece interactions.
Category: Method		
Complex Job Shop [18]	Penalties	DRL algorithm for optimizing scheduling, improving adaptability, visibility, and optimization.
Flow Shop [25]	Finished order vs. overdue penalty	Efficient schedule considering labour skills and machinery interactions.
Flexible Job Shop [24]	Tardiness/machine utilization rate; energy cost; late products	Reinforcement learning minimizing completion times in dynamic job scheduling.
Category: Reward		
Complex Job Shop [62]	Penalties	Job scheduling with multi agent in resource pre-emption learning
Flow Shop [60]	Finished order vs. overdue penalty; energy cost; late products	Optimizing production plants for efficiency and sustainability.
Flexible Job Shop [19]	Tardiness/machine utilization rate; energy cost; late products	Addressing reinforcement algorithm in scheduling, aiming at decision making in Flexible Job Shop.

6. Bibliometric Analysis of Studies on RL in Production Scheduling

The bibliometric analysis of RL in the context of production scheduling is focusing here on its theoretical foundations and practical implications, between the years 1996 and 2024. The first two phases involve the collection of bibliographic data, which was gathered via Scopus database. The search was restricted to this database due to its prominence as a comprehensive repository of scientific literature and its frequent utilization in academic assessments. The inclusion criteria for the purpose of analysis presented in Sections 6.1–6.4 encompassed publications that contained the terms "reinforcement learning" and 'production' and 'scheduling'. Besides that, the terms "reinforcement learning" and "deterministic scheduling" or "reinforcement learning" and "uncertain scheduling" were used for analysis carried out in Section 6.5. In the next two phases of the data sorting and presentation, the

Microsoft Excel and VOSviewer software 1.6.20 were employed to extract the necessary information, such as the annual scientific outputs, most relevant sources, most cited author, and keyword co-occurrence.

The process of selected studies for mentioned research methodology is synthetized in Figure 4, according to PRISMA guidelines.

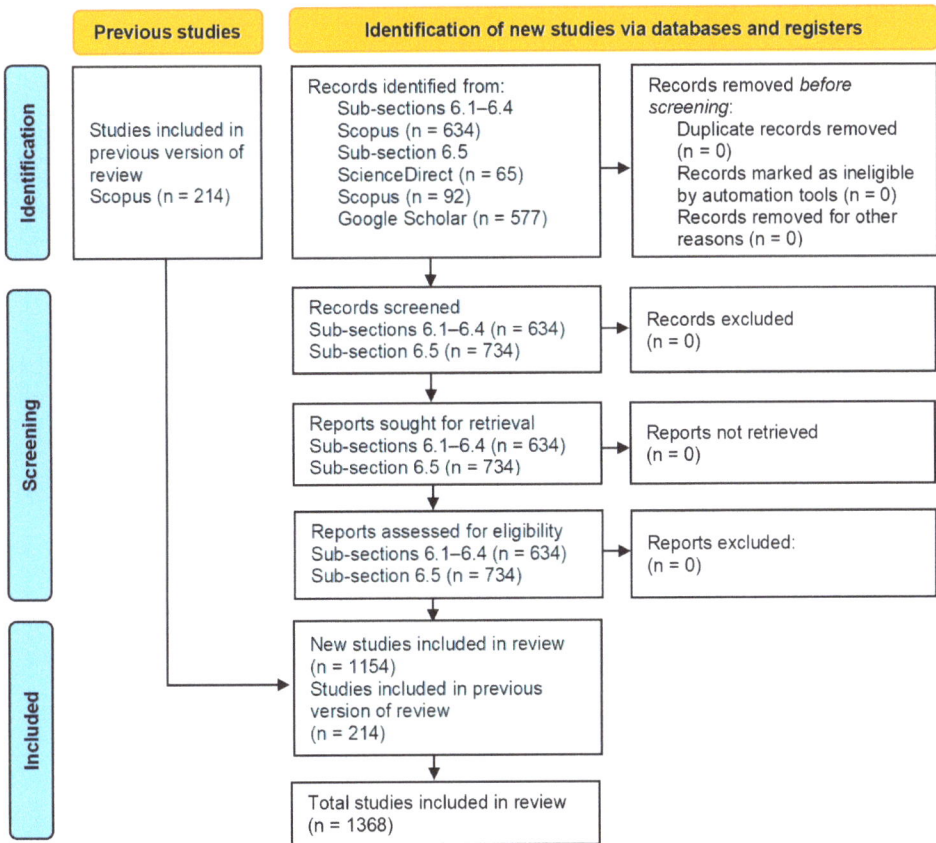

Figure 4. PRISMA 2020 flow diagram for updated systematic reviews which included searches of databases.

Using the above-specified keywords and search criteria (for Sections 6.1–6.4 n = 634 publications and for Section 6.5 n = 734 publications), together 1368 co-authored articles were found until 27 May 2024, when all document types were included in review analysis (new studies n = 1154 and studies included in previous version of review n = 214).

Review analysis of Sections 6.1–6.4 included 634 co-authored articles searched within "Article title, Abstract and Keywords". The primary research areas that receive significant attention in the articles include Computer Science, Engineering, Mathematics, Decision Sciences, Business, Management and Counting, Energy, Chemical Engineering, Material Science, and other topics. The 634 publications in our sample were categorized into 19 distinct research topics. The eight primary research areas, along with their article distribution are displayed in Table 2.

Table 2. Associated research disciplines.

Research Areas	Number of Publications	Percentage
Computer Science	429	32.7%
Engineering	402	30.6%
Mathematics	159	12%
Decision Sciences	85	6.5%
Business, Management and Counting	49	3.7%
Energy	44	3.4%
Chemical Engineering	34	2.6%
Materials Science	25	2%
Others	85	6.5%

6.1. Trends of Publications and Citations

Numbers of published articles and their citations usually provide sufficiently reliable information to anticipate further development of examined research domain. Considering the numbers of publications and citations in the field of production planning using learning algorithms keeping around 29 years of data, the trend analysis graph has been derived. For this purpose, the same search terms and keywords were applied as in case of identification of major research categories, but the types of documents were extended to all the types. The reason of changing document types was to find out the initial research initiatives in this domain. The same search conditions were applied in the rest of the paper to include the larger sample of publications for the purpose of the investigation. The annual distribution of publications (out of the total 634 items) and their citations from the same database during the period from 1996 to 2024 is illustrated in Figure 5.

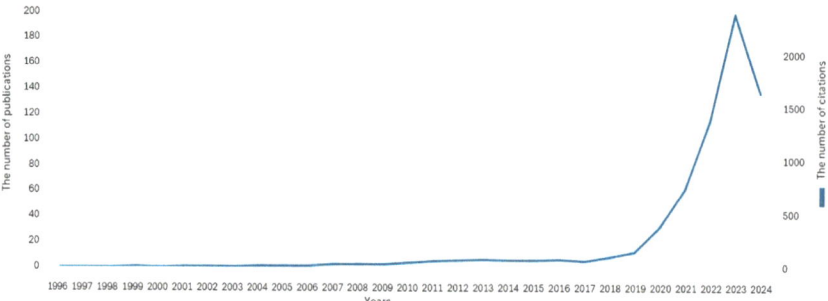

Figure 5. Publication and citation trends for RL in production scheduling field from 1996 to 2024.

An examination of the yearly scientific outputs between 1996 and 2018 amply demonstrated a relatively stable low number of articles published annually. Throughout these two decenniums, the need for RL in production scheduling in real conditions apparently did not appear. During the 2019–2023 era, there was a noticeable rise in the number of publications that were registered in the most recognized database for peer reviewed content. This phenomenon can be primarily attributed to the advancements in artificial intelligence. It is noteworthy to emphasize that if this exponential trend of increasing the number of publications continues as can be seen in year 2024, then one can anticipate that during the next decade the importance of RL in manufacturing scheduling will significantly increase.

6.2. Most Relevant Sources

An identification of the most relevant publications from an initial dataset presents common approach in bibliometric research since such sources usually publish influential research that attracts widespread interest. As a rule, the most productive journals have the greatest influence on the development of science in a particular field since they publish more articles and generate more citations [77–79]. As for as the relevancy of literature in the explored field, the top ten journals that have published the most articles, are identified here. Also, the top ten most cited scientific journals are mentioned in this Sub-section. Figures 6 and 7 categorize journals according to these two criteria to show that they represent documents that exhibit the utmost relevance to RL in production scheduling.

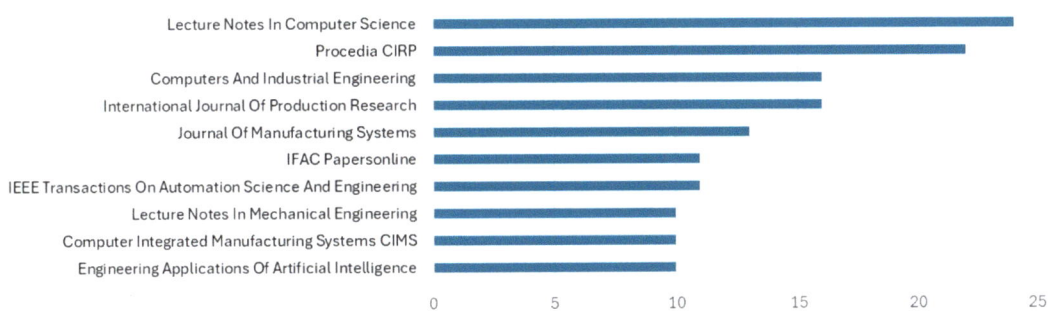

Figure 6. Top ten published journals for RL on production scheduling field from 1996 to 2024.

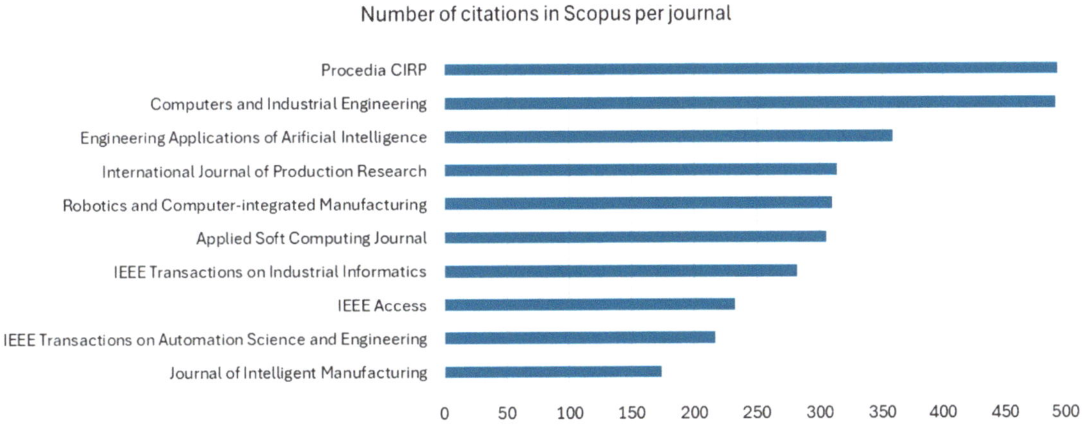

Figure 7. Top ten cited journals for RL on production scheduling field from 1996 to 2024.

The Lecture Notes in Computer Science, Procedia CIRP and Computers and Industrial Engineering along with the twelve other journals are considered the most relevant scientific publications in this field. It can also be noted that all fifteen journals listed in Figures 6 and 7, regardless of the results of the metrics used, can be empirically ranked as widely recognized for disseminating advanced research on reinforcement learning applied to production scheduling. In addition, their scientific rigor is also indicated by the fact that out of the fifteen identified journals, eight met high standards for quality as they are indexed for Current Content Connect journals with a verifiable impact on steering research practices and behaviors [80,81].

6.3. Most Cited Authors

Since the 1996s, many authors have made significant contributions to the development of this field. In this Sub-section, the intention is to present some of those authors who made significant intellectual contributions to the research. The analysis of the most cited authors was performed using data from Scopus database. In addition, co-citation analysis was carried out for each publication source (out of the total 634 items) to reveal the network between the studies. For this purpose, VOSviewer software [82] has been used. To obtain relevant information and clear graphic representation of complex relations, the following filters were employed. Filter 1: Maximum number of authors per document—15; Filter 2: Minimum number of documents of an author—3; Filter 3: Minimum number of citations of an author—10. Moreover, the full counting method has been applied meaning that the publications that have co-authors from multiple countries are counted as a full publication for each of those countries. The co-citation network of the selected sample of scholars using these settings is visualized in Figure 8.

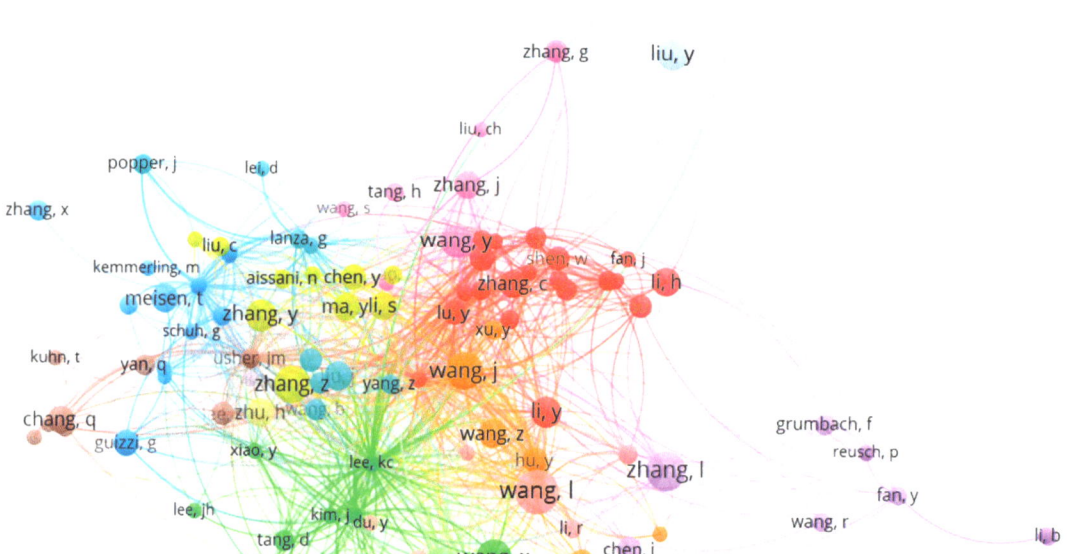

Figure 8. Co-citation network of the authors that have made significant contributions to the development of this field from 1996 to 2024.

This co-citation network map shows, among other things, scholars that have received the highest number of citations in the last 29 years. Of the 1376 cited authors, 138 meet the above-mentioned criteria. Each scholar from each included publication is represented by a node in this network. The size of each node indicates frequency of citation of the subject's scholarly works. An edge is drawn between two nodes if the two scholars were cited by a common document. To rank influential scholars in the given domain based on their citation rates, the ten most cited authors were selected. Those ten authors are listed in Table 3.

Table 3. Most influential authors.

Name	Number of Citations	Country	Name	Number of Citations	Country
Waschenck, B.	386	Germany	Wang, Y. C.	265	Taiwan
Wang, L.	375	China	Wang, H.	224	China
Wang, J.	354	China	Lin, C.C.	216	Taiwan
Bauernhansl, T.	342	Germany	Li, S.	209	China
Usher, J.M.	265	USA	Beldjilali, B.	207	Algeria

6.4. Identification of the Related Research Areas

The goal of this part of the article is to identify areas of research in which the issue of production scheduling based on RL is of interest. For this purpose, the keyword analysis application has been employed to help separate important research themes which has received a high interest of researchers from less important ones. To obtain relevant and representative categories not including less significant ones, the following setting has been used: Minimum number of occurrence of keywords—14. Based on this restriction, 88 keywords meet the threshold from the total 3767 keywords. Those main keywords that were produced automatically from the titles in the papers on production scheduling based on RL along with their occurrence are shown in Figure 9.

As can be seen, topics can be divided into five clusters based on a computer algorithm, while each cluster has a different color as shown in Figure 9. The keywords co-occurrence map highlights these clusters where the darker the color, the greater the density value is. It allows to identify relevant research topics and their mutual relationships. Based on the obtained bibliometric results extracted from VOSviewer, ten related topics that are very close to the explored research domain were identified as shown in Table 4.

The results from Table 4 point to their consistency with practical reality and operation research goals. For example, in recent years, there has been evidently increased interest in using reinforcement learning for optimization of real-time job scheduling tasks [76–86]. This fact can be correlated with the continuing trend of mass customization in the production of consumer goods [87,88]. As known, for mass customization is characteristic to meet dynamically changing user requirements in time, while customized products need to be completed by different deadlines. Accordingly, efficient real-time job-scheduling algorithms based on DRL become essential. The next important method that is ranked among the top 10 co-occurrences keywords is production control. It uses different control techniques to meet production targets regarding production schedules and quality (see, e.g., [89–92]). The next important co-occurred keyword in Table 3—multi agent systems. In general, incorporating multi-agent systems into reinforcement learning for production scheduling offers numerous advantages in terms of flexibility, scalability, and adaptability [93–95]. By enabling decentralized decision-making and continuous learning, these systems can effectively handle the complexities and dynamics of modern production environments leading to more efficient and resilient scheduling solutions [96]. Among the co-occurrences keywords it is possible to highlight also 'smart manufacturing' that represents the implementation domain of production scheduling based on RL. Even though smart manufacturing has also become a buzzword, which also has its drawbacks, this conception is gradually being established as the new manufacturing paradigm. On the other hand, complexity of smart manufacturing network infrastructures becomes higher and higher, and the uncertainty of such manufacturing environment becomes a serious problem [25]. These facts lead to the necessity of applying advanced dynamic planning solutions that also includes production scheduling using RL. This paragraph simultaneously answers to the main research question formulated in Section 1.

Further, application of RL in production scheduling will be here analyzed through bibliometric means from a viewpoint of different scheduling problems.

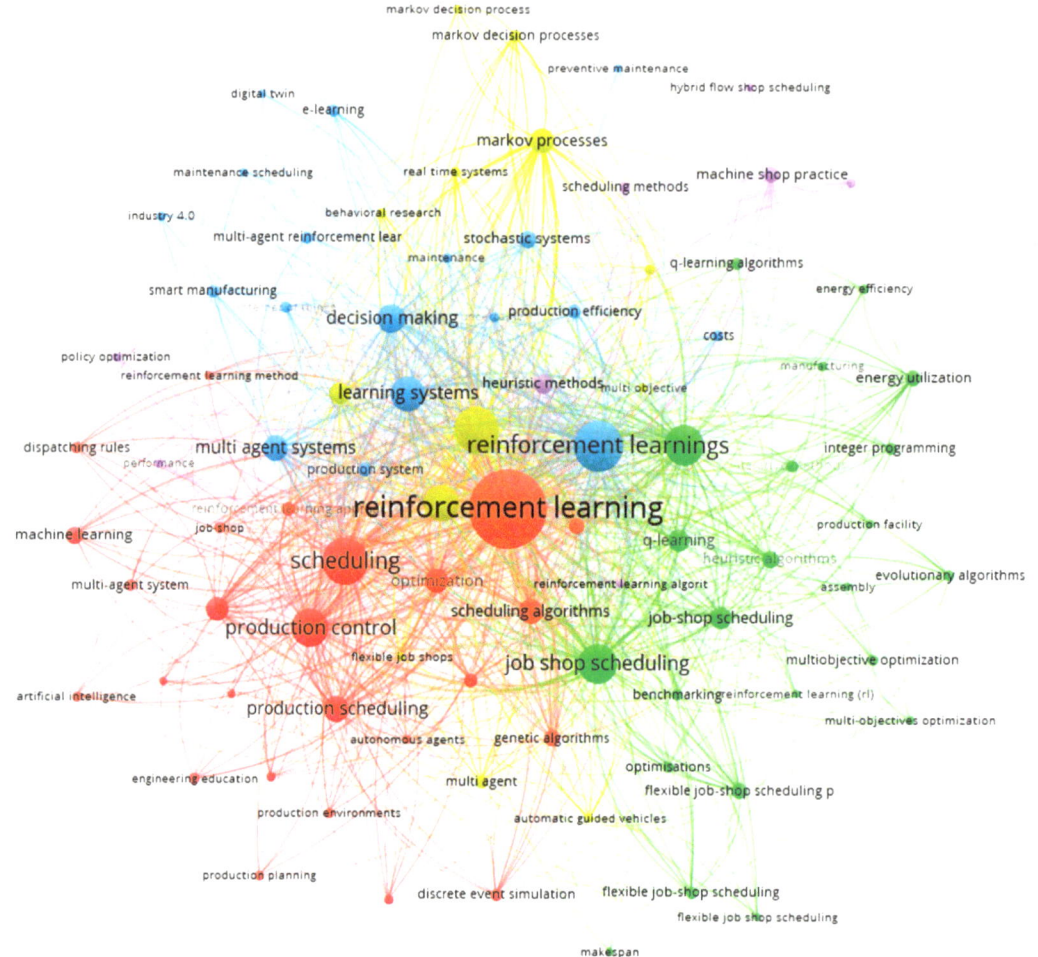

Figure 9. Co-occurrences keywords for RL on production scheduling field from 1996 to 2024.

Table 4. Most related methodologies and implementation areas of production scheduling based on RL.

Related Research Areas	Number of Co-Occurrence	Related Terms/Topics	Number of Co-Occurrence
Reinforcement learning	526	Production control	161
Scheduling	220	Deep reinforcement learning	148
Deep learning	215	Learning systems	134
Learning algorithms	178	Decision making	99
Job shop scheduling	168	Multi agent systems	86

6.5. Comparison of Applications of RL in Different Scheduling Problems

In general, scheduling methods are categorized based on time at which decision is taken into dynamic and static ones. Dynamic scheduling is related to real-time systems that require responding to changing demand requirements, while static scheduling is off-line and focuses on short-term time horizon by setting a fixed timeline for process completion. It has been found by Wang et al. [28] that production scheduling based on RL approaches are largely adopted to solve dynamic scheduling problems. Scheduling problems can also be categorized by the nature of scheduling environment as deterministic, when processing parameters are known and invariable, and non-deterministic, when input parameters are uncertain [97]. Production scheduling problems under this second criterion can be classified as shown in Figure 10.

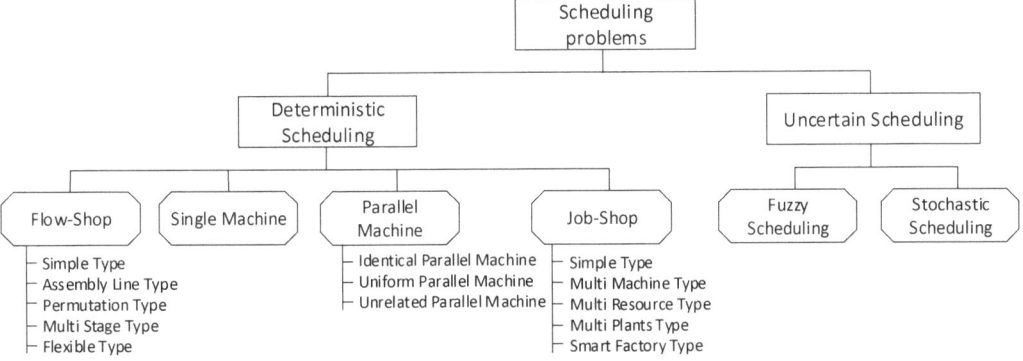

Figure 10. Basic classification of scheduling problems.

Understanding differences among specific scheduling problems is crucial for selection of the appropriate optimization and scheduling techniques with the aim to improve efficiency and productivity in various industries. The main difference among scheduling problems can be seen, e.g., in routing flexibility and complexity. For instance, job-shop problems have a high routing flexibility and complexity, while for flow-shop and single machine problems is typical low flexibility, and parallel machine problem has moderate routing flexibility and complexity [98,99]. Their differences also lie in nature of application domains for which they are intended. For example, for a customized manufacturing is typical job-shop scheduling [100,101], for assembly lines is mostly considered flow-shop scheduling problems [102,103], and open job shop scheduling is frequently applicable in healthcare [104,105].

The classification is further used to explore an application frequency of RL in the identified categories of the scheduling problems. First, deterministic versus uncertain scheduling is compared according to this view. For this purpose, the search terms were defined by combining the following keywords: "Reinforcement Learning" along with "Deterministic scheduling" or "Uncertain scheduling", respectively. Data together with inclusion criteria were collated by searching: (i) ScienceDirect database—All fields, All years, and All document types; (ii) Scopus database—All fields, All years, All document types, and (iii) Google Scholar database—All years and All document types. Together 734 publications were analyzed. Web of Science was not used in this procedure due to the low occurrence of scientific works on the subjects. The obtained data in this way are provided in Table 5.

Table 5. Comparison of deterministic and uncertain scheduling methods based on RL.

Search Terms Used	Science Direct Database	Scopus Database	Google Scholar Database
"Deterministic scheduling" and "reinforcement learning"	53	68	474
"Uncertain scheduling" and "reinforcement learning"	12	24	103

From Table 5 is clear that deterministic scheduling based on RL is in a dominant position against uncertain scheduling using RL. Therefore, to identify the most promising area(s) of production scheduling in the context of RL, deterministic scheduling and uncertain scheduling approaches has been examined in the following. Key words used for that purpose were:

(a) Scheduling AND "reinforcement learning" AND specific deterministic scheduling problems ("job shop", "flow shop", "open shop", "single machine", and "parallel machines").
(b) "Reinforcement learning" AND specific uncertain scheduling problems ("fuzzy scheduling" and "stochastic scheduling").

Data were retrieved from ScienceDirect database using filters 'Research articles', and 'All years'; Scopus database using filter 'Article titles', 'Abstracts', 'Keywords', All years, and All document types, and Google Scholar database—All years and All document types. Obtained results are graphically presented and compared in percentage with each other in Figure 11.

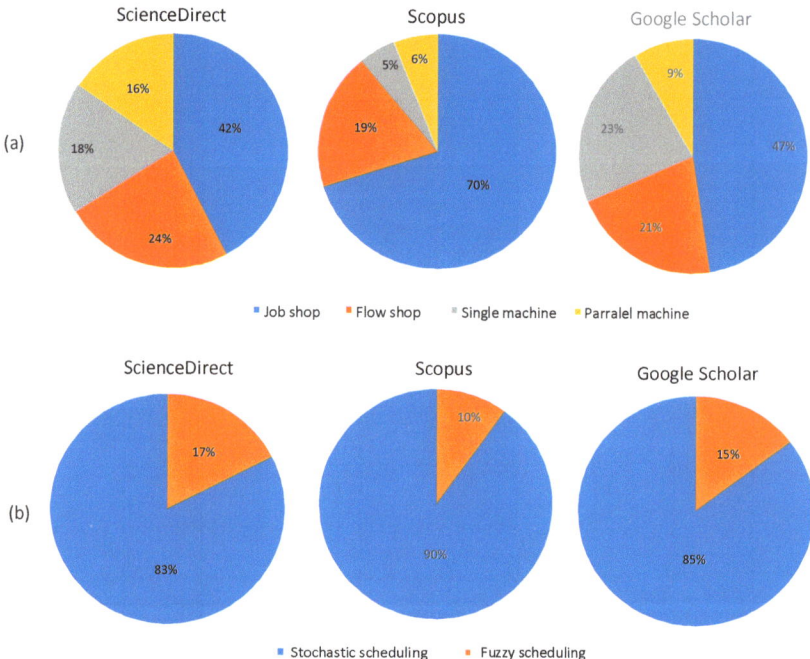

Figure 11. Comparison of (**a**) deterministic scheduling methods and (**b**) uncertain scheduling methods from their occurrences in literature.

One can see from Figure 11a that RL-based scheduling algorithms are mostly used to solve job shop scheduling problems [106], while flow shop production environment is the second most important type of scheduling problems, where RL is applied. Obviously, RL-based algorithms found application in other types of scheduling problems. As the most noticeable of them, it is possible to mention energy efficiency scheduling, multi-objective scheduling, and distributive scheduling. The last-mentioned scheduling problem is exploited especially in intelligent manufacturing systems [107]. Analyzing the results from Figure 11b, it is observed that RL is predominantly used in stochastic scheduling methods comparing with its application in fuzzy scheduling methods. Moreover, the effectiveness of stochastic scheduling using RL has been also demonstrated through benchmarking studies [29,108,109]. Although the application of RL in fuzzy scheduling is promising, it remains less common due to additional complexities involved in integrating fuzzy logic with RL methods [110,111]. However, the results of this quantitative approach for comparison of application of RL in different scheduling problems provide some useful managerial insights into scheduling practice. Nevertheless, further exploration and research on qualitative aspects of RL-based scheduling, particularly in the context of smart manufacturing, is required.

7. Comparison of the Presented Research and Previous Review Articles

As was already mentioned in introduction, this review paper continues the work of the two earlier articles [28,29] by analyzing some new relevant aspects of production scheduling methods using RL and provides some updated information regarding recent developments in the field. The purpose of this section is to provide a clear view on differences and similarities of the three works in terms of their subject matters. The following Table 6 contains a summary comparison of investigation areas included in the mentioned works.

Table 6. The comparison of the review papers on RL in Production Scheduling.

The Focus of Investigation	The Compared Review Papers		
	Wang et al., 2021 [28]	Kayhan and Yildiz, 2021 [29]	Offered Research
The citation trend for RL in production scheduling from 1996 to 2024			✓
The most relevant publications in the field	✓		✓
The most influential authors in the field			✓
The comparison of deterministic and uncertain scheduling methods based on RL			✓
The comparison of stochastic and fuzzy scheduling methods based on RL			✓
The publication trend for RL in production scheduling	✓	✓	✓
The most relevant sources published research on RL in production scheduling			✓
The comparison of the most frequent deterministic scheduling methods based on RL	✓	✓	✓
The comparison of the value-based and policy-based scheduling methods based on RL	✓		
The comparison of static and dynamic scheduling methods based on RL	✓		
The categorization of the literature on RL in production scheduling according to multiple aspects		✓	
The publication trend for RL in production scheduling according to manufacturing environment		✓	
The comparison of different types of RL algorithms for production scheduling		✓	
The comparison of stochastic and deterministic scheduling methods based on RL		✓	

From this table it can be see that the compared papers are mostly complementary to each other.

8. Conclusions

The existing body of research on production scheduling primarily consists of studies conducted within the domains of Computer Science, Engineering, Mathematics, Decision Sciences, Business, Management and Counting, Energy, Chemical Engineering, and Material Science. These scientific disciplines, notably 'Engineering' and 'Computer Science' have exerted significant influence on development of production scheduling based on RL.

The examination of bibliometric findings frequently indicates that an increase in the quantity of published articles is associated with recognition of progressive trends in the subject. Also, for this reason, a bibliometric analysis is becoming more and more beneficial in a variety of academic fields since it makes mapping scientific information and analyzing research development objective and repeatable. The use of this method enables us to identify the networks of scientific collaboration, to establish connections between novel study themes and research streams, as well as show the connections between citations, co-citations and published productivity in the field.

The main contribution of this article can be summarized by two steps:

(i) This review brings additional insights into RL in production scheduling by providing the following new features:
- The citation trend for RL on production scheduling field from 1996 to 2024 (see Figure 5) has been carried out that shows that increasing trend starting from 2019 to present rapidly continues in noticeable rise in their number.
- The analysis of the most relevant sources from the viewpoint of number of their citations (see Figure 7) has been performed to identify the most impacted sources where the latest knowledge in this field is available.
- The most influential authors in this domain were identified (see Table 3) for the determination of the cutting-edge state in RL-based production scheduling.
- The quantitative comparison of deterministic and uncertain scheduling methods based on RL has been conducted (see in Table 5). It showed that deterministic scheduling methods using RL is in a dominant position against RL-based uncertain scheduling techniques.
- The quantitative comparison of stochastic and fuzzy scheduling methods has been given in Figure 11b. From the comparison, it has been observed that RL is predominantly used in stochastic scheduling methods comparing with its application in fuzzy scheduling methods.

(ii) The contribution of this paper can be also seen in the following activities and resulting statements:
- The publication trend for RL in production scheduling field has been updated by mapping period from 1996 to 2024 (see Figure 5). It showed that exponential growth of the publications starting from 2019 [28] rapidly continues in noticeable rise in their number.
- The updated list of the most relevant sources published research on RL in production scheduling was compiled in Figure 6. It has been found that five of ten sources identified until 2021 belong among top ten sources identified until 2024. It means that due to the growing interest about this research field, at the same time, the number of journals covering this topic is increasing.
- Actualization of the quantitative comparison of the most frequent deterministic scheduling methods based on RL was provided in Figure 11a. In this context, the previously identified trend has been confirmed that RL-based scheduling algorithms are mostly used to solve job shop scheduling problems, while flow shop production presents the second most important type of scheduling problems.
- The updated categorization of newly developed RL algorithms has been elaborated and presented in Figure 3 that can provide better implementation support for decision making in real-world problems.

- The updated classification of scheduling methods is provided in Figure 10. In principle, it can be used for easier selection of the scheduling techniques to solve specific types of problems.

In addition to the above-mentioned findings, it would be needed to focus on other challenges to be considered in the future such manufacturing process planning with integrated support for knowledge sharing, increasing demand for improvements in ubiquitous "smartness" in manufacturing processes including designing and implementing smart algorithms, and the need for robust scheduling tools for agile collaborative manufacturing systems.

Author Contributions: Conceptualization, V.M.; methodology, R.S. and A.B.; validation, Z.S.; formal analysis, V.M. and R.S.; investigation, V.M. and A.B.; writing—original draft preparation, A.B. and V.M.; writing—review and editing, R.S. and V.M.; visualization, Z.S.; project administration, V.M. All authors have read and agreed to the published version of the manuscript.

Funding: This research has been funded by the project SME 5.0 with funding received from the European Union's Horizon research and innovation program under the Marie Skłodowska-Curie Grant Agreement No. 101086487 and the KEGA (Cultural and Education Grant Agency) project No. 044TUKE-4/2023 granted by the Ministry of Education of the Slovak Republic.

Institutional Review Board Statement: Not applicable.

Informed Consent Statement: Not applicable.

Data Availability Statement: Data is contained within the article.

Conflicts of Interest: The authors declare no conflicts of interest. The funders had no role in the design of the study; in the collection, analyses, or interpretation of data; in the writing of the manuscript; or in the decision to publish the results.

References

1. Pinedo, M. *Planning and Scheduling in Manufacturing and Services*; Springer: New York, NY, USA, 2005.
2. Beheshti, Z.; Shamsuddin, S.M.H. A review of population-based meta-heuristic algorithms. *Int. J. Adv. Soft Comput. Appl.* **2013**, *5*, 1–35.
3. Xhafa, F.; Abraham, A. (Eds.) *Metaheuristics for Scheduling in Industrial and Manufacturing Applications*; Springer: Berlin/Heidelberg, Germany, 2008; Volume 128.
4. Abdel-Kader, R.F. Particle swarm optimization for constrained instruction scheduling. *VLSI Des.* **2008**, *2008*, 930610. [CrossRef]
5. Balamurugan, A.; Ranjitharamasamy, S.P. A Modified Heuristics for the Batch Size Optimization with Combined Time in a Mass-Customized Manufacturing System. *Int. J. Ind. Eng. Theory Appl. Pract.* **2023**, *30*, 1090–1115.
6. Ghassemi Tari, F.; Olfat, L. Heuristic rules for tardiness problem in flow shop with intermediate due dates. *Int. J. Adv. Manuf. Technol.* **2014**, *71*, 381–393. [CrossRef]
7. Modrak, V.; Pandian, R.S. Flow shop scheduling algorithm to minimize completion time for n-jobs m-machines problem. *Teh. Vjesn.* **2010**, *17*, 273–278.
8. Thenarasu, M.; Rameshkumar, K.; Rousseau, J.; Anbuudayasankar, S.P. Development and analysis of priority decision rules using MCDM approach for a flexible job shop scheduling: A simulation study. *Simul. Model. Pract. Theory* **2022**, *114*, 102416. [CrossRef]
9. Pandian, S.; Modrak, V. Possibilities, obstacles and challenges of genetic algorithm in manufacturing cell formation. *Adv. Logist. Syst.* **2009**, *3*, 63–70.
10. Abdulredha, M.N.; Bara'a, A.A.; Jabir, A.J. Heuristic and meta-heuristic optimization models for task scheduling in cloud-fog systems: A review. *Iraqi J. Electr. Electron. Eng.* **2020**, *16*, 103–112. [CrossRef]
11. Modrak, V.; Pandian, R.S.; Semanco, P. Calibration of GA parameters for layout design optimization problems using design of experiments. *Appl. Sci.* **2021**, *11*, 6940. [CrossRef]
12. Keshanchi, B.; Souri, A.; Navimipour, N.J. An improved genetic algorithm for task scheduling in the cloud environments using the priority queues: Formal verification, simulation, and statistical testing. *J. Syst. Softw.* **2017**, *124*, 1–21. [CrossRef]
13. Jans, R.; Degraeve, Z. Meta-heuristics for dynamic lot sizing: A review and comparison of solution approaches. *Eur. J. Oper. Res.* **2007**, *177*, 1855–1875. [CrossRef]
14. Han, B.A.; Yang, J.J. A deep reinforcement learning based solution for flexible job shop scheduling problem. *Int. J. Simul. Model.* **2021**, *20*, 375–386. [CrossRef]
15. Shyalika, C.; Silva, T.; Karunananda, A. Reinforcement Learning in Dynamic Task Scheduling: A Review. *SN Comput. Sci.* **2020**, *1*, 306. [CrossRef]
16. Wang, X.; Zhang, L.; Ren, L.; Xie, K.; Wang, K.; Ye, F.; Chen, Z. Brief Review on Applying Reinforcement Learning to Job Shop Scheduling Problems. *J. Syst. Simul.* **2022**, *33*, 2782–2791.

17. Dima, I.C.; Gabrara, J.; Modrak, V.; Piotr, P.; Popescu, C. Using the expert systems in the operational management of production. In Proceedings of the 11th WSEAS International Conference on Mathematics and Computers in Business and Economics (MCBE'10), Iasi, Romania, 13–15 June 2010; WSEAS Press: Stevens Point, WI, USA, 2010.
18. Waschneck, B.; Reichstaller, A.; Belzner, L.; Altenmüller, T.; Bauernhansl, T.; Knapp, A.; Kyek, A. Optimization of global production scheduling with deep reinforcement learning. *Procedia CIRP* **2018**, *72*, 1264–1269. [CrossRef]
19. Yan, J.; Liu, Z.; Zhang, T.; Zhang, Y. Autonomous decision-making method of transportation process for flexible job shop scheduling problem based on reinforcement learning. In Proceedings of the 2021 International Conference on Machine Learning and Intelligent Systems Engineering, MLISE, Chongqing, China, 9–11 July 2021; Institute of Electrical and Electronics Engineers Inc.: Piscataway, NJ, USA; pp. 234–238.
20. Modrak, V.; Pandian, R.S. *Operations Management Research and Cellular Manufacturing Systems*; IGI Global: Hershey, PA, USA, 2010.
21. Huang, Z.; Liu, Q.; Zhu, F. Hierarchical reinforcement learning with adaptive scheduling for robot control. *Eng. Appl. Artif. Intell.* **2023**, *126*, 107130. [CrossRef]
22. Arviv, K.; Stern, H.; Edan, Y. Collaborative reinforcement learning for a two-robot job transfer flow-shop scheduling problem. *Int. J. Prod. Res.* **2016**, *54*, 1196–1209. [CrossRef]
23. Wen, X.; Zhang, X.; Xing, H.; Ye, G.; Li, H.; Zhang, Y.; Wang, H. An improved genetic algorithm based on reinforcement learning for aircraft assembly scheduling problem. *Comput. Ind. Eng.* **2024**, *193*, 110263. [CrossRef]
24. Aydin, M.E.; Öztemel, E. Dynamic job-shop scheduling using reinforcement learning agents. *Robot. Auton. Syst.* **2000**, *33*, 169–178. [CrossRef]
25. Qu, S.; Wang, J.; Govil, S.; Leckie, J.O. Optimized Adaptive Scheduling of a Manufacturing Process System with Multi-skill Workforce and Multiple Machine Types: An Ontology-based, Multi-agent Reinforcement Learning Approach. *Procedia CIRP* **2016**, *57*, 55–60. [CrossRef]
26. Luo, S.; Zhang, L.; Fan, Y. Dynamic multi-objective scheduling for flexible job shop by deep reinforcement learning. *Comput. Ind. Eng.* **2021**, *159*, 107489. [CrossRef]
27. Zhou, L.; Zhang, L.; Horn, B.K.P. Deep reinforcement learning-based dynamic scheduling in smart manufacturing. *Procedia CIRP* **2020**, *93*, 383–388. [CrossRef]
28. Wang, L.; Pan, Z.; Wang, J. A Review of Reinforcement Learning Based Intelligent Optimization for Manufacturing Scheduling. *Complex Syst. Model. Simul.* **2021**, *1*, 257–270. [CrossRef]
29. Kayhan, B.M.; Yildiz, G. Reinforcement learning applications to machine scheduling problems: A comprehensive literature review. *J. Intell. Manuf.* **2021**, *34*, 905–929. [CrossRef]
30. Broadus, R.N. Toward a Definition of "Bibliometrics". *Scientometrics* **1987**, *12*, 373–379. [CrossRef]
31. Arunmozhi, B.; Sudhakarapandian, R.; Sultan Batcha, Y.; Rajay Vedaraj, I.S. An inferential analysis of stainless steel in additive manufacturing using bibliometric indicators. *Mater Today Proc.* **2023**, in press. [CrossRef]
32. Randhawa, K.; Wilden, R.; Hohberger, J. A bibliometric review of open innovation: Setting a research agenda. *J. Prod. Innov. Manag.* **2016**, *33*, 750–772. [CrossRef]
33. van Raan, A. Advanced bibliometric methods as quantitative core of peer review based evaluation and foresight exercises. *Scientometrics* **1996**, *36*, 397–420. [CrossRef]
34. Brandom, R.B. *Articulating Reasons: An Introduction to Inferentialism*; Harvard University Press: Cambridge, MA, USA, 2001.
35. Kothari, C.R. *Research Methodology: Methods and Techniques*; New Age International: New Delhi, India, 2004.
36. Suárez, M. An inferential conception of scientific representation. *Philos. Sci.* **2004**, *71*, 767–779. [CrossRef]
37. Contessa, G. Scientific representation, interpretation, and surrogative reasoning. *Philos. Sci.* **2007**, *74*, 48–68. [CrossRef]
38. Govier, T. *Problems in Argument Analysis and Evaluation*; University of Windsor: Windsor, ON, Canada, 2018; Volume 6.
39. Munusamy, R.; Mukherjee, A.; Vasudevan, K.; Venkateswaran, B. Design and Simulation of an Artificial intelligence (AI) Brain for a 2D Vehicle Navigation System. *INCAS Bull.* **2022**, *14*, 53–64. [CrossRef]
40. Dunjko, V.; Briegel, H.J. Machine learning & artificial intelligence in the quantum domain: A review of recent progress. *Rep. Prog. Phys.* **2018**, *81*, 074001.
41. Horvitz, E.; Mulligan, D. Data, privacy, and the greater good. *Science* **2015**, *349*, 253–255. [CrossRef]
42. Sutton, R.S.; Barto, A.G. *Reinforcement Learning: An Introduction*; MIT: New York, NY, USA, 2018.
43. Kuhnle, A.; May, M.C.; Schäfer, L.; Lanza, G. Explainable reinforcement learning in production control of job shop manufacturing system. *Int. J. Prod. Res.* **2022**, *60*, 5812–5834. [CrossRef]
44. Esteso, A.; Peidro, D.; Mula, J.; Díaz-Madroñero, M. Reinforcement learning applied to production planning and control. *Int. J. Prod. Res.* **2023**, *61*, 5772–5789. [CrossRef]
45. Khan, M.A.M.; Khan, M.R.J.; Tooshil, A.; Sikder, N.; Mahmud, M.P.; Kouzani, A.Z.; Nahid, A.A. A systematic review on reinforcement learning-based robotics within the last decade. *IEEE Access* **2020**, *8*, 176598–176623. [CrossRef]
46. AlMahamid, F.; Grolinger, K. Reinforcement learning algorithms: An overview and classification. In Proceedings of the 2021 IEEE Canadian Conference on Electrical and Computer Engineering (CCECE), Kingston, ON, Canada, 12–17 September 2021; IEEE: Piscataway, NJ, USA; pp. 1–7.
47. Akalin, N.; Loutfi, A. Reinforcement learning approaches in social robotics. *Sensors* **2021**, *21*, 1292. [CrossRef]
48. Zhang, H.; Yu, T. Taxonomy of reinforcement learning algorithms. In *Deep Reinforcement Learning: Fundamentals, Research and Applications*; Springer: Singapore, 2020; pp. 125–133.

49. Baker, K.R.; Trietsch, D. *Principles of Sequencing and Scheduling*; John Wiley & Sons: Hoboken, NJ, USA, 2009.
50. Pinedo, M.L. *Scheduling: Theory, Algorithms, and Systems*; Springer: Berlin/Heidelberg, Germany, 2016.
51. Allahverdi, A.; Ng, C.T.; Cheng, T.C.E.; Kovalyov, M.Y. A survey of scheduling problems with setup times or costs. *Eur. J. Oper. Res.* **2008**, *187*, 985–1032. [CrossRef]
52. Panwalkar, S.S.; Smith, M.L. Survey of flow shop scheduling research. *Oper. Res.* **1977**, *25*, 45–84. [CrossRef]
53. Paraschos, P.D.; Koulinas, G.K.; Koulouriotis, D.E. Reinforcement Learning-Based Optimization for Sustainable and Lean Production within the Context of Industry 4.0. *Algorithms* **2024**, *17*, 98. [CrossRef]
54. Wang, S.; Li, J.; Luo, Y. Smart Scheduling for Flexible and Hybrid Production with Multi-Agent Deep Reinforcement Learning. In Proceedings of the 2021 IEEE 2nd International Conference on Information Technology, Big Data and Artificial Intelligence, ICIBA, Chongqing, China, 17–19 December 2021; Institute of Electrical and Electronics Engineers Inc.: Piscataway, NJ, USA; pp. 288–294.
55. Tang, J.; Haddad, Y.; Salonitis, K. Reconfigurable manufacturing system scheduling: A deep reinforcement learning approach. *Procedia CIRP* **2022**, *107*, 1198–1203. [CrossRef]
56. Shahrabi, J.; Adibi, M.A.; Mahootchi, M. A reinforcement learning approach to parameter estimation in dynamic job shop scheduling. *Comput Ind Eng.* **2017**, *110*, 75–82. [CrossRef]
57. Yang, J.; You, X.; Wu, G.; Hassan, M.M.; Almogren, A.; Guna, J. Application of reinforcement learning in UAV cluster task scheduling. *Future Gener. Comput. Syst.* **2019**, *95*, 140–148. [CrossRef]
58. Yuan, X.; Pan, Y.; Yang, J.; Wang, W.; Huang, Z. Study on the application of reinforcement learning in the operation optimization of HVAC system. In *Building Simulation*; Tsinghua University Press: Beijing, China, 2021; Volume 14, pp. 75–87.
59. Kurinov, I.; Orzechowski, G.; Hämäläinen, P.; Mikkola, A. Automated excavator based on reinforcement learning and multibody system dynamics. *IEEE Access* **2020**, *8*, 213998–214006. [CrossRef]
60. Popper, J.; Motsch, W.; David, A.; Petzsche, T.; Ruskowski, M. Utilizing multi-agent deep reinforcement learning for flexible job shop scheduling under sustainable viewpoints. In Proceedings of the International Conference on Electrical, Computer, Communications and Mechatronics Engineering 2021, ICECCME, Mauritius, Mauritius, 7–8 October 2021; Institute of Electrical and Electronics Engineers Inc.: Piscataway, NJ, USA.
61. Xiong, H.; Fan, H.; Jiang, G.; Li, G. A simulation-based study of dispatching rules in a dynamic job shop scheduling problem with batch release and extended technical precedence constraints. *Eur. J. Oper. Res.* **2017**, *257*, 13–24. [CrossRef]
62. Palacio, J.C.; Jiménez, Y.M.; Schietgat, L.; Van Doninck, B.; Nowé, A. A Q-Learning algorithm for flexible job shop scheduling in a real-world manufacturing scenario. *Procedia CIRP* **2022**, *106*, 227–232. [CrossRef]
63. Chang, J.; Yu, D.; Hu, Y.; He, W.; Yu, H. Deep Reinforcement Learning for Dynamic Flexible Job Shop Scheduling with Random Job Arrival. *Processes* **2022**, *10*, 760. [CrossRef]
64. Liu, R.; Piplani, R.; Toro, C. Deep reinforcement learning for dynamic scheduling of a flexible job shop. *Int. J. Prod. Res.* **2022**, *60*, 4049–4069. [CrossRef]
65. Samsonov, V.; Kemmerling, M.; Paegert, M.; Lütticke, D.; Sauermann, F.; Gützlaff, A.; Schuh, G.; Meisen, T. Manufacturing control in job shop environments with reinforcement learning. In Proceedings of the 13th International Conference on Agents and Artificial Intelligence (ICAART 2021), Online, 4–6 February 2021; SciTePress: Setúbal, Portugal; pp. 589–597.
66. Cunha, B.; Madureira, A.M.; Fonseca, B.; Coelho, D. Deep reinforcement learning as a job shop scheduling solver: A literature review. In Proceedings of the 18th International Conference on Hybrid Intelligent Systems (HIS 2018), Porto, Portugal, 13–15 December 2018; Madureira, A.M., Abraham, A., Gandhi, N., Varela, M.L., Eds.; Springer International Publishing: Cham, Switzerland, 2018.
67. Wang, X.; Zhang, L.; Lin, T.; Zhao, C.; Wang, K.; Chen, Z. Solving job scheduling problems in a resource preemption environment with multi-agent reinforcement learning. *Robot. Comput. Integr. Manuf.* **2022**, *77*, 102324. [CrossRef]
68. Oh, S.H.; Cho, Y.I.; Woo, J.H. Distributional reinforcement learning with the independent learners for flexible job shop scheduling problem with high variability. *J. Comput. Des. Eng.* **2022**, *9*, 1157–1174. [CrossRef]
69. Zhang, Y.; Zhu, H.; Tang, D.; Zhou, T.; Gui, Y. Dynamic job shop scheduling based on deep reinforcement learning for multi-agent manufacturing systems. *Robot. Comput. Integr. Manuf.* **2022**, *78*, 102412. [CrossRef]
70. Liang, Y.; Sun, Z.; Song, T.; Chou, Q.; Fan, W.; Fan, J.; Rui, Y.; Zhou, Q.; Bai, J.; Yang, C.; et al. Lenovo Schedules Laptop Manufacturing Using Deep Reinforcement Learning. *Interfaces* **2022**, *52*, 56–68. [CrossRef]
71. Chen, Y.; Guo, W.; Liu, J.; Shen, S.; Lin, J.; Cui, D. A multi-setpoint cooling control approach for air-cooled data centers using the deep Q-network algorithm. *Meas. Control* **2024**, *57*, 782–793. [CrossRef]
72. Théate, T.; Ernst, D. An application of deep reinforcement learning to algorithmic trading. *Expert Syst. Appl.* **2021**, *173*, 114632. [CrossRef]
73. Sanaye, S.; Sarrafi, A. A novel energy management method based on Deep Q Network algorithm for low operating cost of an integrated hybrid system. *Energy Rep.* **2021**, *7*, 2647–2663. [CrossRef]
74. Luo, S. Dynamic scheduling for flexible job shop with new job insertions by deep reinforcement learning. *Appl. Soft Comput. J.* **2020**, *91*, 106208. [CrossRef]
75. Luo, S.; Zhang, L.; Fan, Y. Real-Time Scheduling for Dynamic Partial-No-Wait Multiobjective Flexible Job Shop by Deep Reinforcement Learning. *IEEE Trans. Autom. Sci. Eng.* **2022**, *19*, 3020–3038. [CrossRef]

76. Hu, J.; Wang, H.; Tang, H.-K.; Kanazawa, T.; Gupta, C.; Farahat, A. Knowledge-enhanced reinforcement learning for multi-machine integrated production and maintenance scheduling. *Comput. Ind. Eng.* **2023**, *185*, 109631. [CrossRef]
77. Du, Y.; Li, J.Q.; Chen, X.L.; Duan, P.Y.; Pan, Q.K. Knowledge-Based Reinforcement Learning and Estimation of Distribution Algorithm for Flexible Job Shop Scheduling Problem. *IEEE Trans. Emerg. Top. Comput. Intell.* **2023**, *7*, 1036–1050. [CrossRef]
78. Li, Y.; Gu, W.; Yuan, M.; Tang, Y. Real-time data-driven dynamic scheduling for flexible job shop with insufficient transportation resources using hybrid deep Q network. *Robot. Comput. Integr. Manuf.* **2022**, *74*, 102283. [CrossRef]
79. Zhou, T.; Zhu, H.; Tang, D.; Liu, C.; Cai, Q.; Shi, W.; Gui, Y. Reinforcement learning for online optimization of job-shop scheduling in a smart manufacturing factory. *Adv. Mech. Eng.* **2022**, *14*, 16878132221086120. [CrossRef]
80. Wang, L.; Hu, X.; Wang, Y.; Xu, S.; Ma, S.; Yang, K.; Wang, W. Dynamic job-shop scheduling in smart manufacturing using deep reinforcement learning. *Comput. Netw.* **2021**, *190*, 107969. [CrossRef]
81. Wang, Y.; Usher, J.M. Application of reinforcement learning for agent-based production scheduling. *Eng. Appl. Artif. Intell.* **2005**, *18*, 73–82. [CrossRef]
82. Cancino, C.A.; Merigó, J.M.; Coronado, F.C. A bibliometric analysis of leading universities in innovation research. *J. Innov. Knowl.* **2017**, *2*, 106–124. [CrossRef]
83. Varin, C.; Cattelan, M.; Firth, D. Statistical modelling of citation exchange between statistics journals. *J. R. Stat. Soc. Ser. A Stat. Soc.* **2016**, *179*, 1–63. [CrossRef] [PubMed]
84. Moral-Muñoz, J.A.; Herrera-Viedma, E.; Santisteban-Espejo, A.; Cobo, M.J. Software tools for conducting bibliometric analysis in science: An up-to-date review. *Prof. De La Inf./Inf. Prof.* **2020**, *29*, e290103. [CrossRef]
85. Curry, S. Let's move beyond the rhetoric: It's time to change how we judge research. *Nature* **2018**, *554*, 147–148. [CrossRef] [PubMed]
86. Al-Hoorie, A.; Vitta, J.P. The seven sins of L2 research: A review of 30 journals' statistical quality and their CiteScore, SJR, SNIP, JCR Impact Factors. *Lang. Teach. Res.* **2019**, *23*, 727–744. [CrossRef]
87. Waltman, L.; Van Eck, N.J.; Noyons, E.C.M. A Unified Approach to Mapping and Clustering of Bibliometric Networks. *J. Informetr.* **2010**, *4*, 629–635. [CrossRef]
88. Cheng, F.; Huang, Y.; Tanpure, B.; Sawalani, P.; Cheng, L.; Liu, C. Cost-aware job scheduling for cloud instances using deep reinforcement learning. *Clust. Comput.* **2022**, *25*, 619–631. [CrossRef]
89. Thaipisutikul, T.; Chen, Y.-C.; Hui, L.; Chen, S.-C.; Mongkolwat, P.; Shih, T.K. The matter of deep reinforcement learning towards practical AI applications. In Proceedings of the 12th International Conference on Ubi-Media Computing, Bali, Indonesia, 5–8 August 2019; pp. 24–29.
90. Yan, J.; Huang, Y.; Gupta, A.; Gupta, A.; Liu, C.; Li, J.; Cheng, L. Energy-aware systems for real-time job scheduling in cloud data centers: A deep reinforcement learning approach. *Comput. Electr. Eng.* **2022**, *99*, 107688. [CrossRef]
91. Piller, F.T. Mass customization: Reflections on the state of the concept. *Int. J. Flex. Manuf. Syst.* **2004**, *16*, 313–334. [CrossRef]
92. Suzić, N.; Forza, C.; Trentin, A.; Anišić, Z. Implementation guidelines for mass customization: Current characteristics and suggestions for improvement. *Prod. Plan. Control* **2018**, *29*, 856–871. [CrossRef]
93. Altenmüller, T.; Stüker, T.; Waschneck, B.; Kuhnle, A.; Lanza, G. Reinforcement learning for an intelligent and autonomous production control of complex job-shops under time constraints. *Prod. Eng.* **2020**, *14*, 319–328. [CrossRef]
94. Zhao, Y.; Zhang, H. Application of machine learning and rule scheduling in a job-shop production control system. *Int. J. Simul. Model* **2021**, *20*, 410–421. [CrossRef]
95. Kuhnle, A.; Kaiser, J.P.; Theiß, F.; Stricker, N.; Lanza, G. Designing an adaptive production control system using reinforcement learning. *J. Intell. Manuf.* **2021**, *32*, 855–876. [CrossRef]
96. Panzer, M.; Bender, B.; Gronau, N. Deep reinforcement learning in production planning and control: A systematic literature review. In Proceedings of the Conference on Production Systems and Logistics, Online, 10–11 August 2021.
97. Wojakowski, P.; Warżołek, D. The classification of scheduling problems under production uncertainty. *Res. Logist. Prod.* **2014**, *4*, 245–256.
98. Blackstone, J.H.; Phillips, D.T.; Hogg, G.L. A state-of-the-art survey of dispatching rules for manufacturing job shop operations. *Int. J. Prod. Res.* **1982**, *20*, 27–45. [CrossRef]
99. Blazewicz, J.; Ecker, K.H.; Pesch, E.; Schmidt, G.; Weglarz, J. *Handbook on Scheduling: From Theory to Applications*; Springer: Berlin/Heidelberg, Germany, 2007.
100. Ivanov, D.; Dolgui, A.; Sokolov, B. A dynamic approach to multi-stage job shop scheduling in an industry 4.0-based flexible assembly system. In *Advances in Production Management Systems. The Path to Intelligent, Collaborative and Sustainable Manufacturing: IFIP WG 5.7 International Conference, APMS 2017, Hamburg, Germany, 3–7 September 2017, Proceedings, Part I*; Springer International Publishing: Cham, Switzerland; pp. 475–482.
101. Modrak, V. (Ed.) *Mass Customized Manufacturing: Theoretical Concepts and Practical Approaches*; CRC Press: Boca Raton, FL, USA, 2017.
102. Komaki, G.M.; Sheikh, S.; Malakooti, B. Flow shop scheduling problems with assembly operations: A review and new trends. *Int. J. Prod. Res.* **2019**, *57*, 2926–2955. [CrossRef]
103. Yang, Y.; Li, X. A knowledge-driven constructive heuristic algorithm for the distributed assembly blocking flow shop scheduling problem. *Expert Syst. Appl.* **2022**, *202*, 117269. [CrossRef]

104. Nasiri, M.M.; Yazdanparast, R.; Jolai, F. A simulation optimisation approach for real-time scheduling in an open shop environment using a composite dispatching rule. *Int. J. Comput. Integr. Manuf.* **2017**, *30*, 1239–1252. [CrossRef]
105. Abdelmaguid, T.F. Bi-objective dynamic multiprocessor open shop scheduling for maintenance and healthcare diagnostics. *Expert Syst. Appl.* **2021**, *186*, 115777. [CrossRef]
106. Tremblet, D.; Thevenin, S.; Dolgui, A. Makespan estimation in a flexible job-shop scheduling environment using machine learning. *Int. J. Prod. Res.* **2024**, *62*, 3654–3670. [CrossRef]
107. Fu, Y.; Hou, Y.; Wang, Z.; Wu, X.; Gao, K.; Wang, L. Distributed scheduling problems in intelligent manufacturing systems. *Tsinghua Sci. Technol.* **2021**, *26*, 625–645. [CrossRef]
108. Zhang, Y.; Zhang, X.; Ding, Y. A Reinforcement Learning-Based Approach to Stochastic Job Shop Scheduling. *IEEE Trans. Autom. Sci. Eng.* **2020**, *17*, 72–83.
109. Rinciog, A.; Meyer, A. Towards standardizing reinforcement learning approaches for stochastic production scheduling. *arXiv* **2021**, arXiv:2104.08196.
110. Zeng, B.; Yang, Y. A Hybrid Reinforcement Learning and Fuzzy Logic Approach for Job Shop Scheduling. *J. Intell. Manuf.* **2017**, *28*, 1189–1201.
111. Zhang, G.; Huang, Y. Fuzzy reinforcement learning for multi-objective dynamic scheduling of a flexible manufacturing system. *J. Intell. Manuf.* **2005**, *16*, 293–304.

Disclaimer/Publisher's Note: The statements, opinions and data contained in all publications are solely those of the individual author(s) and contributor(s) and not of MDPI and/or the editor(s). MDPI and/or the editor(s) disclaim responsibility for any injury to people or property resulting from any ideas, methods, instructions or products referred to in the content.

Review

Unlocking the Potential of Remanufacturing Through Machine Learning and Data-Driven Models—A Survey

Yong Han Kim [1], Wei Ye [2], Ritbik Kumar [1], Finn Bail [3], Julia Dvorak [3], Yanchao Tan [2], Marvin Carl May [3], Qing Chang [4], Ragu Athinarayanan [2], Gisela Lanza [3], John W. Sutherland [1], Xingyu Li [2,*] and Chandra Nath [1]

[1] Environmental and Ecological Engineering, Purdue University, 500 Central Dr, West Lafayette, IN 47907, USA
[2] School of Engineering Technology, Purdue University, 401 N. Grant St., West Lafayette, IN 47907, USA
[3] wbk Institute of Production Science, Karlsruhe Institute of Technology (KIT), Kaiserstrasse 12, 76131 Karlsruhe, Germany
[4] Department of Mechanical and Aerospace Engineering, University of Virginia, Charlottesville, VA 22903, USA
* Correspondence: li4558@purdue.edu

Abstract: As a key strategy for achieving a circular economy, remanufacturing involves bringing end-of-use (EoU) products or cores back to a 'like new' condition, providing more affordable and sustainable alternatives to new products. Despite the potential for substantial resources and energy savings, the industry faces operational challenges. These challenges arise from uncertainties surrounding core quality and functionality, return times, process variation required to meet product specifications, and the end-of-use (EoU) product values, as well as their new life expectancy after extended use as a 'market product'. While remanufacturing holds immense promise, its full potential can only be realized through concerted efforts towards resolving the inherent complexities and obstacles that impede its operations. Machine learning (ML) and data-driven models emerge as transformative tools to mitigate numerous challenges encountered by manufacturing industry. Recently, the integration of cutting-edge technologies, such as sensor-based product data acquisition and storage, data analytics, machine health management, artificial intelligence (AI)-driven scheduling, and human–robot collaboration (HRC), in remanufacturing procedures has received significant attention from remanufacturers and the circular economy community. These advanced computational technologies help remanufacturers to implement flexible operation scheduling, enhance quality control, and streamline workflows for EoU products. This study embarks on a comprehensive review and in-depth analysis of state-of-the-art algorithms across various facets of remanufacturing processes and operations. Additionally, it identifies key challenges to advancing remanufacturing practices through data-driven and ML methods and uncovers research opportunities in synergy with smart manufacturing techniques. The study aims to offer guidelines for stakeholders and to reinforce the industry's pivotal role in circular economy initiatives.

Keywords: remanufacturing; circular economy; machine learning; data-driven models; sustainability

Citation: Kim, Y.H.; Ye, W.; Kumar, R.; Bail, F.; Dvorak, J.; Tan, Y.; May, M.C.; Chang, Q.; Athinarayanan, R.; Lanza, G.; et al. Unlocking the Potential of Remanufacturing Through Machine Learning and Data-Driven Models—A Survey. *Algorithms* **2024**, *17*, 562. https://doi.org/10.3390/a17120562

Academic Editor: Frank Werner

Received: 26 August 2024
Revised: 13 November 2024
Accepted: 17 November 2024
Published: 8 December 2024

Copyright: © 2024 by the authors. Licensee MDPI, Basel, Switzerland. This article is an open access article distributed under the terms and conditions of the Creative Commons Attribution (CC BY) license (https://creativecommons.org/licenses/by/4.0/).

1. Introduction

Remanufacturing is one of the key elements in a circular economy, aiming to restore full or partial value of end-of-use (EoU) products to a 'like new' or refurbished condition through processes such as disassembly, cleaning, repair, component replacement, and re-assembly [1,2]. As depicted in Figure 1, through extending the life cycles of products by restoring their values to a near-new condition and keeping the resources in a closed loop as long as possible, remanufacturing conserves valuable resources and reduces the environmental footprint associated with the extraction, processing, and transportation of raw materials for creating brand new products, thereby enhancing sustainability [3,4].

The benefits of remanufacturing are substantial, in terms of resource preservation [5,6], reduced energy intensity [7], lower environmental impact [8], and notable economic gains [9], owing to significant reduction in the use of new materials, water, and other energy sources required for traditional manufacturing processes [10–13].

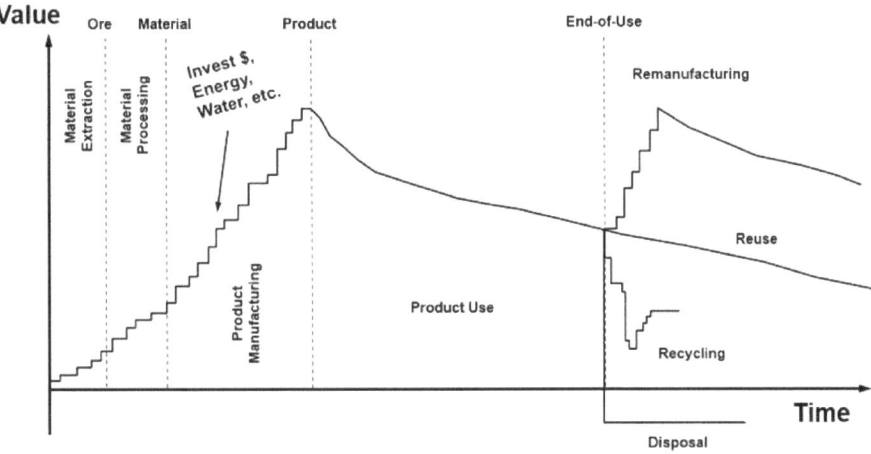

Figure 1. Value recovery over time in a product's life cycle (adapted from [14]).

Among several strategic decisions, in terms of reuse, remanufacturing, recycling, or disposal, as shown in Figure 1, remanufacturing is crucial for enhancing manufacturing sustainability, preserving the value of products, and fostering techno-economic benefits. However, the conceptualization and implementation of remanufacturing involves several significant challenges. First, the inherent uncertainty in product condition and mechanical functionality arises from the duration and environment of the product's use, as well as the consumer's independent decision to return it. Guide et al. highlighted that uncertainties regarding the timing, quantity, and condition of materials recovered from cores are critical factors complicating decision-making in remanufacturing [15]. Factors such as component condition, disassembly sequence, and market values are crucial in trading off between sustainability and profitability [16]. Additionally, the remanufacturing process necessitates an effective reverse logistics system to facilitate the acquisition of cores from the market. The complexity of adapting to customer behaviors and incentives for participating in reverse logistics further complicates the coordination of various stages. This necessitates enhanced data visibility in areas such as product quality, material flow, energy flow, shopfloor operations, and inventory management [17,18]. Therefore, efficient tracking of products and usage information across the life cycle are vital for optimizing remanufacturing efforts [12,19].

The heterogeneous quality conditions of returned products require customized production and planning strategies during remanufacturing and associated procedures. Variability in core conditions leads to fluctuating processing times, different reconditioning paths, variable inventory control and resource allocation, and complex re-entrant routings [20,21], creating a dynamic and challenging operational environment [20]. Accordingly, these variations demand extensive manual operation [22], involving core assessment, operation sequencing, and selection of disassembly and reconditioning techniques. The complexity of planning the remanufacturing process requires a deep knowledge of product design, failure modes, and production capabilities [23]. A study on the remanufacturing procedure of EoU returned products indicated that grading cores into different quality classes by involving humans can enhance profitability by only up to 4% [24]. To address the above-mentioned challenges, thereby improving remanufacturing efficiency and overall plant profits, recent advancements have introduced automation and HRC technologies that facilitate the adaptation of processes to varying core conditions. This includes incorporating advanced in-line/in situ inspection technologies, collaborative robots, decision support systems, and automated disassembly planning tools [1].

The advent of Industry 4.0 and advanced computational methods, such as ML and data-driven analysis, offer promising solutions to address the challenges faced by the remanufacturing industry [25]. Technologies such as the Industrial Internet of Things (IIoT) [26], Digital Twins [27], Cobot [28], Virtual Reality (VR), and Augmented Reality (AR) [29,30] could help fast and accurate data acquisition, real-time data access, and support improving efficiency during remanufacturing activities in different ways [31]. Data-driven and ML methods are poised to improve remanufacturing by enabling more precise prediction and classification of product conditions [32], thereby improving quality control and waste management [21]. Additionally, these advanced techniques can optimize inventory management and operational scheduling [1,33], leading to further cost reductions, improved operational efficiency, and resource utilization. Despite the potential alignment, research on developing ML and data-driven methods for remanufacturing systems is still in its early stages [34], indicating that a comprehensive baseline and critical discussion of existing research opportunities and gaps is critically required.

This review study systematically explores the synergistic impacts of advanced computational technologies on remanufacturing activities. Our approach makes a three-fold contribution to the existing research as follows: (i) a systematic review of the existing literature on remanufacturing to understand current trends, major topics, and potential synergies with advanced computational methods (refer to Section 2); (ii) the development of a conceptual framework that integrates data-driven and ML methods into remanufacturing processes, advancing theoretical understanding of their interactions and impacts (Section 3); and (iii) the identification of research gaps and opportunities related to the implementation of smart technologies and advanced computing methods in remanufacturing procedure in industry (Section 4). Section 5 presents our findings and outlooks in the context of smart manufacturing, followed by concluding remarks in Section 6.

2. Remanufacturing Literature Topic Analysis

A topic model is utilized to understand the underlying topics in remanufacturing related research. This approach enables us to understand the current state, underlying topics, and trend of remanufacturing-related research. By mapping out the existing knowledge base, we can better assess how advanced computational methods intersect with remanufacturing practices and pinpoint areas for further investigation and development. To ensure a comprehensive and technically relevant literature review, we deliberately focused on high-impact journals and peer-reviewed conference papers sourced from the *Web of Science*, prioritizing sources that contribute to the understanding and development of remanufacturing systems. Our query, executed on 10 June 2024, utilized the keyword *"remanufactur*"* (Topic), resulting in a collection of approximately 6000 articles related to remanufacturing.

Figure 2 illustrates the upward trend in remanufacturing-related publications over the past 50 years, with a notably steeper increase since 2008. This surge indicates a significant rise in scholarly interest and activity in the remanufacturing field, likely driven by advancements in smart manufacturing technologies and an increasing emphasis on manufacturing sustainability and global decarbonization goals. Since 2014, propelled by advancements in information and communication technologies, there has been a clear, sustained increase in the application of data-driven and AI/ML methods in remanufacturing research, with a growth rate exceeding 30% annually, underscoring the field's growing attention to and methodological alignment in tackling remanufacturing challenges.

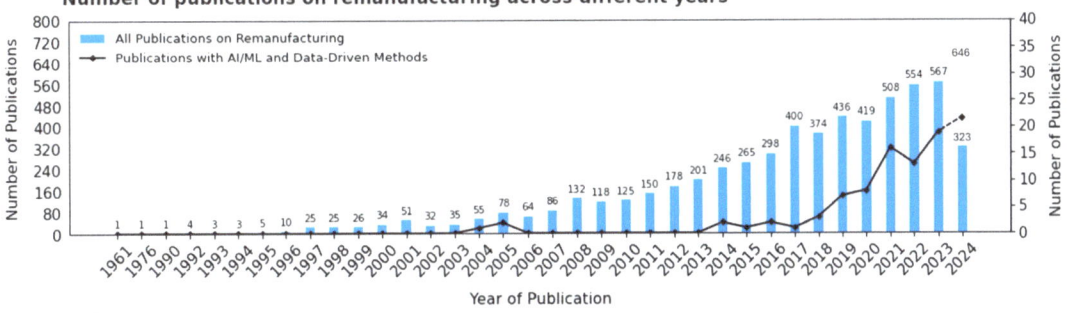

Figure 2. Annual publication trends in remanufacturing (blue bars) and in AI/ML and data-driven methods applied to remanufacturing (black solid line) over the past 60 years (as of July 2024). Projected 2024 values for remanufacturing publications and AI/ML data-driven publications are shown by grey bars and a dashed line, respectively. Source: Web of Science—Remanufacturing—https://www.webofscience.com/wos/woscc/basic-research accessed on 10 July 2024.

To uncover the latent topics and their distributions within the collected remanufacturing literature, we employed the *Latent Dirichlet Allocation* model [35], a widely recognized technique for topic modeling, to the abstracts of all collected articles. Given the limited body of literature specifically addressing AI/ML and data-driven methods in remanufacturing, the topic model may have limitations in identifying themes within this smaller subset. Our analysis seeks to clarify the dominating topics of remanufacturing-related research and reveal potential avenues for understanding the synergistic effects of integrating ML and data-driven methods with remanufacturing practices. Table 1 presents the results of the model, which identified nine distinct topics across the collected 6000 articles. Each topic was named based on the most frequently occurring terms in the associated articles to aid in interpreting the thematic content. For instance, 'Topic 0' prominently features words such as *'closed_loop'* and *'closed_loop supply chain'*, leading to the topic name *'Closed-Loop Supply Chain'*.

Table 1. Overview of identified remanufacturing topics based on their frequent keywords.

Index	Topic Names	Frequent Words
0	Closed-Loop Supply Chain	'closed_loop', 'closed_loop supply chain'
1	Reverse Logistics	'reverse', 'logistics'
2	Carbon Emission	'carbon', 'emission', 'reduction'
3	Life Cycle Management	'life_cycle', 'circular_economy', 'reuse'
4	Inventory Policy	'inventory', 'policy', 'return'
5	Collaborative Business Models	'retailer', 'third-party', 'manufacturer'
6	Process Optimization	'disassembly', 'assembly', 'planning'
7	Repair Technologies	'laser', 'cladding', 'coating'
8	Techno-Economic Assessment	'economic', 'sustainable', 'company'

To further analyze the topics and their interrelationships, we used the *t-distributed Stochastic Neighbor Embedding (or t-SNE)*, which is a nonlinear dimensionality reduction technique that can visualize high-dimensional data in a low-dimensional space. Figure 3 presents the topic distributions in a two-dimensional space to help understand the relationships in the data. The x- and y-axes of the plot represent new abstract coordinates derived by the t-SNE algorithm. These 2-dimensional (2D) coordinates are not tied to any specific features or values from the original data. Instead, they are designed to visualize the high-dimensional topic labels in a lower-dimensional space. Each dot in the scatter data represents an article, with the color of the dot indicating the corresponding topic category. The distance between dots reflects the similarity of topics; dots of the same color are typically located in close topic proximity, while the spatial arrangement of different clusters indicates the degree of similarity among various topics.

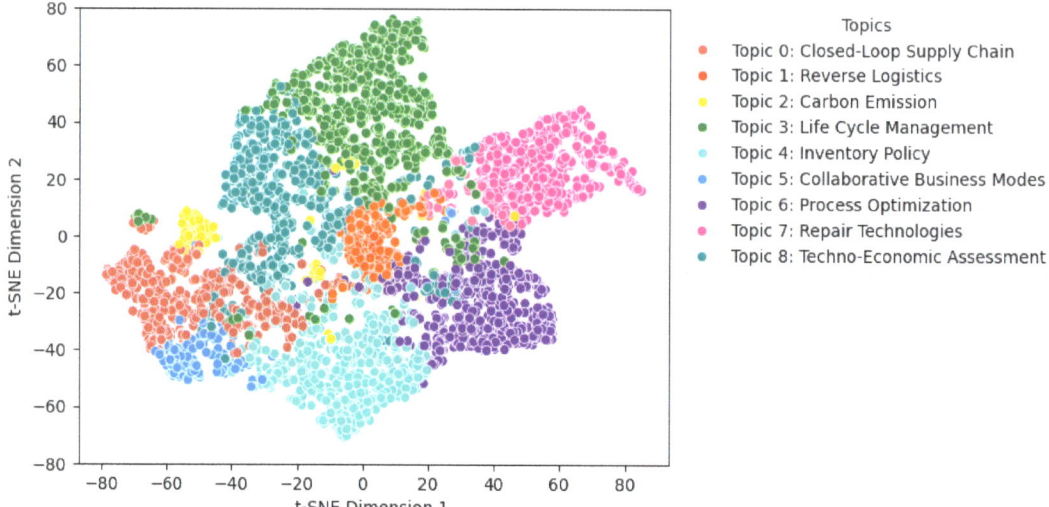

Figure 3. Articles clustered by topics visualized in the 2D space across the collected 6000 articles.

By visualizing the topics and their interrelationships using the *Latent Dirichlet Allocation* model, we identified key themes and areas of focus within the field and pinpointed where advanced computational technologies may have the most impact, particularly in topics such as *closed-loop supply chain, reverse logistics, carbon emission, life cycle management, inventory policy* and *process optimization*. Additionally, the identified individual articles' thematic alignments, and how these themes interact and overlap within themselves underscore the potential for collective advancements across various facets of remanufacturing through the application of ML and data-driven methods.

3. ML and Data-Driven Models for Remanufacturing

ML and data-driven models leverage algorithms and statistical techniques to analyze and interpret complex and high-volume data in many fields including manufacturing [36–39]. In remanufacturing, these technologies offer significant potential to enhance various aspects, such as the automated sorting of a wide range of products, improving asset management, facilitating real-time decision-making, and optimizing the entire product life cycle. These technologies can deliver innovative solutions for sequence optimization, quality control, and predictive analysis throughout remanufacturing processes. In this section, we present a detailed summary of key ML and data-driven methods, including explanations of their potential benefits for remanufacturing.

IIoT: By connecting industrial machinery and devices to data collection systems, cloud platforms, and the internet, the Industrial Internet of Things (IIoT) supports extensive data acquisition and real-time analysis across the manufacturing ecosystem [31,40,41]. For remanufacturing, IIoT facilitates fast and accurate asset tracking and inventory management by providing detailed core histories and spare parts availability. Emerging sensing technologies allow accessibility by installing sensors on the inner structure of machines to better understand the machine's operational statuses [42] and support automation by allowing machines to communicate and coordinate with each other [43], resulting in coherent remanufacturing processes.

Traceability: Traceability systems, such as digital product passports (DPP), track the history, location, and status of products throughout their life cycle [44]. For the purpose of remanufacturing, these tools provide detailed histories of cores, ensuring remanufacturers can access all relevant information about previous repairs, modifications, and usage conditions [45]. These data help in assessing the condition of returned EoU products and determining the best remanufacturing approach. The systems also ensure compliance with regulatory standards and build consumer confidence by offering transparency about the origins of materials and processes involved in remanufactured products [46].

ML models: Supervised and unsupervised learning and reinforcement learning (RL) technologies can analyze vast amounts of data to make informed decisions, optimize processes, and predict future outcomes [47,48]. In remanufacturing, these technologies enable predictive analytics to evaluate which parts will need remanufacturing, provide dynamic planning for the timely streamlining of workflows, and support quality assurance to ensure that remanufactured products meet stringent standards [49,50]. AI can also help in designing and facilitating efficient remanufacturing processes by learning from historical data and continuously improving process quality [42] and equipment healthiness [51]. Key ML models applied in remanufacturing include neural networks, deep learning models, and reinforcement learning algorithms as follows: (i) **Neural Networks and Deep Learning Models**, such as Convolutional Neural Networks (CNNs) and Long Short-Term Memory (LSTM) networks, have found significant applications in remanufacturing. CNNs excel in visual inspection tasks, enabling automated defect detection and quality control in remanufactured products [52]. LSTM networks, with their ability to process sequential data, are particularly useful for predicting equipment health and product life cycles, crucial for optimizing maintenance schedules and remanufacturing timing [53,54]; (ii) **RL models**, including Q-Learning, Deep Q-Network (DQN), and Proximal Policy Optimization (PPO), have emerged as powerful tools for dynamic decision-making in remanufacturing processes. These algorithms can optimize workflows, resource allocation, and adaptive quality control processes, learning from continuous feedback to improve remanufacturing strategies over time [55–57].

Data-Driven and Optimization Models: Data-driven and optimization models utilize quantitative algorithms to enhance decision-making. These models include: (i) **Graph-based models**, such as AND/OR Graphs [58,59] and Petri Nets [60], which provide a framework for modeling complex remanufacturing systems and processes, especially in HRC. These models are particularly effective in optimizing disassembly sequences, modeling production workflows, and task allocation within humans and robots; (ii) **Mathematical Programming Models**, including Convex Optimization [61], Linear Programming (LP) [62] and Nonlinear Integer Programming (NLIP) [63,64], offer robust solutions for complex planning and scheduling problems; (iii) **Meta-Heuristics** are optimization methods designed to generate or select heuristics that provide sufficiently good solutions to complex optimization problems [65,66]. In remanufacturing, meta-heuristics, such as the Genetic Algorithm (GA), Bees Algorithm (BA), and Particle Swarm Optimization (PSO), can be used to solve intricate problems related to scheduling, resource allocation, and process optimization [67]. These techniques are particularly useful when dealing with multiple objectives [68] and dynamic remanufacturing environments [69]; (iv) **Probabilistic Models**, including Monte Carlo simulation [70] and Markov chains [71], play a crucial role in modeling uncertainty and stochastic processes inherent in remanufacturing. These models assist in assessing risks, and optimizing decision-making under uncertainty, which is essential given the variable nature of returned products in remanufacturing.

It is important to highlight advanced manufacturing technologies that can provide additional opportunities that could be synergized with the aforementioned algorithms to further enhance remanufacturing processes. Immersive technologies like VR and AR could enhance remanufacturing by providing real-time, detailed visualization and simulation, thereby improving training, design, and troubleshooting processes. VR simulates complex scenarios, while AR assists in assembly, disassembly, and maintenance activities by overlaying digital information onto the physical world, thus enhancing accuracy and reducing training time [72]. Cobots work alongside humans to increase productivity, precision, and safety by handling automated disassembly, cleaning, and reassembly tasks. Cobots are versatile and can be programmed for various tasks, thereby reducing injury risk and ensuring consistent quality in remanufacturing operations [73].

4. Literature Review

In this section, we aim to gain a comprehensive understanding of the field and identify research gaps and opportunities by providing a literature review on the synergies between data-driven and ML methods in remanufacturing. We systematically sorted the literature by matching identified remanufacturing topics in Table 1 with advanced computational methods, as summarized in Table 2. First, we examined the application and associated impacts of the IIoT on life cycle management and closed-loop supply models, emphasizing how these technologies facilitate data-driven decision-making in support of circular economy initiatives (Topics 0–4 in Figure 2). Next, we discuss the potential of optimization and ML techniques to enhance dynamic scheduling and HRC within remanufacturing processes (Topic 6), enabling optimized decision-making amidst uncertainties. Finally, we present our review work on utilizing ML models to understand and manage the quality of remanufacturing processes and products, addressing Topics 6–7.

Figure 4 provides a comprehensive overview of the interactions between machine learning (ML) and data-driven models within remanufacturing tasks, highlighting their connections to life cycle management, scheduling and planning, quality control, and HRC. These areas are supported by a variety of ML and data-driven models, ranging from neural networks to probabilistic approaches. Each model is associated with specific tasks in remanufacturing research, as identified in our literature review.

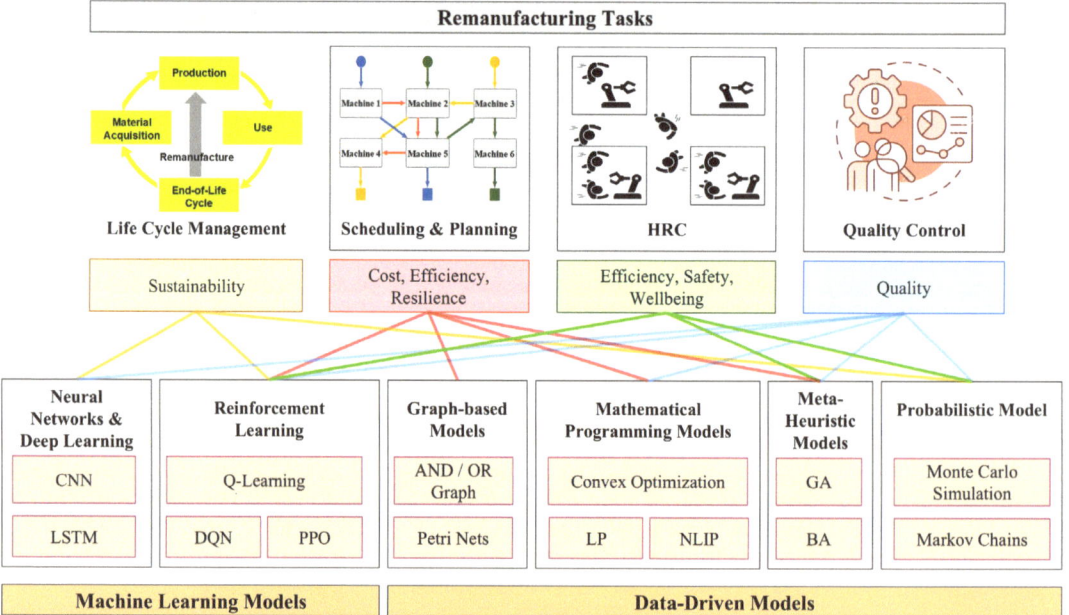

Figure 4. Machine learning and data-driven models and their role in remanufacturing. Abbreviations: CNN—Convolutional Neural Network, LSTM—Long Short-Term Memory, DQN—Deep Q-Network, PPO—Proximal Policy Optimization, LP—Linear Programming, NLIP—Nonlinear Integer Programming, GA—Genetic Algorithms, BA—Bees Algorithm.

Table 2. Applications of machine learning and data-driven models in key remanufacturing topics.

Topics	Applications	Algorithms	Key Findings
Life cycle management	Cylinder heads [44], Energy labeling [46], Aerospace blades [74], E-waste [75], Battery [76,77], Automated vehicle [78], Engine [79]	IIoT [74], Life cycle assessment (LCA) [80], Cobot [77], Digital Twin [78,79], Digital Passport [44–46,75,76]	• Real-time monitoring systems with IIoT and DT enhance the precision, efficiency and success rates of recovering high-value components and materials, thereby contributing to extending product life cycles. • Digital twins and predictive analytics can help forecast EoL scenarios, support proactive maintenance, and ensure that products are effectively remanufactured or recycled.
Reverse logistics	Manufacturers [45], Engine [81], Tactical decisions [82], Solid waste [83], Laptop [84]	Digital passport [45], Digital Twin [81,82], IIoT [81,83,84]	• Digital tools like RFID and cloud-based systems enhance traceability in reverse logistics, minimizing uncertainties in product returns and waste collection. • The integration of advanced technologies supports dynamic management of stochastic demand and material flows, leading to more efficient reverse logistics.
Carbon emission	Food supply chain [85,86], Wind turbine [87]	IIoT [85–87], LCA [80,86], Blockchain [80]	• Integrating LCA with emerging technologies such as IIoT and Blockchain enables accurate real-time monitoring. • IIoT, smart sensors and Blockchain can reduce carbon emissions by optimizing resource utilization, but the energy required for their production and disposal might introduce additional emissions, necessitating a balance in these trade-offs.
Closed-loop supply chain	Manufacturers [45], Food supply chain [85,86], Wind turbine [87], A manufacturing facility [80], Information technology [88], Smartphone [89], Battery [90], Trade-in policy [91]	Digital passport [45], IIoT [85–92], LCA [80,86], Blockchain [88,91]	• Digital integration in the supply chain facilitates better tracking of product returns and efficient materials management, contributing to the overall sustainability of the supply chain. • Successful closed-loop supply chains require improved collaboration among stakeholders, which could be supported by digital platforms that enable data sharing and coordination.
Process optimization	Acquisition strategy [61–64,93–96], Price optimization [97], Process planning [98], Sequence planning [70,99,100], Job shop scheduling [55,101], Carbon footprint [102], System control [56,57,103,104]	Convex Optimization [61], Nonlinear programming [63,64], Linear programming [62], Monte Carlo simulation [70], GA [101], BA [28,100], Deep Q-learning [55,57], PPO [56,103], Root cause analysis [105], Deep belief networks [106]	• Data drive models and ML can help optimize remanufacturing processes through integrating production, planning, and process control mechanisms. • Smart technologies reduce human errors, eliminate individual subjectivity and contribute towards efficient resource utilization.
Repair technology	Process control [107–109], Sorting [105]	RL [32], CNN [105], Transfer learning [106], Gaussian process regression model [107]	• Advanced computational algorithms help devise efficient inspection strategies that play a key part in remanufacturing. • ML assists in continuous improvement and enhances quality assurance through establishing and maintaining product and process key characteristics.
HRC	Assembly [59,60,71,110–112], Quality inspection [58,113], Disassembly [28,70,99,114–121], Remanufacturing [95,100]	AND/OR graphs [58,59], Fuzzification [70], BA [28,99,100], PSO [118], Optimization [115–117,120,122], Transfer learning [121], RNN [111,113], Markov Chains [71], Petri Nets [60], RL [112]	• Balancing of different objectives is essential in HRC • The selection of algorithms varies based on the specific problem types and remanufacturing applications.

4.1. Life Cycle Management

Digital technologies, such as the IIoT, digital twins, and cyber-physical systems, are crucial for implementing data-driven and ML models and for optimizing various facets of the remanufacturing, including process quality control, operational efficiency, LCA, and supply chain management. IIoT techniques facilitate data collection, storage, and analysis, and real-time monitoring, thereby enhancing the visibility and management of the remanufacturing process and the entire life cycle [81]. One study found that integrating machine vision systems and IIoT techniques into aerospace remanufacturing significantly enhances the process by enabling intelligent sensing, real-time data acquisition, and advanced monitoring systems, resulting in higher repair yields, reduced human error, and improved operational safety [74]. Adopting data-driven decision-making in remanufacturing reduces costs, optimizes operations, and enhances quality through real-time insights and predictive analytics [77].

Cyber-physical systems and digital twins create real-time, digital replicas of physical processes, aiming to strengthen synchronization, efficiency, and predictive capabilities across the entire remanufacturing system [123]. A proposed control mechanism based on big data analysis, incorporating cyber-physical systems and digital twin techniques, aims to mitigate uncertainty in remanufacturing using real-time perception and predictive optimization [78]. Moreover, a digital twin model enhanced with a neural network and the Bees Algorithm (BA) for real-time data-driven decisions was presented to optimize remanufacturing planning [79]. Figure 5 presents a proposed conceptual framework to integrate data across the various stages of life cycle management [124].

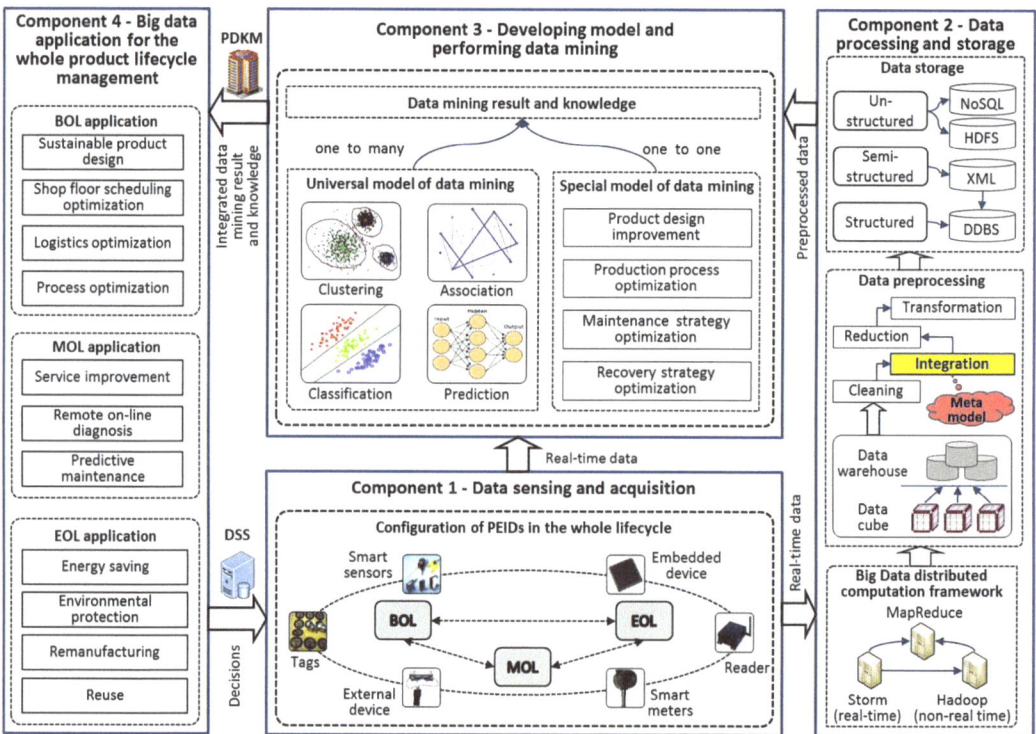

Figure 5. Conceptual framework for integrating big data into product life cycle management (taken from [124]).

The framework includes four major components: data sensing and acquisition, data processing and storage, model development and data mining, and big data application for product life cycle management. The data sensing and acquisition phase gathers information from various life cycle stages through product-embedded devices such as Radio Frequency Identification (RFID) tags and smart sensors, enabling real-time tracking of the status of products, materials and machines. The data processing and storage phase handles the collected data using distributed systems such as Hadoop and Storm, allowing for real-time and non-real-time data analysis and storage. The model development and data mining phase creates models to extract knowledge from big data, including both general models (such as classification, clustering and prediction) and specific models tailored to tasks like enhancing product development and optimizing manufacturing processes. The big data application for product life cycle management phase utilizes the analyzed data to support real-time decision-making, enabling efficient production, logistics and maintenance [124].

Figure 6 illustrates a conceptual model from [125] that integrates IIoT concepts into remanufacturing, establishing a framework for real-time information capture and integration, aiming to facilitate the implementation of data-driven production scheduling on the shop floor [125]. Digital technologies have contributed significantly to LCA methodologies and environmental impact evaluations. LCA is an effective method for measuring the environmental impacts of a system throughout its entire life span [126]. The environmental benefits of smart sensors in reducing food loss were assessed using an LCA model, which highlighted the need to manage potential environmental burdens from sensor manufacturing and disposal for overall sustainability [85]. Zhu et al. introduced a novel four-layer LCA framework integrating IIoT technology to improve real-time data collection and monitoring, demonstrated through a wind turbine case study [87]. Additionally, Zhang et al. developed a new LCA model incorporating blockchain, IIoT, and big data analytics to enhance the efficiency and reliability of LCA, improving data integrity and decision-making [80]. Figure 7 illustrates a multi-level blockchain-based LCA system designed in [80] that connects the manufacturing infrastructures and activities at different stages with a diverse range of applications and users. Moreover, an open-source LCA tool utilizing IIoT to track food quality and assess environmental impacts across multiple stages of the food supply chain was also introduced [86]. Digital technologies have been applied to waste management, playing a critical role in improving product design for remanufacturing. Waste streams of automotive products were analyzed to support product design that facilitates remanufacturing [127] and to determine factors that impede the reuse of parts [128]. Wang et al. introduced WRCloud, a novel service-oriented remanufacturing platform based on cloud manufacturing principles, designed to improve interoperability, intelligence, and adaptability in managing waste electrical and electronic equipment [129].

IIoT is crucial for advancing data acquisition and sharing throughout various closed-loop supply chain stages and remanufacturing processes [130]. AI and blockchain technologies can strengthen supply chain resilience and sustainability by facilitating operations such as just-in-time manufacturing, streamlined automation, and remanufacturing [88]. Additionally, Pan and Miao presented a model for assessing risks in closed-loop supply chains for remanufacturing using neural networks to improve risk assessment accuracy and supply chain management [92]. Yu proposed a novel mathematical model to assist decision-making in reverse logistics for remanufacturing and discussed the impacts of IIoT technology on remanufacturing companies [82]. Innovative approaches in closed-loop supply chain management leverage digital technologies to enhance efficiency and sustainability. For instance, a closed-loop supply chain model utilizing IIoT data has been proposed to optimize the life cycle of products, focusing on EoL recovery processes, including cost and demand for remanufacturing [89]. Similarly, Tavana et al. designed a circular supply chain network for handling electric vehicle lithium-ion batteries, leveraging IIoT and big data technologies to address uncertainties and enhance overall management efficiency [90]. The integration of IIoT with a kanban system has enabled real-time monitoring and dynamic scheduling in reverse logistics, improving waste collection and recycling processes [83]. Additionally, Tozanlı et al. investigated trade-in strategies within closed-loop supply chains, optimizing disassembly decisions through simulations integrated with IIoT and blockchain technologies [91]. The use of embedded IIoT devices to evaluate product designs for EoL recovery helps determine the most effective designs for remanufacturing, increasing profitability and reducing waste [84].

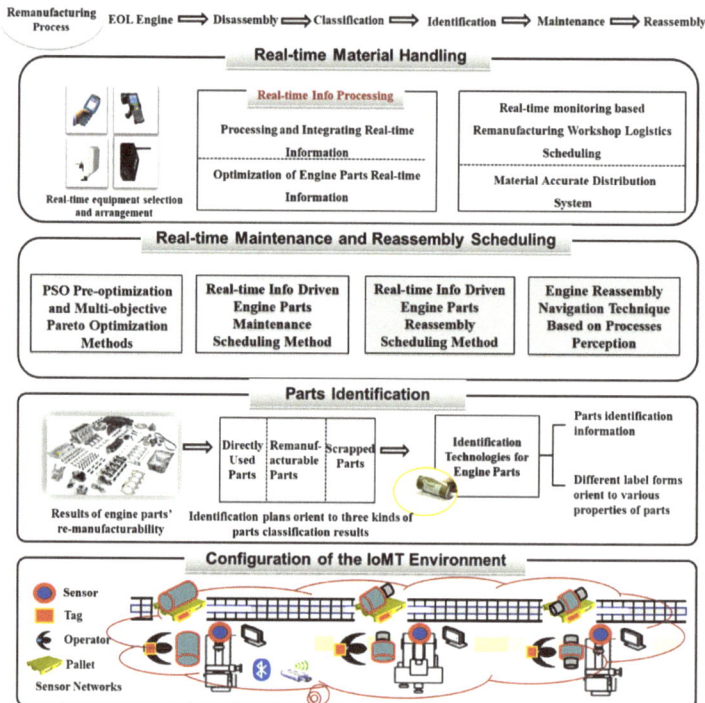

Figure 6. IIoT-integrated scheduling model for engine remanufacturing (adopted from [125]).

The acquisition and collection of cores depend not only on customers and usage history as identical products can be different in quality [131]. A DPP can enhance the acquisition and collection of cores by providing detailed, real-time data on product history and condition, which improves the predictability of recovery processes and differentiates between varying quality levels [132]. Plociennik et al. introduced a Digital Life Cycle Passport, utilizing a cloud-based platform and the Asset Administration Shell, which enabled comprehensive data sharing across the product life cycle, as described in Figure 8. This was exemplified by an e-waste sorting case study that showcased its potential to automate and optimize sorting decisions [75]. Adisorn et al. also explored the role of DPPs as a policy tool for supporting a circular economy, emphasizing their capacity to provide critical product-related information to stakeholders throughout the product life cycle [46]. Additionally, Berger et al. identified key information requirements for Digital Battery Passports, including specifications, diagnostics, and maintenance data, which were essential for managing and making decisions throughout the electric vehicle battery life cycle [76]. Jensen et al. further detailed the data needs for DPPs to enhance circular supply chain management, identifying seven crucial data clusters through a mechatronics case study [45]. Szaller et al. investigated the impact of DPPs on information sharing in remanufacturing processes, demonstrating that increased information availability through DPPs reduced production uncertainties, lowered non-productive time, and improved the remanufacturing ratio [44].

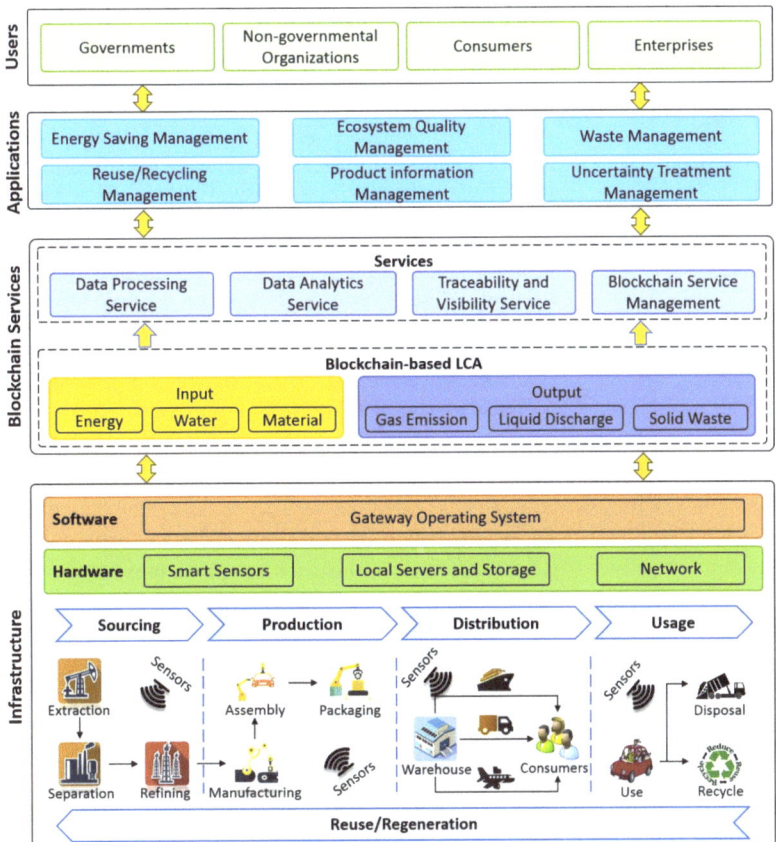

Figure 7. LCA system utilizing blockchain technology (taken from [80]).

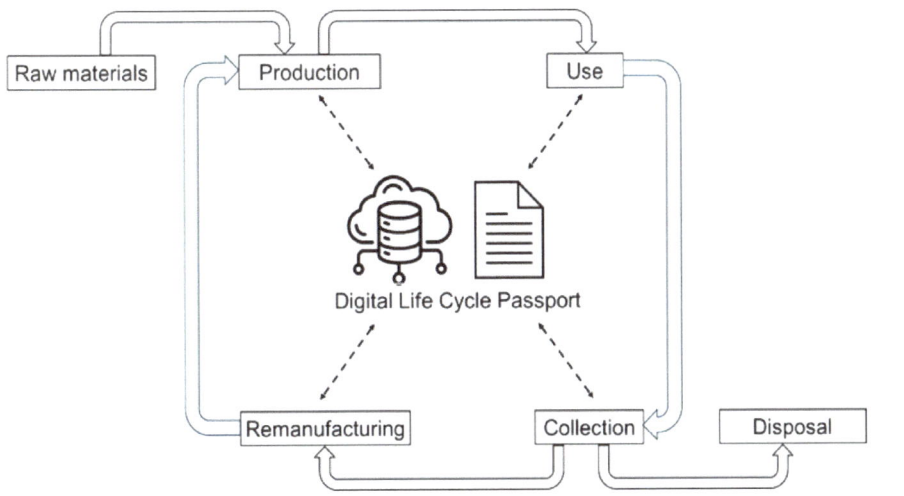

Figure 8. Data management via the digital life cycle passport (DLCP) (modified from [75]).

4.2. Scheduling and Planning

Effective scheduling and planning are essential for remanufacturing management as they ensure optimal resource allocation, minimize downtime, and enhance overall operational efficiency. To address the challenges of process complexity and demand uncertainties, data-driven optimization and RL models have been developed. Various types of uncertainties impact the scheduling and planning of the remanufacturing process. The most studied uncertainty is the quality of returned cores [55,61,62,93–95,97,98,103], which significantly impacts the remanufacturing process requirements, resource needed, and cost estimates. Another crucial uncertainty is the disassembly time [70,99,101,102], which affects process planning and resource management. Additionally, uncertainties related to the cores and demands [93,94,96] affect production planning and inventory management, with variations arising from differences in core return timing and quality [61,63]. Furthermore, remanufacturing failure rates [55,101,102] are crucial for robust process planning and quality assurance. While these uncertainties are well documented, others like the resources needed for remanufacturing [63], are less discussed.

ML and data-driven models are powerful tools to address the challenges in scheduling and planning, particularly through meta-heuristic, mathematical optimization, and RL techniques. Mathematical optimization techniques are utilized to maximize profit and minimize costs in scheduling and planning in remanufacturing. These methods typically target optimizing acquisition qualities and quantities, remanufacturing decisions, and resource allocation. For instance, Yang et al. formulated a convex optimization, an extended multi-product Newsvendor Problem, to maximize overall profit [62]. Similarly, a nonlinear integer programming (NLIP) model was developed to minimize the total cost of acquisition, remanufacturing, and scrapping of cores [63]. Other data-driven approaches integrate with linear programming to maximize total profit [62], applying nonlinear programming models considering carbon emissions [64]. The objectives of these models are often costs, revenue, and environmental benefits. Meta-heuristic techniques address complex, multi-objective optimization problems in scheduling and planning. Examples include a modified discrete BA for disassembly sequence planning [100], and an improved discrete BA for workstation optimization [28]. Zheng et al. proposed a GA combined with an improved random forest classifier to intelligently select the optimal rescheduling method based on system status, as shown in Figure 9. The system status is characterized by factors such as machine utilization, job processing times, and the total time required for reworked operations [101].

RL has proven to be effective in handling uncertainties in remanufacturing, such as the quality of returned products, machine failures, and varying initial states. Bai et al. used Q-learning and DQN algorithms to minimize total production time, continuously adapting to dynamic conditions [55]. Wurster et al. dynamically controlled a hybrid disassembly system, consisting of various types of stations, using DQN to minimize labor costs, idling costs, makespan, and failures [57]. Paschko et al. dealt with the control of job release in a hybrid disassembly line, minimizing work in progress and maximizing throughput using PPO [56]. Peng et al. employed PPO to optimize disassembly scheduling and minimize makespan, utilizing the strength of RL to adapt to various uncertainties and improve decision-making over time [103].

Hybrid approaches that combine multiple algorithms have also demonstrated effectiveness. For example, one study integrated fuzzy dynamic modeling and Monte Carlo simulations with RL for robotic disassembly optimization [70]. The combination of different techniques holds significant potential for developing robust and adaptive systems capable of navigating the dynamic landscape of remanufacturing scheduling and planning. Future research could focus on further integrating these approaches to leverage their respective strengths and address increasingly complex challenges in remanufacturing.

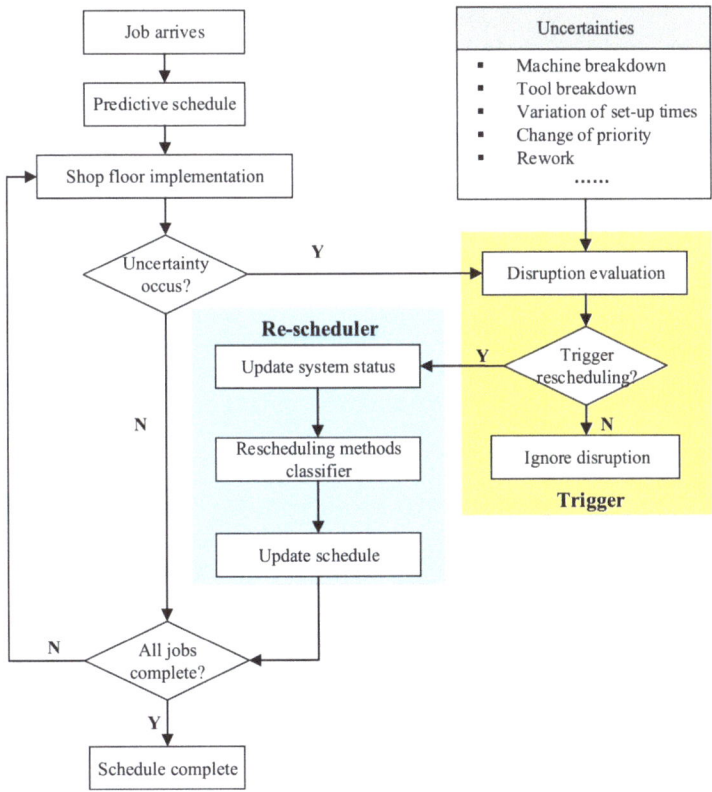

Figure 9. Flowchart of adaptive (re)scheduling strategy (taken from [101]).

4.3. Quality Control

Quality control in remanufacturing involves assessing and validating the condition of returned components or remanufactured products to ensure they meet specified standards before reprocessing or market release. Remanufacturing models in the literature often assume quality to be homogeneous; however, it has wide variations due to customer usage, usage length, and special product characteristics [133]. These variations make inspection processes in remanufacturing labor-intensive and time-consuming. Advanced computational methods, such as object detection and defect identification, can aid in evaluating the condition, reusability, and quality grade of returned cores, addressing the high uncertainty and subjective bias associated with manual assessments [134]. In this section, we review and categorize the literature on the use of data-driven and ML methods for automating remanufacturing quality control. These technologies help overcome issues related to individual subjectivity, time constraints, and high labor costs by excelling in learning complex geometries and patterns [135].

Kaiser et al. highlighted the challenges of high uncertainty in the inspection process related to cores and addressed these by utilizing RL models to capture cores, and an unsupervised learning model for anomaly detection [32], as demonstrated in Figure 10. The figure demonstrates the model capability of handling uncertainty in remanufacturing through its adaptable architecture. As shown in the figure, the model starts with processing, comparing the core's expected and inspected conditions. Deviations are flagged for review. Sensors capture data during the perception stage, which the quality controller analyzes for defects. Finally, during decision-making, the system decides if the core is reusable or should be rejected, automating the entire inspection process. Few-shot learning techniques were employed to categorize anomalies and to precisely assess the core's quality grade [32]. Nwankpa et al. presented a novel inspection process with a deep convolution neural network for mild steel plates to detect eight fault conditions and their combinations [105]. The high accuracy of the model on a small dataset demonstrated its robustness and efficiency, making it an ideal solution for smart inspection strategy in remanufacturing.

Islam et al. presented an automated sorting system utilizing a smart conveyor with multiple cameras, reflective sensors, and a PC running Python applications. It leverages inception transfer learning for image classification and the YOLO model for object detection, ensuring robust and high-accuracy identification and sorting of remanufacturing parts through the combination of classifiers [106]. Mongan et al. used a Gaussian process regression model to predict the performance of ultrasonically welded joints and unanticipated process variation based on the process inputs and feedback (integrated sensor data) [107]. The proposed method, capable of detecting process variations and anomalies, has proven effective in both manufacturing and remanufacturing environments. It enhances quality control by identifying anomalies throughout operations and enabling informed decisions regarding the reusability and remanufacturability of cores and parts.

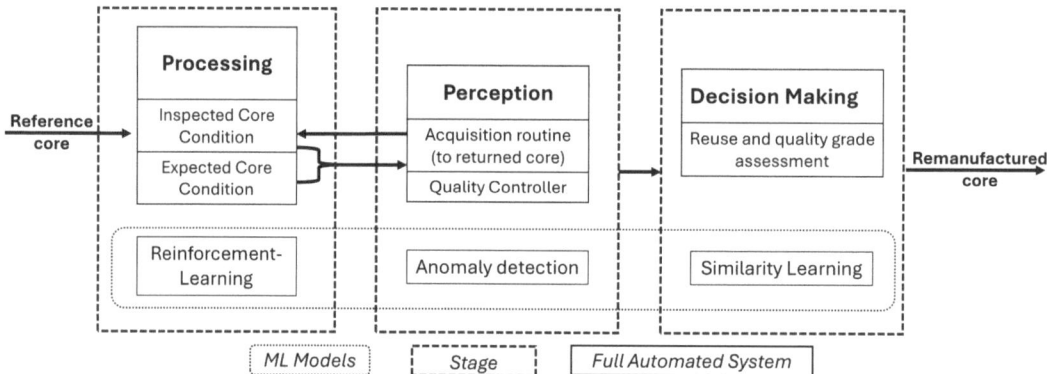

Figure 10. A scheme of core condition assessment through image and point cloud analysis, detecting quality deviations like corrosion or missing parts, which are then compared to expected conditions to determine reusability and quality grade (recreated from [32]).

In addition to implementing an effective inspection strategy for cores and remanufactured products, it is crucial to monitor various processes within remanufacturing operations. Statistical process control is a valuable tool for achieving process stability and reducing variability [136]. It facilitates continuous improvement and enhances quality assurance throughout the operations [137], which can be significantly augmented by ML models. ML excels in pattern recognition, allowing control charts to detect complex patterns, automate root cause analysis, and examine relationships between process data [108]. The integration of AI and ML into remanufacturing process control ensures adherence to high quality and standards. Moreover, the remanufacturing time of the equipment also influences quality standards and the economic effectiveness of remanufacturing decisions. Wang. et al. proposed a deep belief networks model to predict the optimal remanufacturing time by analyzing the historical equipment multi-life cycle and cost composition data [109]. The integrated automated inspection, condition monitoring and optimized planning and production can make the remanufacturing and maintenance plan more efficient and cost-effective [138].

In remanufacturing, it is necessary to define an optimal inspection plan following the identification of critical-to-quality parameters—key product characteristics (KPCs) and key control characteristics (KCCs) [139]. Product characteristics may be categorized into standard and key product characteristics. KPCs dictate quality parameters that could be determined through quality engineering tools and techniques such as Quality Function

Deployment, Failure Mode and Effects Analysis, Design for Manufacture and Assembly [140]. KCCs are established to precisely control them within specified limits to check variability within the processes to maintain both the process and KPC target values [141]. The remanufacturing scenario presents a complex challenge regarding the efficiency and effectiveness of inspection owing to the products designed and manufactured by some third-party enterprises and the high variability in the core inputs [142]. ML and data-driven models offer significant potential to improve parameter evaluation and maintain inspection efficiency in complex and variable remanufacturing scenarios [143].

4.4. HRC

HRC in remanufacturing enhances productivity and precision by merging human dexterity and decision-making capabilities with the consistency and strength of robots. This synergy not only boosts efficiency and adaptability to uncertainties but also holds promise for effectively managing process complexities and uncertainties in product disassembly, component inspection, and reassembly through the strategic allocation of tasks between humans and robots/cobots. This synergy forms effective teams with unique capabilities in operational tasks, information perception, and learning [144]. HRC enhances precision and adaptability in assembly [110], integrates human expertise with robotic sensing in inspection [58], and addresses the unpredictable challenges of disassembly. While full automation is often impractical, HRC enables efficient task distribution between humans and robots [114]. This approach addresses the unpredictable nature of returned products while balancing workload and economic outcomes. However, implementing HRC in remanufacturing systems faces challenges ranging from technological integration to worker adaptation and process changes [114].

In HRC for remanufacturing, process planning objectives include human-related factors alongside traditional profit-oriented goals like minimizing disassembly time, cost, and workstation numbers [28,59,70,95,99,100,115–118,122]. While efficiency remains crucial, its definition shifts in HRC scenarios. Instead of focusing solely on throughput and resource utilization, efficiency in HRC emphasizes optimal task allocation between humans and robots [28,59,100,115–118,122]. This addresses the challenges of workload distribution in manual and automated operations, as noted by [114]. Unique to HRC are objectives related to worker well-being, including human fatigue, safety, and workload [59,115–117,122]. These human-centric considerations are crucial in HRC scenarios, recognizing the importance of worker well-being and safety in the remanufacturing process. Environmental factors such as energy consumption are sometimes considered [59], further expanding the multifaceted nature of HRC in remanufacturing planning and scheduling. Balancing these diverse objectives makes optimal task allocation between humans and robots a central research question in HRC for remanufacturing.

ML and data-driven methods drive the utilization of HRC to enhance the efficiency and quality of remanufacturing processes. For example, Belhadj et al. conducted an extensive product analysis based on a CAD file to customize suitable operations for each returned core [119]. This has been extended to access the properties, complexity of parts and tool requirements [120]. Connecting elements are often of particular interest because their detachment affects the complexity and forces required for a remanufacturing operation, which, in turn, influences whether a task is best performed by a human or a robot [121]. To effectively allocate tasks in inspection, Karami et al. propose an AND/OR graph-based approach, improving efficiency by enabling parallel operations like simultaneous retrieval and inspection, allowing human intervention for issue management [58]. Another study implemented a voice-controlled collaborative inspection system where robots performed AI-powered visual inspections of predefined areas while humans provided oversight and performed parallel tasks, reducing the cycle time by 33.4% compared to manual inspection [113].

While the remanufacturing literature rarely focuses specifically on reassembly, research on general assembly has identified various ML and data-driven approaches for task allocation in HRC. Traditional methods such as Markov chains [71] and Petri nets [60] have been successfully applied, showing significant improvements in efficiency and cycle times. Figure 11 shows an exemplary workflow of HRC for disassembly designed to flexibly and efficiently complete the disassembly process in remanufacturing [100]. The disassembly process begins with establishing a model to define the disassembly precedence of products, allowing the generation of feasible disassembly sequences. Disassembly tasks are then classified, and the disassembly sequence for the robot and operator is optimized and evaluated based on time, cost, and difficulty [100]. Specifically, a prediction mechanism is employed to infer the human's current activity and anticipate their next assembly steps. The results from this algorithm are then fed into a scheduling algorithm, enabling the robot to determine its actions in a way that is both assistive and productive. Deep learning techniques like LSTM have been employed for multimodal recognition of subtasks in collaborative human–robot tasks [111]. Additionally, RL approaches have shown promise in adaptive task scheduling for interactive HRC assembly processes [112].

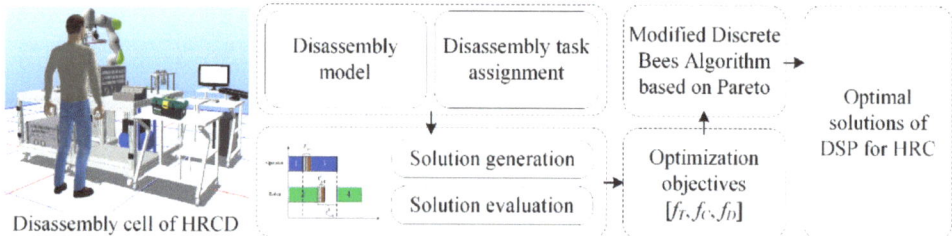

Figure 11. The workflow of HRC for disassembly (taken from [100]).

5. Discussion

The literature analysis reveals that integrating data-driven and ML models advances remanufacturing systems by enabling real-time monitoring, enhancing quality control, and facilitating dynamic scheduling, thereby supporting circular economy initiatives. Leveraging advanced sensors and connectivity, the IIoT and DPP enable comprehensive data collection and analysis across various stages of the remanufacturing process. Data-driven models derived from IIoT data play a vital role in supporting LCA and closed-loop supply chain management. They provide a thorough evaluation of environmental impacts throughout the product life cycle and aid in making informed decisions to promote sustainability. This capability provides critical insights into operational performance and product life cycle management. It is particularly effective in addressing uncertainties associated with the timing, quality, and quantity of returned parts, which significantly impact inventory control, product design, and production planning for remanufactured products [145].

Advanced ML techniques, such as deep learning and RL, further refine this process by enabling precise defect detection, anomaly management, and dynamic scheduling, thereby addressing uncertainties and improving operational effectiveness. For example, CNNs and YOLO models can be used in automated quality inspection systems to analyze images of remanufactured components, detecting defects with high accuracy, reducing inspection time, and ensuring consistent adherence to quality specifications. Predictive analytics can forecast potential failures, allowing for preemptive interventions that minimize operational disruptions and associated costs. RL optimizes dynamic scheduling and operational strategies to address uncertainties effectively. These advanced techniques not only improve operational effectiveness but also ensure that remanufactured products meet high standards of quality and reliability.

From the literature review, it is understood that, despite their advantages, the implementation of data-driven and ML methods in remanufacturing presents several challenges and may require the comprehensive adoption of smart manufacturing technologies. Smart manufacturing technologies utilize cutting-edge solutions, such as the IIoT, AI, ML algorithms, advanced sensor networks, and cyber-physical systems, to create digital simulations of production processes, manage computer-controlled equipment, and track and report real-time production data [146]. ML and data-driven models, as part of smart manufacturing techniques, support predictive maintenance, and analytics, enabling more accurate control and optimization of manufacturing processes [147]. Existing studies have discussed smart manufacturing in support of environmental sustainability. Huang et al. reviewed the literature on Industry 4.0, emphasizing its potential to enhance manufacturing sustainability through interconnected, smart technologies. The review examines how internet-connected machines and sensors improve productivity, energy efficiency, and environmental impact by optimizing processes and reducing waste [37]. Sutherland et al. reviewed recent research on the environmental impacts of industrial activities, focusing on work from the past 10–20 years, organizing their findings around the product life cycle and key topics in environmental impact [148]. Their review also systematically summarizes challenges in design, process improvement, and material efficiency within the framework of a circular economy, all within the context of Industry 4.0 advancements [148]. Kara et al. reviewed the evolution of emerging information and communication technologies to enhance material efficiency and environmental sustainability, adopting a holistic approach that redefines human–nature relations within planetary boundaries [149]. In this study, we further investigate the opportunities offered by smart manufacturing in remanufacturing, as illustrated in Figure 12, emphasizing how the integration of data-driven and ML methods with advanced manufacturing technologies can significantly enhance remanufacturing practices.

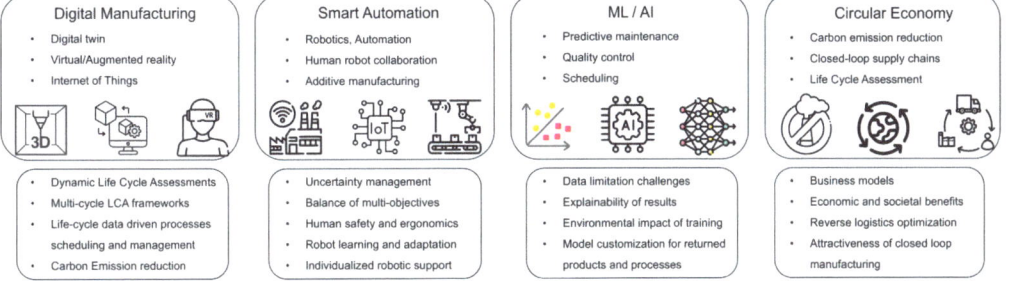

Figure 12. Future research directions in using smart manufacturing technologies for remanufacturing.

Developing smart manufacturing methodologies for dynamic LCA is essential for providing real-time feedback on the environmental impacts of remanufacturing processes. Identifying effective methods for measuring and reducing carbon emissions, as well as creating new LCA frameworks that capture the long-term benefits of remanufacturing across multiple life cycles, is crucial. Digital manufacturing technologies significantly enhance remanufacturing processes by enabling dynamic LCA that provides real-time feedback on environmental impacts, allowing for immediate adjustments to improve sustainability. These technologies also support the development of multi-cycle LCA frameworks, which accurately capture the long-term benefits of remanufacturing across multiple product life cycles. Additionally, life-cycle data-driven scheduling and management optimize processes by leveraging detailed insights into product histories to improve efficiency and decision-making. Moreover, digital tools play a crucial role in reducing carbon emissions by identifying and mitigating inefficiencies in processes and logistics, contributing to more environmentally responsible remanufacturing practices.

For remanufacturing system automation, it is important to balance conflicting objectives, such as profit maximization, cost reduction, environmental benefits, and adaptability to real-time changes and uncertainties. Furthermore, enabling robots to effectively learn from human operators and developing adaptive robotic support systems tailored to individual worker's skills, work styles, and ergonomic needs are critical. Additionally, using AI and ML in remanufacturing presents several significant challenges. One key challenge is the curation of data. Unlike in other manufacturing applications where data are often assumed to be complete due to the continuous monitoring and collecting from mass production lines, remanufacturing deals with highly heterogeneous data spanning a wide range of temporal scales, core specifications, and process requirements. This diversity makes it extremely difficult to align and fuse data to build the necessary context for effective AI analysis.

The explainability of results is another critical issue, as many AI models, particularly complex ones, operate as "black boxes", making it difficult to interpret their decisions and ensure they align with industry standards and expectations. The environmental impact of training is also a concern, as training sophisticated AI models can require substantial computational resources, leading to significant energy consumption, substantial data computing/storage costs, and a larger carbon footprint. Finally, model customization for returned products and processes poses a challenge. AI systems need to be tailored to handle the variability and complexity of returned items and diverse remanufacturing processes, which can vary greatly in terms of quality and characteristics. Addressing these challenges is essential for effectively integrating AI and ML into remanufacturing. To address remanufacturing challenges, cohesive models should integrate automated inspection, production planning, and time prediction, with a focus on low data storage and computational efficiency to support enterprises in different scales. Research may also target effective predictive maintenance methods, anomaly detection algorithms, and model architecture design and optimization to customize models for diverse products and processes.

Applying digital technologies to remanufacturing could focus on exploring innovative business models that enhance economic competitiveness while offering societal benefits. These models might leverage the circular economy by promoting closed-loop manufacturing practices, helping to reduce waste, conserve resources, and create sustainable jobs. Additionally, research could aim to optimize reverse logistics through digital solutions, potentially improving the efficiency of handling returned products by refining inventory management, reducing transportation costs, and enhancing product quality control. Such efforts could be important for demonstrating the economic and environmental benefits of closed-loop manufacturing, thereby increasing its attractiveness and encouraging broader industry adoption. Moreover, future studies could consider using life cycle data to further refine process optimization and emphasize economic advantages, while also considering the broader economic, environmental, and social benefits of closed-loop supply chains in remanufacturing.

The potential of integrating data-driven and ML methods into remanufacturing extends well beyond the computational techniques examined within the smart manufacturing framework. The advent of emerging advanced manufacturing technologies, when coupled with these data-driven and ML methods, unveils opportunities that remain largely untapped. Additive manufacturing (e.g., 3D-printing) offers significant benefits for remanufacturing by enabling the rapid repair of damaged components and the production of custom parts on demand [150,151]. This technology allows for precise material deposition and can create complex geometries that traditional manufacturing methods cannot easily achieve, potentially reducing lead times and lowering costs. Laser cladding, another advanced technology, provides a method for adding material to worn or damaged surfaces with high precision, restoring parts to their original dimensions and enhancing their performance [152]. Significant challenges involve addressing material compatibility issues in advanced manufacturing processes, overcoming barriers to fully automating remanufacturing systems. Data-driven models enhance this process by accurately predicting material properties and optimizing process parameters, while ML supports the customization and personalization of parts and improves quality control through real-time defect detection [153]. Together, these integrated approaches hold great promise for advancing the efficiency and sustainability of remanufacturing processes.

6. Conclusions

In this study, we investigated the integration of data-driven and ML technologies into remanufacturing processes to improve both operational efficiency and sustainability. Our findings highlighted how technologies such as the IIoT and DPP facilitate real-time monitoring, thereby supporting real-time LCA and closed-loop supply chain management. We further explored advanced ML techniques for precise defect detection, anomaly management, and process optimization. Additionally, we evaluated the impact of dynamic scheduling and HRC on mitigating uncertainties in remanufacturing. This research review effort not only identifies key gaps and challenges but also uncovers opportunities for advancing remanufacturing practices through advanced computational methods and smart manufacturing technologies, emphasizing their potential to deliver economic, environmental, and societal benefits.

Future work should focus on providing clearer categorizations of the challenges and pros and cons of ML and data-driven methods in remanufacturing, along with guidelines for selecting the most effective AI techniques for specific problems. Additionally, summarizing and comparing various AI applications in remanufacturing, providing practical examples of AI adoption in remanufacturing, would also be valuable for industry practitioners and researchers. Furthermore, future research should also explore the human-centric benefits of advanced computational algorithms and smart manufacturing technologies, considering not only personal well-being but also higher-level human needs, such as personal growth and self-actualization. This approach will ensure that advanced computational algorithms contribute positively to the workforce and create broader societal benefits.

Author Contributions: Conceptualization, X.L., J.W.S., C.N., R.A., M.C.M., G.L. and Q.C.; methodology, Y.H.K., W.Y., R.K., F.B., J.D., Y.T., X.L. and C.N.; software, Y.H.K., W.Y., R.K., F.B., J.D. and Y.T.; validation, Q.C., R.A., G.L. and J.W.S.; formal analysis, W.Y., F.B., Y.T., Y.H.K., R.K. and M.C.M.; investigation, W.Y., Y.H.K., R.K., F.B., Y.T., X.L. and C.N.; resources, C.N., J.W.S., M.C.M., X.L., G.L. and R.A.; data curation, F.B., J.D., W.Y., Y.H.K., R.K. and Y.T.; writing—original draft preparation, Y.H.K., W.Y., R.K., F.B. and Y.T.; writing—review and editing, X.L., C.N., M.C.M., Q.C., R.A., J.W.S. and G.L.; visualization, Y.T., W.Y., Y.H.K., R.K., J.D. and F.B.; supervision, J.W.S., C.N., X.L., M.C.M., R.A., G.L. and Q.C.; project administration, C.N. and X.L.; funding acquisition, J.W.S., G.L., M.C.M., R.A., C.N. and X.L. All authors have read and agreed to the published version of the manuscript.

Funding: This work was supported by the Deutsche Forschungsgemeinschaft (DFG, German Research Foundation) [grant number: SFB-1574-471687386], the Clean Energy Smart Manufacturing Innovation Institute (CESMII) [grant number: DE-EE0007613/45500000058651], and the National Institute of Standards and Technology (NIST) [grant number: 70NANB23H266].

Data Availability Statement: No new data were created or analyzed in this study.

Conflicts of Interest: The authors declare no conflicts of interest.

References

1. Tolio, T.; Bernard, A.; Colledani, M.; Kara, S.; Seliger, G.; Duflou, J.; Battaia, O.; Takata, S. Design, management and control of demanufacturing and remanufacturing systems. *CIRP Ann.* **2017**, *66*, 585–609. [CrossRef]
2. Singhal, D.; Tripathy, S.; Jena, S.K. Remanufacturing for the circular economy: Study and evaluation of critical factors. *Resour. Conserv. Recycl.* **2020**, *156*, 104681. [CrossRef]
3. Sundin, E.; Bras, B. Making functional sales environmentally and economically beneficial through product remanufacturing. *J. Clean. Prod.* **2005**, *13*, 913–925. [CrossRef]
4. Lieder, M.; Rashid, A. Towards circular economy implementation: A comprehensive review in context of manufacturing industry. *J. Clean. Prod.* **2016**, *115*, 36–51. [CrossRef]
5. Liu, C.; Cai, W.; Zhang, C.; Wei, F. Data-driven intelligent control system in remanufacturing assembly for production and resource efficiency. *Int. J. Adv. Manuf. Technol.* **2023**, *128*, 3531–3544. [CrossRef]
6. Hatcher, G.; Ijomah, W.; Windmill, J. Design for remanufacture: A literature review and future research needs. *J. Clean. Prod.* **2011**, *19*, 2004–2014. [CrossRef]
7. Sutherland, J.W.; Adler, D.P.; Haapala, K.R.; Kumar, V. A comparison of manufacturing and remanufacturing energy intensities with application to diesel engine production. *CIRP Ann.* **2008**, *57*, 5–8. [CrossRef]

8. Liu, M.; Chen, L.; Sheng, X.; Yang, Y.; Yu, F.; Li, Y.; Yuan, X.; Li, Y.; Wang, Q.; Ma, Q. Dynamic simulation of life cycle environmental benefits of remanufacturing asynchronous motors to permanent magnet synchronous motors. *J. Clean. Prod.* **2023**, *426*, 138932. [CrossRef]
9. Ramírez, F.J.; Aledo, J.A.; Gamez, J.A.; Pham, D.T. Economic modelling of robotic disassembly in end-of-life product recovery for remanufacturing. *Comput. Ind. Eng.* **2020**, *142*, 106339. [CrossRef]
10. Atasu, A.; Sarvary, M.; Van Wassenhove, L.N. Remanufacturing as a marketing strategy. *Manag. Sci.* **2008**, *54*, 1731–1746. [CrossRef]
11. Zhang, X.; Zhang, M.; Zhang, H.; Jiang, Z.; Liu, C.; Cai, W. A review on energy, environment and economic assessment in remanufacturing based on life cycle assessment method. *J. Clean. Prod.* **2020**, *255*, 120160. [CrossRef]
12. Yu, M.; Bai, B.; Xiong, S.; Liao, X. Evaluating environmental impacts and economic performance of remanufacturing electric vehicle lithium-ion batteries. *J. Clean. Prod.* **2021**, *321*, 128935. [CrossRef]
13. Van Loon, P.; Van Wassenhove, L.N. Assessing the economic and environmental impact of remanufacturing: A decision support tool for OEM suppliers. *Int. J. Prod. Res.* **2018**, *56*, 1662–1674. [CrossRef]
14. Jiang, Z.; Wang, H.; Zhang, H.; Mendis, G.; Sutherland, J.W. Value recovery options portfolio optimization for remanufacturing end of life product. *J. Clean. Prod.* **2019**, *210*, 419–431. [CrossRef]
15. Guide, V.D.R., Jr.; Vanwassenhove, L.N. Managing product returns for remanufacturing. *Prod. Oper. Manag.* **2001**, *10*, 142–155. [CrossRef]
16. Alfaro-Algaba, M.; Ramirez, F.J. Techno-economic and environmental disassembly planning of lithium-ion electric vehicle battery packs for remanufacturing. *Resour. Conserv. Recycl.* **2020**, *154*, 104461. [CrossRef]
17. Wang, J.; Zhao, J.; Wang, X. Optimum policy in hybrid manufacturing/remanufacturing system. *Comput. Ind. Eng.* **2011**, *60*, 411–419. [CrossRef]
18. Alinovi, A.; Bottani, E.; Montanari, R. Reverse logistics: A stochastic EOQ-based inventory control model for mixed manufacturing/remanufacturing systems with return policies. *Int. J. Prod. Res.* **2012**, *50*, 1243–1264. [CrossRef]
19. Xu, F.; Li, Y.; Feng, L. The influence of big data system for used product management on manufacturing–remanufacturing operations. *J. Clean. Prod.* **2019**, *209*, 782–794. [CrossRef]
20. Li, C.; Tang, Y.; Li, C.; Li, L. A modeling approach to analyze variability of remanufacturing process routing. *IEEE Trans. Autom. Sci. Eng.* **2012**, *10*, 86–98. [CrossRef]
21. Kin, S.T.M.; Ong, S.; Nee, A. Remanufacturing process planning. *Procedia Cirp* **2014**, *15*, 189–194. [CrossRef]
22. Sakao, T.; Sundin, E. How to improve remanufacturing?—A systematic analysis of practices and theories. *J. Manuf. Sci. Eng.* **2019**, *141*, 021004. [CrossRef]
23. He, Y.; Hao, C.; Wang, Y.; Li, Y.; Wang, Y.; Huang, L.; Tian, X. An ontology-based method of knowledge modelling for remanufacturing process planning. *J. Clean. Prod.* **2020**, *258*, 120952. [CrossRef]
24. Ferguson, M.; Guide Jr, V.D.; Koca, E.; Souza, G.C. The value of quality grading in remanufacturing. *Prod. Oper. Manag.* **2009**, *18*, 300–314. [CrossRef]
25. Sahoo, S.; Jakhar, S.K. Industry 4.0 deployment for circular economy performance—Understanding the role of green procurement and remanufacturing activities. *Bus. Strategy Environ.* **2024**, *33*, 1144–1160. [CrossRef]
26. Chau, M.Q.; Nguyen, X.P.; Huynh, T.T.; Chu, V.D.; Le, T.H.; Nguyen, T.P.; Nguyen, D.T. Prospects of application of IoT-based advanced technologies in remanufacturing process towards sustainable development and energy-efficient use. In *Energy Sources, Part A: Recovery, Utilization, and Environmental Effects*; Taylor & Francis: Abingdon, UK, 2021; pp. 1–25.
27. Wang, X.V.; Wang, L. Digital twin-based WEEE recycling, recovery and remanufacturing in the background of Industry 4.0. *Int. J. Prod. Res.* **2019**, *57*, 3892–3902. [CrossRef]
28. Xu, W.; Cui, J.; Liu, B.; Liu, J.; Yao, B.; Zhou, Z. Human-robot collaborative disassembly line balancing considering the safe strategy in remanufacturing. *J. Clean. Prod.* **2021**, *324*, 129158. [CrossRef]
29. Siddiqi, M.U.; Ijomah, W.L.; Dobie, G.I.; Hafeez, M.; Gareth Pierce, S.; Ion, W.; Mineo, C.; MacLeod, C.N. Low cost three-dimensional virtual model construction for remanufacturing industry. *J. Remanuf.* **2019**, *9*, 129–139. [CrossRef]
30. Yang, Y.; Keivanpour, S.; Imbeau, D. Integrating X-reality and lean into end-of-life aircraft parts disassembly sequence planning: A critical review and research agenda. *Int. J. Adv. Manuf. Technol.* **2023**, *127*, 2181–2210. [CrossRef]
31. Teixeira, E.L.S.; Tjahjono, B.; Beltran, M.; Julião, J. Demystifying the digital transition of remanufacturing: A systematic review of literature. *Comput. Ind.* **2022**, *134*, 103567. [CrossRef]
32. Kaiser, J.P.; Lang, S.; Wurster, M.; Lanza, G. A concept for autonomous quality control for core inspection in remanufacturing. *Procedia CIRP* **2022**, *105*, 374–379. [CrossRef]
33. Liu, Z.; Afrinaldi, F.; Zhang, H.C.; Jiang, Q. Exploring optimal timing for remanufacturing based on replacement theory. *CIRP Ann.* **2016**, *65*, 447–450. [CrossRef]
34. Kerin, M.; Pham, D.T. Smart remanufacturing: A review and research framework. *J. Manuf. Technol. Manag.* **2020**, *31*, 1205–1235. [CrossRef]
35. Blei, D.M.; Ng, A.Y.; Jordan, M.I. Latent dirichlet allocation. *J. Mach. Learn. Res.* **2003**, *3*, 993–1022.
36. Nath, C. Integrated tool condition monitoring systems and their applications: A comprehensive review. *Procedia Manuf.* **2020**, *48*, 852–863. [CrossRef]

37. Huang, A.; Triebe, M.; Li, Z.; Wu, H.; Joung, B.G.; Sutherland, J.W. A review of research on smart manufacturing in support of environmental sustainability. *Int. J. Sustain. Manuf.* **2022**, *5*, 132–163. [CrossRef]
38. Abdallah, M.; Joung, B.G.; Lee, W.J.; Mousoulis, C.; Raghunathan, N.; Shakouri, A.; Sutherland, J.W.; Bagchi, S. Anomaly detection and inter-sensor transfer learning on smart manufacturing datasets. *Sensors* **2023**, *23*, 486. [CrossRef]
39. Joung, B.G.; Nath, C.; Li, Z.; Sutherland, J.W. *Bearing Anomaly Detection in an Air Compressor Using an LSTM and RNN-Based Machine Learning Model*; Springer: Berlin/Heidelberg, Germany, 2024.
40. May, M.C.; Glatter, D.; Arnold, D.; Pfeffer, D.; Lanza, G. IIoT System Canvas—From architecture patterns towards an IIoT development framework. *J. Manuf. Syst.* **2024**, *72*, 437–459. [CrossRef]
41. Lynn, R.; Chen, A.; Locks, S.; Nath, C.; Kurfess, T. Intelligent and accessible data flow architectures for manufacturing system optimization. In Proceedings of the Advances in Production Management Systems: Innovative Production Management Towards Sustainable Growth: IFIP WG 5.7 International Conference, APMS 2015, Tokyo, Japan, 7–9 September 2015; Proceedings, Part I0; Springer: Berlin/Heidelberg, Germany, 2015; pp. 27–35.
42. Gao, R.X.; Wang, P. Through life analysis for machine tools: From design to remanufacture. *Procedia CIRP* **2017**, *59*, 2–7. [CrossRef]
43. Li, X.; Bayrak, A.E.; Epureanu, B.I.; Koren, Y. Real-time teaming of multiple reconfigurable manufacturing systems. *CIRP Ann.* **2018**, *67*, 437–440. [CrossRef]
44. Szaller, Á.; Gallina, V.; Gal, B.; Gaal, A.; Fries, C. Quantitative benefits of the digital product passport and data sharing in remanufacturing. *Procedia CIRP* **2023**, *120*, 928–933. [CrossRef]
45. Jensen, S.F.; Kristensen, J.H.; Adamsen, S.; Christensen, A.; Waehrens, B.V. Digital product passports for a circular economy: Data needs for product life cycle decision-making. *Sustain. Prod. Consum.* **2023**, *37*, 242–255. [CrossRef]
46. Adisorn, T.; Tholen, L.; Götz, T. Towards a digital product passport fit for contributing to a circular economy. *Energies* **2021**, *14*, 2289. [CrossRef]
47. Shah, P.; Gosavi, A.; Nagi, R. A machine learning approach to optimise the usage of recycled material in a remanufacturing environment. *Int. J. Prod. Res.* **2010**, *48*, 933–955. [CrossRef]
48. Nassehi, A.; Zhong, R.Y.; Li, X.; Epureanu, B.I. Review of machine learning technologies and artificial intelligence in modern manufacturing systems. In *Design and Operation of Production Networks for Mass Personalization in the Era of Cloud Technology*; Elsevier: Amsterdam, The Netherlands, 2022; pp. 317–348.
49. Song, C.; Guan, X.; Zhao, Q.; Ho, Y.C. Machine learning approach for determining feasible plans of a remanufacturing system. *IEEE Trans. Autom. Sci. Eng.* **2005**, *2*, 262–275. [CrossRef]
50. Schlüter, M.; Lickert, H.; Schweitzer, K.; Bilge, P.; Briese, C.; Dietrich, F.; Krüger, J. AI-enhanced identification, inspection and sorting for reverse logistics in remanufacturing. *Procedia CIRP* **2021**, *98*, 300–305. [CrossRef]
51. Xu, Z.; Saleh, J.H. Machine learning for reliability engineering and safety applications: Review of current status and future opportunities. *Reliab. Eng. Syst. Saf.* **2021**, *211*, 107530. [CrossRef]
52. Lee, K.B.; Cheon, S.; Kim, C.O. A convolutional neural network for fault classification and diagnosis in semiconductor manufacturing processes. *IEEE Trans. Semicond. Manuf.* **2017**, *30*, 135–142. [CrossRef]
53. Wang, B.; Li, Y.; Luo, Y.; Li, X.; Freiheit, T. Early event detection in a deep-learning driven quality prediction model for ultrasonic welding. *J. Manuf. Syst.* **2021**, *60*, 325–336. [CrossRef]
54. Zeybek, S. Prediction of the remaining useful life of engines for remanufacturing using a semi-supervised deep learning model trained by the Bees Algorithm. In *Intelligent Production and Manufacturing Optimisation—The Bees Algorithm Approach*; Springer: Berlin/Heidelberg, Germany, 2022; pp. 383–397.
55. Bai, Y.; Lv, Y. Reinforcement learning-based job shop scheduling for remanufacturing production. In Proceedings of the 2022 IEEE International Conference on Industrial Engineering and Engineering Management (IEEM), Kuala Lumpur, Malaysia, 7–10 December 2022; pp. 0246–0251.
56. Paschko, F.; Knorn, S.; Krini, A.; Kemke, M. Material flow control in Remanufacturing Systems with random failures and variable processing times. *J. Remanuf.* **2023**, *13*, 161–185. [CrossRef]
57. Wurster, M.; Michel, M.; May, M.C.; Kuhnle, A.; Stricker, N.; Lanza, G. Modelling and condition-based control of a flexible and hybrid disassembly system with manual and autonomous workstations using reinforcement learning. *J. Intell. Manuf.* **2022**, *33*, 575–591. [CrossRef]
58. Karami, H.; Darvish, K.; Mastrogiovanni, F. A task allocation approach for human-robot collaboration in product defects inspection scenarios. In Proceedings of the 2020 29th IEEE International Conference on Robot and Human Interactive Communication (RO-MAN), Naples, Italy, 31 August–4 September 2020; pp. 1127–1134.
59. Johannsmeier, L.; Haddadin, S. A hierarchical human-robot interaction-planning framework for task allocation in collaborative industrial assembly processes. *IEEE Robot. Autom. Lett.* **2016**, *2*, 41–48. [CrossRef]
60. Casalino, A.; Cividini, F.; Zanchettin, A.M.; Piroddi, L.; Rocco, P. Human-robot collaborative assembly: A use-case application. *IFAC-PapersOnLine* **2018**, *51*, 194–199. [CrossRef]
61. Yang, C.H.; Liu, H.b.; Ji, P.; Ma, X. Optimal acquisition and remanufacturing policies for multi-product remanufacturing systems. *J. Clean. Prod.* **2016**, *135*, 1571–1579. [CrossRef]
62. Yanıkoğlu, İ.; Denizel, M. The value of quality grading in remanufacturing under quality level uncertainty. *Int. J. Prod. Res.* **2021**, *59*, 839–859. [CrossRef]

63. Yang, C.H.; Wang, J.; Ji, P. Optimal acquisition policy in remanufacturing under general core quality distributions. *Int. J. Prod. Res.* **2015**, *53*, 1425–1438. [CrossRef]
64. Zhou, J.; Deng, Q.; Li, T. Optimal acquisition and remanufacturing policies considering the effect of quality uncertainty on carbon emissions. *J. Clean. Prod.* **2018**, *186*, 180–190. [CrossRef]
65. Kesavan, V.; Kamalakannan, R.; Sudhakarapandian, R.; Sivakumar, P. Heuristic and meta-heuristic algorithms for solving medium and large scale sized cellular manufacturing system NP-hard problems: A comprehensive review. *Mater. Today Proc.* **2020**, *21*, 66–72. [CrossRef]
66. Papalambros, P.Y.; Wilde, D.J. *Principles of Optimal Design: Modeling and Computation*; Cambridge University Press: Cambridge, UK, 2000.
67. Peng, H.; Wang, H.; Chen, D. Optimization of remanufacturing process routes oriented toward eco-efficiency. *Front. Mech. Eng.* **2019**, *14*, 422–433. [CrossRef]
68. Jiang, Z.; Zhou, T.; Zhang, H.; Wang, Y.; Cao, H.; Tian, G. Reliability and cost optimization for remanufacturing process planning. *J. Clean. Prod.* **2016**, *135*, 1602–1610. [CrossRef]
69. Li, L.; Li, C.; Ma, H.; Tang, Y. An optimization method for the remanufacturing dynamic facility layout problem with uncertainties. *Discret. Dyn. Nat. Soc.* **2015**, *2015*, 685408. [CrossRef]
70. Ye, F.; Perrett, J.; Zhang, L.; Laili, Y.; Wang, Y. A self-evolving system for robotic disassembly sequence planning under uncertain interference conditions. *Robot. Comput.-Integr. Manuf.* **2022**, *78*, 102392. [CrossRef]
71. Zanchettin, A.M.; Casalino, A.; Piroddi, L.; Rocco, P. Prediction of human activity patterns for human–robot collaborative assembly tasks. *IEEE Trans. Ind. Inform.* **2018**, *15*, 3934–3942. [CrossRef]
72. Fang, W.; Chen, L.; Zhang, T.; Chen, C.; Teng, Z.; Wang, L. Head-mounted display augmented reality in manufacturing: A systematic review. *Robot. Comput.-Integr. Manuf.* **2023**, *83*, 102567. [CrossRef]
73. Djuric, A.M.; Urbanic, R.; Rickli, J. A framework for collaborative robot (CoBot) integration in advanced manufacturing systems. *SAE Int. J. Mater. Manuf.* **2016**, *9*, 457–464. [CrossRef]
74. French, R.; Benakis, M.; Marin-Reyes, H. Intelligent sensing for robotic re-manufacturing in aerospace—An industry 4.0 design based prototype. In Proceedings of the 2017 IEEE International Symposium on Robotics and Intelligent Sensors (IRIS), Ottawa, ON, Canada, 5–7 October 2017; pp. 272–277.
75. Plociennik, C.; Pourjafarian, M.; Nazeri, A.; Windholz, W.; Knetsch, S.; Rickert, J.; Ciroth, A.; Lopes, A.d.C.P.; Hagedorn, T.; Vogelgesang, M.; et al. Towards a digital lifecycle passport for the circular economy. *Procedia CIRP* **2022**, *105*, 122–127. [CrossRef]
76. Berger, K.; Schöggl, J.P.; Baumgartner, R.J. Digital battery passports to enable circular and sustainable value chains: Conceptualization and use cases. *J. Clean. Prod.* **2022**, *353*, 131492. [CrossRef]
77. Blömeke, S.; Rickert, J.; Mennenga, M.; Thiede, S.; Spengler, T.S.; Herrmann, C. Recycling 4.0–Mapping smart manufacturing solutions to remanufacturing and recycling operations. *Procedia CIRP* **2020**, *90*, 600–605. [CrossRef]
78. Wang, Y.; Wang, S.; Yang, B.; Zhu, L.; Liu, F. Big data driven Hierarchical Digital Twin Predictive Remanufacturing paradigm: Architecture, control mechanism, application scenario and benefits. *J. Clean. Prod.* **2020**, *248*, 119299. [CrossRef]
79. Kerin, M.; Hartono, N.; Pham, D. Optimising remanufacturing decision-making using the bees algorithm in product digital twins. *Sci. Rep.* **2023**, *13*, 701. [CrossRef]
80. Zhang, A.; Zhong, R.Y.; Farooque, M.; Kang, K.; Venkatesh, V.G. Blockchain-based life cycle assessment: An implementation framework and system architecture. *Resour. Conserv. Recycl.* **2020**, *152*, 104512. [CrossRef]
81. Kerin, M.; Pham, D.T.; Huang, J.; Hadall, J. A generic asset model for implementing product digital twins in smart remanufacturing. *Int. J. Adv. Manuf. Technol.* **2023**, *124*, 3021–3038. [CrossRef]
82. Yu, H. Modeling a remanufacturing reverse logistics planning problem: Some insights into disruptive technology adoption. *Int. J. Adv. Manuf. Technol.* **2022**, *123*, 4231–4249. [CrossRef]
83. Thürer, M.; Pan, Y.; Qu, T.; Luo, H.; Li, C.; Huang, G.Q. Internet of Things (IoT) driven kanban system for reverse logistics: Solid waste collection. *J. Intell. Manuf.* **2019**, *30*, 2621–2630. [CrossRef]
84. Joshi, A.D.; Gupta, S.M. Evaluation of design alternatives of End-of-Life products using internet of things. *Int. J. Prod. Econ.* **2019**, *208*, 281–293. [CrossRef]
85. Zhu, J.; Luo, Z.; Liu, Y.; Tong, H.; Yin, K. Environmental perspectives for food loss reduction via smart sensors: A global life cycle assessment. *J. Clean. Prod.* **2022**, *374*, 133852. [CrossRef]
86. Costa, T.P.d.; Gillespie, J.; Pelc, K.; Adefisan, A.; Adefisan, M.; Ramanathan, R.; Murphy, F. Life cycle assessment tool for food supply chain environmental evaluation. *Sustainability* **2022**, *15*, 718. [CrossRef]
87. An, J.; Zou, Z.; Chen, G.; Sun, Y.; Liu, R.; Zheng, L. An IoT-based life cycle assessment platform of wind turbines. *Sensors* **2021**, *21*, 1233. [CrossRef]
88. Yang, Z.; Guo, X.; Sun, J.; Zhang, Y.; Wang, Y. What does not kill you makes you stronger: Supply chain resilience and corporate sustainability through emerging IT capability. *IEEE Trans. Eng. Manag.* **2022**, *17*, 10507–10521. [CrossRef]
89. Delpla, V.; Kenné, J.P.; Hof, L.A. Circular manufacturing 4.0: Towards internet of things embedded closed-loop supply chains. *Int. J. Adv. Manuf. Technol.* **2022**, *118*, 1–24. [CrossRef]
90. Tavana, M.; Sohrabi, M.; Rezaei, H.; Sorooshian, S.; Mina, H. A sustainable circular supply chain network design model for electric vehicle battery production using internet of things and big data. *Expert Syst.* **2024**, *41*, e13395. [CrossRef]

91. Tozanlı, Ö.; Kongar, E.; Gupta, S.M. Trade-in-to-upgrade as a marketing strategy in disassembly-to-order systems at the edge of blockchain technology. *Int. J. Prod. Res.* **2020**, *58*, 7183–7200. [CrossRef]
92. Pan, W.; Miao, L. Dynamics and risk assessment of a remanufacturing closed-loop supply chain system using the internet of things and neural network approach. *J. Supercomput.* **2023**, *79*, 3878–3901. [CrossRef]
93. Liao, H.; Zhang, Q.; Shen, N.; Li, L. Stochastic analysis of quality uncertainty and optimal acquisition strategies for engine remanufacturing. *J. Clean. Prod.* **2020**, *261*, 121088. [CrossRef]
94. Teunter, R.H.; Flapper, S.D.P. Optimal core acquisition and remanufacturing policies under uncertain core quality fractions. *Eur. J. Oper. Res.* **2011**, *210*, 241–248. [CrossRef]
95. Liao, H.; Zhang, Q.; Li, L. Optimal procurement strategy for multi-echelon remanufacturing systems under quality uncertainty. *Transp. Res. Part E: Logist. Transp. Rev.* **2023**, *170*, 103023. [CrossRef]
96. Mutha, A.; Bansal, S.; Guide, V.D.R. Managing demand uncertainty through core acquisition in remanufacturing. *Prod. Oper. Manag.* **2016**, *25*, 1449–1464. [CrossRef]
97. Bhattacharya, R.; Kaur, A.; Amit, R. Price optimization of multi-stage remanufacturing in a closed loop supply chain. *J. Clean. Prod.* **2018**, *186*, 943–962. [CrossRef]
98. Jiang, Z.; Jiang, Y.; Wang, Y.; Zhang, H.; Cao, H.; Tian, G. A hybrid approach of rough set and case-based reasoning to remanufacturing process planning. *J. Intell. Manuf.* **2019**, *30*, 19–32. [CrossRef]
99. Li, K.; Liu, Q.; Xu, W.; Liu, J.; Zhou, Z.; Feng, H. Sequence planning considering human fatigue for human-robot collaboration in disassembly. *Procedia CIRP* **2019**, *83*, 95–104. [CrossRef]
100. Xu, W.; Tang, Q.; Liu, J.; Liu, Z.; Zhou, Z.; Pham, D.T. Disassembly sequence planning using discrete Bees algorithm for human-robot collaboration in remanufacturing. *Robot. Comput.-Integr. Manuf.* **2020**, *62*, 101860. [CrossRef]
101. Zheng, P.; Wang, J.; Zhang, J.; Yang, C.; Jin, Y. An adaptive CGAN/IRF-based rescheduling strategy for aircraft parts remanufacturing system under dynamic environment. *Robot. Comput.-Integr. Manuf.* **2019**, *58*, 230–238. [CrossRef]
102. Liao, H.; Shi, Y.; Liu, X.; Shen, N.; Deng, Q. A non-probabilistic model of carbon footprints in remanufacture under multiple uncertainties. *J. Clean. Prod.* **2019**, *211*, 1127–1140. [CrossRef]
103. Peng, Y.; Li, W.; Liang, Y.; Pham, D.T. Robotic disassembly of screws for end-of-life product remanufacturing enabled by deep reinforcement learning. *J. Clean. Prod.* **2024**, *439*, 140863. [CrossRef]
104. Li, X.; Li, N.; Kolmanovsky, I.; Epureanu, B.I. Stochastic model predictive control for remanufacturing system management. *J. Manuf. Syst.* **2021**, *59*, 355–366. [CrossRef]
105. Nwankpa, C.E.; Eze, S.C. Deep learning based visual automated sorting system for remanufacturing. In Proceedings of the 2020 IEEE green technologies conference (GreenTech), Oklahoma City, OK, USA, 1–3 April 2020; pp. 196–198.
106. Islam, A.; Jain, S.; Nenadic, N.G.; Thurston, M.G.; Greenberg, J.; Moss, B. Image-Based Machine Learning in Automotive Used Parts Identification for Remanufacturing. *Technology Innovation for the Circular Economy: Recycling, Remanufacturing, Design, Systems Analysis and Logistics*; Wiley: Hoboken, NJ, USA, 2024; pp. 507–526.
107. Mongan, P.; Hinchy, E.; O'Dowd, N.; McCarthy, C. Increasing Quality Control of Ultrasonically Welded Joints Through Gaussian Process Regression. In *Proceedings of the International Conference on Flexible Automation and Intelligent Manufacturing*; Springer: Berlin/Heidelberg, Germany, 2022; pp. 368–378.
108. Zan, T.; Liu, Z.; Su, Z.; Wang, M.; Gao, X.; Chen, D. Statistical process control with intelligence based on the deep learning model. *Appl. Sci.* **2019**, *10*, 308. [CrossRef]
109. Wang, L.; Xia, X.; Cao, J.; Liu, X. Modeling and predicting remanufacturing time of equipment using deep belief networks. *Clust. Comput.* **2019**, *22*, 2677–2688. [CrossRef]
110. Wang, L.; Gao, R.; Váncza, J.; Krüger, J.; Wang, X.V.; Makris, S.; Chryssolouris, G. Symbiotic human-robot collaborative assembly. *CIRP Ann.* **2019**, *68*, 701–726. [CrossRef]
111. Brooks, C.; Atreya, M.; Szafir, D. Proactive robot assistants for freeform collaborative tasks through multimodal recognition of generic subtasks. In Proceedings of the 2018 IEEE/RSJ International Conference on Intelligent Robots and Systems (IROS), Madrid, Spain, 1–5 October 2018; pp. 8567–8573.
112. Akkaladevi, S.C.; Plasch, M.; Maddukuri, S.; Eitzinger, C.; Pichler, A.; Rinner, B. Toward an interactive reinforcement based learning framework for human robot collaborative assembly processes. *Front. Robot. AI* **2018**, *5*, 126. [CrossRef]
113. Papavasileiou, A.; Nikoladakis, S.; Basamakis, F.P.; Aivaliotis, S.; Michalos, G.; Makris, S. A Voice-Enabled ROS2 Framework for Human–Robot Collaborative Inspection. *Appl. Sci.* **2024**, *14*, 4138. [CrossRef]
114. Lee, M.L.; Liang, X.; Hu, B.; Onel, G.; Behdad, S.; Zheng, M. A review of prospects and opportunities in disassembly with human–robot collaboration. *J. Manuf. Sci. Eng.* **2024**, *146*. [CrossRef]
115. Liao, H.y.; Chen, Y.; Hu, B.; Behdad, S. Optimization-based disassembly sequence planning under uncertainty for human–robot collaboration. *J. Mech. Des.* **2023**, *145*, 022001. [CrossRef]
116. Lee, M.L.; Behdad, S.; Liang, X.; Zheng, M. Task allocation and planning for product disassembly with human–robot collaboration. *Robot. Comput.-Integr. Manuf.* **2022**, *76*, 102306. [CrossRef]
117. Lee, M.L.; Liu, W.; Behdad, S.; Liang, X.; Zheng, M. Robot-assisted disassembly sequence planning with real-time human motion prediction. *IEEE Trans. Syst. Man Cybern. Syst.* **2022**, *53*, 438–450. [CrossRef]
118. Chu, M.; Chen, W. Human-robot collaboration disassembly planning for end-of-life power batteries. *J. Manuf. Syst.* **2023**, *69*, 271–291. [CrossRef]

119. Belhadj, I.; Aicha, M.; Aifaoui, N. Product disassembly planning and task allocation based on human and robot collaboration. *Int. J. Interact. Des. Manuf. (IJIDeM)* **2022**, *16*, 803–819. [CrossRef]
120. Lou, S.; Tan, R.; Zhang, Y.; Lv, C. Human-robot interactive disassembly planning in Industry 5.0. In Proceedings of the 2023 IEEE/ASME International Conference on Advanced Intelligent Mechatronics (AIM), Seattle, WA, USA, 28–30 June 2023; pp. 891–895.
121. Qu, W.; Li, J.; Zhang, R.; Liu, S.; Bao, J. Adaptive planning of human–robot collaborative disassembly for end-of-life lithium-ion batteries based on digital twin. *J. Intell. Manuf.* **2024**, *35*, 2021–2043. [CrossRef]
122. Zhang, M.; Li, C.; Shang, Y.; Liu, Z. Cycle time and human fatigue minimization for human-robot collaborative assembly cell. *IEEE Robot. Autom. Lett.* **2022**, *7*, 6147–6154. [CrossRef]
123. Lee, J.; Bagheri, B.; Kao, H.A. A cyber-physical systems architecture for industry 4.0-based manufacturing systems. *Manuf. Lett.* **2015**, *3*, 18–23. [CrossRef]
124. Zhang, Y.; Ren, S.; Liu, Y.; Sakao, T.; Huisingh, D. A framework for Big Data driven product lifecycle management. *J. Clean. Prod.* **2017**, *159*, 229–240. [CrossRef]
125. Zhang, Y.; Liu, S.; Liu, Y.; Yang, H.; Li, M.; Huisingh, D.; Wang, L. The 'Internet of Things' enabled real-time scheduling for remanufacturing of automobile engines. *J. Clean. Prod.* **2018**, *185*, 562–575. [CrossRef]
126. Ding, T.; Liang, L.; Zhou, K.; Yang, M.; Wei, Y. Water-energy nexus: The origin, development and prospect. *Ecol. Model.* **2020**, *419*, 108943. [CrossRef]
127. Williams, J.; Shu, L.; Fenton, R. Analysis of remanufacturer waste streams across product sectors. *CIRP Ann.* **2001**, *50*, 101–104. [CrossRef]
128. Sherwood, M.; Shu, L.; Fenton, R. Supporting design for remanufacture through waste-stream analysis of automotive remanufacturers. *CIRP Ann.* **2000**, *49*, 87–90. [CrossRef]
129. Wang, L.; Wang, X.V.; Gao, L.; Váncza, J. A cloud-based approach for WEEE remanufacturing. *CIRP Ann.* **2014**, *63*, 409–412. [CrossRef]
130. Fofou, R.F.; Jiang, Z.; Wang, Y. A review on the lifecycle strategies enhancing remanufacturing. *Appl. Sci.* **2021**, *11*, 5937. [CrossRef]
131. Cao, H.; Folan, P.; Potter, D.; Browne, J. Knowledge-enriched shop floor control in end-of-life business. *Prod. Plan. Control* **2011**, *22*, 174–193. [CrossRef]
132. Langley, D.J.; Rosco, E.; Angelopoulos, M.; Kamminga, O.; Hooijer, C. Orchestrating a smart circular economy: Guiding principles for digital product passports. *J. Bus. Res.* **2023**, *169*, 114259. [CrossRef]
133. Ponte, B.; Cannella, S.; Dominguez, R.; Naim, M.M.; Syntetos, A.A. Quality grading of returns and the dynamics of remanufacturing. *Int. J. Prod. Econ.* **2021**, *236*, 108129. [CrossRef]
134. Du, Y.; Cao, H.; Liu, F.; Li, C.; Chen, X. An integrated method for evaluating the remanufacturability of used machine tool. *J. Clean. Prod.* **2012**, *20*, 82–91. [CrossRef]
135. Saiz, F.A.; Alfaro, G.; Barandiaran, I. An inspection and classification system for automotive component remanufacturing industry based on ensemble learning. *Information* **2021**, *12*, 489. [CrossRef]
136. Date, K.; Tanaka, Y. Quality-oriented statistical process control utilizing bayesian modeling. *IEEE Trans. Semicond. Manuf.* **2021**, *34*, 307–311. [CrossRef]
137. Viharos, Z.J.; Jakab, R. Reinforcement learning for statistical process control in manufacturing. *Measurement* **2021**, *182*, 109616. [CrossRef]
138. Wang, Z.; Xu, Y.; Ma, X.; Thomson, G. Towards smart remanufacturing and maintenance of machinery-review of automated inspection, condition monitoring and production optimisation. In Proceedings of the 2020 25th IEEE International Conference on Emerging Technologies and Factory Automation (ETFA), Vienna, Austria, 8–11 September 2020; Volume 1, pp. 1731–1738.
139. Errington, M.; Childe, S.J. A business process model of inspection in remanufacturing. *J. Remanuf.* **2013**, *3*, 1–22. [CrossRef]
140. Zheng, L.; Liu, Q.; McMahon, C.A. Integration of process FMEA with product and process design based on key characteristics. In *Proceedings of the 6th CIRP-Sponsored International Conference on Digital Enterprise Technology*; Springer: Berlin/Heidelberg, Germany, 2010; pp. 1673–1686.
141. Wang, K.; Yin, Y.; Du, S.; Xi, L. Variation management of key control characteristics in multistage machining processes considering quality-cost equilibrium. *J. Manuf. Syst.* **2021**, *59*, 441–452. [CrossRef]
142. Zhao, S.; You, Z.; Zhu, Q. Quality choice for product recovery considering a trade-in program and third-party remanufacturing competition. *Int. J. Prod. Econ.* **2021**, *240*, 108239. [CrossRef]
143. Van Nguyen, T.; Zhou, L.; Chong, A.Y.L.; Li, B.; Pu, X. Predicting customer demand for remanufactured products: A data-mining approach. *Eur. J. Oper. Res.* **2020**, *281*, 543–558. [CrossRef]
144. Li, X.; Koren, Y.; Epureanu, B.I. Complementary learning-team machines to enlighten and exploit human expertise. *CIRP Ann.* **2022**, *71*, 417–420. [CrossRef]
145. Lee, C.M.; Woo, W.S.; Roh, Y.H. Remanufacturing: Trends and issues. *Int. J. Precis. Eng. Manuf.-Green Technol.* **2017**, *4*, 113–125. [CrossRef]
146. Kusiak, A. Smart manufacturing. *Int. J. Prod. Res.* **2018**, *56*, 508–517. [CrossRef]
147. Clausen, J.B.B.; Li, H. Big data driven order-up to level model: Application of machine learning. *Comput. Oper. Res.* **2022**, *139*, 105641. [CrossRef]

148. Sutherland, J.W.; Skerlos, S.J.; Haapala, K.R.; Cooper, D.; Zhao, F.; Huang, A. Industrial sustainability: Reviewing the past and envisioning the future. *J. Manuf. Sci. Eng.* **2020**, *142*, 110806. [CrossRef]
149. Kara, S.; Hauschild, M.; Sutherland, J.; McAloone, T. Closed-loop systems to circular economy: A pathway to environmental sustainability? *CIRP Ann.* **2022**, *71*, 505–528. [CrossRef]
150. Kanishka, K.; Acherjee, B. A systematic review of additive manufacturing-based remanufacturing techniques for component repair and restoration. *J. Manuf. Process.* **2023**, *89*, 220–283. [CrossRef]
151. Yusoh, S.S.M.; Abd Wahab, D.; Habeeb, H.A.; Azman, A.H. Intelligent systems for additive manufacturing-based repair in remanufacturing: A systematic review of its potential. *PeerJ Comput. Sci.* **2021**, *7*, e808. [CrossRef]
152. Liu, Z.; Jiang, Q.; Li, T.; Dong, S.; Yan, S.; Zhang, H.; Xu, B. Environmental benefits of remanufacturing: A case study of cylinder heads remanufactured through laser cladding. *J. Clean. Prod.* **2016**, *133*, 1027–1033. [CrossRef]
153. Liu, W.W.; Tang, Z.J.; Liu, X.Y.; Wang, H.J.; Zhang, H.C. A review on in-situ monitoring and adaptive control technology for laser cladding remanufacturing. *Procedia CIRP* **2017**, *61*, 235–240. [CrossRef]

Disclaimer/Publisher's Note: The statements, opinions and data contained in all publications are solely those of the individual author(s) and contributor(s) and not of MDPI and/or the editor(s). MDPI and/or the editor(s) disclaim responsibility for any injury to people or property resulting from any ideas, methods, instructions or products referred to in the content.

Article

Reducing Nervousness in Master Production Planning: A Systematic Approach Incorporating Product-Driven Strategies

Patricio Sáez [1],*, Carlos Herrera [2] and Victor Parada [3,4]

1. Department of Statistics, Universidad de Concepción, Concepción 4030000, Chile
2. Department of Industrial Engineering, Universidad de Concepción, Concepción 4030000, Chile; cherreral@udec.cl
3. Department of Informatics Engineering, Universidad de Santiago de Chile, Santiago 8320000, Chile; victor.parada@usach.cl
4. Instituto Sistemas Complejos de Ingeniería (ISCI), Santiago 8320000, Chile
* Correspondence: patricsaez@udec.cl

Abstract: Manufacturing companies face a significant challenge when developing their master production schedule, navigating unforeseen disruptions during daily operations. Moreover, fluctuations in demand pose a substantial risk to scheduling and are the main cause of instability and uncertainty in the system. To address these challenges, employing flexible systems to mitigate uncertainty without incurring additional costs and generate sustainable responses in industrial applications is crucial. This paper proposes a product-driven system to complement the master production plan generated by a mathematical model. This system incorporates intelligent agents that make production decisions with a function capable of reducing uncertainty without significantly increasing production costs. The agents modify or determine the forecasted production quantities for each cycle or period. In the case study conducted, a master production plan was established for 12 products over a one-year time horizon. The proposed solution achieved an 11.42% reduction in uncertainty, albeit with a 2.39% cost increase.

Keywords: product-driven; nervousness; schedule; planning; intelligent product; agent-based model; holonic manufacturing system

Citation: Sáez, P.; Herrera, C.; Parada, V. Reducing Nervousness in Master Production Planning: A Systematic Approach Incorporating Product-Driven Strategies. *Algorithms* **2023**, *16*, 386. https://doi.org/10.3390/a16080386

Academic Editors: Alexandre Dolgui, David Lemoine, María I. Restrepo and Frank Werner

Received: 20 June 2023
Revised: 3 August 2023
Accepted: 4 August 2023
Published: 11 August 2023

Copyright: © 2023 by the authors. Licensee MDPI, Basel, Switzerland. This article is an open access article distributed under the terms and conditions of the Creative Commons Attribution (CC BY) license (https://creativecommons.org/licenses/by/4.0/).

1. Introduction

Conventional manufacturing management is constantly evolving due to the incorporation of new technologies. These technologies make it possible to reduce the problems caused by fluctuations in market demand and operational disturbances. As a result, conventional production planning and control models have been transformed into new flexible models that react dynamically during the production period. These models react dynamically to changes in scheduling, including disturbances arising from various factors such as operating machinery, production expansion, processes, products, and production volumes [1–4].

When developing their master production plan, which serves as the basis for strategic decision making, manufacturing companies often consider flexibility in their production systems. This plan outlines the production quantities of each product based on market demands and requirements. Manufacturing companies typically develop the master production plan using optimization models that may not consider the operational details, leading to potential feasibility issues and production challenges. To mitigate these issues, companies often modify their operations, which can destabilize the system and lead to production plan nervousness [5].

Production plan nervousness can make achieving stable production systems challenging, resulting in a need for constant supervision and distrust in planning [6]. Incorporating demand fluctuations, the leading cause of production plan nervousness, into a model is complex [7]. Nevertheless, advancements in technology, including artificial intelligence tools and new manufacturing systems, have made it possible to mitigate the effects of nervousness [8].

The literature has given limited attention to the impact of production plan nervousness on production stability. Conversely, instability is also a cause of nervousness because as nervousness increases, production plan instability increases [9,10]. Hence, it is reasonable to consider both concepts as interdependent [11,12]. The most common approach to reduce nervousness and instability is automatic reprogramming, allowing the system to respond to exceptional conditions [13]. However, conventional routines are inflexible in practice, making it impossible to reprogram jobs.

Experimental studies and quantitative modeling have recently addressed nervousness in production systems [14]. However, the literature lacks clarity on the most effective approach to mitigate nervousness. Some studies have suggested frequent rescheduling for better responsiveness to demand fluctuations, while others have recommended avoiding frequent schedule changes [11]. In addition, considering the cost of production has shown that improved stability does not necessarily significantly increase the total cost [15]. To better understand the performance of a specific model, computational simulations of the proposed approach are necessary for more clarity.

Product-driven production systems (PDSs) are models that naturally allow for the inclusion of the nervousness phenomenon. A PDS regards the products as intelligent and artificial entities that execute and coordinate the control process. Thus, in a PDS, products function as controllers of resources and adapt to disturbances in an interoperable system [16–18]. Therefore, products enable the dynamic reconfiguration of resources to provide agility in the face of production changes generated by nervousness. The implementation of a PDS is achieved through the concept of a holonic system (HMS) using a multiagent system (MAS). A holonic system (HMS) is used within a multiagent system (MAS) to implement a PDS. A MAS is a development approach based on the distribution, autonomy, and cooperation of virtual entities known as agents [19]. In an HMS, machines, robots, or workers are modeled as holons consisting of physical and virtual components capable of autonomous self-organization and blending the physical and virtual worlds [16]. However, there is no clarity on the effect of including these issues on the computational performance of a PDS.

Measuring and analyzing the concept of nervousness can be complex because, unlike other objective measures such as productivity or efficiency, nervousness lacks a direct quantitative measure. Additionally, nervousness can vary widely depending on the production environment, with factors such as market dynamics, task complexity, and labor relations (human resources) influencing it. These contextual differences make comparing and generalizing nervousness levels across production situations difficult.

This paper presents a PDS that considers the nervousness management of a production planning system. The PDS considers intelligent products as functional units and makes autonomous production decisions to manage nervousness in an environment under realistic conditions. A decrease in system nervousness occurs due to decentralized decision making based on information from intelligent products. We evaluated the computational performance of the proposed PDS by applying it to a production planning scenario that involves 12 products over a one-year planning horizon. This proposal generates flexible production planning that can reduce the nervousness of the system, produce more stable plans, and mitigate production cost increases.

The proposed PDS offers efficient solutions for practical production planning problems in sustainable manufacturing environments, spanning various manufacturing industries, especially those producing different products with fluctuating demand. By employing intelligent agents to make production decisions and adjust production quantities, the system has the potential to assist companies in creating a more flexible and adaptable master production schedule.

This study contributes to production planning research by integrating moving horizon planning with dynamic planning, resulting in improved stability and reduced instability in the production process. Thus, the primary objective of this study is to evaluate the cost and nervousness of the system using synthetic data. By analyzing these factors, the aim is to understand the integrated approach's effectiveness and performance. In addition, this study contributes to developing an effective PDS that addresses nervousness in production planning. The PDS incorporates intelligent products as functional units, enabling decentralized decision making and autonomous adjustments in production to mitigate nervousness under realistic conditions. Including intelligent agents empowers companies to create a flexible and adaptable master production schedule that ensures stable production plans and reduced costs.

This paper is organized as follows: Section 2 reviews the literature and explains the essential terms, such as master production plan, nervousness, PDSs, and intelligent products. Section 3 outlines the proposed PDS and is followed by Section 4, which presents the results. Section 5 discusses the results and Section 6 concludes the paper.

2. Related Work

Production planning involves determining a product's quantity, timing, and production stage location, often represented by a mathematical model that optimizes decision making to minimize costs or maximize profits. The model determines the production quantity for each period within a finite horizon while meeting future demand and not exceeding the system's capacity. Lot sizing is a commonly used modeling technique for production planning [20].

Several studies in the literature have addressed time-based production planning using moving horizon planning for different production processes [21–24]. However, although it is a widely used approach in the industry, the impact of combining moving horizon planning with artificial intelligence tools on the stability of the production process still lacks clarity in the literature [25]. A real-world data study was conducted in the automotive industry, considering multiple impact assessment tests to meet plant requirements [23].

In modern industry, it is crucial for production planning to respond effectively to dynamic market conditions and mitigate the adverse effects of production instability, commonly referred to as nervousness. The objectives of production planning include reducing lead times, enhancing process agility, improving product quality, and reducing manufacturing costs [26]. However, achieving these objectives requires a series of operational reconfigurations that result in permanent modifications to the established schedule, leading to instability and increased production nervousness [27].

Several studies have presented methodologies and tools for measuring, detecting, and eliminating production instability [28]. The concepts of instability and nervousness have been studied interchangeably in some cases [11,12], while other works have considered instability as a consequence of system nervousness [9,10]. Tunc et al. [29] provided a higher level of specificity by identifying two types of nervousness that occur due to the quantities involved or the configurations made.

Several studies have considered the mitigation of nervousness based on the quantity of production, inventory, or safety stock [12,30,31]. Other proposals for nervousness mitigation have focused on the planning horizon and the amount of production or storage. In the former, planning horizon freezing has been used [7,23,32,33]. Additionally, the rolling horizon method [34–37] and increases in the forecast horizon [38,39] have been studied. Other authors have considered the dynamic lot-sizing model [40,41] and control rules [42].

The concept of an intelligent product is a fundamental component in the design of a PDS, and it has been defined in various ways in the existing literature [43–47]. We have adopted Wong et al.'s [43] definition of an intelligent product in our proposal. Their definition stipulates that an intelligent product must possess five essential characteristics: a unique identity, the ability to communicate effectively with its environment, the capability to retain or store data, the ability to participate in decision making relevant to its destiny, and a communication language to express its characteristics. Thus, including intelligent products in the PDS facilitates the synchronization of material and information flows in a specific direction.

The characteristics of intelligent products provide the basis for the product-controlled production approach. They are entities that take the initiative during the execution of the production plan by reacting appropriately to disturbances that might occur [15]. This approach facilitates the design, distribution, and operation phases of production. The consequence is improved product quality and performance resulting from self-learning, self-diagnosis, self-adaptation, and self-optimization [48].

A PDS is a distributed control system to support operational decision making, the design of which is facilitated by including the holonic paradigm, which specifies that each product is represented by physical and virtual components [49]. The virtual component is interpreted as an agent, making a PDS a multiagent system. Agent-based models have autonomous roles, originating actions without direct human intervention. Herrera et al. [50] conducted a simulation to coordinate different decision levels in a production system with intelligent product characteristics. They observed that coordination among active batches was more effective at distributed levels than traditional approaches. In another study, Campos et al. [8] proposed a solution to a dynamic scheduling problem by dividing the process into three stages and assigning specific roles to different agents. However, their approach did not directly include a master scheduling model.

Integrating a PDS with a holonic system and its implementation through a multiagent system could generate computational times that do not allow for real-time production control. Decentralized decision making in these systems could provide feasible solutions that minimize nervousness for a given period but with higher production costs. Additionally, the industry has adopted static production modeling as a practical solution, which could be initially integrated into a PDS and subsequently adjusted with individual decisions made by intelligent products. However, the production planning literature has given limited attention to these topics, and the computational performance of a PDS with such features is not yet clear.

Despite the significance of integrating a DPS with a holonic system and its implementation through a multi-agent system, there is a need for more research that addresses this approach. This lack of information hinders a comprehensive understanding of the computational performance associated with a DPS and its distinctive characteristics. Hence, the conducted study generates novel insights in this field, maximizing the potential of these systems and achieving more efficient and adaptable production planning.

3. Proposed PDS

The proposed PDS implements a master plan for a production system that operates with production cycles and periods, considering the presence of nervousness. The master production plan is obtained by solving an optimization problem and determining the optimal quantity for each product in each cycle and period. Each product is represented by a virtual agent that translates the information into valuable data for decision making, resulting in a highly distributed architecture. Furthermore, each agent incorporates an intelligence function that assesses individual and collective performance. Nervousness is the variance between the planned quantity for each product in a given cycle and period. The optimization model is presented in Section 3.1, the nervousness evaluation in Section 3.2, and the PDS architecture in Section 3.3.

3.1. The Optimization Problem

The mathematical model that produces the master production plan considers minimizing the production cost subject to the quantity to be produced at a given time. This formulation extends the formulation presented in the literature for lot-sizing problems by including production costs, inventory, setup, and backorder costs [20,51]. Our specific model uses the following variables, all of which depend on the period 't' and product 'i': production quantity (x_{it}), inventory level (s_{it}), backlog quantity (r_{it}), and setup (y_{it}).

Additionally, we provide the model with the following initial parameters: demand (d_{it}), production cost (p_{it}), inventory holding cost (h_{it}), backorder cost (b_{it}), setup cost (q_{it}), and system capacity (C_t). We define all these parameters for specific periods 't' and product 'i'. Let the following decision variables be defined as follows:

x_{it} = Quantity of product i in period t.
s_{it} = Quantity of inventory product i in period t.
r_{it} = Backlog of product i in period t.
y_{it} = Setup of product i in period t ($y_{it} = 1 \leftrightarrow x_{it} > 0, \forall i, \forall t$).

The model requires the following input:

d_{it} = Demand of product i in period t.
p_{it} = Production cost of product i in period t.
h_{it} = Inventory cost of product i in period t.
b_{it} = Backorder cost of product i in period t.
q_{it} = Setup cost of product i in period t.
C_t = Capacity in period t.

The mathematical formulation is in Equations (1)–(5).

$$min f^k = \sum_{i=1}^{n} \sum_{t=k}^{t'} (p_{it}x_{it} + h_{it}s_{it} + b_{it}r_{it} + q_{it}y_{it}) \tag{1}$$

subject to:

$$x_{it} \leq My_{it}, i \in [1, \ldots, n], t \in [k, \ldots, t'] \tag{2}$$

$$\sum_{i}^{n} x_{it} \leq C_t, t \in [k, \ldots, t'] \tag{3}$$

$$s_{i0}^0 = s_{ini}^0, r_{i0}^0 = r_{ini}^0, i \in [1, \ldots, n] \tag{4}$$

$$s_{i(t-1)} - r_{i(t-1)} + x_{it} = d_{it} + s_{it} - r_{it}, i \in [1, \ldots, n], t \in [k, \ldots, t'] \tag{5}$$

Equations (1)–(5) enable us to compute the production schedule that minimizes costs for each cycle. Specifically, Equation (1) addresses the total cost of the current planning (considering individual costs and production quantities). Meanwhile, Equations (2)–(5) provide us with information related to production and its development, starting from the establishment of the initial parameters (s_{ini}^0 and r_{ini}^0) up to the production dynamics (capacity evolution in each period and production balance per cycle and period).

In greater detail, we have the following: the objective function of model f^k in Equation (1) corresponds to the minimization of the production cost in the intervals of time horizon sliding $[k, \ldots, t']$. In this way, k and $t' = k + n - 1$ are the first and last periods of the mobile planning horizon of length n in each cycle k. Constraint (2) relates production and the corresponding setup, where setup = 1 when there is production and 0 otherwise. Constraint (3) restricts production according to the capacity. Constraints (4) and (5) set the initial inventory conditions, backorders, and the balance between the two. The problem covers each cycle k concerning schedules of precedent cycles. In this problem, the objective function (1) minimizes the value between the production quantity of product i in period t in cycle k (Q_{it}^k) related to the cycle $k-1$.

3.2. Measurement of System Nervousness

Nervousness measures the difference in the quantity of product i to be produced in period t during production cycle k compared to the previous cycle and period. The calculation is based on two parameters (the magnitude of change and the frequency of changes), so significant changes or a high frequency of changes in production imply high values of nervousness. Two metrics express the nervousness per cycle and period. Let C_{ki}

be the number of schedule changes of product i in cycle k and C_{ti} be the number of schedule changes of product i in period t. Furthermore, let Q_{it}^k be the production quantity for product i in period t in cycle k. Then, in Equation (6), N_{cki} is the nervousness in cycle k for product i, and in Equation (7), N_{pti} is the nervousness in period t for product i. Equation (8) presents the measure of nervousness N.

$$N_{cki} = C_{ki} * \left\{ \sum_{t=0}^{n-1} |Q_{i(t+1)}^k - Q_{it}^k| \right\}, \forall k, \forall i \qquad (6)$$

$$N_{pti} = C_{ti} * \left\{ \sum_{t=0}^{n} |Q_{it}^{(k+1)} - Q_{it}^k| \right\}, \forall t, \forall i \qquad (7)$$

$$N = N_{cki} + N_{pti} \qquad (8)$$

Thus, Q_{it}^k represents the quantity of production for product i in period t in cycle k. For the example in Table 1, in period 5, nervousness is measured between Q_{i2}^2, Q_{i3}^2, Q_{i4}^2, and Q_{i5}^2 for N_{cki} and Q_{i5}^2, Q_{i5}^3, Q_{i5}^4, and Q_{i5}^5 or N_{pti}.

Table 1. Example of production scheduling with a rolling horizon.

k/t	1	2	3	4	5	6	7	8
1	Q_{i1}^1	Q_{i2}^1	Q_{i3}^1	Q_{i4}^1				
2		Q_{i2}^2	Q_{i3}^2	Q_{i4}^2	Q_{i5}^2			
3			Q_{i3}^3	Q_{i4}^3	Q_{i5}^3	Q_{i6}^3		
4				Q_{i4}^4	Q_{i5}^4	Q_{i6}^4	Q_{i7}^4	
5					Q_{i5}^5	Q_{i6}^5	Q_{i7}^5	Q_{i8}^5

The parameter Φ_k quantifies the ratio between cost and nervousness for each cycle k. In cycle k, $c(k)$ represents the cost and $N(k)$ represents the nervousness. This parameter identifies the magnitude of the change in each cycle by calculating the area under the curve of cost and nervousness. In addition, let $c = [c_1, \ldots, c_k]$ and $N = [N_1, \ldots, N_k]$ be two vectors to update Φ_k; thus, $\Phi_k, k = 1, 2, \ldots, 60$ is given by Equation (9).

$$\Phi_k = \left| \frac{\sum_{k=1}^{k} c(k)}{\sum_{k=1}^{k} N(k)} \right|, \forall k \in \{k = 1, \ldots, k = 60\} \qquad (9)$$

The following numerical example for $k = 10$ illustrates the updating of Equation (9). Considers values for c and N as follows:

$c = [12.1, 12.44, 12.85, 13.34, 13.97, 14.6, 15.39, 16.3, 17.12, 18.05]$,
$N = [1.79, -3.47, -8.63, -14.07, -19.13, -24.43, -29.74, -34.54, -38.87, -43.37]$.

Such values indicate that a program costing 12.1 monetary units has a nervousness of 1.79 for $k = 0$. Thus, the calculations of Φ are exemplified below for the vectors c and N.

$$\Phi = [\left|\frac{12.1}{1.79}\right| = 6.76, \left|\frac{24.54}{-1.68}\right| = 14.61, \left|\frac{37.39}{-10.3}\right| = 3.63, \ldots, \left|\frac{128.1}{-171.1}\right| = 0.75, \left|\frac{146.2}{-214.5}\right| = 0.68]$$

3.3. PDS Architecture

The system architecture contains physical and virtual layers, each with three levels (configuration, interactions, and results), as shown in Figure 1. An agent represents each product in the virtual layer, transforming the information into valuable data for decision making. The configuration of the virtual layer represents the results generated by the optimization model as data for communication and decision making by each agent. Thus, the physical layer of the system interacts with other physical entities, and its virtual layer interacts with the environment for production control and management. Decision making and communication among agents are distributed on the same hierarchical scale. The intelligence function of the agents considers decision rules for obtaining a global objective considering all of the system's entities. Such decision rules are known and applied by all of the agents of the system through internal and inter-agent communication. This information is processed and stored in the physical part of the components. At the results level, the model outputs correspond to the production planning, virtually and physically representing the planning.

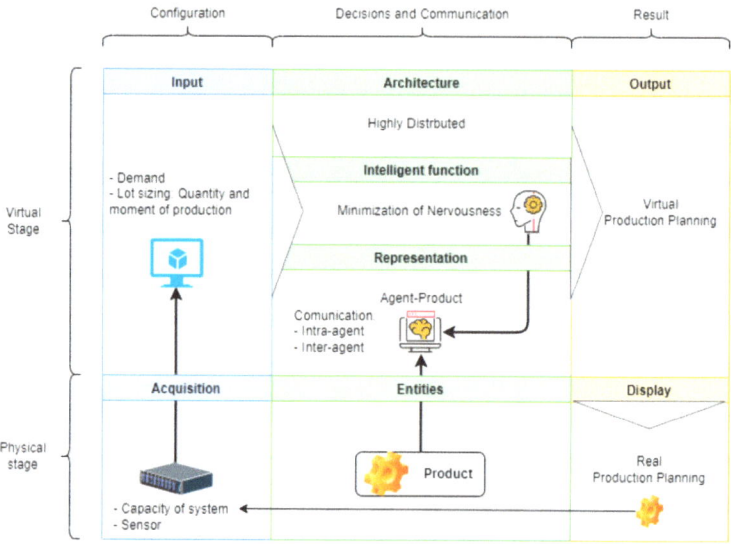

Figure 1. Model characterization matrix.

The virtual layer in Figure 1 contemplates an intelligence function that evaluates individual and collective performance, looking for system stability with a sustained cost increase. To this end, the intelligence function measures the nervousness of each agent using Equation (8). Each agent complies with the characteristics of an intelligent product defined by Wong et al. [43], i.e., they have a unique identifier and can communicate with the surrounding agents of the same product type.

Agent communication occurs within the system's virtual layer, where each product corresponds to an individual agent (Figure 1). This communication converts information into data. Each agent collects and processes data on its current state, production requirements, and resource needs. Interaction between agents occurs through a question-and-answer system. In addition, communication between agents eventually involves transferring data through the system optimization model, including results derived from production planning, capacity, and constraint information and recommendations to support decision making.

Figure 2 depicts the communication process among agents representing various product types within the system. These agents engage in virtual interactions, inquiring about the required production quantity for each period and cycle. Furthermore, when the daily production capacity is exceeded, agents reach out to agents representing other product types. Such interactions constitute internal communication among agents of the same type and external communication between agents of different types. For instance, an agent positioned in the production plan's second cycle and second period would query the production quantities for future periods pertaining to the product it represents. Additionally, this agent would refer to the quantities produced in previous cycles to ensure production stability. This continuous communication facilitates the coordination of production activities and enables informed decision making that aligns with each product's specific needs and capacities.

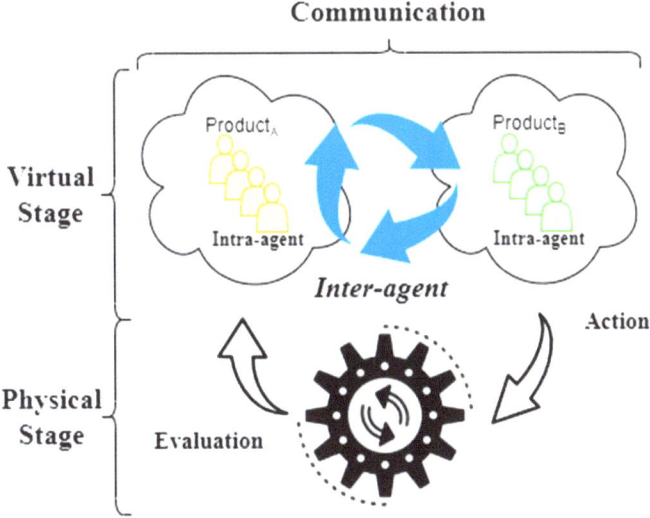

Figure 2. Diagram of communication between intelligent products.

Figure 3 shows the sequence of actions of the proposed architecture. First, the algorithm solves the mathematical model and generates the optimal production. Then, the agents evaluate the nervousness and the planning cost to determine the required production that minimizes the increase in production cost. The objective function of the lot-sizing model (Equation (1)) is the basis of such calculation. Finally, agents communicate with other agents of the same product type in the corresponding cycle and period to evaluate the production quantity. Simultaneously, agents communicate with agents of another product family to avoid exceeding the system's production capacity and to satisfy each product's demand (see Figure 4). Then, the possibilities of decreasing nervousness are evaluated by modifying the production quantities and calculating the costs associated with such modifications. When a production quantity modification occurs that improves the value of nervousness, the agents store the production values. This communication architecture and these agent interactions respond to a perturbation of the system because of the permanent evaluation of quantities.

The production plan considers 12 products and a production horizon of 52 periods. The planning horizon is $n = 8$ with an interval between periods of $\Delta t = 1$. The demand for each product obeys a normal distribution $d_{it}^k \sim \eta(\mu, \rho) = \eta(120, 12), \forall i, \forall t, \forall k$ to simulate different variations. The first stage outputs a master production plan for each product in the active period and a demand projection for subsequent periods. The complete simulation is set up with parameters that resemble a real industrial case, allowing a realistic evaluation of the model's performance. Version 6.2 of the NetLogo simulation platform simulates the scenario providing a suitable environment for testing and monitoring model performance [52].

Figure 5 shows a class diagram to provide a reference model. The system contains a main class called "System", which has two attributes: "PhysicalLayer" and "VirtualLayer". The physical layer ("PhysicalLayer") has a list of physical entities ("PhysicalEntity") and a results attribute ("Results"). In addition, the virtual layer ("VirtualLayer") has a list of agents ("Agent") and a configuration ("Configuration"). Each physical entity and agent has its specific attributes and methods. The physical entities interact through the "Interaction" class, which registers the source and target physical entity. Agents make decisions and communicate with each other using the "Information" class to share valuable data. The "Results" class stores the production planning ("ProductionPlanning"), which has information about the period and production quantities for each product ("Product") in the form of "ProductionQuantity" objects. In addition, the "CommunicationData" class manages the necessary communication data in the virtual layer.

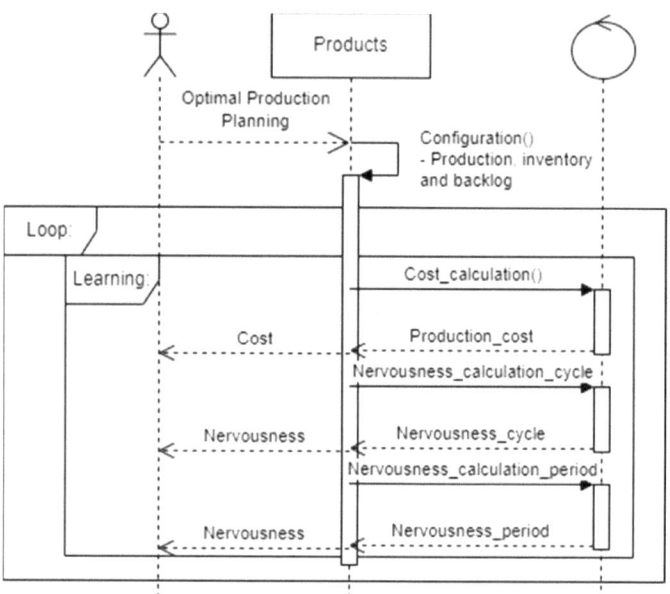

Figure 3. Sequence diagram for the model.

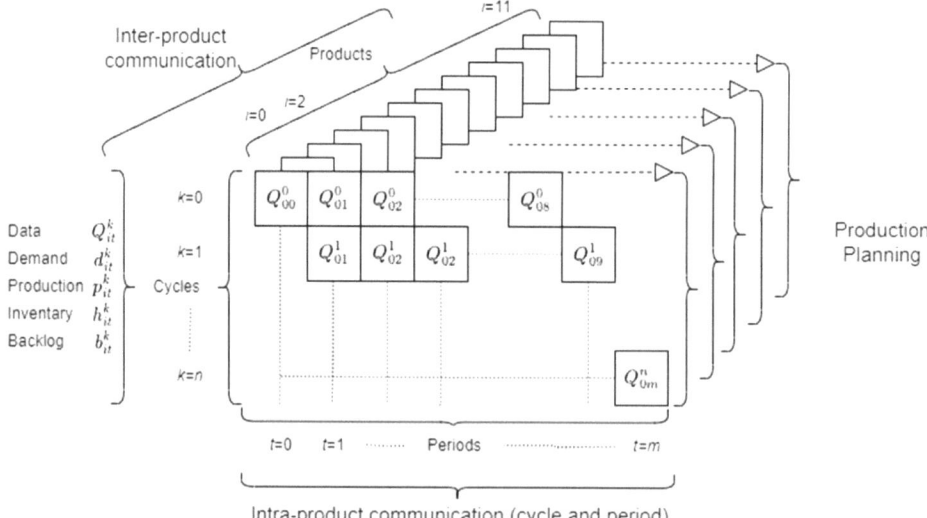

Figure 4. Simulation dynamics and product agent communication.

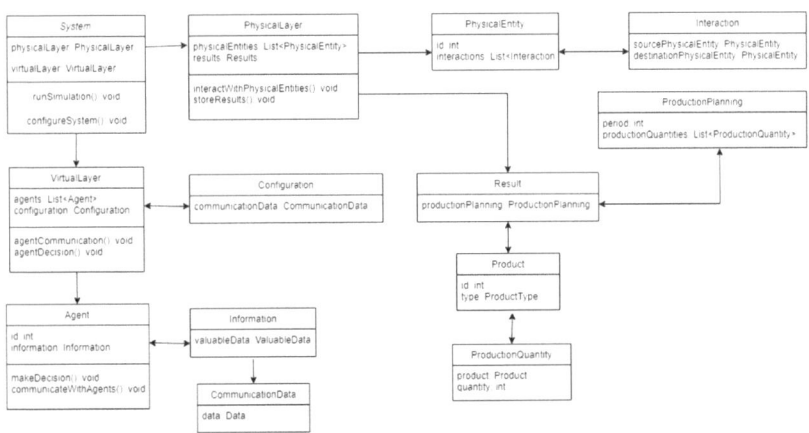

Figure 5. Class diagram for proposed model.

4. Results

The PDS presents an initial phase of significant variation in cost and nervousness until it reaches a steady state. This phenomenon emerges from a simulation with three control variables: per period, per cycle, and per period cycle. In period control, intelligent products monitor production quantities during each period and modify the production plan to reduce nervousness. In cycle control, intelligent products control production quantities over the planning horizon. In period–cycle control, intelligent products look for period and cycle stability by considering consecutive periods of the planning horizon. In each type of control, Equations (6)–(8) update the nervousness.

Table 2 shows the results of analyzing the percentage increase in production costs up to 10%. Our model, with a 1% cost increase, reduces nervousness by 1.78%, 42.41%, and 14.31% in terms of cycle control, period control, and cycle–period control, respectively. This reduction in nervousness is consistent across the studied percentage increases, with period control being the most effective until a 6% cost increase. For cost increases exceeding 7%, cycle–period control becomes more effective, resulting in a 98.61% reduction in accumulative nervousness.

Table 2. Analysis of percentage increase in the cost of the master production plan.

		Increase in Production Plan Cost									
		1%	2%	3%	4%	5%	6%	7%	8%	9%	10%
% Reduction in nervousness	Cycle control	1.78	7.43	10.12	12.83	14.72	16.85	18.99	21.86	23.86	25.93
	Period control	42.41	51.71	56.98	61.89	63.8	67.08	68.63	69.72	71.7	72.97
	Cycle and period control	14.31	24.59	34.44	43.25	55.92	64.18	88.74	95.3	98.5	98.61

However, it is necessary to analyze the three types of control, evaluating the number of cycles required to reduce nervousness expressed in Table 2. Figure 6 shows the results of the cost and nervousness variations for each control type. The decrease in nervousness occurs with the consequent increase in cost concerning the initial values. For example, considering control by period (Figure 6a), there is an increase in cost of 11.21% and a reduction in nervousness of 14.72% in the eighth cycle. In control by cycle (Figure 6b), an increase in cost of 2.39% and a reduction in nervousness of 18.27% are observed. Figure 6c shows the behavior of the PDS according to the period–cycle control. A more significant decrease in nervousness is observed than with the two types of controls. In the same programming cycle, an increase in cost of 11.27% and a reduction in nervousness of 34.44% are observed.

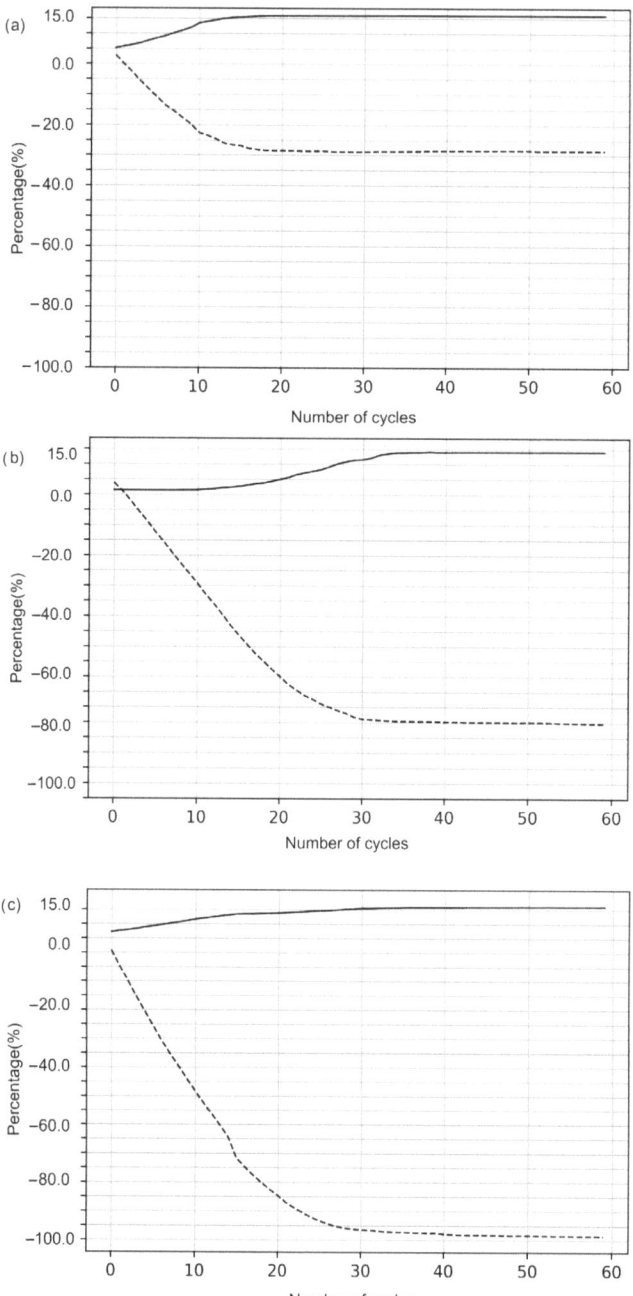

Figure 6. Cost and sensitivity analysis (**a**) Analysis of the model based on control by period. (**b**) Model analysis based on control per cycle. (**c**) Model analysis based on control by period–simultaneous cycle.

5. Discussion

The PDS results indicate an uneven relationship between decreased nervousness and increased costs. The more significant the decrease in nervousness, the smaller the increase in the cost of the production plan. This system-generated dynamic is consistent with the plan modification that minimizes the cost. In other words, any change in the production plan calculated through the mathematical model generates an increase in cost. However, the benefit of such a modification implies more stable plans. As the production cycles proceed, both cost and nervousness reach an equilibrium because modifying production quantities is no longer possible. Figure 7a–c show that the main results of decreasing nervousness and increasing cost occur before production cycle 10. In Figure 7, we observe the results for different values of Φ_k, which compare the initial cost increase with the benefits of nervousness reduction. The behavior is similar in the three types of control applied, obtaining a more noticeable change when using the cycle–period control, which optimizes in a balanced way between cycle and product.

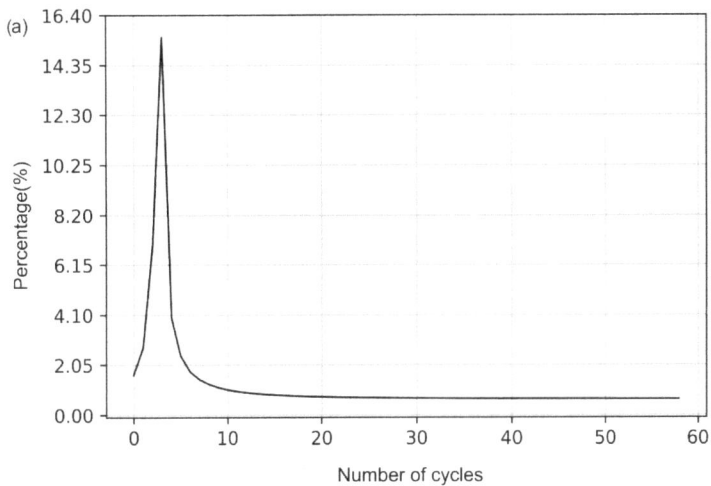

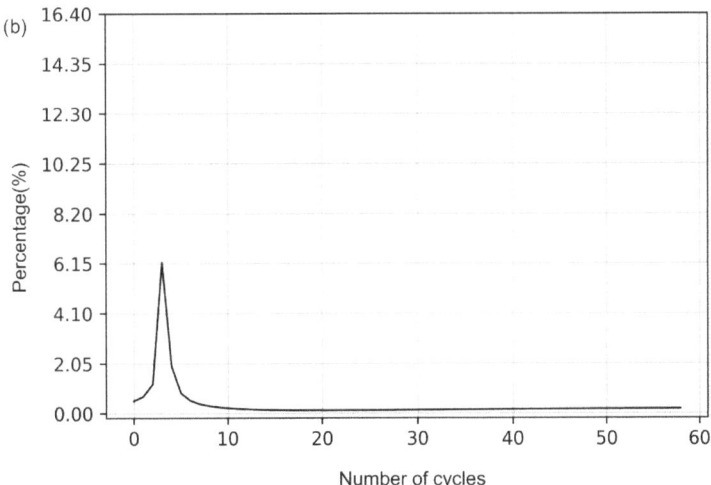

Figure 7. *Cont.*

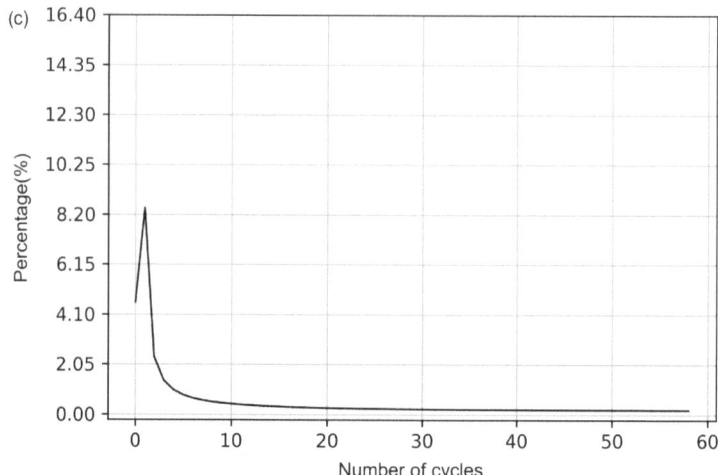

Figure 7. (**a**) Analysis of Φ in a model based on control by period. (**b**) Analysis of Φ in a model based on control per cycle. (**c**) Analysis of Φ in a model based on period–cycle control.

In all types of control, cost increases with decreasing nervousness are observed in the first cycles of the simulation. However, after this initialization stage, a period of stability is reached during which there are no substantial differences in the magnitude of the changes associated with costs and nervousness. The computational results suggest that using a PDS is promising in reducing nervousness without substantial increases in production costs. Thus, a PDS can improve the master production plan by minimizing nervousness and adapting to changing environments.

The proposed system reduced uncertainty by 11.42% for the case study conducted. This is a promising result since uncertainty can be detrimental to production planning. However, a 2.39% increase in production costs was observed. In this case, the increase in production costs could be considered relatively low, especially considering the benefit of more accurate and stable planning. It is essential to consider that cost-effectiveness analysis may vary according to each production system's context and specific priorities. Some companies may accept a slight cost increase if it implies stability in production and a significant reduction in uncertainty. Other companies may prioritize cost minimization and be less willing to accept additional increases. Thus, the precise assessment of cost-effectiveness depends on each company's specific objectives and priorities.

6. Conclusions

This work proposes a production planning system that addresses nervousness management in production systems. The system utilizes intelligent products and starts from an initial production plan for the planning period generated through a mathematical cost minimization model. The numerical evaluation of the proposed system using a 12-product production system and a one-year planning period shows that it effectively reduces nervousness without significantly increasing production costs. For example, using cycle control, a modest increase in cost of 2.39% results in a significant reduction in nervousness of up to 11.42%.

The developed system includes a mathematical model, a metric for measuring uncertainty, and a definition of intelligent products. It is worth noting that there are several options and variants in the literature for each component, allowing for customization based on the specific needs of different industries. Future research could further explore these combinations of possibilities to develop production planning control systems tailored to industry-specific requirements.

It is relevant to emphasize that the proposed system generates flexible solutions without requiring multiple executions of a mathematical model, thus avoiding the resolution of computationally slow problems. This approach enables improved decision making in the modern industry by leveraging real-time process data that feed algorithms optimizing resource utilization. In turn, this fosters the development of a more sustainable industry, contributing to the innovation of new perspectives for uncertainty management in production planning.

Integrating new technologies into conventional manufacturing management is revolutionizing the industry, primarily to address challenges arising from demand fluctuations and operational disruptions. Product-driven production systems emerge as a promising solution by incorporating intelligent products capable of autonomous decision making and adaptation to disruptions. This approach enables more flexible planning, reduces nervousness, and mitigates increases in production costs. By implementing these approaches based on artificial intelligence and holonic systems, efficient solutions for production planning can be achieved across various industries. This integration enhances adaptability and optimizes resource allocation in sustainable manufacturing environments.

Overall, the findings of this study demonstrate the potential of using a production planning system to manage uncertainty in production planning, resulting in enhanced system performance in terms of reducing uncertainty and optimizing production costs. This work contributes to the existing literature on production planning and lays the groundwork for future research in this field.

As a future research direction, we propose exploring novel forms of embedded intelligence to improve response times and outcomes. These new forms would align with heuristics or machine learning techniques. In addition, it is possible to consider dynamism in the agent decision making, including functionalities that allow selecting the best decision at each moment according to different optimization criteria. Further study would determine the level of dynamism that does not exceed a certain threshold of computational time. Furthermore, expanding our study and considering real-world industrial cases is recommended. This would provide a more comprehensive understanding of the applicability and effectiveness of the proposed approach in diverse production environments.

Author Contributions: Conceptualization: P.S. and C.H.; Data Curation: P.S.; Formal Analysis: P.S.; Investigation: C.H. and P.S.; Methodology: P.S. and C.H.; Software: P.S.; Supervision: C.H. and V.P.; Validation: C.H., P.S. and V.P.; Visualization: P.S., C.H. and V.P.; Writing—Original Draft Preparation: P.S., C.H. and V.P.; Writing—Review and Editing: P.S., C.H. and V.P. All authors have read and agreed to the published version of the manuscript.

Funding: This research received no external funding.

Data Availability Statement: The data that support the findings of this study are available from the corresponding author, Patricio Sáez, upon request.

Acknowledgments: V. Parada gratefully acknowledges financial support from ANID PIA/PUENTE AFB220003 and DICYT-USACH 061919PD.

Conflicts of Interest: The authors declare no conflict of interest.

References

1. Gräßler, I.; Pöhler, A. Implementation of an Adapted Holonic Production Architecture. *Procedia CIRP* **2017**, *63*, 138–143. [CrossRef]
2. Cardin, O.; Derigent, W.; Trentesaux, D. Evolution of holonic control architectures towards Industry 4.0: A short overview. *IFAC-PapersOnLine* **2018**, *51*, 1243–1248. [CrossRef]
3. Kovalenko, I.; Tilbury, D.; Barton, K. The model-based product agent: A control oriented architecture for intelligent products in multi-agent manufacturing systems. *Control Eng. Pract.* **2019**, *86*, 105–117. [CrossRef]
4. Yadav, A.; Jayswal, S.C. Evaluation of batching and layout on the performance of flexible manufacturing system. *Int. J. Adv. Manuf. Technol.* **2019**, *101*, 1435–1449. [CrossRef]
5. Mortezaei, N.; Zulkifli, N. Integration of lot sizing and flow shop scheduling with lot streaming. *J. Appl. Math.* **2013**, *2013*, 216595. [CrossRef]

6. Damand, D.; Derrouiche, R.; Barth, M. Parameterisation of the MRP method: Automatic identification and extraction of properties. *Int. J. Prod. Res.* **2013**, *51*, 5658–5669. [CrossRef]
7. Atadeniz, S.N.; Sridharan, S.V. Effectiveness of nervousness reduction policies when capacity is constrained. *Int. J. Prod. Res.* **2020**, *58*, 4121–4137. [CrossRef]
8. Campos, J.T.d.G.A.A.; Blumelova, J.; Lepikson, H.A.; Freires, F.G.M. Agent-based dynamic scheduling model for product-driven production. *Braz. J. Oper. Prod. Manag.* **2020**, *17*, 1–10. [CrossRef]
9. Kabak, K.E.; Ornek, A.M. An improved metric for measuring multi-item multi-level schedule instability under rolling schedules. *Comput. Ind. Eng.* **2009**, *56*, 691–707. [CrossRef]
10. Sivadasan, S.; Smart, J.; Huatuco, L.H.; Calinescu, A. Reducing schedule instability by identifying and omitting complexity-adding information flows at the supplier-customer interface. *Int. J. Prod. Econ.* **2013**, *145*, 253–262. [CrossRef]
11. Pujawan, I.N.; Smart, A.U. Factors affecting schedule instability in manufacturing companies. *Int. J. Prod. Res.* **2012**, *50*, 2252–2266. [CrossRef]
12. Sridharan, V.; LaForge, L. An analysis of alternative policies to achieve schedule stability. *J. Manuf. Oper. Manag.* **1990**, *3*, 53–73.
13. Li, Q.; Disney, S.M. Revisiting rescheduling: MRP nervousness and the bullwhip effect. *Int. J. Prod. Res.* **2017**, *55*, 1992–2012. [CrossRef]
14. Azouz, N.; Belisário, L.S.; Ammar, A.; Pierreval, H. Addressing over-correction in adaptive card-based pull control systems. *Int. J. Comput. Integr. Manuf.* **2018**, *31*, 1189–1204. [CrossRef]
15. Herrera, C.; Belmokhtar-berraf, S.; Thomas, A.; Parada, V. A reactive decision-making approach to reduce instability in a master production schedule. *Int. J. Prod. Res.* **2016**, *7543*, 2394–2404. [CrossRef]
16. Mcfarlane, D.; Sarma, S.; Chirn, J.L.; Wong, C.Y.; Ashton, K. The intelligent product in manufacturing control and management. *IFAC Proc. Vol.* **2002**, *35*, 49–54. [CrossRef]
17. Meyer, G.G.; Holmstro, J.; Fra, K. Computers in Industry Intelligent Products: A survey. *Comput. Ind.* **2009**, *60*, 137–148. [CrossRef]
18. Herrera, C. Cadre générique de planification logistique dans un contexte de décisions centralisées et distribuées. Ph.D. Thesis, Université Henry Poincaré, Nancy, Francais, 2011.
19. Leitão, P.; Rodrigues, N.; Barbosa, J.; Turrin, C.; Pagani, A. Intelligent products: The grace experience. *Control Eng. Pract.* **2015**, *42*, 95–105. [CrossRef]
20. Ramya, R.; Rajendran, C.; Ziegler, H.; Mohapatra, S.; Ganesh, K. *Capacitated Lot Sizing Problems in Process Industries*; Springer: Cham, Switzerland, 2019. [CrossRef]
21. Lin, P.C.; Uzsoy, R. Chance-constrained formulations in rolling horizon production planning: An experimental study. *Int. J. Prod. Res.* **2016**, *54*, 3927–3942. [CrossRef]
22. Demirel, E.; Özelkan, E.C.; Lim, C. Aggregate planning with Flexibility Requirements Profile. *Int. J. Prod. Econ.* **2018**, *202*, 45–58. [CrossRef]
23. Lalami, I.; Frein, Y.; Gayon, J.P. Production planning in automotive powertrain plants: A case study. *Int. J. Prod. Res.* **2017**, *55*, 5378–5393. [CrossRef]
24. Ju, L.; Zhang, Q.; Tan, Z.; Wang, W.; Xin, H.; Zhang, Z. Multi-agent-system-based coupling control optimization model for micro-grid group intelligent scheduling considering autonomy-cooperative operation strategy. *Energy* **2018**, *157*, 1035–1052. [CrossRef]
25. Ziarnetzky, T.; Mönch, L.; Uzsoy, R. Rolling horizon, multi-product production planning with chance constraints and forecast evolution for wafer fabs. *Int. J. Prod. Res.* **2018**, *56*, 6112–6134. [CrossRef]
26. Koh, S.C.L.; Saad, S.M.; Jones, M.H. Uncertainty under MRP-planned manufacture: Review and categorization. *Int. J. Prod. Res.* **2002**, *40*, 2399–2421. [CrossRef]
27. Salido, M.A.; Escamilla, J.; Barber, F.; Giret, A. Rescheduling in job-shop problems for sustainable manufacturing systems. *J. Clean. Prod.* **2017**, *162*, S121–S132. [CrossRef]
28. Schuh, G.; Prote, J.P.; Luckert, M.; Hünnekes, P.; Schmidhuber, M. Effects of the update frequency of production plans on the logistical performance of production planning and control. *Procedia CIRP* **2019**, *79*, 421–426. [CrossRef]
29. Tunc, H.; Kilic, O.A.; Tarim, S.A.; Eksioglu, B. A simple approach for assessing the cost of system nervousness. *Int. J. Prod. Econ.* **2013**, *141*, 619–625. [CrossRef]
30. Hasachoo, N.; Masuchun, R. Factors affecting schedule nervousness in the production operations of airline catering industry. *IEEE Int. Conf. Ind. Eng. Eng. Manag.* **2016**, *2016*, 499–503. [CrossRef]
31. Koh, S.C.L.; Saad, S.M. Managing uncertainty in ERP-controlled manufacturing environments in SMEs. *Int. J. Prod. Econ.* **2006**, *101*, 109–127. [CrossRef]
32. Kadipasaoglu, S.N.; Sridharan, V. Alternative approaches for reducing schedule instability in multistage manufacturing under demand uncertainty. *J. Oper. Manag.* **1995**, *13*, 193–211. [CrossRef]
33. Vanajakumari, M.; Sun, H.; Jones, A.; Sriskandarajah, C. Supply chain planning: A case for Hybrid Cross-Docks. *Omega* **2022**, *108*, 102585. [CrossRef]
34. Inderfurth, K. Nervousness in inventory control: Analytical results. *OR Spektrum* **1994**, *16*, 113–123. [CrossRef]
35. Kazan, O.; Nagi, R.; Rump, C.M. New lot-sizing formulations for less nervous production schedules. *Comput. Oper. Res.* **2000**, *27*, 1325–1345. [CrossRef]

36. Mönch, L.; Zimmermann, J. A computational study of a shifting bottleneck heuristic for multi-product complex job shops. *Prod. Plan. Control* **2011**, *22*, 25–40. [CrossRef]
37. van der Sluis, E. Reducing system nervousness in multi-product inventory systems. *Int. J. Prod. Econ.* **1993**, *30–31*, 551–562. [CrossRef]
38. Torabzadeh, S.; Ozelkan, E.C. Fuzzy aggregate production planning with flexible requirement profile for plan stability in uncertain environments. *Eur. J. Ind. Eng.* **2021**, *15*, 514–549. [CrossRef]
39. Hasachoo, N.; Masuchun, R. Reducing schedule nervousness in production and operations under non-stationary stochastic demand: The case of an airline catering company. *IEEE Int. Conf. Ind. Eng. Eng. Manag.* **2016**, *2016*, 941–945. [CrossRef]
40. Özelkan, E.C.; Torabzadeh, S.; Demirel, E.; Lim, C. Bi-objective aggregate production planning for managing plan stability. *Comput. Ind. Eng.* **2023**, *178*, 109105. [CrossRef]
41. Xie, J.; Zhao, X.; Lee, T.S. Freezing the master production schedule under single resource constraint and demand uncertainty. *Int. J. Prod. Econ.* **2003**, *83*, 65–84. [CrossRef]
42. de Kok, T.; Inderfurth, K. Nervousness in inventory management: Comparison of basic control rules. *Eur. J. Oper. Res.* **1997**, *103*, 55–82. [CrossRef]
43. Wong, C.Y.; Mcfarlane, D.; Zaharudin, A.A.; Agarwal, V. The intelligent product driven supply chain. In Proceedings of the IEEE International Conference on Systems, Man and Cybernetics, Yasmine Hammamet, Tunisia, 6–9 October 2002. [CrossRef]
44. Valckenaers, P.; Germain, B.S.; Verstraete, P.; Van Belle, J.; Van Brussel, H. Computers in Industry Intelligent products : Agere versus Essere. *Comput. Ind.* **2009**, *60*, 217–228. [CrossRef]
45. Kiritsis, D. Computer-Aided Design Closed-loop PLM for intelligent products in the era of the Internet of things. *Comput.-Aided Des.* **2011**, *43*, 479–501. [CrossRef]
46. Kärkkäinen, M.; Ala-Risku, T.; Främling, K. The product centric approach: A solution to supply network information management problems? *Comput. Ind.* **2003**, *52*, 147–159. [CrossRef]
47. Ventä, O. *Intelligent Products and Systems: Technology Theme—Final Report*; VTT Technical Research Centre of Finland: Espoo, Finland, 2007.
48. Barbosa, J.; Leitão, P.; Adam, E.; Trentesaux, D. Dynamic self-organization in holonic multi-agent manufacturing systems: The ADACOR evolution. *Comput. Ind.* **2015**, *66*, 99–111. [CrossRef]
49. Mihoubi, B.; Bouzouia, B.; Tebani, K.; Gaham, M. Hardware in the loop simulation for product driven control of a cyber-physical manufacturing system. *Prod. Eng.* **2020**, *14*, 329–343. [CrossRef]
50. Herrera, C.; Thomas, A.; Parada, V. A product-driven system approach for multilevel decisions in manufacturing planning and control. *Prod. Manuf. Res.* **2014**, *2*, 756–766. [CrossRef]
51. Quadt, D. *Lot-Sizing and Scheduling for Flexible Flow Lines*; Lecture Notes in Economics and Mathematical Systems, 546; Springer Nature: Basel, Switzerland, 2004; ISBN 978-3-642-17101-7.
52. Wilensky, U. 'NetLogo'. Center for Connected Learning and Computer-Based Modeling. Northwestern University Evanston. 1999. Available online: http://ccl.northwestern.edu/netlogo/ (accessed on 23 August 2022).

Disclaimer/Publisher's Note: The statements, opinions and data contained in all publications are solely those of the individual author(s) and contributor(s) and not of MDPI and/or the editor(s). MDPI and/or the editor(s) disclaim responsibility for any injury to people or property resulting from any ideas, methods, instructions or products referred to in the content.

Article

Multiprocessor Fair Scheduling Based on an Improved Slime Mold Algorithm

Manli Dai [†] and Zhongyi Jiang *,[†]

School of Computer Science and Artificial Intelligence, Changzhou University, Changzhou 213164, China; dml6891@outlook.com
* Correspondence: jzy@cczu.edu.cn
[†] These authors contributed equally to this work.

Abstract: An improved slime mold algorithm (IMSMA) is presented in this paper for a multiprocessor multitask fair scheduling problem, which aims to reduce the average processing time. An initial population strategy based on Bernoulli mapping reverse learning is proposed for the slime mold algorithm. A Cauchy mutation strategy is employed to escape local optima, and the boundary-check mechanism of the slime mold swarm is optimized. The boundary conditions of the slime mold population are transformed into nonlinear, dynamically changing boundaries. This adjustment strengthens the slime mold algorithm's global search capabilities in early iterations and strengthens its local search capability in later iterations, which accelerates the algorithm's convergence speed. Two unimodal and two multimodal test functions from the CEC2019 benchmark are chosen for comparative experiments. The experiment results show the algorithm's robust convergence and its capacity to escape local optima. The improved slime mold algorithm is applied to the multiprocessor fair scheduling problem to reduce the average execution time on each processor. Numerical experiments showed that the IMSMA performs better than other algorithms in terms of precision and convergence effectiveness.

Keywords: slime mold algorithm; fair scheduling; Bernoulli mapping; reverse learning; Cauchy mutation

Citation: Dai, M.; Jiang, Z. Multiprocessor Fair Scheduling Based on an Improved Slime Mold Algorithm. *Algorithms* **2023**, *16*, 473. https://doi.org/10.3390/a16100473

Academic Editors: Alexandre Dolgui, David Lemoine, María I. Restrepo, Frank Werner

Received: 25 September 2023
Revised: 4 October 2023
Accepted: 4 October 2023
Published: 7 October 2023

Copyright: © 2023 by the authors. Licensee MDPI, Basel, Switzerland. This article is an open access article distributed under the terms and conditions of the Creative Commons Attribution (CC BY) license (https://creativecommons.org/licenses/by/4.0/).

1. Introduction

Multiprocessor systems are widely used in various fields, including medical systems, smartphones, aerospace, and more [1]. With the increasing demand for high performance and low power consumption in today's society, the use of multiprocessor systems has been greatly promoted [2], leading to extensive research on task scheduling problems on multiprocessors. This paper investigates the problem of fair scheduling on multiprocessors, aiming to achieve a balanced average processing time across the processors when executing multiple independent nonpreemptive tasks. The motivation for this problem stems from a factory scenario, where there is a desire to allocate tasks to transportation vehicles in such a way that the average mileage for each vehicle is balanced. This model is also applicable to the fair scheduling problem of taxis, ensuring that the average distance covered by each taxi for deliveries is the same.

The fairness problem in scheduling was initially introduced by Fagin and Williams [3], who abstracted it as the carpool problem for their study. Subsequently, fairness scheduling problems started to emerge in the context of online machine scheduling. The goal of the scheduling problems is to minimize the maximum sum of processing time of the machines. In recent years, there has been an increasing focus on fairness in scheduling, particularly in the context of optimal real-time multiprocessor scheduling algorithms [4]. Research on proportionate fairness scheduling has long been conducted in the fields of operating systems, computer networks, and real-time systems [5]. The scheduling strategies for proportionate fairness are largely based on the concept of maintaining proportional progress rates among all tasks [6]. Due to its ability to balance system throughput and fairness, proportionate fairness scheduling has gained widespread adoption in practice [7].

Ensuring a fair allocation of resources can significantly impact the performance of scheduling algorithms. While various fair scheduling algorithms have been emerging rapidly, research on fair scheduling on multiprocessors is relatively limited. It has been established that the job scheduling problem for processors is NP-hard, and ensuring fairness in scheduling can improve the utilization of processor resources to some extent. The typical objective of fairness scheduling problems is usually to minimize the maximum total processing time on machines. This paper, however, sets the fairness scheduling objective as minimizing the average execution time on each processor.

Scheduling problems with the objective of minimizing the maximum average processing time can be applied to tasks such as taxi and courier dispatch, which require handling a large number of scheduling tasks in a short time, necessitating algorithms that are efficient and have short processing times. The fair scheduling issue for multiprocessor multitasking is addressed in this research using a modified slime mold method.

Swarm intelligence algorithms are mainly inspired by the evolution of organisms in the natural environment and the hunting, foraging, and survival processes of populations [8]. Some common swarm intelligence algorithms include particle swarm optimization (PSO) [9], the whale optimization algorithm (WOA) [10], the sparrow search algorithm (SSA) [11], the butterfly optimization algorithm (BOA) [12], and so on. These swarm intelligence algorithms have been studied and used extensively in a variety of fields, such as photovoltaic maximum power point tracking [13], multiobjective optimization problems [14], and COVID-19 infection prediction [15]. They have demonstrated good performance in solving problems in specific domains. A recently developed metaheuristic algorithm called the slime mold algorithm (SMA), which was introduced by Li et al. [16] in 2020, simulates the behavior and morphological changes of slime molds during natural foraging. Compared with other intelligent optimization algorithms, slime mold algorithm has the advantages of a simple principle, few adjustment parameters, a strong optimization ability, and an easy implementation.

The slime mold algorithm has been successfully applied in many fields, especially in engineering optimization. Premkumar et al. [14] proposed a multiobjective slime mold algorithm based on elite undominated ranking. They applied the slime mold algorithms to solving multiobjective optimization problems and proved that the proposed algorithm was effective in solving complex multiobjective problems. Gong et al. [17] proposed a hybrid algorithm based on a state-adaptive slime mold model and fractional order ant system (SSMFAS) to solve the traveling salesman problem (TSP). Experimental results showed that the algorithm had the competitiveness to find better solutions on TSP instances. By integrating chaos mapping and differing evolution strategies for overall optimization, Chen et al. [18] devised an enhanced slime mold algorithm, which was applied to engineering optimization problems. The whale optimization algorithm and the slime mold algorithm were combined by Abdel-Basset et al. [19] to tackle a chest X-ray separation of images issue. Gush et al. [20] used slime mold algorithms to optimize the optimal intelligent inverter control system of photovoltaic and energy storage systems to improve the photovoltaic carrying capacity of the distribution network.

In this paper, an improved slime mold algorithm is considered to study the fair scheduling of multiprocessor and multitasking. Through in-depth research on slime mold algorithms, it was found that there were still certain limitations. For example, the population diversity is not rich enough, the convergence speed is slow, and it is easy to fall into a local optimal solution. In the standard iteration process of the SMA, the random initialization of the slime mold swarm reduces the potential for population diversity. It also lacks effective solutions when addressing population converged to local optima. The fixed boundary check strategy in the standard SMA makes it difficult to return to the better positions when slime molds exceed the boundaries. This paper makes multistrategy improvements to the standard slime mold algorithm.

The main contributions of this paper are as follows:

1. A reverse learning initialization population strategy based on Bernoulli chaotic mapping is introduced to increase the diversity of populations.
2. Cauchy mutations are introduced to help slime mold populations jump out of a local optimal solution.
3. A nonlinear dynamic boundary improvement strategy is introduced to accelerate the convergence rate of the population.
4. The IMSMA is applied to solving the fair scheduling problem on multiprocessors to minimize the average processing time on each processor.

The article organization is as follows. Section 1 introduces the research about fair scheduling problems and the slime mold algorithm. Section 2 describes some relevant literature on fair scheduling. The conventional slime mold algorithm is presented in Section 3. Section 4 provides detailed improvement strategies for the improved slime mold algorithm (IMSMA). The simulation tests are presented in Section 5. Section 6 models the fair scheduling problem on multiprocessors and applies the IMSMA to solve it. Section 7 provides numerical experiments for fair scheduling on multiple processors. Conclusions are given in Section 8.

2. Related Work

Guaranteeing the fair distribution of resources can have a notable influence on the effectiveness of scheduling algorithms. In the realm of scheduling problems, fairness can be defined in various ways. There exists a wealth of literature dedicated to defining fairness concepts and designing efficient algorithms with fair constraints [21]. Zhong et al. [22] addressed the fair scheduling problem of multicloud workflow tasks and proposed a reinforcement learning-based algorithm. In response to cache contention issues in on-chip multiprocessors, a thread cooperative scheduling technique considering fairness was proposed by Xiao et al. [23]. It was based on non-cooperative game theory. They wanted to ensure equitable thread scheduling in order to improve the performance of the entire system. On heterogeneous processors with multiple cores, Salami et al. [24] suggested an energy-efficient framework for addressing fairness-aware schedules. This framework simultaneously addressed fairness and efficiency issues in multicore processors. For multiprocess contexts, Mohtasham et al. [25] developed a fair resource distribution method that aimed to maximize the overall system utility and fairness. This technique enabled the concurrent execution of multiple scalable processes even under CPU load constraints. Jung et al. [26] presented a multiprocessor-system fair scheduling algorithm based on task satisfaction metrics, which achieved a high proportion of fairness even under highly skewed weight distributions. Their algorithm quantified and evaluated fairness using service-time errors. A review of pertinent research on fair scheduling is given in Table 1.

Table 1. Research on fair scheduling in the relevant literature.

Zhong et al. [22]	To optimize the scheduling order for multiple workflow tasks, they designed a reinforcement learning-based fair scheduling algorithm for multiworkflow tasks.	The authors created an evolving priority-driven method to avoid service level agreement violations through dynamic scheduling. Additionally, they implemented load balancing between virtual machines using a reinforcement learning algorithm.
Xiao et al. [23]	They proposed a fairness-aware thread collaborative scheduling algorithm based on uncooperative game theory, and the on-chip multiprocessor cache congestion problem was addressed.	The authors aimed to enhance the overall system performance by fairly scheduling threads. They employed an uncooperative game approach to address the thread collaborative schedule problem and introduced an iterative algorithm for finding the Nash equilibrium in non-cooperative games. This allowed them to obtain a collaborative scheduling solution for all threads.

Table 1. Cont.

Salami et al. [24]	Specifically addressing the different multicore processors' fair energy-effective schedule dilemma, they proposed an energy-efficient framework that took into account fairness in a heterogeneous context.	Dynamic voltage and frequency scaling was used in the authors' suggested energy-effective framework with a heterogeneous fairness awareness in order to satisfy fairness restrictions and offer an efficient energy-effective schedule. In comparison to the Linux regular scheduler, experimental results showed a significant improvement in both efficiency of energy and fairness.
Mohtasham et al. [25]	The authors proposed a fair distribution of resources method for a multiprocess context aimed at maximizing overall system utility and fairness.	The allocation of resources issue was first formalized as an NP-hard issue. Then, in pseudo-polynomial time, they employed approximation strategies and the convex optimization theory to identify the best answer to the posed problem. This fair resource allocation technique could run multiple scalable processes under CPU load constraints.
Jung et al. [26]	They proposed a multiprocessor-system fair scheduling algorithm based on task satisfaction metrics.	Their algorithm quantified and evaluated fairness using service time errors. It achieved a high proportion of fairness even under highly skewed weight distributions.

3. Standard Slime Mold Algorithm (SMA)

The slime mold algorithm was inspired by the foraging behavior of multicephalic velvet fungus, and the corresponding mathematical model was established. There are three phases: approaching food, surrounding food, and grabbing food [16]. In the stage of approaching food, the slime mold is spontaneously approaching food according to the smell in the environment. The expansion law can be expressed by the formula:

$$X(t+1) = \begin{cases} X_b(t) + vb \times (W \times X_A(t) - X_B(t)), r_1 < p \\ vc \times X(t), r_1 \geq p \end{cases} \quad (1)$$

where $X(t+1)$ and $X(t)$ indicate the position of slime molds at the $(t+1)$th and tth iterations, respectively. The operation "×" represents multiplication. $X_b(t)$ represents the fittest location of the slime molds in terms of fitness from the beginning to the current iteration. $X_A(t)$ and $X_B(t)$ stand for two random positions of the slime mold in the population chosen randomly. r_1 is a random number between zero and one. vb is an arbitrary quantity within $[-a, a]$, where the variation of vb simulates the slime mold's choice between approaching food or continuing the search. vc is the oscillation vector of the slime mold, which modifies its search trajectory. It ranges linearly from one to zero. The parameter a and the selection probability p are determined as follows:

$$a = \arctan h(1 - t/T) \quad (2)$$

$$p = \tan h(|S(i) - DF|) \quad (3)$$

The population size of slime molds is expressed by the number $i = 1, 2, \ldots, N$. t embodies the current iteration number, and T is the maximum number of iterations. $S(i)$ symbolizes the fitness score of the ith slime mold, and DF stands for the best fitness score obtained throughout all iterations.

The following is the weight W's updating formula:

$$W(IndexSorted(i)) \begin{cases} 1 + r_2 \times \log \frac{bF - S(i)}{bF - wF} + 1, i = condition \\ 1 - r_2 \times \log \frac{bF - S(i)}{bF - wF} + 1, i = others \end{cases} \quad (4)$$

$$IndexSorted = sort(S) \tag{5}$$

where *condition* represents slime mold individuals with the top half of fitness values; and *others* represents the remaining individuals. r_1 is a random number between zero and one. *bF* and *wF* represent the best and worst fitness scores of the present iteration, respectively. The operation "×" represents multiplication. The logarithm function is applied in the formula to slow down the rate of numerical changes caused by the contraction of the slime mold, stabilizing the frequency of contraction. *Condition* simulates the process where the slime mold alters its location based on the quantity of food, with higher food concentrations leading to higher weights for slime molds in the vicinity. The sorted list of fitness values is expressed by *IndexSorted*.

During the course of looking for food, slime mold individuals separate a portion of the population to discover new territory and attempt to discover better quality solutions. This increases the possibilities of solution. The position update formula for the slime mold algorithm is expressed by:

$$X(t+1) = \begin{cases} rand \times (ub - lb) + lb, rand < z \\ X_b(t) + vb \times (W \times X_A(t) - X_B(t)), rand \geq z, r_1 < p \\ vc \times X(t), rand \geq z, r_1 \geq p \end{cases} \tag{6}$$

where *rand* represents a random number between zero and one; *ub* and *lb* represent the lower and upper boundaries of the searching area. The operation "×" represents multiplication, and *z* represents the probability of slime mold individuals separating from the population to search for alternative food sources. Typically, *z* is set to 0.03.

4. Improved Slime Mold Algorithm (IMSMA)

4.1. Population Initialization Strategy Based on Bernoulli Mapping and Reverse Learning

The effectiveness of an algorithm is greatly influenced by the population initialization. Chaotic mapping methods possess the characteristics of traversing and randomness, which are appropriate for early-stage exploration of possible regions and can increase the algorithm's variety [18]. Common chaotic mapping models include tent mapping [27] and logistics mapping [28]. Compared to them, Bernoulli mapping [29] exhibits a more uniform distribution. Therefore, this study incorporated Bernoulli chaotic mapping into the population's initialization method in of the slime mold algorithm. The equation is

$$y_{k+1} = \begin{cases} y_k/(1-\lambda), y_k \in (0, 1-\lambda] \\ (y_k - 1 + \lambda)/\lambda, y_k \in (1-\lambda, 1) \end{cases} \tag{7}$$

$$X = lb + (ub - lb) \times y. \tag{8}$$

In Equation (7), *k* stands for the times of chaotic iterations, and λ is the chaotic mapping's parameter, typically set to 0.4. The generated chaotic sequence *y* is mapped to the search space of solutions, as shown in Equation (8). Here, *X* represents the value mapped within the solution interval *lb* and *ub* are the slime mold's boundaries. The operation "×" represents multiplication.

In addition, the opposite learning approach adopts the idea of obtaining reverse solutions from the initial population. By adding reverse solutions, it is possible to further boost population variety [30], enhancing the search capability of the algorithm. Therefore, in this study, after applying the Bernoulli mapping to the population, the opposite learning approach was employed. The opposite learning approach is an improvement approach proposed by Tizhoosh in the field of swarm intelligence in 2005 [31]. Its concept is to generate a reverse solution based on the current solution in the course of the optimization procedure. In order to choose the best solution for the subsequent iteration, the objective function values of the present solution and the opposite solution are compared. The following is the formula for producing the opposite solution:

$$X^* = lb + ub - X. \tag{9}$$

In Equation (9), X^* denotes the reverse solution of the slime mold population, lb and ub are the highest and lowest boundaries of the searching space for the slime mold population, and X represents the current solution of the slime mold population. The obtained reverse solution is then merged with the original solution to form a new population $X = (X^* \cup X)$. According to their objective function values, the new population's fitness values are computed. Subsequently, the fitness values are sorted, and the first half of the population is selected as the initial population.

4.2. Cauchy Mutation Strategy for Escaping Local Optima

The Cauchy distribution is where the Cauchy mutation comes from [32]. The following describes the standard Cauchy distribution's probability density function:

$$f(x) = \frac{1}{\pi} \cdot \frac{1}{1+x^2}, x \in (-\infty, \infty). \tag{10}$$

Figure 1 illustrates the probability density function curved lines of the standard Gaussian distribution, the standard Cauchy distribution, and the standard t-distribution. Through an analysis of the curves, it can be observed that comparing the Gaussian and t-distributions to the Cauchy distribution reveals that it is broader and flatter, and it approaches zero more slowly. Additionally, in comparison to the Gaussian and t-distributions, the Cauchy distribution's origin peak is smaller. This smaller peak guides individuals to use a lesser time trying to find the optimal position [33]. Therefore, the Cauchy mutation exhibits a stronger perturbation and is more conducive to helping the slime mold population escape local optima.

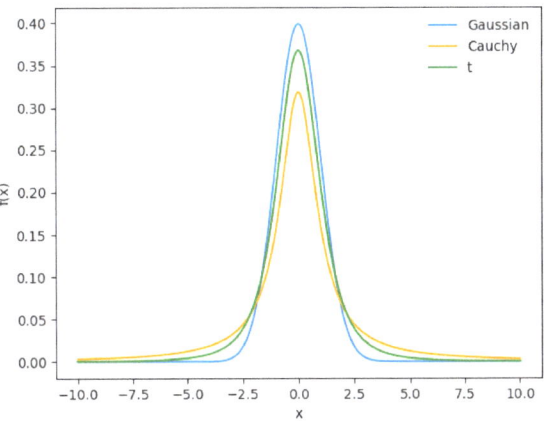

Figure 1. Probability density functions for t-distribution, Gaussian distribution, and Cauchy distribution.

The update strategy for the current best solution is as follows:

$$X_{ij}^{new} = X_{ij} + cauchy(0,1) \cdot X_{ij}. \tag{11}$$

In Equation (11), $cauchy(0,1)$ represents the common Cauchy distribution. The Cauchy distribution's randomly generating function is written as $\eta = \tan(\pi \cdot (\xi - 0.5))$, where ξ indicates a randomly vector ranging from 0 to 1. x_{ij} symbolizes the location of the ith individual at the jth dimension, and x_{ij}^{new} stands for the fresh location of the ith individual at the jth dimension after undergoing a Cauchy mutation.

If the population's global best solution has not been updated for more than 5 iterations throughout the iterative updating procedure of the slime mold algorithm, it is considered that the population may be stuck in its local optimum. In order to boost the likelihood of escape the regional optimal, a Cauchy mutation is applied. The condition for defining that the population's global best value was not updated is that the absolute difference between the fitness value f_{best}^t obtained from the current iteration's best position and the global best value f_{Gbest} is less than Δ, as shown in the following equation:

$$\Delta \geq |f_{best}^t - f_{Gbest}| \quad (12)$$

where t is the current iteration number, and by definition, when $\Delta = 0.001$, the algorithm is stuck at a local optimum. In this instance, the slime mold population utilizes the Cauchy mutation to assist it in eluding the local optimum.

4.3. Nonlinear Dynamic Boundary Conditions

The traditional SMA often experiences the issue of slime mold positions exceeding the boundaries during the early iterations. The typical approach for handling boundary conditions is to set the value of individuals exceeding the top edge to the top border value, and set the value of individuals exceeding the lower border to the lower border value. However, this boundary condition handling method is not conducive to algorithm convergence [13]. In this study, we propose a nonlinear dynamic boundary condition, as shown in the following equation:

$$X_{ij}(t) = \begin{cases} X_{ij}^{rand}(t) + c_1 \cdot k\left(ub - X_{ij}^{rand}(t)\right), & X_{ij}(t) > ub \\ X_{ij}^{rand}(t) - c_2 \cdot k\left(X_{ij}^{rand}(t) - lb\right), & X_{ij}(t) \leq lb \end{cases} \quad (13)$$

$$k = k_1 \left(\frac{T-t}{T}\right)^{k_2 \frac{t}{T}} \quad (14)$$

where $X_{ij}^{rand}(t)$ represents a random slime mold position; c_1 and c_2 are two random numbers between 0 and 1; k_1 and k_2 are amplitude adjustment coefficients that control the magnitude of parameter k, with k_1 and k_2 set to 1.5 and 5, respectively. During the early iterations when the slime mold positions are far from the global optimum, the value of k decreases slowly. Slime molds that exceed the position range are greatly influenced by the coefficient k, enhancing the slime mold algorithm's capability to search globally. During the later iterations, the slime mold positions are less affected by the value of k and more influenced by the best position, leading to a stronger local search capability and quicker algorithm convergence rate.

4.4. IMSMA Flowchart and Pseudocode

The flowchart of the improved slime mold algorithm (IMSMA) is shown in Figure 2.

First, the initialization of the slime mold population is performed using the direction learning strategy based on the Bernoulli map. Subsequently, the weights (W) of the slime molds and the value of parameter a are calculated. Random number r is compared to parameter z. If r is less than z, the slime mold positions are updated using the first equation in Equation (6). If r is greater than or equal to z, the values of parameters p, vb, and vc are updated, and then r is compared to p. If r is less than p, the slime mold positions are updated using the second equation in Equation (6). If r is greater than or equal to p, the slime mold positions are updated using the third equation in Equation (6). Next, nonlinear boundary conditions are applied to modify the positions of the slime molds. The fitness values of the slime molds are calculated, and the global optimal value is updated. It is then checked whether the global optimal value has not been updated for more than five times.

If it has, it is considered that the algorithm has converged to a global optimal value. In this case, the Cauchy mutation strategy is applied to update the positions, and the global optimal value is recalculated and updated. If the global optimal value has changed at least once within a continuous span of 5 times, it is checked whether the termination condition is met. If the condition is not met, the iteration continues. If the condition is met, the algorithm terminates, and the optimal solution and the optimal fitness value are outputted.

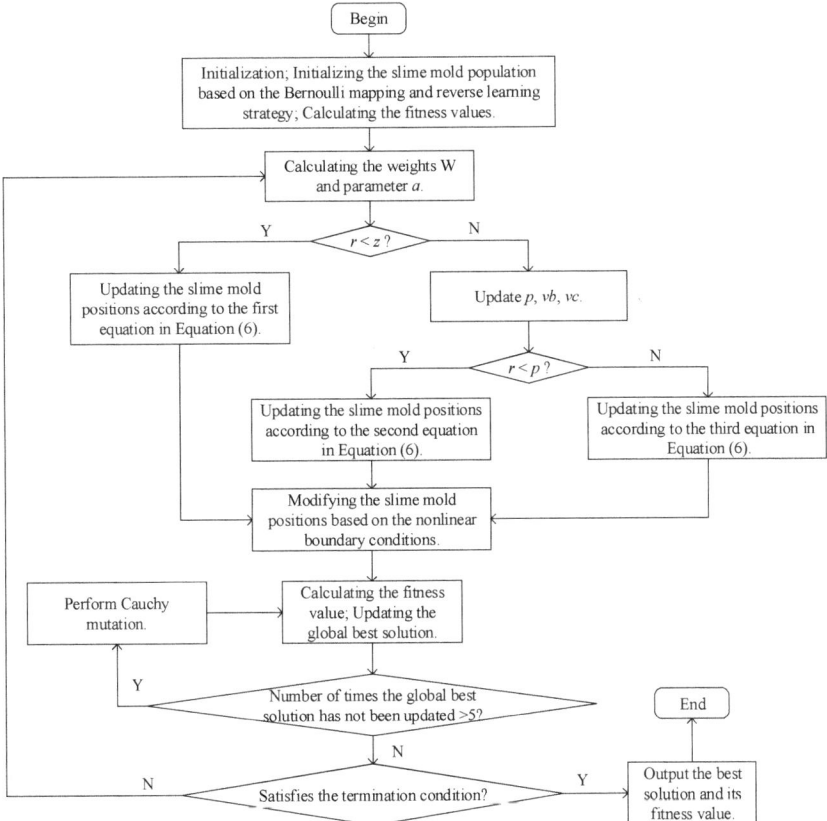

Figure 2. IMSMA Flowchart.

The pseudocode for the improved slime mold algorithm (IMSMA) is as follows:

Step 1. Initialization: T, Dim, slime mold population N, z, lb, ub.
Step 2. Based on the Bernoulli mapping reverse learning strategy, initialize the positions of the slime mold population. Do the fitness calculations and rank them in order to find the best fitness value bF and the poorest fitness value wF.
Step 3. Calculate the values of the weight W and the parameter a.
Step 4. If $rand < z$: on the basis of the first equation in Equation (6), adjust the locations of the slime molds; go to step 6.

Else: update p, vb, vc; go to step 5.

Step 5. If $r < p$: on the basis of the second equation in Equation (6), adjust the locations of the slime molds; go to step 6.

Else: on the basis of the third equation in Equation (6), adjust the locations of the slime molds; go to step 6.

Step 6. Revise the locations of the slime molds based on the nonlinear dynamic boundary conditions. Update the global optimal solution after calculating the fitness values.
Step 7. If the global best solution has not changed more than five times, perform a Cauchy mutation on the positions of the slime molds; go to step 6.
Step 8. If the termination condition is not satisfied, go to step 3.

Else: generate the best answer and its fitness value, and terminate the program.

5. Performance Testing and Analysis of the Improved Slime Mold Algorithm

To test the performance of the improved slime mold algorithm, simulation experiments were conducted. The experimental environment utilized an 11th Gen Intel® Core™ i5-11400H CPU with a clock speed of 2.70 GHz (Intel Corporation, Santa Clara, CA, USA), 16 GB of RAM, and a 64-bit Windows 11 operating system. The programming language used was Python, version 3.6. Four test functions, namely F1 to F4, were selected for the experiments. F1 and F2 are unimodal functions, while F3 and F4 are multimodal functions from the CEC2019 benchmark test functions. Detailed information about these four benchmark test functions is provided in Table 2.

Table 2. Benchmark test functions details.

Function	Function Expressions	Number of Peaks	Variable Range
F1	$f_1(x) = \sum_{i=1}^{n} |x_i| + \prod_{i=1}^{n} |x_i|$	Unimodal	$[-10, 10]$
F2	$f_2(x) = \sum_{i=1}^{n} \left(\sum_{j=1}^{i} x_j \right)^2$	Unimodal	$[-100, 100]$
F3	$f_3(x) = \frac{1}{4000} \sum_{i=1}^{n} x_i^2 - \prod_{i=1}^{n} \cos\left(\frac{x_i}{\sqrt{i}}\right) + 1$	Multimodal	$[-600, 600]$
F4	$f_4 = \sum_{i=1}^{n} \left(x_i^2 - 10\cos(2\pi x_i) + 10 \right)$	Multimodal	$[-5.12, 5.12]$

The algorithm's performance was assessed using the four chosen test functions, and a comparison was made among the WOA, BOA, SSA, SMA, and the IMSMA proposed in this paper. To ensure fairness in the experiments, the testing environment and algorithm parameters were set to the same values. The swarm size was fixed at 30 for all intelligent algorithms, with a dimension of 30 and a maximum iteration of 500. The convergence curved lines of the five algorithms are displayed in Figure 3 after each benchmark function was executed 30 times.

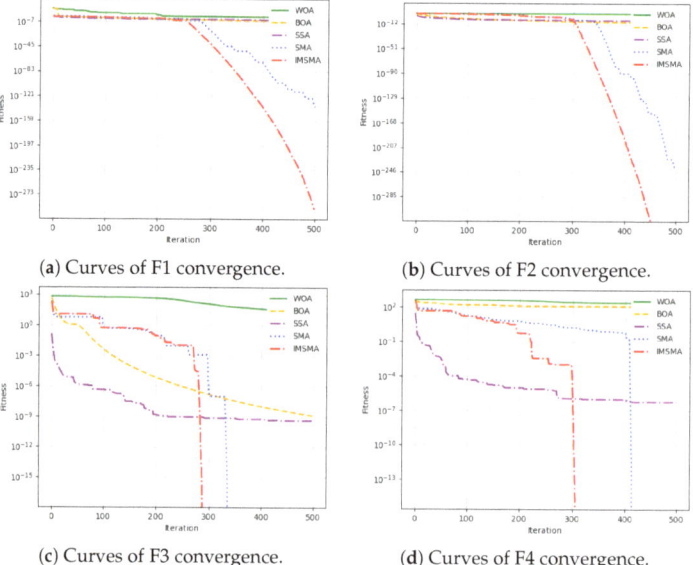

(a) Curves of F1 convergence.   (b) Curves of F2 convergence.

(c) Curves of F3 convergence.   (d) Curves of F4 convergence.

Figure 3. Curves of the test functions' convergence.

The specific test results of the five algorithms are shown in Table 3.

Table 3. Comparison table of algorithms' test results.

Function	Algorithms	Average Fitness Value	Standard Deviation	Best Value	Worst Value
F1	WOA	8.5850×10^0	5.3670×10^0	1.3076×10^0	2.2033×10^1
	BOA	1.2247×10^{-6}	4.0456×10^{-7}	3.7431×10^{-7}	2.1905×10^{-6}
	SSA	4.1472×10^{-5}	0.0002×10^0	1.5931×10^{-96}	0.0010×10^0
	SMA	3.2471×10^{-138}	1.7486×10^{-137}	2.9324×10^{-278}	9.7413×10^{-137}
	IMSMA	$\mathbf{1.1214 \times 10^{-295}}$	0.0000×10^0	0.0000×10^0	3.3642×10^{-294}
F2	WOA	9.2021×10^4	2.6686×10^4	4.9993×10^4	1.4113×10^5
	BOA	5.5098×10^{-10}	3.9426×10^{-11}	4.7340×10^{-10}	6.3100×10^{-10}
	SSA	8.0274×10^{-8}	3.2021×10^{-7}	0.0000×10^0	1.7711×10^{-6}
	SMA	5.3711×10^{-241}	0.0000×10^0	0.0000×10^0	1.6113×10^{-239}
	IMSMA	0.0000×10^0	0.0000×10^0	0.0000×10^0	0.0000×10^0
F3	WOA	2.5141×10^1	2.5713×10^1	1.5288×10^0	1.0146×10^2
	BOA	1.2962×10^{-9}	2.4117×10^{-10}	9.6035×10^{-10}	2.0675×10^{-9}
	SSA	4.2729×10^{-10}	1.5760×10^{-10}	0.0000×10^0	7.3477×10^{-9}
	SMA	0.0000×10^0	0.0000×10^0	0.0000×10^0	0.0000×10^0
	IMSMA	0.0000×10^0	0.0000×10^0	0.0000×10^0	0.0000×10^0
F4	WOA	2.4084×10^2	8.0646×10^1	6.5122×10^1	3.4340×10^2
	BOA	1.1291×10^2	8.6531×10^1	8.1465×10^{-9}	2.0361×10^2
	SSA	5.8915×10^{-7}	2.5701×10^{-6}	0.0000×10^0	1.4265×10^{-5}
	SMA	0.0000×10^0	0.0000×10^0	0.0000×10^0	0.0000×10^0
	IMSMA	0.0000×10^0	0.0000×10^0	0.0000×10^0	0.0000×10^0

Analyzing the experimental results and the convergence curves of algorithms, for function F1, from its convergence curve, it can be observed that the IMSMA starts to converge around 260 iterations, while SMA starts to converge around 280 iterations. The IMSMA exhibits a slightly faster convergence speed. From the final results of 30 experiments, the IMSMA achieves an average fitness value of 1.1214×10^{-295}, as can be observed, which is even closer to the theoretical optimum value of 0. For function F2, the IMSMA starts to converge around 300 iterations, and it exhibits the fastest convergence speed. From Table 3, it is evident that the IMSMA obtains a fitness value of zero on average, indicating that it can find the optimal result. For function F3, the convergence curve plot shows that the SSA and BOA have better convergence performance than the IMSMA in the first 300 iterations. However, after 300 iterations, the SSA gets trapped in local optima and struggles to escape, while BOA's convergence curve becomes flatter, resulting in a slower convergence speed. On the other hand, the IMSMA and SMA quickly converge and find the optimal value around 300 iterations. Comparing the IMSMA and SMA individually, it can be observed that the IMSMA rapidly converges at around 270 iterations and finds the optimal value of zero, while SMA converges faster at around 330 iterations. Table 3 also shows that the IMSMA has an average fitness value, best value, and worst value of zero, indicating that the IMSMA outperforms the SMA. For function F4, the early versions of the SSA provide the best convergence performance, as can be seen from the graphic of the convergence curves. However, in subsequent iterations, its convergence speed becomes significantly slower. On the other hand, the IMSMA shows a good ability to escape local optima between the 200th and 300th iterations, and it reaches the ideal value after only 300 iterations. The SMA converges to the optimal value at around 410 iterations. Through testing the algorithms on the four functions, it can be concluded that the WOA performs the worst and exhibits a convergence stagnation. The IMSMA achieves the best performance with the fastest convergence speed and a good ability to escape local optima.

6. Solving Multiprocessor Fair Scheduling Problem with IMSMA

6.1. Establishment of the Multiprocessor Fair Scheduling Problem Model

The task scheduling problem on multiprocessors has been proven to be an NP-hard problem. Ensuring fairness in scheduling can improve the utilization of processor resources to some extent. Depending on different application scenarios, the definition of fairness may vary. To accomplish fair scheduling, we focused on the average process time on each processor and aimed to minimize the maximum average execution time on each processor to achieve fair scheduling. We established a model for the multiprocessor fair scheduling problem based on this objective. Assuming n jobs and m processors, let P_{ij} represent the time required for job i to be executed on processor j. We introduce a binary variable x_{ij} to indicate whether job i is run on processor j or not. The formulation is as follows:

$$x_{ij} = \begin{cases} 1, condition \\ 0, other \end{cases}. \tag{15}$$

The *condition* represents the case where job i is run on processor j, and *other* represents all other cases. One processor can handle only one task at a time, so the constraint conditions are as follows:

$$\sum_{j=1}^{m} x_{ij} = 1, i = 1 \cdots n. \tag{16}$$

Assuming the total execution time on each processor is P, we have the following constraint:

$$P_j = \sum_{i=1}^{n} P_{ij} x_{ij}, j = 1 \cdots m. \tag{17}$$

The average execution time on each processor P_j^{avg} is represented as follows:

$$P_j^{avg} = \frac{P_j}{\sum_{i=1}^{n} x_{ij}}, j = 1 \cdots m. \tag{18}$$

The following is a representation of the objective function:

$$F(x) = \min\left(\max\left\{P_1^{avg}, P_2^{avg}, P_3^{avg}, \cdots, P_m^{avg}\right\}\right) \tag{19}$$

$$s.t. = \begin{cases} (15) \\ (16) \\ (17) \\ (18) \end{cases} \tag{20}$$

The objective function is constrained by Equations (15)–(18). To facilitate solving the equation, let us consider the continuous approximation of the discrete objective function:

$$F(x) = \min\left(P_1^{avg} + P_2^{avg} + \cdots + P_m^{avg}\right) + \mu_1 \sum_{i=1}^{n} (x_{i1} + x_{i2} + \cdots + x_{im} - 1) + \mu_2 \sum_{i=1}^{n} \sum_{j=1}^{m} \left(x_{ij} - x_{ij}^2\right). \tag{21}$$

In the equation, μ_1 and μ_2 are two random numbers between zero and one. The two additional terms added afterwards are introduced to represent that x_{ij} is a binary variable.

6.2. Description of Multiprocessor Fair Scheduling Algorithm Based on IMSMA

Suppose a system with n tasks and m processors. When initializing the slime mold population, it is important to set the dimension of the slime mold swarm size to $n \times m$. The description of the IMSMA for multiprocessor fair scheduling is as follows:

Step 1. Initialization: T, Dim, slime mold population N, z, lb, ub, n, m.

Step 2. Based on the Bernoulli mapping reverse learning strategy, initialize the positions of the slime mold population.
Step 3. Input the objective function for multiprocessor fair scheduling. Calculate the fitness values and sort them to obtain the greatest fitness value bF and the poorest fitness value wF.
Step 4. Calculate the values of the weight W and the parameter a.
Step 5. If $rand < z$: on the basis of the first equation in Equation (6), adjust the locations of the slime molds; go to step 7.

Else: update p, vb, vc; go to step 6.

Step 6. If $r < p$: on the basis of the second equation in Equation (6), adjust the locations of the slime molds; go to step 7.

Else: determine the location of the slime molds using the third equation in Equation (6); go to step 7.

Step 7. Revise the locations of the slime molds based on the nonlinear dynamic boundary conditions. Update the global optimal solution after calculating the fitness values.
Step 8. If the global best solution has not been changed more than five times, perform Cauchy mutation on the positions of the slime molds; go to step 7.
Step 9. If the termination condition is not satisfied, go to step 4;

Else: generate the best answer and its fitness value, and terminate the program.

7. Numerical Experiment

We performed simulation experiments on the multiprocessor fair scheduling problem, with the same experimental environment as the performance testing of the improved slime mold algorithm. Assuming there were 1000 tasks and 10 processors with varying efficiencies, we randomly initialized a matrix P_{ij} with dimensions 1000 rows by 10 columns. The elements of the matrix were set to values between 1 and 1000. The value at the ith row and jth column corresponded to the execution time of the ith task when executed on the jth processor. We used the IMSMA to solve the multiprocessor fair scheduling problem. The swarm size of the slime mold was fixed to 30, and the dimension was fixed to $n \times m$, which corresponded to the size of matrix P_{ij}.

Experiments were carried out on a range of problem sizes with a 100-iteration setting. The results for the objective values obtained by each algorithm are presented in Table 4.

Table 4. Comparison of objective values obtained by different algorithms for various problem sizes.

Number of Experiments	n	m	IMSMA	SMA	WOA	BOA	SSA
Experiment 1	500	10	**3378**	3434	3534	4639	4293
Experiment 2	500	20	**6544**	6797	6854	9352	8753
Experiment 3	500	30	**9915**	10,409	10,173	13,966	13,155
Experiment 4	1000	10	**3761**	3953	3935	4804	4679
Experiment 5	1000	20	**7593**	7932	7925	9483	9428
Experiment 6	1000	30	**11,634**	11,709	11,858	14,483	13,878
Experiment 7	1500	10	**4070**	4092	4114	4788	4746
Experiment 8	1500	20	**8092**	8145	8235	9713	9519
Experiment 9	1500	30	**12,038**	12,205	12,152	14,321	14,398

The convergence curves of various algorithms for solving problems of different scales are shown in Figure 4.

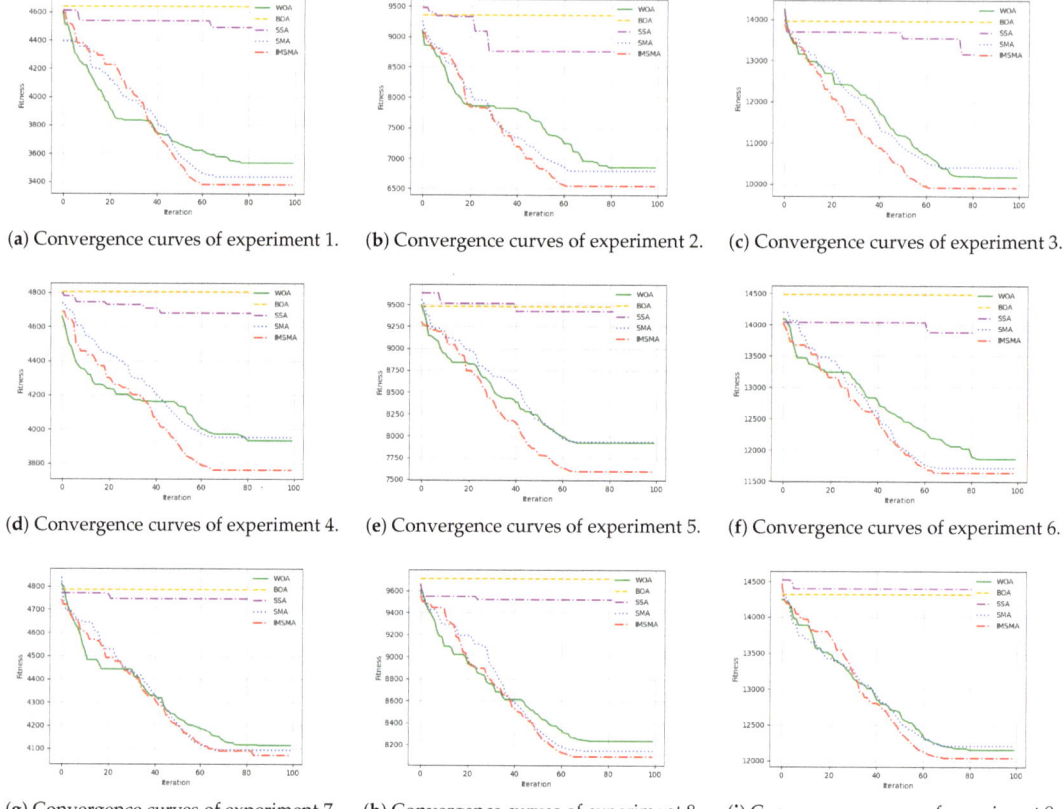

Figure 4. Curves of test functions' convergence.

Based on the data shown in Figure 4 and Table 4, it can be concluded that the IMSMA achieves the lowest objective function values and performs the best in solving the fair scheduling problem on multiple processors. The IMSMA effectively enhances the efficiency of solving the fair scheduling problem on multiple processors.

8. Conclusions

This paper investigated the fair scheduling problem on multiprocessors and proposed a new improved slime mold algorithm (IMSMA) built upon the original slime mold algorithm. The IMSMA introduces a population initialization strategy based on the Bernoulli mapping and reverse learning to enhance the population's diversity of slime mold. It employs a Cauchy mutation strategy to facilitate escaping from local optima when the algorithm gets trapped. Furthermore, the boundary conditions of the slime mold algorithm were modified to nonlinear dynamic boundary conditions to improve the convergence efficiency and accuracy. Simulation experiments were conducted using two unimodal functions and two multimodal test functions to examine the algorithm's effectiveness. The results demonstrated that the IMSMA exhibited a good convergence efficiency and the ability to escape local optima. Then, the paper modeled the fair scheduling problem on multiple processors, with the objective function set to minimize the average execution time on each processor. Finally, the IMSMA was utilized to solve the fair scheduling problem on multiple processors, and the outcomes were assessed against those of other algorithms. The comparison revealed that IMSMA achieved the best objective value and exhibited superior convergence performance compared to the other algorithms. The IMSMA can be applied not only to solve the fair scheduling problem on multiprocessors but also in various scenarios such as taxi dispatch systems and courier scheduling.

Author Contributions: Conceptualization, M.D. and Z.J.; methodology, M.D. and Z.J.; software, M.D.; validation, M.D. and Z.J.; formal analysis, Z.J.; investigation, M.D. and Z.J.; resources, Z.J.; data curation M.D.; writing—original draft preparation, M.D.; writing—review and editing, M.D. and Z.J.; visualization, M.D.; supervision, Z.J.; project administration, M.D.; funding acquisition, M.D. and Z.J. All authors have read and agreed to the published version of the manuscript.

Funding: This research was funded in part by the Jiangsu Postgraduate Research and Practice Innovation Program grant number KYCX233076, in part by the Changzhou university research project grant number KYP2202236C, KYP2202735C, in part by the Jiangsu Engineering Research Center of Digital Twinning Technology for Key Equipment in Petrochemical Process grant number DT2020720. The APC was funded by the Changzhou university research project grant number KYP2202236C.

Data Availability Statement: Not applicable.

Conflicts of Interest: The funders had no role in the design of the study; in the collection, analyses, or interpretation of data; in the writing of the manuscript, or in the decision to publish the results.

References

1. Agarwal, G.; Gupta, S.; Ahuja, R.; Rai, A.K. Multiprocessor task scheduling using multi-objective hybrid genetic Algorithm in Fog–cloud computing. *Knowl.-Based Syst.* **2023**, *272*, 110563.
2. Tang, Q.; Zhu, L.H.; Zhou, L.; Xiong, J.; Wei, J.B. Scheduling directed acyclic graphs with optimal duplication strategy on homogeneous multiprocessor systems. *J. Parallel Distrib. Comput.* **2020**, *138*, 115–127.
3. Fagin, R.; Williams, J.H. A fair carpool scheduling algorithm. *IBM J. Res. Dev.* **1983**, *27*, 133–139.
4. Alhussian, H.; Zakaria, N.; Hussin, F.A. An efficient real-time multiprocessor scheduling algorithm. *J. Converg. Inf. Technol.* **2014**, *9*, 136.
5. Li, T.; Baumberger, D.; Hahn, S. Efficient and scalable multiprocessor fair scheduling using distributed weighted round-robin. *ACM Sigplan Not.* **2009**, *44*, 65–74.
6. Nair, P.P.; Sarkar, A.; Biswas, S. Fault-tolerant real-time fair scheduling on multiprocessor systems with cold-standby. *IEEE Trans. Dependable Secur. Comput.* **2019**, *18*, 1718–1732.
7. Li, Z.; Bai, Y.; Liu, J.; Chen, J.; Chang, Z. Adaptive proportional fair scheduling with global-fairness. *Wirel. Netw.* **2019**, *25*, 5011–5025.
8. Wei, D.; Wang, Z.; Si, L.; Tan, C. Preaching-inspired swarm intelligence algorithm and its applications. *Knowl.-Based Syst.* **2021**, *211*, 106552.
9. Hou, J.; Liu, Z.; Wang, S.; Chen, Z.; Han, J.; Xie, W.; Fang, C.; Liu, J. Intelligent coordinated damping control in active distribution network based on PSO. *Energy Rep.* **2022**, *8*, 1302–1312.
10. Nasiri, J.; Khiyabani, F.M. A whale optimization algorithm (WOA) approach for clustering. *Cogent Math. Stat.* **2018**, *5*, 1483565.
11. Xue, J.; Shen, B. A novel swarm intelligence optimization approach: Sparrow search algorithm. *Syst. Sci. Control Eng.* **2020**, *8*, 22–34. [CrossRef]
12. Arora, S.; Singh, S. Butterfly optimization algorithm: A novel approach for global optimization. *Soft Comput.* **2019**, *23*, 715–734.
13. Dong, M.; Hu, J.; Yang, J.; Song, D.; Wan, J. Jiyu gaijin nianjun youhua shuanfa de guangfu duofeng MPPT kongzhi celue [Multi-peak MPPT Control Strategy for Photovoltaic Systems Based on Improved Slime Mould Optimization Algorithm]. *Control Theory Appl.* **2023**, *40*, 1440–1448. (In Chinese)
14. Premkumar, M.; Jangir, P.; Sowmya, R.; Alhelou, H.H.; Heidari, A.A.; Chen, H. MOSMA: Multi-objective slime mould algorithm based on elitist non-dominated sorting. *IEEE Access* **2020**, *9*, 3229–3248. [CrossRef]
15. Al-Qaness, M.A.; Ewees, A.A.; Fan, H.; Abualigah, L.; Abd Elaziz, M. Marine predators algorithm for forecasting confirmed cases of COVID-19 in Italy, USA, Iran and Korea. *Int. J. Environ. Res. Public Health* **2020**, *17*, 3520.
16. Li, S.; Chen, H.; Wang, M.; Heidari, A.A.; Mirjalili, S. Slime mould algorithm: A new method for stochastic optimization. *Future Gener. Comput. Syst.* **2020**, *111*, 300–323.
17. Gong, X.; Rong, Z.; Wang, J.; Zhang, K.; Yang, S. A hybrid algorithm based on state-adaptive slime mold model and fractional-order ant system for the travelling salesman problem. *Complex Intell. Syst.* **2023**, *9*, 3951–3970.
18. Chen, H.; Li, X.; Li, S.; Zhao, Y.; Dong, J. Improved slime mould algorithm hybridizing chaotic maps and differential evolution strategy for global optimization. *IEEE Access* **2022**, *10*, 66811–66830.
19. Abdel-Basset, M.; Chang, V.; Mohamed, R. HSMA_WOA: A hybrid novel Slime mould algorithm with whale optimization algorithm for tackling the image segmentation problem of chest X-ray images. *Appl. Soft Comput.* **2020**, *95*, 106642.

20. Gush, T.; Kim, C.H.; Admasie, S.; Kim, J.S.; Song, J.S. Optimal Smart Inverter Control for PV and BESS to Improve PV Hosting Capacity of Distribution Networks Using Slime Mould Algorithm. *IEEE Access* **2021**, *9*, 52164–52176. [CrossRef]
21. Vakilian, A.; Yalciner, M. Improved approximation algorithms for individually fair clustering. *Proc. Mach. Learn. Res.* **2022**, *151*, 8758–8779.
22. Zhong, J.H.; Peng, Z.P.; Li, Q.R.; He, J.G. Multi workflow fair scheduling scheme research based on reinforcement learning. *Procedia Comput. Sci.* **2019**, *154*, 117–123.
23. Xiao, Z.; Chen, L.; Wang, B.; Du, J.; Li, K. Novel fairness-aware co-scheduling for shared cache contention game on chip multiprocessors. *Inf. Sci.* **2020**, *526*, 68–85.
24. Salami, B.; Noori, H.; Naghibzadeh, M. Fairness-aware energy efficient scheduling on heterogeneous multi-core processors. *IEEE Trans. Comput.* **2020**, *70*, 72–82.
25. Mohtasham, A.; Filipe, R.; Barreto, J. FRAME: Fair resource allocation in multi-process environments. In Proceedings of the 2015 IEEE 21st International Conference on Parallel and Distributed Systems (ICPADS), Melbourne, Australia, 14–17 December 2015; pp. 601–608.
26. Jung, J.; Shin, J.; Hong, J.; Lee, J.; Kuo, T.W. A fair scheduling algorithm for multiprocessor systems using a task satisfaction index. In Proceedings of the International Conference on Research in Adaptive and Convergent Systems, Kraków, Poland, 20–23 September 2017; pp. 269–274.
27. Kanwal, S.; Inam, S.; Othman, M.T.B.; Waqar, A.; Ibrahim, M.; Nawaz, F.; Nawaz, Z.; Hamam, H. An Effective Color Image Encryption Based on Henon Map, Tent Chaotic Map, and Orthogonal Matrices. *Sensors* **2022**, *22*, 4359. [CrossRef]
28. Zhang, C.; Ding, S. A stochastic configuration network based on chaotic sparrow search algorithm. *Knowl.-Based Syst.* **2021**, *220*, 106924.
29. Yang, C.; Pan, P.; Ding, Q. Image encryption scheme based on mixed chaotic bernoulli measurement matrix block compressive sensing. *Entropy* **2022**, *24*, 273. [CrossRef]
30. He, J.; Guo, X.; Chen, H.; Chai, F.; Liu, S.; Zhang, H.; Zang, W.; Wang, S. Application of HSMAAOA Algorithm in Flood Control Optimal Operation of Reservoir Groups. *Sustainability* **2023**, *15*, 933.
31. Tizhoosh, H.R. Opposition-based learning: A new scheme for machine intelligence. In Proceedings of the International Conference on Computational Intelligence for Modelling, Control and Automation and International Conference on Intelligent Agents, Web Technologies and Internet Commerce (CIMCA-IAWTIC'06), Vienna, Austria, 28–30 November 2005; Volume 1, pp. 695–701.
32. Yu, H.; Song, J.; Chen, C.; Heidari, A.A.; Liu, J.; Chen, H.; Zaguia, A.; Mafarja, M. Image segmentation of Leaf Spot Diseases on Maize using multi-stage Cauchy-enabled grey wolf algorithm. *Eng. Appl. Artif. Intell.* **2022**, *109*, 104653.
33. Zhang, X.; Liu, Q.; Bai, X. Improved slime mould algorithm based on hybrid strategy optimization of Cauchy mutation and simulated annealing. *PLoS ONE* **2023**, *18*, e0280512.

Disclaimer/Publisher's Note: The statements, opinions and data contained in all publications are solely those of the individual author(s) and contributor(s) and not of MDPI and/or the editor(s). MDPI and/or the editor(s) disclaim responsibility for any injury to people or property resulting from any ideas, methods, instructions or products referred to in the content.

Article

Mitigating Co-Activity Conflicts and Resource Overallocation in Construction Projects: A Modular Heuristic Scheduling Approach with Primavera P6 EPPM Integration

Khwansiri Ninpan [1,*], Shuzhang Huang [1], Francesco Vitillo [2], Mohamad Ali Assaad [1], Lies Benmiloud Bechet [1] and Robert Plana [3]

[1] Digital Excellence Center, Assystem, 92400 Courbevoie, France; shuang@assystem.com (S.H.); maassaad@assystem.com (M.A.A.); lbenmiloud@assystem.com (L.B.B.)
[2] Digital Transformation Services, Assystem, 92400 Courbevoie, France; fvitillo@assystem.com
[3] Technology & Innovation, Assystem, 92400 Courbevoie, France; rplana@assystem.com
* Correspondence: kninpan@assystem.com

Abstract: This paper proposes a heuristic approach for managing complex construction projects. The tool incorporates Primavera P6 EPPM and Synchro 4D, enabling proactive clash detection and resolution of spatial conflicts during concurrent tasks. Additionally, it performs resource verification for sufficient allocation before task initiation. This integrated approach facilitates the generation of conflict-free and feasible construction schedules. By adhering to project constraints and seamlessly integrating with existing industry tools, the proposed solution offers a comprehensive and robust approach to construction project management. This constitutes, to our knowledge, the first dynamic digital twin for the delivery of a complex project.

Keywords: heuristics; scheduling algorithms; constraint satisfaction problems; resource allocation; co-activity conflict mitigation

Citation: Ninpan, K.; Huang, S.; Vitillo, F.; Assaad, M.A.; Benmiloud Bechet, L.; Plana, R. Mitigating Co-Activity Conflicts and Resource Overallocation in Construction Projects: A Modular Heuristic Scheduling Approach with Primavera P6 EPPM Integration. *Algorithms* **2024**, *17*, 230. https://doi.org/10.3390/a17060230

Academic Editors: Frank Werner, David Lemoine, María I. Restrepo and Alexandre Dolgui

Received: 30 April 2024
Revised: 17 May 2024
Accepted: 22 May 2024
Published: 24 May 2024

Copyright: © 2024 by the authors. Licensee MDPI, Basel, Switzerland. This article is an open access article distributed under the terms and conditions of the Creative Commons Attribution (CC BY) license (https://creativecommons.org/licenses/by/4.0/).

1. Introduction

The successful delivery of large-scale industrial construction projects often necessitates the development of requisite venues and infrastructural facilities. This undertaking presents a significant industrial project with complex logistical challenges. A central challenge lies in formulating a cohesive construction schedule, which can be categorized as a resource-constrained project scheduling problem (RCPSP). The RCPSP is a well-studied problem in the field of project management, where the objective is to determine the optimal sequence and timing of activities. This paradigm addresses the intricate interplay of various resources such as workspace, machinery, and manpower, all of which are subject to inherent limitations and constraints, alongside a network of tasks characterized by precedence relations and resource requisitions [1–4]. The implementation of the RCPSP in construction projects can potentially minimize project duration, ultimately translating into lower overall project costs [2,5,6]. Additionally, the RCPSP offers a multi-scenario simulation framework, providing valuable insights into the potential outcomes and trade-offs of different scheduling strategies [7–10]. This comprehensive analysis empowers project managers to make informed decisions that enhance both project efficiency and resource utilization.

However, basic RCPSP models may not capture all the complexities of construction projects. While traditional RCPSP models assume deterministic activity durations and resource availabilities, construction projects are inherently stochastic, with unforeseen delays and resource availability fluctuations [11]. In the context of complex construction projects, as exemplified in this study, the RCPSP is further complicated by the need to address spatial conflicts and ensure efficient resource utilization. Spatial conflicts arise when the physical locations of concurrent construction activities overlap, leading to potential clashes and disruptions. Efficient resource utilization is crucial to minimizing delays and optimizing project costs. Addressing these challenges is essential for the successful and timely completion of a project.

Another limitation to consider when applying the RCPSP in construction projects is the complexity involved in solving large-scale instances. Optimizing schedules for extensive construction projects with numerous activities and resource constraints often necessitates the use of specialized scheduling software, which may not be readily accessible or user-friendly for all construction professionals. Diverse solutions have been offered to mitigate the complexities inherent in project scheduling. Notably, Primavera P6 is a preeminent project management tool developed by Oracle [12]. With over three decades of development and widespread adoption across industries, Primavera P6 has established itself as a leader in project management software. It offers robust functionality for both local deployment (P6 PPM) and scalable service provision (P6 EPPM), seamlessly integrating with Oracle databases and supporting external data import. It excels at addressing scheduling constraints such as workspace clashes, enabling the formulation of optimized schedules [13]. However, its multifaceted functionalities require comprehensive training for proficiency.

While Primavera P6 provides advanced features for project scheduling, it lacks the inherent functionality to detect potential spatial conflicts that may arise during the construction-planning phase. Traditionally, this verification has been conducted as a separate and disconnected process, often requiring the use of specialized 4D simulation software, such as Synchro4D [14] (chap. 6). Through integration with project scheduling tools, such as Primavera P6, Synchro 4D can import the project plan and link it to a corresponding 3D building information model (BIM). This BIM serves as a digital representation of the construction plan, enabling Synchro 4D to simulate and visualize the construction sequence over time. This capability allows for the proactive identification of potential spatial conflicts between construction elements. Early detection of such clashes is crucial for managing complex projects where coordinating concurrent activities and resources is paramount. However, while Synchro is effective at spatial conflict detection, it has limitations in fully resolving these conflicts. The tool does not possess advanced functionalities for automatically adjusting the construction schedule or resource allocation to eliminate the identified conflicts. Consequently, project managers may need to manually manipulate the schedule or resource plans within Primavera P6 to sequence activities differently and find a feasible, conflict-free solution.

This paper presents Optimizio [8–10], a heuristic scheduling tool enhanced with functionalities that address the limitations associated with conventional resource leveling and conflict resolution processes. Optimizio automates the entire workflow, offering significant advantages for project management, including the ability to tackle complex scheduling problems, flexibility, and ease of use, which eliminates the need for additional training. The proposed approach offers seamless integration from Primavera P6's project planning data to spatial conflict reports from Synchro 4D. This facilitates the streamlined execution of resource leveling and clash resolution while adhering to all predefined project constraints. The resulting feasible schedule is generated in a format that is directly compatible with Primavera P6, enabling efficient workflows for industry professionals. Through rigorous validation by domain experts, the solution demonstrates its promise for addressing real-world challenges in industrial applications.

The proposed Optimizio approach and its implementation details are thoroughly discussed in this paper. The organization of the paper is as follows: Section 2 presents the materials and methods, providing a detailed description of the problem, a benchmark instance utilized for evaluation purposes, and the overall methodology employed by Optimizio. Section 3 showcases the results of the proposed algorithms. Finally, the major findings, implications, and future research directions are explored in Section 4.

2. Materials and Methods

2.1. Statement of the Problem

This study addresses a real-world construction scheduling challenge that extends beyond the core RCPSP formulation. While the RCPSP provides a solid foundation for scheduling activities under logical dependencies and resource constraints, the use case in this study introduces additional complexities, which are given below.

2.1.1. Data Exchange and Software Integration

One such complexity involves establishing seamless data exchange between existing project management software. Construction projects typically involve a multitude of stakeholders and software platforms, each with its own data formats and workflows. Facilitating efficient data exchange and integration among these tools is crucial for leveraging existing project data and enabling streamlined workflows.

In this study, the initial project plan was obtained from the Oracle Primavera P6 Enterprise Project Portfolio Management (EPPM) cloud solution in an extensible markup language (XML) format, which is suitable for automated data parsing. Subsequently, the analysis of spatial conflicts commenced with the generation of a 3D BIM representing the digital construction plan. The model elements were then spatially mapped to their corresponding activities within the Primavera P6 schedule. This integrated data allowed Synchro 4D to simulate and visualize the construction sequence over time, enabling a four-dimensional (4D) representation. This 4D simulation facilitated the identification of potential spatial conflicts, defined as situations where two or more BIM elements occupy the same physical space concurrently.

These spatial incompatibilities need to be resolved to generate a new, conflict-free schedule. However, merging the identified spatial conflicts with the updated Primavera schedule is not a straightforward task. The integration of the spatial conflict information with the revised scheduling approach presents a significant challenge that must be overcome to ensure the successful and efficient execution of the construction project.

2.1.2. Spatial Conflicts and Contractor Coordination

In the construction projects considered here, the work areas are managed by different contractors, necessitating coordination to mitigate spatial incompatibilities and ensure efficient execution. Inappropriately addressed conflicts can lead to suboptimal schedules, rework, and potential project delays.

Resolving spatial conflicts through conventional manual approaches is frequently a time-intensive and resource-demanding process. While techniques such as adjusting activity dates in Primavera P6 or modifying component positions within 3D models can address certain conflicts, the process is inherently iterative. Teams must repeatedly review and update the 4D simulation, which combines scheduling data with 3D models, until an acceptable solution is achieved. This iterative cycle can be time-consuming and inefficient, particularly for complex projects with intricate spatial constraints. In addition, they are prone to errors, as the manual analysis and coordination processes may overlook intricate interdependencies between activities, resource allocations, and spatial constraints. This necessitates the development of automated and optimized solutions to facilitate seamless coordination among contractors and enhance project execution efficiency.

2.1.3. Suboptimal Resource Allocation

Effective resource management is another critical aspect of successful project execution. Project managers must meticulously assess resource needs, availability, and potential limitations to create a comprehensive resource plan aligned with project goals and timelines.

In this study, instances of suboptimal resource allocation in the initial planning stages were identified. Resources were frequently requested in excess of their available units, potentially leading to a bottleneck during project execution, jeopardizing timely completion, and impacting project delivery performance.

While Primavera P6's resource leveling tool is a valuable asset for resource management, it has limitations when dealing with resource allocation within individual activities. The tool is designed to resolve resource conflicts between activities that compete for the same resources, but it cannot address situations where a single activity is overloaded with resource requirements. Additionally, the leveling tool may encounter challenges when handling activities that involve a mix of labor and non-labor resources, potentially leading to inaccurate or incomplete leveling results. Consequently, the leveled schedule may require manual adjustments to ensure it aligns with practical constraints and project execution plans. To address this challenge, a robust methodology that seamlessly integrates resource management considerations into the project planning process is crucial for overall project efficiency and optimal results.

2.2. Problem Instance

This problem instance is an original contribution of this research and has not been previously reported in the existing literature. This study evaluates the proposed solution's effectiveness in handling complex project scheduling scenarios with diverse activity types, resource constraints, and project-specific limitations.

A benchmark instance comprises 24 logically linked activities categorized into two distinct types: level of effort (LoE) and task dependent. These categories exhibit distinct characteristics regarding resource demand, calendar utilization, and workload computation based on duration. The planning process involves the management of three types of resources: Resources A, B, and C. The initial planning revealed an overallocation of Resource A, indicating that the requirement for this resource exceeded its available capacity. Additionally, Resources B and C exhibit incompatibility, precluding their simultaneous utilization.

The objective of this instance is to generate a feasible schedule that adheres to all activity precedence relationships, resource availability constraints, and project-specific limitations.

2.3. Proposed Solution

To address the complex project scheduling problem, we propose Optimizio [8–10], an approach to model and solve complex scheduling problems. Optimizio leverages a greedy heuristic algorithm that dynamically assigns scores to unscheduled tasks at each decision point. These scores are calculated using a cost function that incorporates relevant scheduling criteria [8]. Based on these calculations and the satisfaction of constraints, our tool schedules as many feasible tasks as possible at each time step, ultimately yielding a feasible and relatively optimal schedule. The efficacy of Optimizio has been validated through extensive testing on large-scale industrial scheduling problems encompassing diverse domains [9], including nuclear, defense, and construction industries.

Optimizio is built upon an object-oriented programming (OOP) solution that encapsulates key components of the RCPSP model through three fundamental classes:

- Project class: This class encapsulates the overall project information, including the decision time step for recalculating the cost function, definition of calendars used in the planning, start and end dates of the project, etc. It also serves as a container for tasks and resources and manages the interactions between them.
- Task class: Instances of this class represent individual tasks within the project. Each task object captures task-specific attributes, such as duration, precedence relationships, and resource requirements.
- Resource class: This class represents available resources within the project. These resources can include personnel, equipment, materials, or any other assets that are required to complete the project tasks.

The core Optimizio platform was extended through the integration of additional modules to address specific project scheduling challenges encountered in this use case. These extensions are given below.

2.3.1. Connector Module

This module offers user-configurable parameters for Primavera P6 data input. This functionality enables users to define the specific Primavera version used for the project schedule. Additionally, users can specify XML tags to be excluded or included during the parsing process. This granular control ensures that the extraction of relevant data points is tailored to the specific project requirements. Following the user configuration and project data upload, a dedicated data preprocessing step is initiated. This step extracts information from the uploaded project data encompassing comprehensive information about the scheduled activities, including the activity name, unique identification code, duration, start and finish dates, predecessor and successor relationships, resource assignments, and user-defined parameters specified during the configuration phase. The extracted data are then transformed into instances of the Optimizio–RCPSP classes. This transformation process essentially converts the raw project data into a structured format that is specifically designed for subsequent analysis within the Optimizio application framework.

This module extends its functionality by facilitating the import of a clash report generated by Synchro4D in an Excel format. This report contains pre-identified pairs of locations that are deemed incompatible due to potential spatial conflicts arising during the 4D simulation process. The imported clash report data undergo a transformation process to integrate them with the Optimizio model. Each resource identified in the clash report is converted into a corresponding resource class instance containing an additional attribute that stores information regarding all incompatible resources associated with that particular resource. This process creates a mapping between resources and their associated incompatibility constraints, effectively capturing the spatial conflict information within the model. By incorporating this information, the model accounts for potential spatial conflicts that may arise during the construction-planning phase. The verification of these resource incompatibilities will be addressed in the subsequent section, the resource incompatibility verification module.

In addition to facilitating the retrieval of input data, this module is responsible for exporting the output of the Optimizio solver to Primavera P6, enabling further analysis and integration with downstream processes. The module generates an XML representation of the feasible schedule produced by the Optimizio solver. This output adheres to the Primavera P6 EPPM data format, ensuring seamless interoperability and enhancing usability for project managers and their teams.

2.3.2. Resource Incompatibility Verification Module

To prevent resource conflicts during project execution, this extension verifies the compatibility of resources assigned to concurrent tasks. It checks for predefined incompatibility constraints within the resource class before task execution. These constraints act as rules specifying which resources cannot be used together on overlapping tasks. If incoming tasks require resources incompatible with those used by ongoing tasks, the incoming task is automatically delayed. They will remain in a waiting state until all incompatible resources are freed by completing ongoing tasks. This proactive approach guarantees the feasibility of the project plan by eliminating the risk of resource conflicts.

2.3.3. Resource Availability Verification Module

This module simulates resource unit availability throughout the project schedule. It tracks assigned resource units for each task, considering factors like resource quantities, work calendars, and potential constraints. This ensures resource assignments align with actual availability before tasks begin. By factoring in resource availability alongside other scheduling constraints, Optimizio could generate more realistic and achievable schedules, ultimately increasing the project's success rate.

The integration of the Optimizio algorithm with the latter two modules is shown in Algorithm 1.

Algorithm 1 Heuristic-Based Project Scheduling with Co-Activity and Resource Considerations

1: Set empty list PT for planned tasks
2: **while** $PT \neq J$ **do**
3:    **for** each time step t **do**
4:       **for** activities J_i **do**
5:          **if** predecessor relationships are respected **then**
6:             **if** required resources are available **then**
7:                **if** required resources have no conflict with resources already allocated to other concurrently scheduled activities **then**
8:                   **if** required resources possess sufficient capacity to accommodate the task launch **then**
9:                      Calculate objective score
10:                 **end if**
11:               **end if**
12:             **end if**
13:          **end if**
14:       **end for**
15:       Sort activities to be scheduled
16:       Execute activities based on sorted list
17:       Append finished activities to the list PT
18:    **end for**
19: **end while**
20: **return** PT

3. Results

The entire benchmark execution achieved a runtime of approximately 0.5 s on an eight-core CPU. This process encompassed data retrieval from Primavera P6 EPPM and Synchro 4D to obtain the initial project plan and resource conflict information. The extracted data were then preprocessed to facilitate the generation of an RCPSP model that captured project requirements and constraints. Subsequently, a heuristic-based scheduling algorithm was employed to simulate and generate feasible project schedules. The quality and feasibility of the generated schedules were then assessed using user-defined key performance indicators (KPIs). Finally, the optimized schedule was exported in an XML format compatible with Primavera P6 EPPM project management software, enabling further analysis and decision-making within the familiar project management environment.

The resource overallocation identified in the initial project plan, as shown in Figure 1a, could lead to various challenges during project execution, such as delays, conflicts, and inefficient resource utilization. By incorporating the Optimizio algorithm integrated with the resource availability verification module, the output schedule exported to Primavera P6 EPPM showed no more resource overallocation issues, demonstrating the effectiveness of the integrated scheduling optimization approach, as demonstrated in Figure 1b.

The baseline project schedule demonstrated the occurrence of spatial conflict. This conflict is visualized in Figure 2 for a comprehensive understanding, showcasing two distinct perspectives: a 3D representation (a) and a top-down view (b). To address this incompatibility, the proposed approach offered useful insights into the scheduling simulation process. The tool generated KPIs that quantified resource occupancy, illustrating the time periods when resources were utilized throughout the simulated project schedule. Figure 2c revealed the overlapping usage of incompatible resources, Resource B and Resource C, in the initial plan. In contrast, the output from Optimizio, as illustrated in Figure 2d, showcased the successful elimination of overlapping occupancy for these two resources. Furthermore, the tool possesses the capability to generate a report of identified spatial conflicts during the simulation (Figure 2e). This report details the resources involved and time frames of the clashes as well as the total duration of the conflicts. These detailed KPIs serve as a valuable tool for project managers, enabling them to anticipate and address co-activity conflicts before they disrupt the project's execution.

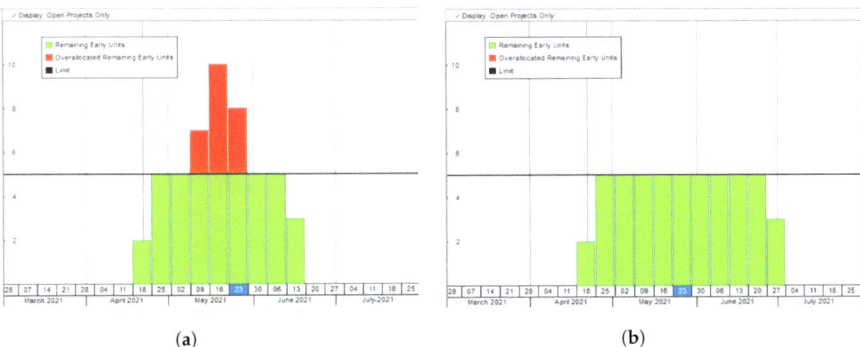

Figure 1. Resource allocation verification. Resource overallocation in the initial project plan, indicating potential issues during project execution (**a**). The schedule generated by Optimizio, demonstrating improved resource allocation for a more efficient and feasible execution plan (**b**).

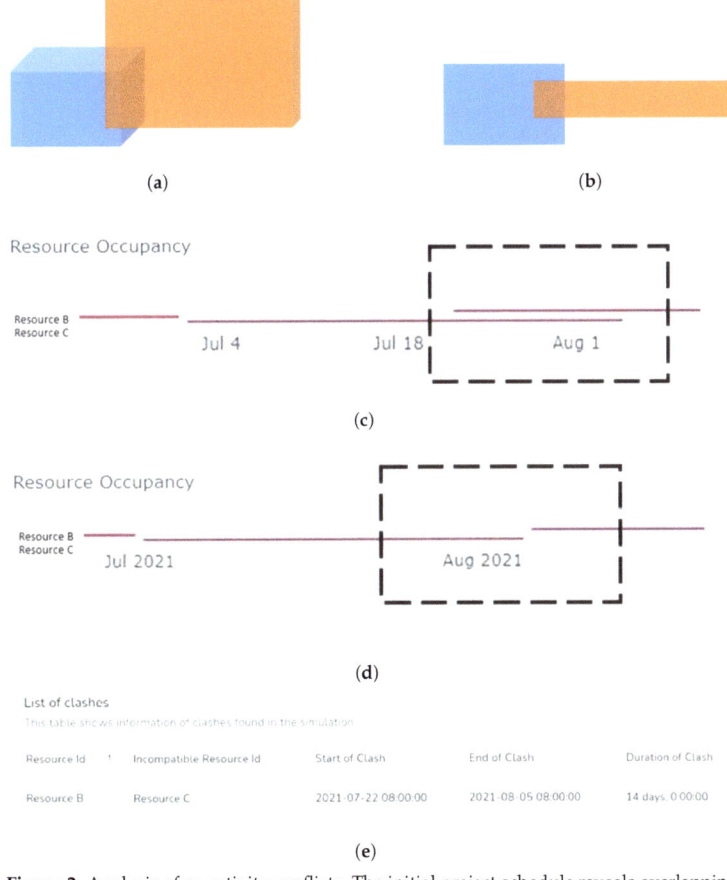

Figure 2. Analysis of co-activity conflicts. The initial project schedule reveals overlapping workspace requirements when visualized from multiple viewpoints, including a three-dimensional representation (**a**), a top-down perspective (**b**), and the aspect reflected by Optimizio's KPI (**c**). (**d**) The updated schedule generated by Optimizio, highlighting conflict resolution. (**e**) List of identified spatial conflicts, including resources involved, start/end times, and total duration of the conflict.

4. Discussion

This work proposes algorithms that bridge the information gap between industrial tools and proactively address scheduling issues caused by resource incompatibility and overallocation. The integration of these approaches into the project management workflow enhances the ability to plan, execute, and monitor projects with greater precision and confidence. Ultimately, this leads to improved project outcomes by minimizing disruptions and delays caused by unforeseen circumstances.

The use case highlights the strategic integration of three key modules. The first module facilitates seamless integration between project management softwares, resulting in the comprehensive consideration of all project perspectives. This integration enables the tool to read input directly from Primavera, along with information on spatial conflicts from Synchro4D. Limited research on Primavera–Synchro4D integration suggests our proposed solution is among the first attempts to bridge the gap between the separate functionalities of these tools. The unified data stream ensures the proposed solution leverages the most accurate project constraints and scheduling information for optimal results. Furthermore, the tool's outputs, which include feasible schedules, can be directly exported back to Primavera P6 EPPM. This bidirectional data flow allows project managers to leverage the capabilities of the proposed tool while maintaining the familiarity and functionality of the Primavera platform.

Additionally, the proposed solution expands its connector capabilities beyond those covered in this publication. Construction projects often face a data integration challenge due to the involvement of multiple stakeholders with distinct project management software preferences. To accommodate this heterogeneity, an additional module was developed to facilitate the transformation of schedules from Microsoft Project, another widely used project planning platform [15], into a format readily interpretable by Primavera. This functionality addresses potential inconsistencies that may arise when utilizing Primavera's built-in conversion features, ensuring seamless data exchange and fostering improved project collaboration.

To further maximize the connector capabilities, the tool offers an additional module that leverages Oracle Web Services to directly interact with project schedules within Primavera. This eliminates the need for manual data exchange through XML files. Users can simply provide their Primavera Oracle account credentials and identify the target project using elements like project object ID, ID, name, or other user-defined identifiers. This streamlines the connection process and facilitates real-time data access.

Acknowledging the widespread use of Primavera P6 EPPM as a leading project management software, one of Optimizio research goals is to facilitate seamless adoption for Primavera users. The ideal approach would involve integrating the proposed tool directly within the Primavera platform as a third-party add-on. This direct integration would streamline the user experience and enhance the accessibility of our constraints engine for the vast user base of Primavera P6 EPPM.

While seamless data integration streamlines processes, real-world project management remains susceptible to unforeseen circumstances. One of the major challenges lies in managing resource overallocation, which occurs when the demands placed on a resource exceed its available capacity. This situation can arise due to various factors, such as improper resource planning, inefficient coordination among stakeholders and contractors, or unexpected changes in project scope. One widely adopted approach is the resource leveling technique, which creates a balanced workload by reallocating resources [16,17]. Primavera's built-in resource leveling features provide effective workload analysis across multiple activities. These features enable project managers to identify instances where a resource is overbooked or assigned to different tasks during the same period, leading to potential overallocation [18]. However, the methods lack the capability to handle situations where a single activity is overloaded or where the requirements are of mixed heterogeneous types.

Construction sites are inherently dynamic environments where numerous activities compete for limited space. By proactively identifying, preventing, and resolving spatial conflicts in construction planning, projects can achieve improved efficiency, enhanced safety, and, ultimately, greater project success. Various optimization methods have been explored to resolve spatial conflicts in construction projects, such as genetic algorithms (GAs) [19,20], particle swarm optimization (PSO) [21], and the building displacement operation (BDGSA) [22]. Alongside optimization approaches, leveraging discrete event simulation (DES) and Unity-based path planning offers a promising automated solution for identifying and resolving potential time–space conflicts [23]. However, the necessity of integrating these algorithms with project planning processes remains a challenge that needs to be addressed.

Several studies propose integrating 4D/5D planning with advanced tools for conflict management in construction projects. One such example is the nD Planning System, which integrates workspace management with critical path method (CPM) scheduling and building information modeling (BIM) data [24]. It provides analytical capabilities for conflict resolution, including adjusting activity schedules, modifying workspace sizes and locations, and exploring alternative construction methods. Nevertheless, a potential limitation of this approach lies in its iterative conflict resolution process, where conflicts are tackled one by one, which may not be optimal for highly complex projects with intricate dependencies.

Our proposed approach addresses limitations in existing methods by incorporating two additional modules that enhance resource management in a practical and efficient way. These modules focus on proactive conflict identification and real-time resource availability verification before tasks commence. While this combined approach may extend the overall project duration, it represents a strategic trade-off. A marginally prolonged yet demonstrably more feasible and executable schedule is a prudent compromise, as it mitigates the risks associated with unforeseen delays, rework, or safety incidents that could potentially arise due to resource incompatibility or unavailability issues.

In this study, the identified spatial overlaps and resource overallocation necessitate delaying the upcoming task's initiation to adhere to stakeholder requirements. Beyond this primary function, the tool offers additional features successfully employed in other scenarios that could be adapted here. Notably, it can compare task priorities and recommend pausing the ongoing task if it has lower priority than the upcoming one. Alternatively, a user-defined rule-based algorithm could be implemented to highlight the tool's versatility.

While the proposed solution offers significant advantages, it is essential to acknowledge its current limitations and outline potential future research directions. At present, Optimizio lacks a cloud-based solution, restricting its usage to local machines. This limitation hinders the ability to directly link team member information to simulations, potentially impacting collaboration and accessibility. To address this limitation, future developments should focus on creating a cloud-based solution for Optimizio. By transitioning to a cloud-based platform, users would gain the ability to access and run Optimizio simulations from anywhere with an internet connection. This enhancement would significantly improve accessibility and facilitate seamless collaboration among geographically dispersed teams.

Despite this current limitation, the scheduling approach presented in this paper offers a comprehensive solution to the complex problem of industrial project scheduling by addressing the key challenges of compatibility with existing tools, flexibility, and domain-specific validation. The successful implementation and evaluation of this approach demonstrate its potential to improve resource utilization, reduce delays, and enhance the overall efficiency of industrial projects. By ensuring data continuity and transparency, this dynamic rule-based engine enriches the capabilities of project management and BIM 4D platforms, ultimately creating a digital twin of the project delivery process.

Author Contributions: Conceptualization, K.N., L.B.B., and R.P.; Funding acquisition, L.B.B. and R.P.; Investigation, K.N.; Methodology, K.N.; Project administration, L.B.B.; Supervision, F.V., M.A.A., L.B.B., and R.P.; Validation, L.B.B. and R.P.; Writing—original draft, K.N. and S.H.; Writing—review and editing, K.N., F.V., and R.P. All authors have read and agreed to the published version of the manuscript.

Funding: This research received no external funding.

Data Availability Statement: The raw data supporting the conclusions of this article will be made available by the authors on request.

Acknowledgments: The authors would like to express their gratitude to the following individuals for their valuable contributions to this work. We acknowledge Mohamed Ali Kabbadj's investigation of existing tools and trends within the field. His research helped shape the direction of our work. We extend our thanks to Habib Benhassine for his insightful guidance. His expertise and understanding of Primavera P6 were instrumental in shaping the conception and development of our proposed approach. Furthermore, his suggestions on presentation helped us to clearly communicate the potential benefits this work could bring to the field.

Conflicts of Interest: The authors declare no conflicts of interest.

References

1. Coelho, J.; Vanhoucke, M. Going to the core of hard resource-constrained project scheduling instances. *Comput. Oper. Res.* **2020**, *121*, 104976. [CrossRef]
2. Ding, H.; Zhuang, C.; Liu, J. Extensions of the resource-constrained project scheduling problem. *Autom. Constr.* **2023**, *153*, 104958. [CrossRef]
3. Wang, H.W.; Lin, J.R.; Zhang, J.P. Work package-based information modeling for resource-constrained scheduling of construction projects. *Autom. Constr.* **2020**, *109*, 102958. [CrossRef]
4. García-Nieves, J.D.; Ponz-Tienda, J.L.; Salcedo-Bernal, A.; Pellicer, E. The Multimode Resource-Constrained Project Scheduling Problem for Repetitive Activities in Construction Projects. *Comput. Aided Civ. Infrastruct. Eng.* **2018**, *33*, 655–671. [CrossRef]
5. Devagekar, P.; Balasubramanian, M. Investing the Application of Resource-Constrained Project Scheduling Problem in a Single-Mode Construction Project. In *Advances in Construction Management: Select Proceedings of ACMM*; Loon, L.Y., Subramaniyan, M., Gunasekaran, K., Eds.; Springer: Singapore, 2022; pp. 513–522. [CrossRef]
6. Liu, J.; Liu, Y.; Shi, Y.; Li, J. Solving Resource-Constrained Project Scheduling Problem via Genetic Algorithm. *J. Comput. Civ. Eng.* **2020**, *34*, 04019055. [CrossRef]
7. Chapman, C.; Ward, S. *Project Risk Management: Processes, Techniques and Insights*, 2nd ed.; Wiley: Hoboken, NJ, USA, 2003.
8. Rai, A.; Atamuradov, V.; Mahe, S.; Deroui, H.; Allali, A.; Aumont, A.; Wacyk, J.G.; Plana, R. A Dynamic Heuristic Optimization for Condition-based Maintenance Planning. In *EasyChair Preprint*; 2020; 2576. Available online: https://easychair.org/publications/preprint_open/SkBc (accessed on 1 May 2024).
9. Rai, A.; Deroui, H.; Vacher, B.; Ninpan, K.; Aumont, A.; Vitillo, F.; Plana, R. A Modular Solution for Large-Scale Critical Industrial Scheduling Problems with Coupling of Other Optimization Problems. *Int. J. Mech. Ind. Eng.* **2022**, *16*. Available online: https://publications.waset.org/abstracts/search?q=Khwansiri%20Ninpan (accessed on 1 May 2024)
10. Ninpan, K.; Kondratenko, K.; Huang, S.; Plancon, A.; Aumont, A.; Artaud, L.; Baker, M.; Roumili, E.; Vitillo, F.; Bechet, L.B.; et al. An Extension of a Dynamic Heuristic Solution for Solving a Multi-Objective Optimization Problem in the Defense Industry. In *Proceedings of the International Conference on Optimization, Learning Algorithms and Applications*; Pereira, A.I., Mendes, A., Fernandes, F.P., Pacheco, M.F., Coelho, J.P., Lima, J., Eds.; Springer: Cham, Switzerland, 2024; pp. 377–390.
11. Elena Bruni, M.; Beraldi, P.; Guerriero, F.; Pinto, E. A scheduling methodology for dealing with uncertainty in construction projects. *Eng. Comput.* **2011**, *28*, 1064–1078. [CrossRef]
12. Williams, D.L. *Oracle Primavera P6 Version 8: Project and Portfolio Management*; Packt Publishing Ltd.: Birmingham, UK, 2012.
13. Aravindhan, C.; Santhoshkumar, R.; Bonny, K.; Vidhya, K.; Manishankar, S.; Dhamodharam, P. Delay analysis in construction project using Primavera & SPSS. *Mater. Today Proc.* **2023**, *80*, 3171–3177. [CrossRef]
14. Sacks, R.; Eastman, C.; Lee, G.; Teicholz, P. *BIM Handbook: A Guide to Building Information Modeling for Owners, Designers, Engineers, Contractors, and Facility Managers*; John Wiley & Sons: Hoboken, NJ, USA, 2018.
15. Biafore, B. *Successful Project Management: Applying Best Practices, Proven Methods, and Real-World Techniques with Microsoft Project*; Pearson Education: London, UK, 2011.
16. Kastor, A.; Sirakoulis, K. The effectiveness of resource levelling tools for Resource Constraint Project Scheduling Problem. *Int. J. Proj. Manag.* **2009**, *27*, 493–500. [CrossRef]
17. Damci, A.; Polat, G.; Akin, F.D.; Turkoglu, H. Resource Levelling with Float Consumption Rate. In Proceedings of the Creative Construction Conference, Budapest, Hungary, 29 June–2 July 2019; Budapest University of Technology and Economics: Budapest, Hungary, 2019; pp. 597–602. [CrossRef]

18. Oracle Primavera P6 User's Guide. Available online: https://docs.oracle.com/cd/F51301_01/English/User_Guides/p6_eppm_user/p6_eppm_user.pdf (accessed on 1 May 2024).
19. Wilson, I.D.; Ware, J.M.; Ware, J.A. A Genetic Algorithm approach to cartographic map generalisation. *Comput. Ind.* **2003**, *52*, 291–304. [CrossRef]
20. Sun, Y.; Guo, Q.; Liu, Y.; Ma, X.; Weng, J. An Immune Genetic Algorithm to Buildings Displacement in Cartographic Generalization-Sun. *Trans. GIS* **2016**, *20*, 585–612. [CrossRef]
21. Huang, H.; Guo, Q.; Sun, Y.; Liu, Y. Reducing Building Conflicts in Map Generalization with an Improved PSO Algorithm. *ISPRS Int. J. Geo-Inf.* **2017**, *6*, 127. [CrossRef]
22. Li, W.; Yan, H.; Lu, X.; Shen, Y. A Heuristic Approach for Resolving Spatial Conflicts of Buildings in Urban Villages. *ISPRS Int. J. Geo-Inf.* **2023**, *12*, 392. [CrossRef]
23. Fathi, S.; Fathi, S.; Balali, V. Time–Space Conflict Management in Construction Sites Using Discrete Event Simulation (DES) and Path Planning in Unity. *Appl. Sci.* **2023**, *13*, 8128. [CrossRef]
24. Chavada, R.; Dawood, N.; Kassem, M. Construction Workspace Management: The Development and application of a Novel nD Planning Approach and Tool. *J. Inf. Technol. Constr.* **2012**, *17*, 213–236.

Disclaimer/Publisher's Note: The statements, opinions and data contained in all publications are solely those of the individual author(s) and contributor(s) and not of MDPI and/or the editor(s). MDPI and/or the editor(s) disclaim responsibility for any injury to people or property resulting from any ideas, methods, instructions or products referred to in the content.

Article

Towards Sustainable Inventory Management: A Many-Objective Approach to Stock Optimization in Multi-Storage Supply Chains

João A. M. Santos [1,2,*], Miguel S. E. Martins [1], Rui M. Pinto [2] and Susana M. Vieira [1]

[1] IDMEC, Instituto Superior Técnico, Universidade de Lisboa, 1049-001 Lisboa, Portugal; miguelsemartins@tecnico.ulisboa.pt (M.S.E.M.); susana.vieira@tecnico.ulisboa.pt (S.M.V.)
[2] Hovione Farmaciência SA, 1649-038 Lisboa, Portugal
* Correspondence: joaoasantos@tecnico.ulisboa.pt

Citation: Santos, J.A.M.; Martins, M.S.E.; Pinto, R.M.; Vieira, S.M. Towards Sustainable Inventory Management: A Many-Objective Approach to Stock Optimization in Multi-Storage Supply Chains. *Algorithms* 2024, 17, 271. https://doi.org/10.3390/a17060271

Academic Editors: Alexandre Dolgui, David Lemoine, María I. Restrepo and Frank Werner

Received: 8 May 2024
Revised: 7 June 2024
Accepted: 11 June 2024
Published: 20 June 2024

Copyright: © 2024 by the authors. Licensee MDPI, Basel, Switzerland. This article is an open access article distributed under the terms and conditions of the Creative Commons Attribution (CC BY) license (https://creativecommons.org/licenses/by/4.0/).

Abstract: Within the framework of sustainable supply chain management and logistics, this work tackles the complex challenge of optimizing inventory levels across varied storage facilities. It introduces a comprehensive many-objective optimization model designed to minimize holding costs, energy consumption, and shortage risk concurrently, thereby integrating sustainability considerations into inventory management. The model incorporates the distinct energy consumption profiles associated with various storage types and evaluates the influence of stock levels on energy usage. Through an examination of a 60-day production schedule, the dynamic relationship between inventory levels and operational objectives is investigated, revealing a well-defined set of optimal solutions that highlight the trade-off between energy savings and shortage risk. Employing a 30-day rolling forward analysis with daily optimization provides insights into the evolving nature of inventory optimization. Additionally, the model is extended to encompass a five-objective optimization by decomposing shortage risk, offering a nuanced comprehension of inventory risks. The outcomes of this research provide a range of optimal solutions, empowering supply chain managers to make informed decisions that strike a balance among cost, energy efficiency, and supply chain resilience.

Keywords: many-objective optimization; ideal stock optimization; sustainable supply chain; stock management; cost-effective logistics

1. Introduction

Supply chain management is a topic of great relevance in today's industrial environment, and a widely researched topic in academia [1]. Resilience of the supply chain (SC) to external unpredictable factors is greatly sought after by companies, and the current data-heavy industrial scene allows the leverage of computational techniques in order to minimize disruptions [2]. Resilience to these SC disruptions has become of paramount importance as industries become more globalized and disruptions more frequent, stemming from natural disasters to geo-political conflicts [3] or global pandemics, such as the COVID-19 pandemic [4]. One of the final stages of the upstream supply chain is the storage of raw materials in companies' warehouses. This is a very complex problem on its own, as keeping, e.g., large amounts of stock can help companies reduce the risk of having a shortage of materials in unpredictable supply chain events, but it comes at a hefty cost, since holding stock has inherent costs—the longer and the greater the quantities of stock being held, the larger the costs.

At the same time, environmental conscience has risen significantly in the last few years. Increasingly, more companies start to take environmental aspects into considerations in their decision-making processes, diverging from purely profit-focused approaches. Nevertheless, it is very commonplace for sustainable solutions to also reduce costs—a solution that is focused on reducing energy consumption will invariably reduce energy costs.

In the supply chain literature this sustainability trend has also been verified, with many publications on green (or sustainable) supply chains [5–10]. Indeed, according to Khan et al. [11], publications on sustainable supply chains have been steadily increasing, especially after 2013, where the yearly number of publications increased from 21 in 2013 to 66 in 2018. More recent publications on the subject show that this trend has continued, with Hmouda et al. [12] showing a continuing increase up until 2021 (note that the publication was submitted in 2022).

The concept of safety stock determination and optimization has been widely researched for decades [13], as establishing the minimum amount of stock necessary for companies to be resilient to most unpredictable phenomena is paramount. Different approaches towards the problem are found throughout the literature. Some researchers use statistical methods for the determination of the safety stock [14]; some tackle the safety stock placement of multi-stage supply chains using optimization and decomposition techniques [15], the combination of base stock and base backlog in a make-to-stock setting [16], and others deal with inventory control in conjunction with pricing and production rates [17,18].

A less researched and more complex problem is the optimization of the ideal stock levels. In contrast to determining safety stock, ideal stock optimization is not static in time and depends on many factors, some fixed, like warehouse capacity, and some highly changeable, like the production schedule and consequent stock requirements. While being a less researched topic than safety stock optimization, several publications are available on this topic. Daniel and Rajendran [19] deal with the problem of determining installation base-stock levels in a serial supply chain, using heuristics to expedite the convergence of the optimization algorithms used. The problem is formulated as a single-objective problem, focused on minimizing the total supply chain cost, comprised of the total holding cost and the total shortage cost; the problem is also solved as a bi-objective problem, considering as objectives the two costs separately. Haijema and Minner [20] analyse hybrid base-stock and constant order policies. The authors address the issue as a simulation-based optimization. Király et al. [21] use simulation to address the issue of inventory control of multi-echelon supply chains. The sustainability in supply chains is also considered as the distance travelled between nodes of the supply chains is also taken into account.

Multiobjective optimization is an optimization area focused on optimizing more than one objective. This means that when the problem has conflicting objectives, multiple non-dominated solutions can be found. This approach has been applied on a plethora of problems in industrial settings, namely, on a multi-effect desalination unit integrated with a fuel cell-based trigeneration system [22] or on data-driven soft sensors for a cleaner papermaking process [23]. Many-objective optimization is a subset of multiobjective optimization that regards optimization problems with three or more objectives. This allows more flexibility in modelling the problem but also comes at the cost—and with the opportunity—of substantially increasing the number of non-dominated solutions. This type of optimization has been applied in, e.g., semiconductor manufacturing [24] or pharmaceutical supply chains [25].

1.1. State-of-the-Art Review

Given the identified research gaps and the context of Industry 5.0, the research question for this study is the following: In a dynamic production environment with heterogeneous storage, how can data-driven inventory management strategies and decision-making frameworks be designed to simultaneously mitigate shortage risk, minimize holding costs, and promote sustainability? This research questions can be separated into three components of inventory management: sustainable inventory management; data-driven inventory management; multiobjective inventory management.

Recent advancements in inventory management have underscored the importance of incorporating components of sustainability and environment impact. Becerra et al. [26] provide a review on sustainable inventory management. The authors show that the majority of the articles analysed have their environmental focus on reducing, mostly resorting to approaches of either simulation or exact programming methods. Lv and Sun [27] propose a bi-objective robust optimization focused on carbon emissions and total system cost, by changing routing decisions. Vu and Ko [28] optimize a single-objective problem, which weighs different costs, including greenhouse gas emissions, and considers cold storage on a trans-shipment problem. Zhou et al. [29] minimize a single objective comprised of weighed factors that include CO_2 emissions and holding costs, by optimizing a set of binary routing variables and order quantities. Mishra et al. [30] present an optimal replenishment strategy, focused on a single-objective optimization with environmental emissions reduction and holding cost as components of their objective.

With the surge of big data, an increasing number of optimization strategies with a data-driven component have appeared. This trend has also been seen in inventory management. Beutel and Minner [31] focus their work on safety stock under causal demand forecast. A single objective is optimized which includes holding and shortage costs, by balancing inventory levels and satisfied demands. The aforementioned work by Lv and Sun [27] is focused on robust optimization, which captures the multi-period uncertain production demand.

Many publications on inventory management consider multiple objectives. To simplify the designation, as the definition is not consensual, in this work, an optimization with two objectives is classified as bi-objective optimization; three or more objectives are considered many-objective optimization—the main difference being that representation of the Pareto front is possible (with sufficient clarity) for only two objectives. The previously stated work by Lv and Sun [27] is an example of a bi-objective optimization approach, but there are additional instances. Sarwar et al. [32] present a bi-objective inventory control system, focused on minimizing the cost of inventory and carbon emissions. Tsai and Chen [33] present a many-objective approach to inventory optimization, considering three objectives, total inventory cost, average inventory level, frequency of inventory shortage, by changing the reorder point and order quantity.

Besides the publications described here, additional state-of-the-art research was considered. Table 1 shows the classification of all articles considered in terms of how many objectives there were, what the decision variables were, what the objectives were, what storage types were considered and whether or not the work featured any data-driven components. These publications are compared with the proposed approach in the following subsection.

1.2. Proposed Approach

This article sets out to answer the previously introduced research question through the optimization of the ideal stock at the warehouse of a company, considered a multi-layered warehouse system with regular warehousing, storage tanks, and cold storage. It brings novelty as the under-researched topic of ideal stock is addressed through a many-objective optimization problem, considering the risk of shortage, holding costs, and sustainability, through energy consumption. This combination was not found in any published research. In contrast to safety stock-based strategies, the optimization of the ideal stock offers a more resilient alternative, with the capacity of being focused on the overarching goal of optimizing output, instead of purely offering a safety level. Furthermore, different storage locations are considered for the stocks to be optimized, each with their respective energy consumption. This strategy and the energy consumption modelling is also novel. It is modelled uniquely for each type of storage location, heavily influenced by the works conducted by Sabegh and Bingham [34], Zavvar Sabegh and Bingham [35], Wolisz et al. [36], Lewczuk et al. [37]. Finally, the shortage risk is modelled through a novel, dimensionless approach, comprised of three components—a risk of immediate shortage, shortage considering one standard deviation from the suppliers' lead time, and a general measure of capacity to fulfil material requirements.

The research is focused on many-objective optimization due to its role in the industry, where decision-makers are not substituted, but rather, their work is facilitated. This comes from the fact that the optimization does not output a single solution but rather a series of optimal solutions. Sustainability can also have a bigger role, as profit does not have to be the only objective any longer—while profit tends to be the biggest focus of companies, adding a sustainability objective in a problem may skew the decision-making process, if the results show that some solutions may have considerable improvements in sustainability at a small cost in profit. Bringing forward these scenarios and effectively improving decision-makers' visibility into possible decision strategies has extensive advantages. Not only are they cost-effective analyses, as cost is always an objective, but they also contribute to smart planning, energy efficiency, and overall environmentally friendly logistics systems. Furthermore, this approach contributes to energy management in manufacturing execution systems (MES), as stock management is a central aspect of it.

Table 1. Classification of inventory management state-of-the-art research regarding the type of optimization used, the decision variables considered, whether or not holding, shortage, and sustainability are considered objectives; whether or not cold storage, general warehousing, or tanks are addressed and modelled; and whether or not the approach has any data-driven component. Publications are ordered according to publication date (older publications first). Publications classified as single-objective approaches but with multiple objectives simply mean that those objectives are considered in the objective function, e.g., by adding holding and shortage costs.

Article	Optimization Type	Decision Variables	Objective			Storage Type			Data-Driven
			Holding	Shortage	Sustainability	Cold Storage	Warehouse	Tanks	
Daniel and Rajendran [19]	Bi	Installation base-stock levels	X	X			X		
Tsou [38]	Many	Order size and safety factor	X	X			X		
Liao et al. [39]	Many	Order quantities	X				X		
Beutel and Minner [31]	Single	Inventory levels, satisfied demands	X	X			X		X
Bouchery et al. [40]	Bi	Batch quantity and binary decision	X		X		X		
Tsai and Chen [33]	Many	Reorder point and order quantity	X	X			X		
Mishra et al. [30]	Single	Cycle time, selling price, preservation and environmental emission cost, ordering cost per cycle and per order	X		X		X		
Sarwar et al. [32]	Bi	Order quantity	X	X	X		X		
Singh et al. [41]	Single	Cycle length, credit period, production rate	X		X		X		
Sepehri et al. [42]	Single	Production run time, selling price, and two investment components	X		X		X		
Lv and Sun [27]	Bi	Binary routing decisions	X		X		X		X
Vu and Ko [28]	Single	Routing decisions			X	X			
Zhou et al. [29]	Single	Routing decisions and order quantities	X		X		X		
Proposed Approach	Many	Stored quantities	X	X	X	X	X	X	X

The results from Table 1 show that the proposed approach tackles a not very explored problem. Regarding the optimization type, six works considered a single objective, four considered two objectives, and three considered more than two (specifically, they all considered three objectives). The proposed approach is initially formulated as a three-objective problem but is relaxed into a five-objective optimization problem. The advantages of many-objective optimization problems have been addressed. Regarding the objectives considered, it can be seen that only a single publication simultaneously addresses holding, shortage, and sustainability. Unsurprisingly for inventory management problems, all publications consider the holding cost, and many (8 out of 13) consider a sustainability component—interestingly, only the older publication disregards sustainability. Only five publications consider shortage costs, with most not allowing for shortage. The least explored component in inventory management regards storage type. Indeed, most publications simply disregard this component—in these cases, articles were classified as regarding general warehouses. The proposed approach gives a considerable focus on the storage type and considers three different types, as the implication in terms of energy consumptions changes drastically. Finally, not many publications have data-driven considerations—however, with the advent of big data, it becomes easier and more necessary to include data as a driving aspect of optimization problems.

This work is also within the scope of the advent Industry 5.0, as the pillars of this new evolution of industrial technology are based on sustainability, human centricity, and resilience [43]. To this end, this research is greatly centred on the pillars of Industry 5.0: human-centric, as the solution outputted by the many-objective optimization model requires a human decision-maker with field expertise; sustainable, as one of the objectives is the reduction in energy consumption; resilient, as the risk of shortage is also minimized, and the optimization is data-driven, based on the production schedule of the company.

This study was inspired by the pharmaceutical industry. However, the methodology detailed ahead is perfectly applicable to any other industries with dynamic production schedules, as the balancing act of storing raw materials is a complex process that has to take into account many considerations. In this problem, a single warehouse, a single cold storage, and multiple tanks were considered; other industries may feature a different configuration of storage locations. Some may not require, e.g., cold storage, depending on the industry. These changes should be easily implemented as there is large flexibility to adapt to different companies.

2. Mathematical Formulation

As stated in the introduction, the objectives used for the optimization problem were the energy consumption, holding cost, and risk of shortage. These objectives were selected based on previous work on the topic (namely, the components of total holding cost and total shortage cost presented in [19]), and sustainability considerations required by the pillars of Industry 5.0. The specific objectives considered are shown below.

- $E \equiv$ energy consumption : total daily consumption of energy derived from acclimatizing the raw materials.
- $C_{Hold} \equiv$ holding cost: total daily cost of holding the stocks at the different storage locations.
- $R_{Sh} \equiv$ risk of shortage: measure of risk of not having sufficient raw materials for production, given the suppliers' lead time and the near-future raw material requirements.

While the holding costs are linearly dependant on the occupation degree of each storage location, the formulation of the energy consumption and risk of shortage are more complex and requires novel implementations with the specific conditions of the problem in mind. The main rationale for these changes stems from the opportunities provided by a many-objective formulation—as the objectives are independent of each other, they do not have to be in the same units, nor be weighed to evaluate their impact on a single solution. This justifies, for instance, why the risk of shortage is directly measured in lead times of the materials and their standard deviations.

2.1. Theoretical Background

To correctly formulate the objectives of the problem, a series of theorems supported by the existing literature can be used. Out of the three objectives, modelling the energy consumption is the most complex component. Each type of storage location has a different model for the energy consumption, as it varies in magnitude and dynamics. The energy consumed in the cold storage is the more nuanced component. Theorem 1 and its corresponding proof define the energy consumption dynamics of a refrigerator unit, with changing degrees of fullness and hysteresis bands.

Theorem 1. *The energy consumption of a refrigerator varies depending on its degree of fullness and the allowed hysteresis band.*

Proof of Theorem 1. According to Sabegh and Bingham [34] and Zavvar Sabegh and Bingham [35], a refrigerator filled with products has a higher specific heat capacity than a empty one. The authors present experimental data showing that an empty refrigerator increases its energy consumption with the increase in the hysteresis band, while one at 40% useful capacity reduces its energy consumption with the increase in the hysteresis band. □

Consider Theorems 2 and 3. These theorems regard the energy consumption in the warehouse.

Theorem 2. *The total energy consumption of a warehouse is calculated as the sum of the energy consumptions for the transportation of equipment, building heating and cooling, ventilation, lighting, IT networks, and other energy consumptions.*

Proof of Theorem 2. According to the practical case study by Lewczuk et al. [37], the total energy consumption is the combination of the stated components, regardless of the warehouse technology and level of automation. □

Theorem 3. *When subjected to heating at the same power output, an empty room increases its temperature faster than a furnished one but also cools down faster.*

Proof of Theorem 3. The emptier a warehouse is, the larger the ratio of air in it; the fuller a warehouse is, the more solid materials there are, and the ratio of air to contents decreases. The mechanisms of heat transfer to the air and to solid objects are different, and their capacity to retain and emit heat also differs. The thermal conductivity of air is smaller than most solid and liquid materials, meaning that it has a lower capacity to exchange heat from and to the environment. According to the experimental work by Wolisz et al. [36], an empty room subjected to the same heating power of a furnished one increases the temperature faster than a furnished one. The authors performed a test on an empty and furnished room, where the room was heated for 4 h (starting at 21 °C), and then allowed to cool for 4 more hours. The empty room increased to 23.3 °C and then reduced to 20.4 °C; the furnished room increased to 22.7 °C and then reduced to 20.7 °C. This experiment proves Theorem 3. □

Finally, a theorem regarding how the holding costs are modelled according to the storage degree of fullness can be seen in Theorem 4.

Theorem 4. *The holding costs of a warehouse are proportional to its degree of fullness.*

Proof of Theorem 4. As stated by Harrison et al. [44], *"holding costs are continuously incurred at a rate proportional to the storage level"*. □

To mathematically formulate each of the objectives, additional notation must be introduced and defined. Table 2 presents the variables required for this problem.

Table 2. Required variables for the problem formulation. All units are presented within square brackets. Variables without unit are dimensionless.

Variable	Description
General Variables	
X_i	Total stock of product i, $[IU]$ $[n_i \times 1]$
$A_{i,k}$	Binary matrix of association of product i to storage location k $[n_i \times n_k]$
S_k	Total quantities in storage location k, $[IU]$.
Lim_k	Limits for storage location k, $[IU]$.
H_k	Holding cost at storage k, per inventory unit of product, $[CU/IU]$.
n_i	Total number of products.
n_k	Total number of storage locations.
n_{kt}	Total number of tanks.
n_t	Total number of days considered for the future material requirements.

Table 2. *Cont.*

Variable	Description
Cold Storage Variables	
ET_{cold}	Correspondence of which storage location k is a cold storage $[n_k \times 1]$
S_{cold}	Total stock at the cold storage location, $[IU]$ $[1 \times 1]$
α_1	Individual freezer unit capacity, $[IU]$
α_2	Ratio of energy consumption increase in freezer units, with degree of fullness
α_3	Nominal daily energy consumption of each freezer unit, $[EU]$
α_4	Mid-point of the sigmoid energy consumption increase
α_5	Width of the sigmoid energy consumption increase
Warehouse Variables	
$ET_{warehouse}$	Correspondence of which storage location k is a warehouse $[n_k \times 1]$
$S_{warehouse}$	Total stock in the warehouse, $[IU]$ $[1 \times 1]$
$FC_{warehouse}$	Fixed energy consumption in the warehouse, $[EU]$ $[1 \times 1]$
β_1	Energy consumption per unit of material in the warehouse, consumed by transportation of stock, $[EU/IU]$ $[1 \times 1]$
β_2	Base energy consumed by HVAC in the warehouse, considering an empty warehouse, $[EU]$ $[1 \times 1]$
β_3	Linear decay rate of HVAC energy consumption in the warehouse, per unit of material, $[EU/IU]$ $[1 \times 1]$
Tank Variables	
ET_{tank}	Correspondence of which storage location k is a tank, with multiple tanks allowed $[n_k \times n_{kt}]$
S_{tank}	Total stock in each tank, $[IU]$ $[1 \times n_{kt}]$
γ	Energy consumption per tank, considering the tank at full capacity, $[EU]$ $[n_{kt} \times 1]$
Stock Shortage Calculation Variables	
L_i	Average lead time of purchasing product i, $[day]$.
σ_i	Standard deviation of the lead time of purchasing product i, $[day]$.
$N_{i,t}$	Requirements of material i for the t-th day after the problem, $[IU]$.
$B_{i,t}$	Stock of material i on day t after consumption has been subtracted and without stock replenishment. The values only contain the sign of the quantities, i.e., whether they are negative, null, or positive quantities.
ShD_i	Day when the base stock is exhausted. Takes the value $n_k + 1$ for materials whose base stock is never exhausted.
$Sh1_i$	Shortage value of type 1 for each material.
$Sh2_i$	Shortage value of type 2 for each material.
$Sh3_i$	Shortage value of type 3 for each material.
$SW1$	Weight of shortage type 1.
$SW2$	Weight of shortage type 2.
$SW3$	Weight of shortage type 3.

The decision variables for this problem are the total stocks of each product, i.e., X_i. These establish the ideal stocks for a given day, based on the near future conditions. Index i corresponds to the material, ranging from 1 to n_i; index k corresponds to the storage location, ranging from 1 to n_k; index t corresponds to the day, ranging from 1 to n_t. $n_{i,cold}$, $n_{i,warehouse}$, and $n_{i,tanks}$ correspond to the number of products in the cold storage, warehouse, and tanks, respectively, verifying the condition $n_{i,cold} + n_{i,warehouse} + n_{i,tanks} = n_i$.

2.2. Assumptions

A number of assumptions were considered for this problem's formulation.

- Three types of storage location were considered: warehouse, cold storage, and tanks. Each type could be in different locations and had different holding costs.
- The formulation considered a single warehouse and cold storage, but multiple tanks were allowed.
- Lead time for transportation of stock between storage locations was considered to be negligible.
- Holding cost was assumed to be linear with the amount of stock.
- While there was only one cold storage location, it contained multiple freezer units.
- For the calculation of the risk of shortage, a horizon of 60 days was considered.
- Filling a storage location more than its maximum capacity was not allowed.
- The problem was considered deterministic.

- All quantities were considered to be in generic units. Materials were in inventory units, $[IU]$, costs were in cost units, $[CU]$, and energy were in energy units, $[EU]$.
- The total energy consumption of a tank was linearly proportional to the rate of fullness of the tank.

Additionally, a few assumptions related to the proposed theorems can be presented.

- The energy consumption dynamics with the degree of fullness and allowed hysteresis band were assumed to be identical for industrial freezers as the ones proposed in [34,35] and presented in Theorem 1.
- The considered industrial freezers could automatically (or manually) adapt their hysteresis band according to the usage level, with a maximum allowed hysteresis of 2 °C—this means that according to Theorem 1, by changing the hysteresis band, the energy consumption could be kept the same with increasing occupation.
- The maximum allowed hysteresis of 2 °C allowed a constant energy consumption up to a utilization of 40%—after that, the energy consumption started to increase from nominal values. This increase stagnated after a certain capacity was reached.
- The increase in energy consumption was modelled as a sigmoid function, approximately constant at lower values, then increasing when the maximum hysteresis band was reached, and returning to constant values.
- The warehouse energy consumption components of transportation of equipment, building heating and cooling, and ventilation were considered to be dependent on the degree of fullness of the warehouse. The remaining components of lighting, IT networks, and other energy consumptions were considered to be fixed values.
- The energy consumption of the warehouse from the transportation of equipment was modelled linearly with the degree of fullness of the warehouse—more occupation required more movement of stock.
- Considering that a warehouse is required to be kept at a specific temperature, and ignoring the transient period required to increase the warehouse contents' inner temperature up to the environment temperature, the greater the ratio of fullness of the warehouse, the lower its non-transient energy consumption, as proved in Theorem 3. This means that the warehouse's energy consumption elements of heating, cooling, and ventilation were modelled as inversely proportional to its degree of fullness.

2.3. Objectives Formulation

The calculation of the energy consumption was performed separately for each type of storage location, cold storage, warehouse, or tank. The general formulation is as shown in Equation (1).

$$E = E_{cold} + E_{warehouse} + E_{tank} \quad [EU] \tag{1}$$

2.3.1. Energy Consumption

The energy consumption of freezer units followed Theorem 1 and the assumptions previously identified. Figure 1 shows an example of the evolution of the energy consumption with the amount of stock. The example considered 3 individual freezer units, and the second freezer was only used after the first was completely full.

The energy consumption of the cold storage E_{cold} can then be formulated as shown in Equation (2). Note that the square brackets with no upper horizontal segments correspond to the floor operator, while the square brackets with no lower horizontal segments correspond to the ceiling operator.

$$E_{cold} = \left[\frac{\alpha_2}{1 + \exp\left(-\left(\frac{S_{cold} - 1}{\alpha_1} - \left\lfloor \frac{S_{cold} - 1}{\alpha_1} \right\rfloor\right) \cdot \frac{\alpha_5}{\alpha_4} + \alpha_5\right)} + \left\lceil \frac{S_{cold}}{\alpha_1} \right\rceil \right] \cdot \alpha_3 \quad [EU] \tag{2}$$

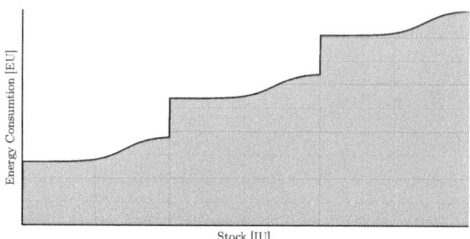

Figure 1. Example of energy consumption evolution with the stock.

Variable S_{cold}, the total stock in the cold storage, can be calculated as shown in Equation (3).

$$S_{cold} = \left(X^{[n_i \times 1]}\right)^T \cdot \left(A^{[n_i \times n_k]} \cdot ET_{cold}^{[n_k \times 1]}\right) \quad [IU] \quad (3)$$

Regarding the energy consumption of the warehouse, $E_{warehouse}$, Theorems 2 and 3 were considered, along with the assumptions provided. The formulation of the energy consumption of the warehouse is shown in expressions (4) and (5).

$$E_{warehouse} = FC_{warehouse} + E_{WH_{transport}} + E_{WH_{HVAC}} \quad [EU] \quad (4)$$

$$\begin{cases} E_{WH_{transport}} = S_{warehouse} \cdot \beta_1 \quad [EU] \\ E_{WH_{HVAC}} = \beta_2 - S_{warehouse} \cdot \beta_3 \quad [EU] \end{cases} \quad (5)$$

Variable $S_{warehouse}$, the total stock in the warehouse, can be calculated as shown in Equation (6).

$$S_{warehouse} = \left(X^{[n_i \times 1]}\right)^T \cdot \left(A^{[n_i \times n_k]} \cdot ET_{warehouse}^{[n_k \times 1]}\right) \quad [IU] \quad (6)$$

Tanks are generally simpler in terms of their energy consumption. For these reasons, the total energy consumption of the tanks is linearly proportional to the rate of fullness of the tank.

$$E_{tank} = \sum_{kt=1}^{n_{kt}} \frac{\gamma_{kt} \cdot S_{tank_{kt}}}{Lim_{kt}} \quad [EU] \quad (7)$$

The stock on each tank can be calculated as shown in expression (8). Contrarily to the stocks in the warehouse and cold storage, S_{tank} has a size of $[1 \times n_{kt}]$, that is, a stock for each tank.

$$S_{tank} = \left(X^{[n_i \times 1]}\right)^T \cdot \left(A^{[n_i \times n_k]} \cdot ET_{tank}^{[n_k \times n_{kt}]}\right) \quad [IU] \quad (8)$$

2.3.2. Holding Cost

The calculation of the holding costs required the holding costs per inventory unit for each storage location (H_k) and the conclusion from Theorem 4 showing that the holding costs are proportional to storage level. This calculation was performed as shown in expression (9). Note that the cost per unit of material in each storage location does not necessarily have to have a monetary value. If, e.g., storage location 1 has a cost per unit of 1 and storage location 2 has a cost of 0.9, this means that storage location 2 has 90% of the cost of storage location 1. Since this optimization was conducted in a many-objective way, the different objective values did not have to be comparable in absolute terms. For a correct analysis, the total stock in each storage location, S_k, was divided by the limit of each storage location, to convert the value into a percentage of fill of each storage location.

$$C_{Hold} = \sum_{k=1}^{n_k} \left(\frac{S_k \cdot H_k}{Lim_k}\right) \quad [CU] \quad (9)$$

The total stock in each storage location was calculated as shown in expression (10)

$$S_k = \sum_{i=1}^{n_i} (X_i \cdot A_{ik}) \quad [IU] \tag{10}$$

While it may seem that the holding costs and the energy consumption objectives may be similar and evolve in a similar way, it does not necessarily take place that way, e.g., a tank without substantial energy consumption per inventory unit of stock may have a very high holding cost, for business-related reasons, such as concurrency with other raw materials.

2.3.3. Risk of Shortage

One of the major advantages of many-objective optimization is that objectives do not have to match their units, as they are compared separately. This means that there is no effort to obtain a monetary cost for shortage, and the risk of shortage can be calculated directly based on the lead time from the suppliers and given the production schedule of how soon a given material is completely consumed.

The final objective evaluated the risk of the optimized stocks not satisfying the production requirements. This considered the daily material requirements for an horizon of 60 days ($N_{i,t}$), the average lead time of the suppliers of each material (L_i), and the standard deviation of the lead time of the materials (σ_i). The first step was the calculation of the evolution of the daily stocks $B_{i,t}$, based on the optimized stocks X_i and on the daily material requirements $N_{i,t}$. This is shown in expression (11).

$$B_{i,t} = \begin{cases} X_i - N_{i,t} & t = 1 \\ B_{i,t-1} - N_{i,t} & t > 1 \end{cases} \tag{11}$$

This expression simply establishes whether the stock of a material on a given day is positive or negative. The next stage was the calculation of the shortage day of each material ShD_i, as shown in expression (12). The function *sign* was used to collapse the value from $B_{i,t}$ into either 1 or -1. For consistency of the expression, if a value of $B_{i,t}$ was 0, the function *sign* returned the value 1, while the original *sign* function would return the value 0; this was to ensure that the expression below worked properly if such a case took place.

$$ShD_i = n_t - \left[\frac{n_t}{2} - \left(\sum_{t=1}^{n_t} \frac{sign(B_{i,t})}{2} \right) - 1 \right] \tag{12}$$

After obtaining on which days the stock of each material was exhausted, the calculation of the risk was performed. Three types of risk were considered:

- The first and gravest type occurred when the shortage day was closer to the day of the optimization than the materials' mean lead time. This means that in average conditions, the stock would not be able to be replenished and there would be material shortage.
- The second type of shortage took place when the shortage day was closer to the day of the optimization than the materials' average lead time with one standard deviation.
- The third type of shortage was inversely proportional to the shortage day of each material without restocking; the further away the day when a material ran out, the smaller the risk.

If a material had a shortage of the first type, the other two shortages were null; if the material had the second shortage type, the third type was null. This means that for each material, only the gravest type of shortage was considered. The calculation of the 3 types of shortage is shown in expressions (13)–(15).

$$Sh1_i = \max(L_i - ShD_i, 0) \tag{13}$$

$$Sh2_i = \begin{cases} 0, & Sh1_i > 0 \\ \max(L_i + \sigma_i - ShD_i, 0), & Sh1_i = 0 \end{cases} \quad (14)$$

$$Sh3_i = \begin{cases} 0, & Sh1_i > 0 \vee Sh2_i > 0 \vee ShD_i = n_t + 1 \\ [-\max(-(L_i + \sigma_i - ShD_i), 0) + n_t], & otherwise \end{cases} \quad (15)$$

Finally, the shortage risk was calculated. This calculation weighed the types of risk differently. Generally speaking, the first type of risk should be weighted larger than the second, and the second larger than the third, to prioritize their reduction in the optimization. The calculation of the shortage risk was performed has shown in expression (16).

$$R_{Sh} = \sum_{i=1}^{n_i} \left(Sh1_i \cdot SW1 + Sh2_i \cdot SW2 + Sh3_i \cdot SW3\right) \quad (16)$$

2.4. Constraints

The only constraint applied to this problem, besides the non-negativity constraint of the decision variables, was the total stock per storage location not exceeding its capacity. This is the formulation shown in Equation (17).

$$S_k \leq Lim_k \quad [IU], \quad \forall_{k \in \{1, \cdots, n_k\}} \quad (17)$$

The complete formulation of the problem is as shown in expression (18).

$$\begin{aligned} \min_{\mathbf{X}} \quad & F_1 = E \quad [EU] \\ & F_2 = C_{Hold} \quad [CU] \\ & F_3 = R_{Sh} \\ s.t. \quad & \mathbf{X} \geq 0 \\ & S_k \leq Lim_k \quad [IU], \quad \forall_{k \in \{1, \cdots, n_k\}} \end{aligned} \quad (18)$$

3. Optimization Approach

The formulated problem is a nonlinear, convex, constrained, many-objective problem. This is a very complex problem that requires the usage of metaheuristic optimization algorithms. Considering this, the algorithm used for the optimization was the non-dominated sorting genetic algorithm NSGA-III [45]. This algorithm is an evolutionary algorithm suited to many-objective problems. While the NSGA-II algorithm could also be applied to many-objective problems, some researchers have shown the advantages of using NSGA-III. Ishibuchi et al. [46] presented a plethora of benchmarks tested on both algorithms; NSGA-III outperformed NSGA-II on all problems except knapsack ones. Ciro et al. [47] showed that NSGA-III obtained better results on an open shop-scheduling problem with resource constraints. While there are many ways of dealing with constraints, the implementation used for this approach was a simple feasibility-first approach that did not compute the objective values for unfeasible solutions but rather assigned them the value of the worst objective value out of the entire population plus the constraint violation [48]. Furthermore, all variables and solutions were encoded as real numbers, and box constraints were in place on all variables to disable negative quantities and exploding quantities. To this end, the box constraints required decision variables to be greater or equal to 0 and smaller than the capacity of their storage location (e.g., a product in cold storage was allowed to have values as high as the capacity of the entire cold storage). The formulation described was implemented in Python, specifically using the Pymoo library [49].

Table 3 shows the values selected for each parameter used for the results' analysis. Refer back to Table 2 for a further description of the parameters.

Table 3. Values used for the aforementioned formulation. Check the parameters' descriptions in Table 2. The column value shows either the value of the parameter or a range of values. Parameters Lim_1 and H_1 regard cold storage; Lim_2 and H_2 regard the warehouse; $Lim_{3:n_k}$ and $H_{3:n_k}$ regard the tanks.

Parameter	Value
$n_{i,cold}$	50
$n_{i,warehouse}$	250
$n_{i,tanks}$	24
n_t	60
α_1	50,000 [IU]
α_2	40%
α_3	135 [EU]
α_4	0.7
α_5	8
$FC_{warehouse}$	100 [EU]
β_1	0.0004 [EU/IU]
β_2	250 [EU]
β_3	0.00003 [EU/IU]
γ	[30, 90] [EU]
SW_1	100
SW_2	10
SW_3	0.1
Lim_1	2.5×10^6 [IU]
Lim_2	1.25×10^7 [IU]
$Lim_{3:n_k}$	[50, 150] [IU]
H_1	1 [CU/IU]
H_2	0.5 [CU/IU]
$H_{3:n_k}$	[0.3, 0.7] [CU/IU]
L_i	[5, 20] [day]
σ_i	[1, 20] [day]

Table 4 shows the parameters used for the three components that control the optimization algorithm: the determination of the reference directions; the NSGA-III algorithm's parameters themselves, and the parameters of the termination criterion.

Table 4. Parameters used for the determination of the reference directions, NSGA-III algorithm, and termination criterion. Duplicate individuals are eliminated.

Parameter	Value
Reference direction method	Das–Dennis
Reference direction dimensions	3
Reference direction number of partitions	12
Population size	200
Initial sampling	Random
Selection method	Tournament selection
Selection pressure	2
Crossover method	Simulated binary crossover
Crossover Eta	30
Number of offspring	2
Mutation method	Polynomial mutation
Mutation Eta	20
Termination tolerance	0.1
Generation window	30
Termination criterion calculation generation period	10
Maximum number of generations	2000

After obtaining the results from the optimization, if the number of solutions was sufficiently large that the advantages and trade-offs of each solution were not easily analysed, a filter was applied for each objective. The algorithm design is shown in Algorithm 1, which details in pseudocode the proposed optimization process, considering the NSGA-III optimization algorithm and the parameters found in Table 4.

Algorithm 1 Ideal stock many-objective optimization

1: **procedure** IDEAL STOCK PROBLEM(X, $Pars$)
2:     Calculate $S_{cold}(X)$ ▷ Equation (3)
3:     Calculate $S_{warehouse}(X)$ ▷ Equation (6)
4:     Calculate $S_{tank}(X)$ ▷ Equation (8)
5:     Calculate E_{cold}, $E_{warehouse}$, and E_{tank} ▷ Equations (2), (4) and (7)
6:     Calculate E ▷ Equation (1)
7:     Calculate $S(X)$ ▷ Equation (10)
8:     Calculate C_{hold} ▷ Equation (9)
9:     Calculate $B(X)$ ▷ Equation (11)
10:    Calculate ShD ▷ Equation (12)
11:    Calculate $Sh1$, $Sh2$, and $Sh3$ ▷ Equations (13)–(15)
12:    Calculate R_{Sh} ▷ Equation (16)
13:    Calculate constraint violation $S_k - Lim_k$ ▷ Equation (17)
14:    Introduce the parameters of the formulation problem into the ideal stock problem function (Table 3)
15:    Obtain the reference direction using the Das–Dennis method. Consider the number of dimensions of the problem and an adequate number of partitions
16:    Define the optimization's termination criteria
17:    **while** Termination criteria not met **do**
18:        Run the optimization
19:    **while** Number of solutions is large **do**
20:        Apply a filter to objective i
21:        Store the non-dominant solutions that adhere to the filter

4. Results' Analysis

The optimization was run for the specified conditions. For consistency, this optimization was repeated 10 times. Regarding the algorithm analysis, the 10 optimizations took an average of 114.2 s, varying from 78.7 s to 128.9 s. As previously mentioned, duplicate individuals were eliminated, meaning that each of the 10 optimizations achieved a different final population; this varied from 19 to 30 members, with an average size of 26.7. While the optimization was run for a maximum of 2000 iterations, the implemented termination criterion caused the optimization to end beforehand. The optimization took between 1370 and 2000 iterations, with an average of 1874 iterations.

Figure 2 shows a parallel plot of the optimization solutions for the first test run. Additionally, Figure 3 shows the Pareto fronts between the three objectives. To reduce the clutter, only 3 out of the 10 optimization results are shown, randomly selected.

The first conclusion that can be drawn from the plots is the nicely shaped Pareto front between the energy consumption and the risk, which can also be seen by the inverse behaviour of the results seen in the parallel plot. This simply means that generally, a reduction in energy consumption (caused by a reduction in the stock kept) leads to a higher shortage risk. The slope of the Pareto front between these two objectives also indicates that a small relative increase in energy consumption leads to a substantial reduction in shortage risk.

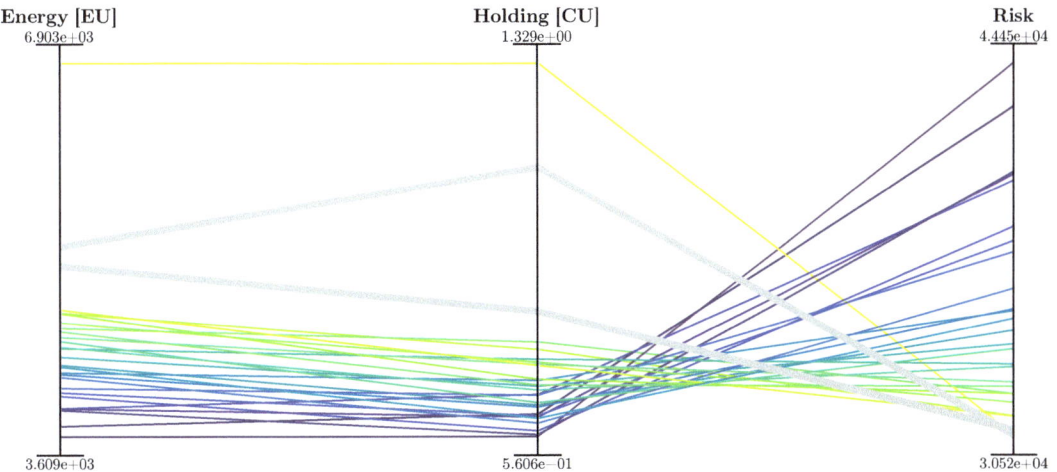

Figure 2. Parallel plot of the many-objective optimization solutions. Each line corresponds to an optimal solution. The colour scale supplied regards the first objective, the energy consumption, simply to aid in identifying the solutions across the remaining objectives.

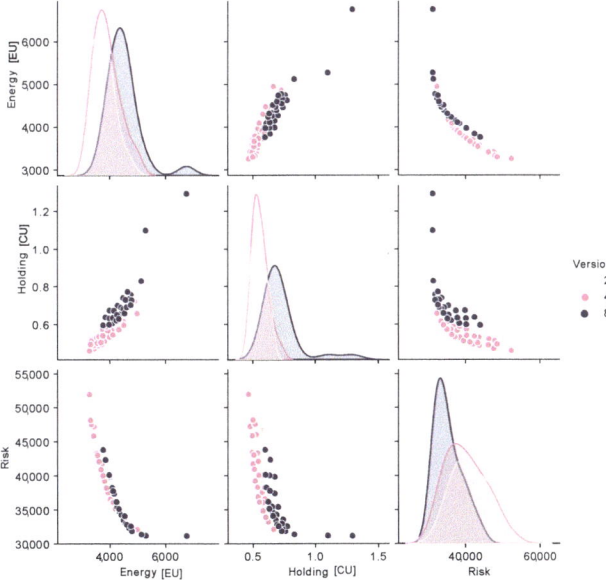

Figure 3. Pareto fronts between each objective for 3 distinct optimization results, out of the 10 repetitions.

The holding costs had a slightly different relation to the two other objectives. They had an approximate proportionality with the energy consumption. This is an expected behaviour, as both objectives were directly proportional to the amount of stock in the storage locations. However, the relation between the two was not always direct, since the holding costs per storage location were not necessarily proportional to the energy costs per storage location. This simply means that a storage location may have a large energy consumption but a small holding cost, as is the case with the cold storage in this setting. From Figure 2, the general rule is that the more similar the slope between the energy consumption and holding costs between two optimization solutions, the more proportional the stocks considered. Solutions with contrasting slopes tended to have non-proportional stocks of each type of storage location. An example of this can be seen in the two solutions shown in Figure 2 as the grey lines. For clarity, these solutions were indexed as solution 4 (the one with the largest holding cost) and solution 14.

Table 5 shows that the stock mix was indeed very different between the two solutions, even though these shared similar energy consumption and shortage risk values. The overarching conclusion that can be drawn from this comparison is that for a small reduction in the shortage risk, without substantially changing the level of energy consumption, the stocks would have to be increased, especially in the tanks, which tripled from scenario 14 to 4.

Table 5. Total inventory units at each storage location (tanks' inventory levels are aggregated) for each of the optimal solutions tested.

Storage	Solution Index	
Location	4	14
Cold	7.67×10^5	7.55×10^5
Tanks	6.93×10^1	2.19×10^1
Warehouse	7.37×10^6	7.03×10^6

4.1. Results' Evolution

As previously stated, the daily product requirements were collected for 90 days, while the optimization only considered 60. This means that the ideal stocks could be calculated for 30 days to observe the temporal evolution of the ideal stocks. The optimizations ran for each of the rolling forward periods and were run 10 times each. Figure 4 shows the 30 Pareto fronts of risk against energy. It is important to mention that for each day, only one version is shown: the one whose median values of the three objectives had the smallest Euclidean distance to the origin. Note that the Pareto curves shown are smoothed approximations to reduce the visual clutter and allow an easier analysis.

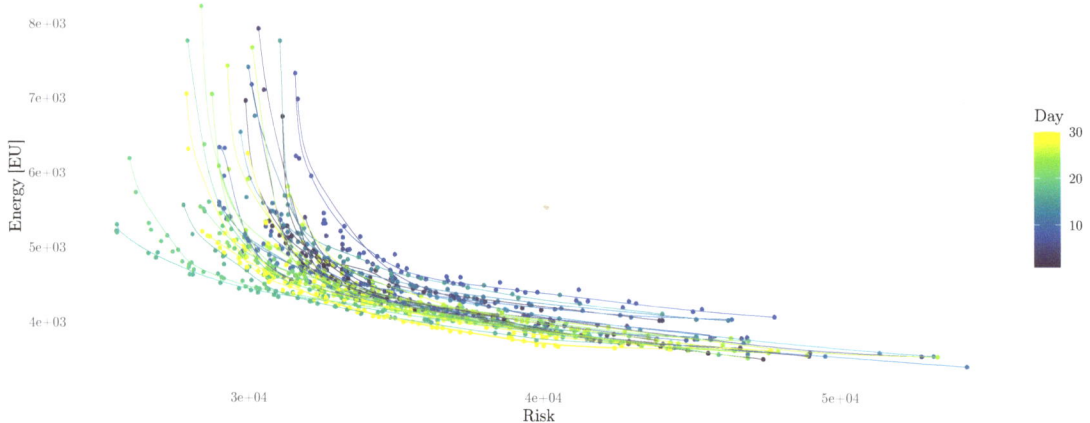

Figure 4. Approximated Pareto fronts for the optimizations with the lowest median objectives of each day of the rolling-forward schedule. The Pareto front's lines are smoothed for easier comprehension.

The figure shows that the Pareto fronts at the initial days tended to be slightly worst than the average (in regards to their distance to the origin), worsening their values until the 10th day. The Pareto fronts then moved closer to the origin, with the closest results around the 20th day. Finally, the fronts degraded slightly, ending on the 30th day slightly closer to the origin than on the first day. The distance to the origin broadly indicated the material requirements—Pareto fronts closer to the origin tended to regard production schedules with larger material requirements.

While there were some variations along the month, the stocks did not change extensively. This was a desirable behaviour, as the changes in the stock requirements from one day to the next were not very substantial—there were only changes in one day out of the 60 days considered, since when t changed to $t+1$, the material requirements changed from $N_{i,t:t+60}$ to $N_{i,t+1:t+61}$. Nevertheless, the figure shows that the Pareto fronts were further from the origin in the initial days, then improved until around $t = 20$ and ended at a reasonable distance. A smaller distance of one front to the origin meant that both objectives had better values than the one farther from the origin—this means that the problem's conditions changed sufficiently between those two scenarios, and the stock requirements in the front farther from the original were larger than the ones from the closer front.

4.2. Shortage Risk Segregation

The final analysis focused on separating the shortage risk formulation into its three components and using them independently when running the optimization. The formulation of this problem became as shown in expression (19). In terms of algorithm, the only change required in Algorithm 1 was to disregard row 12.

$$\begin{aligned}
\min_{\mathbf{X}} \quad & F_1 = E\ [EU] \\
& F_2 = C_{Hold}\ [CU] \\
& F_3 = \sum Sh1_i \\
& F_4 = \sum Sh2_i \\
& F_5 = \sum Sh3_i \\
\text{s.t.} \quad & \mathbf{X} \geq 0 \\
& S_k \leq Lim_k\ [IU],\quad \forall_{k \in \{1,\cdots,n_k\}}
\end{aligned} \quad (19)$$

The only alterations to the parameters presented in Table 4 were an increase in the number of reference direction dimensions from three to five and an increase in the population size from 200 to 2000. The optimization was then run 10 times to allow for a better representation of the solution space. As for the algorithm analysis, the average execution time was 453.4 s (358.5 s–524.4 s), the average final population size was 453.5 (410–514), and the average total number of iterations was 329 (270–390). The parallel plot of the complete solution space (including the unique solutions from the 10 optimization runs) is shown in Figure 5.

The parallel plot is a very complex display of information, showing an aggregation of many varied optimal solutions, each prioritizing a different set of objectives. Since the colour coding simply scales the energy consumption of the solution it regards, so as to allow for better tracking of solution along the other objectives, it can be seen that the first component of the risk is the one which is most closely related to the energy consumption, in an inverse proportion. This means that the higher the energy consumption, the lower the risk of type 1—since the larger the total stock the higher the energy consumption.

A many-objective optimization such as the one presented can be extremely useful for decision-makers to make their decision in a more informed way. A decision could determine that only solutions with a type 1 risk smaller than 400 would be acceptable. The result to this requirement would be the solutions shown in Figure 6.

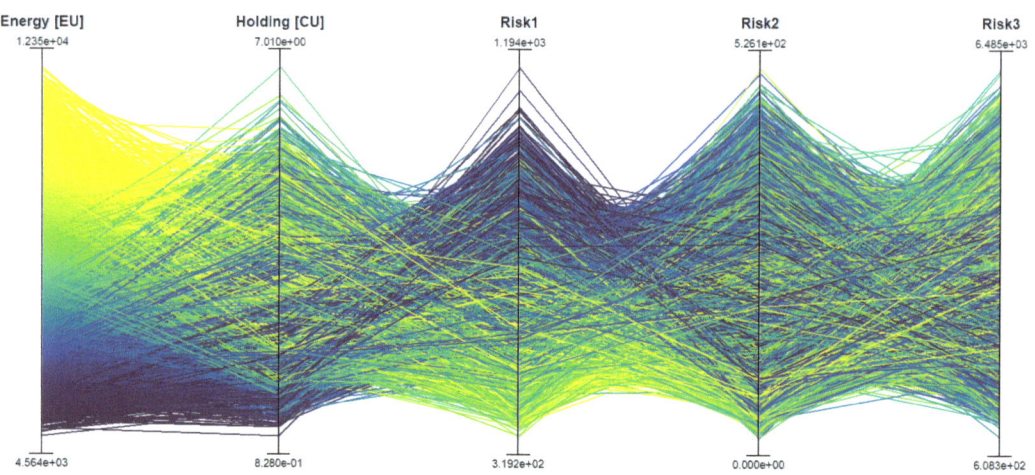

Figure 5. Parallel plot of the separated risk optimization for the complete solution space.

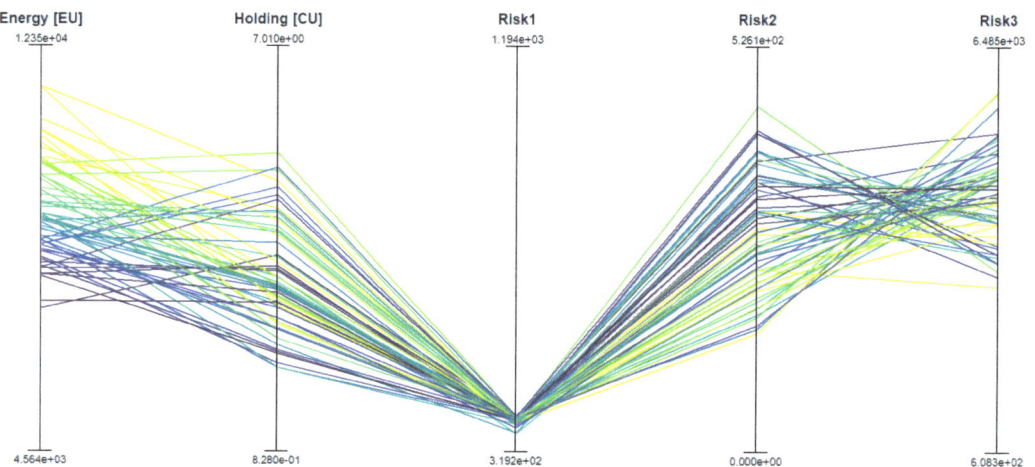

Figure 6. Parallel plot of the separated risk optimization for the complete solution space, only considering solutions with a risk of type 1 smaller than 400.

After obtaining this subset of parallel plots, the decision-maker could specify that only solutions with a holding cost higher than 4.8 are acceptable. The results would be as shown in Figure 7.

As can be seen, sequentially combining different requirements for the objectives allows the decision-makers to arrive at a restricted set of solutions that best fit the company's requirements.

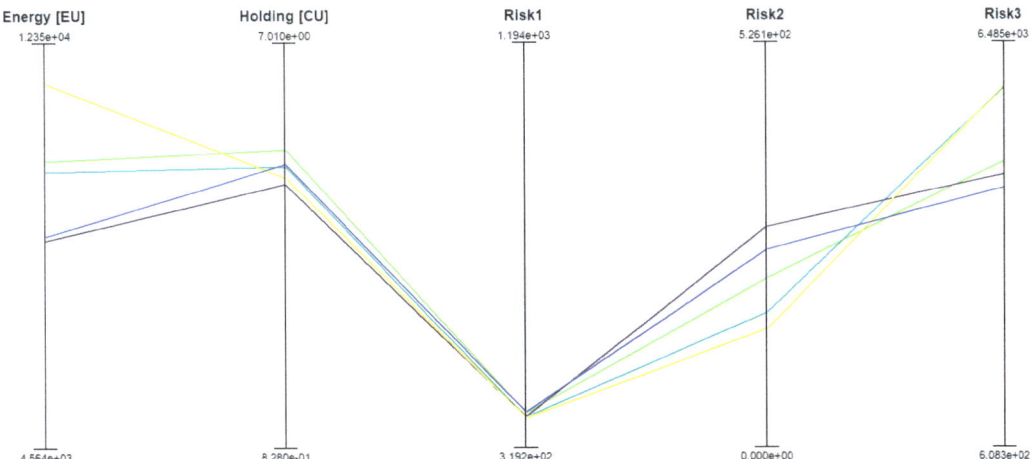

Figure 7. Parallel plot of the separated risk optimization for the complete solution space, only considering solutions with a risk of type 1 smaller than 400 and a holding cost larger than 4.8.

5. Conclusions

This research tackled a very important issue—stock management—using a methodology that complemented the decision-making process of stakeholders, rather than substituting it, with greater focus on the energy consumption of the solutions, in line with current environmental awareness.

The study revealed a diverse array of promising solutions, effectively balancing energy consumption, holding costs, and shortage risk. This many-objective optimization approach highlighted an inherent trade-off: minimizing one objective inevitably led to increases in others. This places the decision-maker in a pivotal role, tasked with selecting the solution that best aligns with the company's broader strategic goals. These findings also echo the concept of Pareto optimality, a state where it is impossible to improve one objective without compromising another. In a business context, this often translates into making strategic choices regarding resource allocation—for instance, optimizing energy consumption might necessitate higher holding costs. While this study's unique modelling and objectives preclude a direct comparison with the existing literature, it underscores the importance of Pareto efficient solutions in navigating complex, multi-faceted challenges like energy management and inventory control. The absence of a one-size-fits-all answer reinforces the need for bespoke strategies that reflect individual company priorities and risk tolerance.

The inclusion of energy consumption in the decision-making process can at first glance worsen the results—more energy efficient solutions tend to have a larger risk of shortage. However, brining awareness into this dimension can be useful in several ways. First of all, in scenarios were an improvement in energy consumption is achieved at a small cost to the other objectives, it provides a justification for decision-makers to select the said solution. Secondly, while choosing low-energy-consumption strategies may lead to larger risk of shortage, and consequently larger costs to the company, a focus on sustainability can provide marketing opportunities, as some industries benefit greatly from a stronger adherence to sustainability principles. According to Unal and Tascioglu [50], sustainability initiatives *"help companies establish a strong relationship with consumers, [...] which in turn creates a higher level of purchase intent and reduced sensitivity to price premiums"*.

Logistics systems are pivotal components in companies and are often overlooked when it comes to the application of optimization and artificial intelligence algorithms, often applied solely to the shop-floor operations. However, the application of energy-efficient and environmentally friendly planning strategies in logistics systems, such as the present optimization of the ideal stock at storage locations, can improve visibility into the objectives considered and provide better results than fixed stock strategies, while being cost-effective analyses. Additionally, manufacturing execution systems (MES) often overlook the dimension of energy management; the proposed approach tackles both issues: a central issue of MES—stock optimization—with energy consumption considerations.

While this study demonstrates the effectiveness of many-objective optimization in balancing competing objectives in warehouse stock management, the model's focus on a single warehouse with specific storage types limits its generalizability to more complex supply chain configurations. Furthermore, the abundance of Pareto optimal solutions generated by the many-objective optimization model poses a challenge for decision-makers in selecting the most suitable option, as evidenced in Figure 5. Future research should prioritize extending the model to encompass multiple warehouses and diverse storage configurations, while also developing decision support tools or frameworks to facilitate the interpretation and selection of optimal solutions within a vast solution space. Additionally, strategies to reduce the number of quasi-redundant solutions and to prioritize those aligned with specific company strategies could significantly enhance the practicality and decision-making efficiency of the proposed approach. Finally, additional objectives may be added to the problem, taking into consideration, e.g., the actual costs of delivering products after their due date, or buying raw materials from low-lead-time suppliers at a premium.

Author Contributions: J.A.M.S.: conceptualization, methodology, software, validation, investigation, data curation, writing—original draft, visualization; M.S.E.M.: methodology, validation, investigation, resources, writing—review and editing, supervision; R.M.P.: resources, data curation, writing—review and editing, supervision; S.M.V.: methodology, validation, formal analysis, investigation, resources, writing—review and editing, supervision, project administration, funding acquisition. All authors have read and agreed to the published version of the manuscript.

Funding: This work was supported by FCT, Fundação para a Ciência e a Tecnologia, I.P., under the PhD scholarships 2020.06065.BD (João A.M. Santos) and 2020.08776.BD (Miguel S.E. Martins), and Hovione Farmaciência S.A. (João A.M. Santos). Additionally, the authors acknowledge Fundação para a Ciência e a Tecnologia (FCT) for its financial support via the projects LAETA Base Funding (DOI: 10.54499/UIDB/50022/2020) and LAETA Programatic Funding (DOI: 10.54499/UIDP/50022/2020). The authors express their gratitude to the financing institutions.

Data Availability Statement: The software and datasets used for this research can be consulted in [51].

Conflicts of Interest: Author João A. M. Santos was pursuing a PhD hosted by the company Hovione Farmaciência S.A. Author Rui M. Pinto was his co-supervisor and was employed by the company Hovione Farmaciência S.A. The remaining authors declare that the research was conducted in the absence of any commercial or financial relationships that could be construed as a potential conflict of interest.

References

1. Habib, M.M.; Hasan, I. Supply Chain Management (SCM)—Is it Value Addition towards Academia? *IOP Conf. Ser. Mater. Sci. Eng.* **2019**, *528*, 012090. [CrossRef]
2. Gani, M.O.; Yoshi, T.; Rahman, M.S. Optimizing firm's supply chain resilience in data-driven business environment. *J. Glob. Oper. Strateg. Sourc.* **2023**, *16*, 258–281. [CrossRef]
3. Katsaliaki, K.; Galetsi, P.; Kumar, S. Supply chain disruptions and resilience: A major review and future research agenda. *Ann. Oper. Res.* **2022**, *319*, 965–1002. [CrossRef]
4. Veselovská, L. Supply chain disruptions in the context of early stages of the global COVID-19 outbreak. *Probl. Perspect. Manag.* **2020**, *18*, 490–500. [CrossRef]
5. Seuring, S.; Müller, M. From a literature review to a conceptual framework for sustainable supply chain management. *J. Clean. Prod.* **2008**, *16*, 1699–1710. [CrossRef]

6. Seuring, S. A review of modeling approaches for sustainable supply chain management. *Decis. Support Syst.* **2013**, *54*, 1513–1520. [CrossRef]
7. Srivastava, S.K. Green supply-chain management: A state-of-the-art literature review. *Int. J. Manag. Rev.* **2007**, *9*, 53–80. [CrossRef]
8. Min, H.; Kim, I. Green supply chain research: Past, present, and future. *Logist. Res.* **2012**, *4*, 39–47. [CrossRef]
9. Benjaafar, S.; Li, Y.; Daskin, M. Carbon footprint and the management of supply chains: Insights from simple models. *IEEE Trans. Autom. Sci. Eng.* **2012**, *10*, 99–116. [CrossRef]
10. Ahi, P.; Searcy, C. A comparative literature analysis of definitions for green and sustainable supply chain management. *J. Clean. Prod.* **2013**, *52*, 329–341. [CrossRef]
11. Khan, S.A.R.; Yu, Z.; Golpira, H.; Sharif, A.; Mardani, A. A state-of-the-art review and meta-analysis on sustainable supply chain management: Future research directions. *J. Clean. Prod.* **2021**, *278*, 123357. [CrossRef]
12. Hmouda, A.M.; Orzes, G.; Sauer, P.C. Sustainable supply chain management in energy production: A literature review. *Renew. Sustain. Energy Rev.* **2024**, *191*, 114085. [CrossRef]
13. Gonçalves, J.N.; Carvalho, M.S.; Cortez, P. Operations research models and methods for safety stock determination: A review. *Oper. Res. Perspect.* **2020**, *7*, 100164. [CrossRef]
14. Radasanu, A.C. Inventory management, service level and safety stock. *J. Public Adm. Financ. Law* **2016**, *9*, 145–153.
15. Osman, H.; Demirli, K. Integrated safety stock optimization for multiple sourced stockpoints facing variable demand and lead time. *Int. J. Prod. Econ.* **2012**, *135*, 299–307. [CrossRef]
16. Economopoulos, A.A.; Kouikoglou, V.S.; Grigoroudis, E. The base stock/base backlog control policy for a make-to-stock system with impatient customers. *IEEE Trans. Autom. Sci. Eng.* **2010**, *8*, 243–249. [CrossRef]
17. Feng, L.; Zhang, J.; Tang, W. Optimal inventory control and pricing of perishable items without shortages. *IEEE Trans. Autom. Sci. Eng.* **2015**, *13*, 918–931. [CrossRef]
18. Chen, L.; Chen, Y.; Pang, Z. Dynamic pricing and inventory control in a make-to-stock queue with information on the production status. *IEEE Trans. Autom. Sci. Eng.* **2010**, *8*, 361–373. [CrossRef]
19. Daniel, J.S.R.; Rajendran, C. Heuristic approaches to determine base-stock levels in a serial supply chain with a single objective and with multiple objectives. *Eur. J. Oper. Res.* **2006**, *175*, 566–592. [CrossRef]
20. Haijema, R.; Minner, S. Stock-level dependent ordering of perishables: A comparison of hybrid base-stock and constant order policies. *Int. J. Prod. Econ.* **2016**, *181*, 215–225. [CrossRef]
21. Király, A.; Belvárdi, G.; Abonyi, J. Determining optimal stock level in multi-echelon supply chains. *Hung. J. Ind. Chem.* **2011**, *39*, 107–112.
22. Hadavi, H.; Saifoddin, A.; Amirhaeri, Y.; Pourfayaz, F. Hybrid multi-objective optimization and thermo-economic analysis of a multi-effect desalination unit integrated with a fuel cell-based trigeneration system. *J. Clean. Prod.* **2023**, *407*, 137156. [CrossRef]
23. He, Z.; Qian, J.; Li, J.; Hong, M.; Man, Y. Data-driven soft sensors of papermaking process and its application to cleaner production with multi-objective optimization. *J. Clean. Prod.* **2022**, *372*, 133803. [CrossRef]
24. Liao, T.; Zhang, L. High-Dimensional Many-Objective Bayesian Optimization for LDE-Aware Analog IC Sizing. *IEEE Trans. Very Large Scale Integr. (VLSI) Syst.* **2021**, *30*, 15–28. [CrossRef]
25. Santos, J.A.; Sousa, J.M.; Vieira, S.M.; Ferreira, A.F. Many-objective optimization of a three-echelon supply chain: A case study in the pharmaceutical industry. *Comput. Ind. Eng.* **2022**, *173*, 108729. [CrossRef]
26. Becerra, P.; Mula, J.; Sanchis, R. Sustainable inventory management in supply chains: Trends and further research. *Sustainability* **2022**, *14*, 2613. [CrossRef]
27. Lv, A.; Sun, B. Multi-objective robust optimization for the sustainable location-inventory-routing problem of auto parts supply logistics. *Mathematics* **2022**, *10*, 2942. [CrossRef]
28. Vu, H.T.T.; Ko, J. Inventory transshipment considering greenhouse gas emissions for sustainable cross-filling in cold supply chains. *Sustainability* **2023**, *15*, 7311. [CrossRef]
29. Zhou, L.; Zhang, D.; Li, S.; Luo, X. An Integrated Optimization Model of Green Supply Chain Network Design with Inventory Management. *Sustainability* **2023**, *15*, 12583. [CrossRef]
30. Mishra, U.; Wu, J.Z.; Tsao, Y.C.; Tseng, M. Sustainable inventory system with controllable non-instantaneous deterioration and environmental emission rates. *J. Clean. Prod.* **2020**, *244*, 118807. [CrossRef]
31. Beutel, A.L.; Minner, S. Safety Stock Planning Under Causal Demand Forecasting. *Int. J. Prod. Econ.* **2012**, *140*, 637–645. [CrossRef] [PubMed]
32. Sarwar, F.; Ahmed, M.; Rahman, M. Application of nature inspired algorithms for multi-objective inventory control scenarios. *Int. J. Ind. Eng. Comput.* **2021**, *12*, 91–114. [CrossRef]
33. Tsai, S.; Chen, S. A simulation-based multi-objective optimization framework: A case study on inventory management. *Omega-Int. J. Manag. Sci.* **2017**, *70*, 148–159. [CrossRef]
34. Sabegh, M.Z.; Bingham, C. Impact of hysteresis control and internal thermal mass on the energy efficiency of IoT-controlled domestic refrigerators. In Proceedings of the 2019 IEEE 7th International Conference on Smart Energy Grid Engineering (SEGE), Oshawa, ON, Canada, 12–14 August 2019; pp. 103–107.
35. Zavvar Sabegh, M.R.; Bingham, C. Model predictive control with binary quadratic programming for the scheduled operation of domestic refrigerators. *Energies* **2019**, *12*, 4649. [CrossRef]

36. Wolisz, H.; Kull, T.M.; Streblow, R.; Müller, D. The effect of furniture and floor covering upon dynamic thermal building simulations. *Energy Procedia* **2015**, *78*, 2154–2159. [CrossRef]
37. Lewczuk, K.; Kłodawski, M.; Gepner, P. Energy consumption in a distributional warehouse: A practical case study for different warehouse technologies. *Energies* **2021**, *14*, 2709. [CrossRef]
38. Tsou, C.S. Multi-objective inventory planning using MOPSO and TOPSIS. *Expert Syst. Appl.* **2008**, *35*, 136–142. [CrossRef]
39. Liao, S.; Hsieh, C.; Lai, P.J. An evolutionary approach for multi-objective optimization of the integrated location-inventory distribution network problem in vendor-managed inventory. *Expert Syst. Appl.* **2011**, *38*, 6768–6776. [CrossRef]
40. Bouchery, Y.; Ghaffari, A.; Jemaï, Z.; Dallery, Y. Including sustainability criteria into inventory models. *Eur. J. Oper. Res.* **2012**, *222*, 229–240. [CrossRef]
41. Singh, S.; Yadav, D.; Sarkar, B.; Sarkar, M. Impact of energy and carbon emission of a supply chain management with two-level trade-credit policy. *Energies* **2021**, *14*, 1569. [CrossRef]
42. Sepehri, A.; Mishra, U.; Sarkar, B. A sustainable production-inventory model with imperfect quality under preservation technology and quality improvement investment. *J. Clean. Prod.* **2021**, *310*, 127332. [CrossRef]
43. Jin, Q.; Chen, H.; Hu, F. Proposal of Industry 5.0-Enabled Sustainability of Product–Service Systems and Its Quantitative Multi-Criteria Decision-Making Method. *Processes* **2024**, *12*, 473. [CrossRef]
44. Harrison, J.M.; Sellke, T.M.; Taylor, A.J. Impulse control of Brownian motion. *Math. Oper. Res.* **1983**, *8*, 454–466. [CrossRef]
45. Jain, H.; Deb, K. An evolutionary many-objective optimization algorithm using reference-point based nondominated sorting approach, part II: Handling constraints and extending to an adaptive approach. *IEEE Trans. Evol. Comput.* **2013**, *18*, 602–622. [CrossRef]
46. Ishibuchi, H.; Imada, R.; Setoguchi, Y.; Nojima, Y. Performance comparison of NSGA-II and NSGA-III on various many-objective test problems. In Proceedings of the 2016 IEEE Congress on Evolutionary Computation (CEC), Vancouver, BC, Canada, 24–29 July 2016; pp. 3045–3052.
47. Ciro, G.C.; Dugardin, F.; Yalaoui, F.; Kelly, R. A NSGA-II and NSGA-III comparison for solving an open shop scheduling problem with resource constraints. *IFAC-PapersOnLine* **2016**, *49*, 1272–1277. [CrossRef]
48. Dobnikar, A.; Steele, N.C.; Pearson, D.W.; Albrecht, R.F.; Deb, K.; Agrawal, S. A niched-penalty approach for constraint handling in genetic algorithms. In *Proceedings of the Artificial Neural Nets and Genetic Algorithms: Proceedings of the International Conference in Portorož, Portoroz, Slovenia, 6–9 September 1999*; Springer: Berlin/Heidelberg, Germany, 1999; pp. 235–243.
49. Blank, J.; Deb, K. pymoo: Multi-Objective Optimization in Python. *IEEE Access* **2020**, *8*, 89497–89509. [CrossRef]
50. Unal, U.; Tascioglu, B. Sustainable, therefore reputable: Linking sustainability, reputation, and consumer behaviour. *Mark. Intell. Plan.* **2022**, *40*, 497–512. [CrossRef]
51. Santos, J.A.; Martins, M.S.; Ferreira, A.F.; Vieira, S.M. Sustainable Many-Objective Ideal Stock Optimization of a Multi-Storage Supply Chain. 2023. Available online: https://zenodo.org/records/8392704 (accessed on 15 January 2024).

Disclaimer/Publisher's Note: The statements, opinions and data contained in all publications are solely those of the individual author(s) and contributor(s) and not of MDPI and/or the editor(s). MDPI and/or the editor(s) disclaim responsibility for any injury to people or property resulting from any ideas, methods, instructions or products referred to in the content.

Article

Multi-Criteria Decision Support System for Automatically Selecting Photovoltaic Sets to Maximise Micro Solar Generation

Guilherme Zanlorenzi [1,2], Anderson Luis Szejka [2,*] and Osiris Cancíglieri Junior [2]

1 R&D Department, NHS Sistemas Eletrônicos, Curitiba 81260-000, Brazil
2 Industrial and Systems Engineering Graduate Program, Pontifical Catholic University of Parana, Curitiba 80215-901, Brazil; osiris.canciglieri@pucpr.br
* Correspondence: anderson.szejka@pucpr.br; Tel.: +55-41-98415-7430

Abstract: Technological advancements have improved solar energy generation and reduced the cost of installing photovoltaic (PV) systems. However, challenges such as low energy-conversion efficiency and the unpredictability of electricity generation due to shading or climate conditions persist. Despite decreasing costs, access to solar energy generation technologies remains limited. This paper proposes a multi-criteria decision support system (MCDSS) for selecting the most suitable PV set (comprising PV modules, inverters, and batteries) for microgrid installations. The MCDSS employs two multi-criteria decision-making methods (MCDM) for analysis and decision-making: AHP and TOPSIS. The system was tested in two case studies: Barreiras, with a global efficiency of 14.4% and an internal rate of return (IRR) of 56.0%, and Curitiba, with a worldwide efficiency of 14.8% and an IRR of 52.0%. The research provided a framework for assessing and selecting PV sets based on efficiency, cost, and return on investment. Methodologically, it integrates multiple MCDM techniques, demonstrating their applicability in renewable energy. Managerially, it offers a practical tool for decision-makers in the energy sector to enhance the feasibility and attractiveness of microgeneration projects. This research highlights the potential of MCDSS to improve the efficiency and accessibility of solar energy generation.

Keywords: photovoltaic sets; multi-criteria decision making; micro solar generation; generation optimisation

Citation: Zanlorenzi, G.; Szejka, A.L.; Canciglieri Junior, O. Multi-Criteria Decision Support System for Automatically Selecting Photovoltaic Sets to Maximise Micro Solar Generation. *Algorithms* **2024**, *17*, 274. https://doi.org/10.3390/a17070274

Academic Editors: Frank Werner, David Lemoine, María I. Restrepo and Alexandre Dolgui

Received: 16 May 2024
Revised: 11 June 2024
Accepted: 19 June 2024
Published: 22 June 2024

Copyright: © 2024 by the authors. Licensee MDPI, Basel, Switzerland. This article is an open access article distributed under the terms and conditions of the Creative Commons Attribution (CC BY) license (https:// creativecommons.org/licenses/by/ 4.0/).

1. Introduction

Solar generation has seen significant development since 2010 and has become a low-cost source of energy [1]. Solar energy usage has increased mainly because of the drop in investment costs [2,3]. In this way, the microgeneration market has expanded and gradually attracted more attention, according to the database of the U.S. Energy Information Administration (EIA), due to the gradual reduction in the cost of photovoltaic (PV) modules [4]. However, some issues persist with the low efficiency of energy conversion and the uncertainty of electricity generation due to the adverse effects on the modules when they are partially or totally shaded [5]. Despite the reduction in the costs of PV equipment, solar energy generation technologies are not accessible to everyone [1,6].

Recent related works, such as [7–12], have been carried out to increase the energy efficiency of PV components, such as cooling systems, PV cell materials, PV modules and inverters. Identifying a low efficiency or total inefficiency in some microgeneration is possible. This fact occurs when the low-power photovoltaic set is acquired without prior analysis by a specialist to assess the user's consumption, the installation location of the PV set, and the energy generation potential [13]. In addition, some related works [14–16] explore different methods for real-time statistical analysis and forecasting of factors that impact end users' energy and economic performance. However, these studies do not focus on maximising the performance of PV systems based on detailed data and information about installation requirements and constraints.

Although it exists everywhere in the world, solar irradiation has particularities that vary according to geographical position, such as the average amount of irradiation that reaches the Earth in one year, cloudiness index, clearness index, temperature, and so on [17]. This gap highlights the need for a more comprehensive approach considering specific installation conditions to optimise PV system efficiency and effectiveness. Therefore, multiple variables (climatic and geographical data, technical specifications, economic factors, regulatory and policy frameworks) must be simultaneously considered while defining the most suitable PV set (PV modules, inverter and batteries) [18].

This article proposes a multi-criteria decision support system to identify the most suitable PV set (PV modules, inverter, and batteries) for a microgrid installation, considering the maximum potential energy generation and global efficiency system as well as minimum acquisition and installation costs. The main expected contributions of the research presented in this paper are as follows:

- It improves the PV set selection and application to extract the maximum installed energy potential and the maximum efficiency of technologies available based on specific implementation requirements.
- It encourages the use of renewable energy sources, since this tool analyses the available budget versus implementation costs and energy generation capacity.
- It supports the decision of specialists or not in the PV set selection according to the implementation requirements.
- The remainder of the paper is structured as follows: Section 2 presents the materials and methods of the research, including (i) a review to improve the understanding of PV set definition requirements, (ii) MCDM methods available to support this research and (iii) the conceptualising of a multi-criteria decision support system for a solar microgeneration installation. Section 3 discusses the results of applying the system in two specific experimental cases. Section 4 discusses the research's conclusion, main advantages and limitations, and finally, Section 5 presents the future perspectives for this research.

2. Material and Methods

2.1. Photovoltaic (PV) Set Definitions

A photovoltaic (PV) set comprises multiple devices: PV modules, inverter, batteries, cabling, hardware, and protection devices. From these devices, two are the main components for the generation of photovoltaic energy: PV modules and inverters.

PV modules convert the solar radiation focused on its surface into heat and electrical energy [19]. When PV modules are exposed to irradiation, they produce changes in electrical properties, generating a potential difference between their terminals and, consequently, electrical current when applied to a circuit [20].

Many types of PV modules are made mainly from crystalline or amorphous materials. The crystalline ones are commonly more expensive than the amorphous ones, but they have higher efficiencies, especially those of monocrystalline materials [21]. Efficiency mainly reflects the percentage of electrical power over the total photon power received from the incident irradiation [22]. Table 1 explores an efficiency comparison among multiple PV cell types, focusing on composition characteristics such as thin film, rigid film, organic sell, etc., and PV efficiency. With commercial cells, there are three different types: monocrystalline silicon, polycrystalline silicon and thin film.

The solar inverter is the second most crucial piece of equipment for solar energy generation. Solar inverters or PV inverters are responsible for converting the DC output of a PV solar panel into a DC or AC that can be fed into a commercial electrical grid (on-grid) or used by a local electrical network (off-grid). There are two solar inverters: (i) central and (ii) micro-inverter.

- The central inverter is the most common commercially, and its name is derived from the installation method since it needs two or more PV modules to work correctly. It is a central and standard part of all modules of the PV system.

- The micro-inverter is integrated with PV modules due to its small size. Typically, the PV panels + inverter set is named the AC module. This equipment has two types of converters in operation to supply energy to the electric network: a CC-DC and a CC-AC.

Table 2 compares inverters based on the technologies used and their respective efficiencies.

Table 1. Comparison of PV cells: technology vs. efficiency.

PV Material	Status	Efficiency	Characteristics
CdTe (Cadmium Telluride)	Commercial	7%	Thin film on rigid substrates
a-Se:H (Amorphous Silicon)	Commercial	5–10%	Thin film on rigid substrates
Mono-Si (Monocrystalline Silicon)	Commercial	12–18%	Rigid cell
Multi-Si (Polycrystalline Silicon)	Commercial	11–15%	Rigid cell
Ti3C2Tx	Research	17%	Organic cell
c-Si	Special	20%	Rigid cell
In2O3:SnO2	Research	24–26%	Thin film on rigid substrates
GaAs (Gallium Arsenite)	Special	24–28%	Thin film on rigid substrates
Multi-junction PV Cell	Special	39–46%	Thin film on flexible substrates

Source: Based on [23,24].

Table 2. Comparison of solar inverters: technology vs. efficiency.

Author	Characteristics	Efficiency	Specification
SASIDHARAN and SINGH [25]	Full-bridge inverter Single-stage inverter CC-CA isolated Micro-inverter	90.0%	Converter: CC-CA Input: 80 Vdc Output: 220 Vac Potency: 500 W Switching: 4 kHz
WU and CHOU [26]	Multistage inverter (7 stages) Non-isolated Micro-inverter	94.9%	Converter: CC-CA Input: 70 Vdc Output: 110 Vac Potency: 500 W Switching: 15.3 kHz
XUEWEI et al. [27]	Full-bridge inverter Isolated Micro-inverter	95.0%	Converter: DC-DC Input: 21–41 Vdc Output: 200 Vdc Potency: 200 W Switching: 100 kHz
WU et al. [28]	Buck–boost converter Non-isolated Central inverter	95.5%	Converter: DC-DC Input: 0–600 Vdc Output: 380 Vdc Potency: 5000 W Switching: 25 kHz
CHOI e LEE [29]	Fly back Isolated Micro-inverter	96.0%	Converter: DC-DC Input: 24 Vdc Output: 380 Vdc Potency: 180 W Switching: 50 kHz
ARSHADI et al. [30]	Half-bridge inverter Non-isolated Micro-inverter	96.2%	Converter: DC-AC Input: 700 Vdc Output: 220 Vac Potency: 149.5 W Switching: 20 kHz
ZHAO et al. [31]	Half-bridge inverter Non-isolated Micro-inverter	96.5%	Converter: DC-DC Input: 48 Vdc Output: 800 Vdc Potency: 500 W Switching: 100 kHz
CHA et al. [32]	Resonator converter Isolated Micro-inverter	97.5%	Converter: DC-DC Input: 40–80 Vdc Output: 350 Vdc Potency: 370 W Switching: 50 kHz
ARSHADI et al. [30]	Half-bridge inverter Non-isolated Micro-inverter	96.2%	Converter: DC-AC Input: 700 Vdc Output: 220 Vac Potency: 149.5 W Switching: 20 kHz

According to [33], several factors negatively influence the generation of PV energy. Among the identified factors, it is possible to divide them into three categories: (i) geographic, (ii) constructive parameter and installation mistakes. Table 3 presents the impact of each factor on power generation.

Table 3. Impact of external issues in PV.

Category	External Issue	Impact on Power Generation
Geographic position	Temperature	1–10%
	Dust Deposition	0–15%
	Snow	Determined by the Local Installation
	Shading	Determined by the Local Installation
	Spectral distribution	0–5%
Constructive Parameters	Lifetime	0–5%
	Uncertainty of construction parameters	0–5%
Installations Mistakes	Cabling	0–3%
	Installation angle	1–5%

Source: Based on [33].

These factors are relevant for selecting the most suitable set of PV panels, inverters, and other devices for a solar microgrid. Additionally, it is essential to establish how this system will be installed and the maintenance guidelines to be provided to the end user to extract the maximum performance throughout the entire life cycle of the PV system.

2.2. Multi-Criteria Decision-Making: Foundations

Multi-criteria decision-making (MCDM) techniques have emerged to aid decision-making processes involving numerous variables that cannot be easily considered simultaneously to find the optimal solution [34]. These techniques standardise decision-making through mathematical modelling, facilitating the resolution of problems with multiple objectives. Some notable MCDM techniques include PROMETHEE [35], ELECTRE [36], TOPSIS [37], and AHP [38].

- PROMETHEE (Preference Ranking Organization Method for Enrichment Evaluation)—This aids in identifying the most suitable solution when decision-makers have predetermined criteria and alternatives [39]. It prioritises alternatives based on pre-established criteria, providing decision-makers with a comprehensive view of the business and enabling multifunctional decision-making strategies. However, it may encounter ranking issues.
- ELECTRE—This method constructs an over-classification relationship based on decision-makers' preferences towards available alternatives [40]. ELECTRE uses a binary over classification relationship to classify alternatives, employing either a pessimistic or optimistic approach.
- TOPSIS (Technique for Order of Preference by Similarity)—This method is primarily used to rank alternatives based on preference [41]. It selects alternatives closest to the ideal positive solution and farthest from the ideal negative solution, formed using the best and worst values achieved by alternatives across evaluation criteria. Its advantages lie in its simplicity, ability to compare ideal and undesirable scenarios, and quick identification of the best alternative [37].
- AHP (Analytic Hierarchy Process)—This structured decision-making tool helps individuals and organisations solve complex problems by breaking them down into simpler, more manageable components [42]. AHP is especially valuable in scenarios where decisions involve multiple criteria, both qualitative and quantitative. AHP has been extensively utilised across different domains. Studies [43,44] have applied AHP to develop collaborative supplier performance indices, select cleaning systems for parts, choose IoT platforms, assess disaster-response management systems, analyse interoperability, and prioritise software risks [45].

According to [41], the AHP and the TOPSIS are recognised as two of the most effective multi-criteria decision-making (MCDM) methods [46]. Both methods offer unique advantages that make them well-suited for complex decision-making scenarios involving multiple criteria and alternatives.

In this context, AHP enables using qualitative or quantitative data for criterion analysis in various health, industrial, technical, and strategic applications [47,48]. The first step of AHP involves decomposing the decision problem into a hierarchy with several levels, starting from the overall goal at the top, followed by criteria and sub-criteria, and finally, the alternatives at the bottom [38]. This hierarchical structure allows decision makers to focus on smaller, related sets of decision elements, simplifying the analysis.

The core of AHP lies in making pairwise comparisons between elements at each level of the hierarchy. Decision- makers compare the relative importance of criteria, sub-criteria, or alternatives two at a time, using a scale of 1 to 9, where 1 indicates equal significance and 9 indicates extreme importance of one element over the other [49]. These comparisons are used to construct a comparison matrix for each level of the hierarchy. A priority vector is calculated from these matrices, representing each element's relative weight. Additionally, AHP includes a consistency check to ensure that the judgments made in the pairwise comparisons are logically consistent. A consistency index (CI) is calculated, and if the value is less than 0.1, the consistency is considered acceptable; otherwise, the judgments should be reviewed and adjusted. Finally, the priority weights are combined to calculate the overall score for each alternative, helping to identify the best option based on the defined criteria [38].

In parallel, TOPSIS operates on the principle that the chosen alternative should have the shortest distance from the positive ideal solution (PIS), which represents the best possible scenario, and the farthest distance from the negative ideal solution (NIS), representing the worst possible scenario [41]. This dual consideration of the ideal and anti-ideal solutions makes TOPSIS particularly effective in handling trade-offs among multiple conflicting criteria, providing a balanced evaluation of each alternative. The method is straightforward and intuitive, normalising data, calculating distance measures, and ranking other options based on their relative closeness to the ideal solution.

The calculation process of TOPSIS involves different steps, according to [37,50]. First, the decision matrix lists all alternatives and their performance scores across various criteria. Each criterion's values are then normalised to transform them into dimensionless numbers, facilitating comparison. This normalisation is typically performed using the Euclidean distance formula. Next, the weighted normalised decision matrix is formed by multiplying the normalised values by their corresponding criterion weights, reflecting each criterion's relative importance. The positive ideal solution (PIS) and negative ideal solution (NIS) are then determined. The PIS consists of the best values for each criterion (maximum for benefits and minimum for costs), while the NIS consists of the worst values (minimum for benefits and maximum for costs). The Euclidean distances to the PIS and NIS are calculated for each alternative. Finally, the relative closeness of each alternative to the ideal solution is computed, and the other options are ranked accordingly. The alternative with the highest relative closeness to the PIS is considered the best choice.

Therefore, the MCDSS for identifying the most suitable PV sets employs both AHP and TOPSIS methods in parallel to enhance the overall reliability and effectiveness of the decision-making process. Utilising these methods simultaneously allows for a comprehensive evaluation of their performance, helping to identify which method best determines the optimal photovoltaic system according to the criteria specified by the user. The following section explores the steps in developing and implementing this decision support system.

2.3. Multi-Criteria Decision Support System (MCDSS) for Photovoltaic Set Identification

For the correct functioning of the method to be developed, specific data must be inputted as the calculation basis for determining the customised photovoltaic plant for the installation site. Calculating the energy potential estimate of a region requires integrating solar irradiation factors and temperature factors to assess system losses. Since temperature interference varies throughout the day, it is necessary to calculate the behaviour of the photovoltaic system hour by hour for a year to apply temperature losses accurately. Therefore, the system's response will be more precise if the information is more detailed. In addition, monthly averages of solar irradiation data provide better detail than just an annual average.

Based on this context, the multi-criteria decision support system (MCDSS) for photovoltaic set definition was structured in (i) mapped input data, (ii) data pre-processing, (iii) MCDM application, and (iv) output data. Figure 1 presents the MCDSS for photovoltaic set definition architecture.

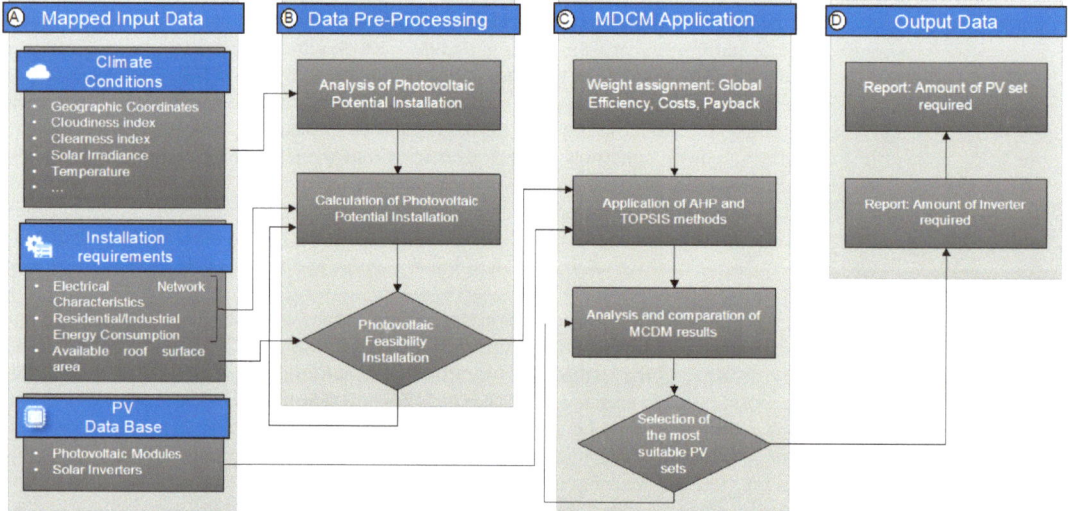

Figure 1. MCDSS for photovoltaic set definition architecture.

- Mapped Input Data (Detail A of Figure 1)—In this section, input data are mapped and collected. These data include crucial information such as climate conditions, installation requirements, and a photovoltaic database. Climate conditions provide insights into solar irradiation patterns and temperature, while installation requirements encompass practical considerations such as available physical space and ideal orientation of solar panels. The photovoltaic database contains details on products and technologies available in the market, essential for comparison and proper equipment selection.
- Data Pre-Processing (Detail B of Figure 1)—Data pre-processing plays a fundamental role in treating and preparing the mapped input data for analysis. This process is divided into sub-steps, including the analysis of available photovoltaic potential, calculation of demanded photovoltaic potential, and evaluation of the feasibility of photovoltaic system installation. These steps help determine the maximum amount of solar energy that can be generated, the system's required capacity to meet electricity demand, and whether installation is viable in each location.
- MCMD Application (Detail C of Figure 1)—The application of multi-criteria decision methods (MCMD) is the heart of the system, where processed data are analysed and used to make decisions. AHP and TOPSIS are applied to determine the best photovoltaic set configuration. Evaluated criteria typically include system efficiency, installation cost, and return on investment time.
- Output Data (Detail D of Figure 1)—The system produces outputs that include specific recommendations for PV sets based on defined criteria. These criteria may include selecting photovoltaic module models, inverters, and other relevant considerations.

These results are presented clearly and comprehensively, providing users with essential information for making informed decisions about implementing photovoltaic systems.

2.3.1. Mapped Input Data

The mapped input data consist of three essential components: (i) climate conditions, (ii) installation requirements, and (iii) PV database. These elements provide information to support the next steps of the MCDSS, allowing the selection and sizing of photovoltaic systems in different contexts and locations.

The first essential component is Climate Conditions, which offer definitions of geographic coordinates, cloudiness index, clearness index, solar irradiation patterns, ambient temperature, and other relevant environmental factors. These data are fundamental for calculating the energy generation capacity of photovoltaic systems at different times of the year and under various weather conditions. The geographic coordinates are obtained directly from the global positioning system (GPS), which provides precise information about the specific location of a given place. These data are essential for analysing and planning photovoltaic systems, as they help determine solar exposure and the ideal angle of solar panels. Information about cloudiness, clarity, and temperature indices is also obtained from reliable meteorological sources, such as national weather websites. In the case of Brazil, for example, these data can be extracted from the National Institute of Meteorology (INMET) [51]. These indices provide valuable insights into local weather conditions, including cloud presence, atmospheric transparency, and temperature variations throughout the day and seasons.

Solar irradiance, measured in units of W/m^2 (watt per square metre), represents the instantaneous amount of energy received from the Sun in a specific region. Accurately sizing a photovoltaic (PV) system for electricity generation requires calculating the maximum, minimum, and average annual solar irradiance throughout the day and the average annual solar irradiance during peak hours. This assessment is crucial for optimising system performance, since these factors collectively impact the availability and intensity of solar energy, highlighting the importance of comprehensive analysis and consideration during system design and implementation.

The amount of solar irradiance reaching the Earth's surface is influenced by various factors, including geographical features, cloud cover, clearness index, temperature, and other atmospheric conditions. Therefore, Equation (1) estimates the irradiation received at the top of the atmosphere in a specific region in each period [52].

$$I_{\Delta t} = \frac{W_0}{r^2} \left\{ (t_2 - t_1) \cdot \sin\delta \cdot \sin\phi + \frac{12}{\pi} \cdot \cos\delta \cdot \cos\phi \cdot [\sin(\tau_2) - \sin(\tau_1)] \right\}, \quad (1)$$

where $I_{\Delta t}$ is the average intensity of local irradiation during the interval (Δ_t), which is measured in W/m^2 (watt per square metre); W_0 is a solar constant whose value is 1380 W/m^2; r is the ratio between the current distance of the Sun in relation to Earth and the average distance from the Sun to Earth; t_1 and t_2 are the beginning and end times of the interval Δ_t; δ is the Sun's declination; ϕ is the latitude of the studied location and τ is the hourly angle of the Sun; τ_1 is the hourly angle of the Sun corresponding to t_1 and τ_2 is the hourly angle of the Sun corresponding to t_2. Equation (2) simplifies Equation (1) for a given period, keeping the variable δ and ϕ.

$$I_0 = \frac{W_0}{r^2} \cdot \sin\alpha, \quad (2)$$

where I_0 is the instantaneous intensity of irradiation at the location, α is the solar elevation angle, and r is the ratio of the current distance from the Sun to the Earth. r is determined by Equation (3), and α is determined by Equation (4).

$$r = 1.0 + 0.017 \cdot \cos\left[\frac{2\pi}{365} \cdot (186 - D)\right] \quad (3)$$

$$sin\alpha = sin\delta \cdot sin\phi + cos\delta \cdot cos\phi \cdot cos\tau \qquad (4)$$

where D is the Julian day in sequential count; α is the solar elevation angle; δ is the Sun's declination; ϕ is the latitude of the studied location, and τ is the hourly angle of the Sun. Based on the equations above, it is possible to estimate the solar irradiance at the top of the atmosphere for any location on planet Earth.

It is important to calculate the maximum, minimum, and average annual solar irradiance throughout the day and the average solar yearly irradiance during peak hours to size the PV set correctly for electricity generation. The amount of solar irradiance received from the Sun on the Earth's surface is directly impacted by multiple factors such as geographical factors, cloudiness and clearness index, temperature, and so on.

The second element is Installation Requirements, which encompass a variety of practical considerations, including the availability of physical space, optimal orientation and angle of solar panels, safety requirements, and local regulations. These data help determine the feasibility and logistics of installing photovoltaic systems in different locations and environments.

Additionally, residential or industrial energy consumption data are fundamental variables across the process to determine the optimal configuration of the photovoltaic system. This information provides crucial insights into energy consumption patterns over time, enabling a precise analysis of the site's energy needs. Additionally, these data help identify peak consumption times, which are essential for properly sizing the system and determining the required energy storage capacity, such as batteries. Therefore, the information needed is the average consumption, the amount charged by the concessionaire for the kW consumed, the installation type, the annual tariff adjustment amount and the available roof surface.

The values entered in the installation requirements are used to calculate the potential to be installed, the investment payback time, and the possibility of installation according to the value entered for the available area. If the area is insufficient, the system will not find any option for a PV module that meets the power required to meet the user's demand.

The last essential component is Photovoltaic Database, which contains detailed information about a wide range of products and technologies available in the market. These data include technical specifications of solar panels, inverters, and other components and performance and efficiency data. This information is essential for comparing and selecting the most suitable equipment to meet the specific needs of each photovoltaic project. Table 4 shows an example of the PV database variables.

Table 4. Example of the data for a PV database.

Brand		Model	Area (m^2)	Weight (kg)	V_{oc} (V)	I_{sc} (A)	V_{mp} (V)	I_{mp} (A)	Power (W)	Eff (%)	Price (USD)
RENESOLA	[53]	RS6535ME3	2.58	29.0	49.5	13.78	41.5	12.90	535	21	116.20
UP SOLAR	[54]	UPM375MH	1.82	19.0	41.5	11.57	34.6	10.93	375	21	128.77
UP SOLAR	[54]	UPB450P	2.17	28.0	49.5	11.60	41.3	10.88	450	22	115.28
CANADIAN	[55]	CS6W535MS	2.56	27.6	49.0	13.85	41.1	13.02	535	21	125.27
CANADIAN	[55]	CS6W550MS	2.56	27.6	49.6	14.00	41.7	13.20	550	21	127.28
CANADIAN	[55]	CS6W560MS	2.56	27.6	50.0	14.10	42.1	13.31	560	22	128.78
SCHUTEN	[56]	STM365/120	1.81	20.5	41.2	11.29	33.9	10.75	365	20	127.27
SCHUTEN	[56]	STM395/120	1.81	20.5	42.0	11.65	35.6	11.05	395	22	137.57

2.3.2. Data Pre-Processing

Data pre-processing handles the mapped input data and supports the multi-criteria decision-making models with structured information. Data pre-processing is divided into sub-steps, which are (i) analysis of available photovoltaic potential, (ii) calculation of demanded photovoltaic potential, and (iii) assessment of the feasibility of photovoltaic system installation.

The analysis of installed photovoltaic potential is the first step of data pre-processing. It focuses on two fundamental analyses for determining the best photovoltaic set, which are (i) defining solar irradiation at the location on the ground where the photovoltaic system will be installed and (ii) determining the average temperature at the location where the photovoltaic system will be installed. The definition of solar irradiation at the location on the ground where the photovoltaic system will be installed is based on Equations (1)–(4), which are available on different platforms such as Weather Spark [57] and Solar Electricity Handbook [58]. Figure 2 demonstrates the potential solar irradiation on the inclined plane of the São Paulo region, Brazil, throughout April 2024. For this report, the geographical coordinates of São Paulo are −23.548 degrees latitude, −46.636 degrees longitude, and 2523 ft elevation.

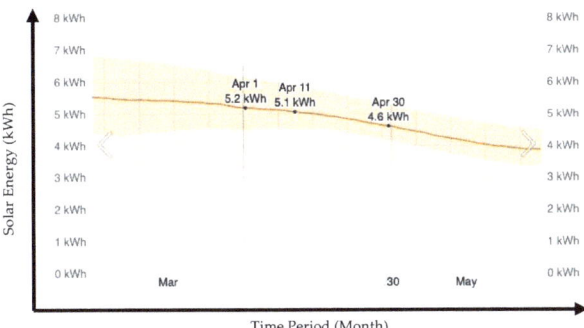

Figure 2. The average daily shortwave solar energy reaches the ground per square metre (orange line), with 25th to 75th and 10th to 90th percentile bands. Source: [57].

With the determination of the irradiation potential, it is necessary to obtain the average temperature of the region. The temperature of the area where the system will be installed strongly influences photovoltaic energy generation, so it must be calculated before estimating the photovoltaic potential of the region. In addition to ambient temperature, it is necessary to assess the temperature of the photovoltaic module, as the higher the temperature of the solar system, the lower its efficiency. The average temperature can be obtained from the Weather Spark and Fabhabs platforms, and the photovoltaic module temperature can be obtained from Equation (5). Figure 3 shows the average temperature of the São Paulo region, Brazil, throughout April 2024.

$$T_{cel} = T_a + \left(\frac{T_{NOCT} - 20}{0.8}\right) \cdot I_{\%} \quad (5)$$

where T_{cel} is the operating temperature of the photovoltaic cell, T_a is the ambient temperature, T_{NOCT} is the value of the operating temperature of the photovoltaic cell provided by the module datasheets, and $I_{\%}$ is the percentage obtained from the behaviour of irradiation at the top of the atmosphere relative to its maximum value. After estimating the operating temperature of the modules, it is possible to calculate the percentage of losses due to temperature, which has a value of −0.40% in power for each °C above 25 °C. Therefore, the photovoltaic potential of the region is given by Equation (6).

$$P_{PV} = I_{\Delta t} \cdot TL_{\%} \quad (6)$$

where P_{PV} is the available photovoltaic potential; $I_{\Delta t}$ is the irradiance reaching the ground; $TL_{\%}$ is the temperature loss expressed as a percentage relative to energy production, which can be directly applied to the value of the irradiance reaching the ground.

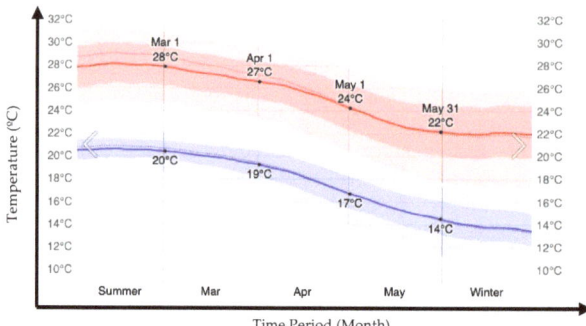

Figure 3. The daily average high (red line) and low (blue line) temperature, with 25th to 75th and 10th to 90th percentile bands. The thin dotted lines are the corresponding average perceived temperatures. Source: [57].

After the analysis of the available photovoltaic potential (Stage 1), which determines the maximum amount of solar energy that the photovoltaic system can generate at a given location, it is necessary to calculate the installed potential (Stage 2) for the photovoltaic system. To calculate the installed photovoltaic potential, it is necessary to consider (i) the historical energy consumption of the residence or industry and (ii) the availability of usable area for the installation of the photovoltaic system.

The local energy consumption history analysis considers consumption patterns over time, seasonality, and daily variations. These data are essential to estimate the amount of electrical energy the photovoltaic system will need to generate to meet consumer demand. On the other hand, the availability of roof area for the installation of solar panels involves evaluating the usable area of the roof, its orientation and tilt relative to the Sun, the presence of shading from nearby trees or buildings, and other possible physical constraints. Based on this information, it is possible to calculate the demanded photovoltaic potential, determining the necessary capacity of the photovoltaic system to meet the electrical energy demand of the location. This calculation is essential to properly size the photovoltaic system and ensure it can efficiently and economically meet the consumer's energy needs. If the available area is insufficient, the user will be informed of the maximum capacity to be installed.

Finally, the feasibility of installing the photovoltaic system is assessed, considering various factors such as installation costs, return on investment, government incentives, regulatory and environmental restrictions, and technical feasibility. This assessment is crucial to determine whether the photovoltaic system installation is viable and economical at a given location. These data pre-processing steps provide a solid foundation for successful planning and implementation of photovoltaic systems, ensuring that they are correctly sized, optimised for maximum utilisation of available solar energy, and economically viable for the customer.

2.3.3. MCDM Application and Output Data

The equipment selection will be carried out using multi-criteria decision support methods, AHP and TOPSIS, to provide a customised installation proposal for each region, as well as the energy demand and specific requirements the user demands. Therefore, combining methods will assist users interested in generating their own energy, aiming to minimise installation costs and reduce energy demand so that only installation availability costs are charged.

The methods allow and provide for the inclusion of qualitative parameters to indicate the preference of one criterion over another. Therefore, the user will be asked to determine the weights for the criteria evaluated by the decision methods, which must meet the consistency index. The criteria assessed by the multi-criteria decision support methods will be (i) system efficiency, (ii) installation cost, and (iii) payback period. All criteria have a direct relationship; for example, the most efficient system may have a higher initial investment, while a cheaper system may not guarantee a shorter payback period for the installed photovoltaic system.

- System efficiency evaluation criterion—the method will indicate the equipment with the best energy utilisation. Priority will be given to photovoltaic modules that can obtain higher electrical power for a certain amount of solar irradiation.
- Installation cost evaluation criterion—the decision will be to select equipment with the lowest cost.
- Financial analysis and evaluation criteria will lead the method to prioritise a balanced installation, aiming to reduce the investment payback time. To conduct an economic analysis of the photovoltaic system to be installed, factors such as payback period, net present value (NPV), and internal rate of return (IRR) will be evaluated. To achieve this, it is necessary to verify the kilowatt-hour rate charged by the local utility company where the equipment will be installed.

Due to the many alternatives, decision support methods will facilitate the decision-making process regarding which photovoltaic module and inverter model will be installed according to the user's needs regarding the evaluated criteria. Therefore, the first recommendation will be the quantity and model of photovoltaic modules that best match the user-entered criteria. Based on the power generated by the photovoltaic modules, the method will exclude some inverter models to avoid errors during selection. Inverters will be excluded if the energy generated by the selected modules is less than 80% of the nominal inverter power or 20% higher. This result prevents an improper choice by the method, such as recommending an oversized inverter based on the "cost" criterion when actual values are input.

For the selection of a photovoltaic module alternative, various factors will be analysed, such as open-circuit voltage (V_{oc}), maximum power (P_{Max}), maximum power current (I_{Max}), area (a), efficiency (η), and cost (C), which will be compared to determine the best alternative. The exact process will be carried out to determine the best inverter alternative, where the analysed factors will include maximum power (P_{Max}), efficiency (η), maximum DC voltage (Vdc), and cost (C). The PV equipment selected by each decision support method will be presented and compared to verify if the chosen alternatives correspond to the trends provided by the user. Two comparisons will be made: first, the photovoltaic modules and inverters will be separately compared, and finally, the components will be integrated to generate the complete system for the final comparison.

Each evaluated criterion's maximum and minimum values will be used for these comparisons, generating a range of values. Subsequently, the value of the respective analysed criterion for the selected alternative will correspond to a percentage within this previously established range, providing a better visualisation of the selected alternative. For example, assuming the global maximum and minimum values for the efficiency criterion of the modules are, respectively, 15% and 18%, and the alternative selected by the multi-criteria decision support method has an efficiency of 17.5%, according to the previous values, the selected module corresponds to 83.33% of the value range of the alternatives. By checking this result, it is possible to observe that there are more efficient modules among the options, but they were not selected due to some other criterion, which could be the high cost. After verifying the comparisons of the alternatives selected by each multi-criteria decision support method, it will be up to the user to choose the most suitable option.

Finally, the method will present which photovoltaic module model and quantity are necessary for the installation to have an average annual capacity equivalent to that established by the user when determining the energy demand of the location where the system will be installed, according to the photovoltaic module models entered in the method's database. The same will be performed with the inverters, but considering the equipment's construction factors, especially the maximum photovoltaic voltage, which could damage the equipment if it exceeds the manufacturer's specification.

3. Results and Discussion

The MCDSS-PV was applied in two scenarios with different locations: (i) Curitiba, Brazil, and (ii) Barreiras, Brazil. Table 5 presents monthly irradiation and temperatures for these regions.

Table 5. Monthly averages of irradiation and temperatures for the cities of Curitiba and Barreiras.

Mapped Data	January 2023	February 2023	March 2023	April 2023	May 2023	June 2023	July 2023	August 2023	September 2023	October 2023	November 2023	December 2023
						Curitiba						
$I_{\Delta t}$ (W/m^2)	6400	6000	5800	4900	3900	3400	3600	4400	5400	5900	6600	6800
T_{max} (°C)	28	28	28	23	21	20	19	21	21	23	25	25
T_{min} (°C)	16	16	15	13	10	8	8	9	11	13	14	15
						Barreiras						
$I_{\Delta t}$ (W/m^2)	6000	6000	5800	5700	5500	5400	5800	6400	6800	6500	6000	6000
T_{max} (°C)	30	31	31	31	33	32	32	34	36	35	32	31
T_{min} (°C)	21	21	21	21	20	19	18	19	22	23	22	21

Source: [57].

For the study of this scenario, a demand of 350 kWh/month will be considered in a three-phase installation, with an available power to be deducted of 100 kWh/month. In other words, the installed capacity must supply 3000 kWh/year, which the PV installation must supply.

3.1. Case Study of Barreiras City, Brazil

Barreiras' City of Bahia state in Brazil, according to [57], is the region with the highest irradiation potential in the northeast of the country, reaching daily average values of 5995 Wh/m^2, as shown in Table 5. This city is located at the following coordinates: latitude: −12.142939, longitude: −45.0089385, altitude: 454 m, and GMT −3. Figure 4 presents the annual irradiance map of northeast Brazil and highlights Barreiras' City in Bahia. Figure 5 demonstrates the average high and low temperatures.

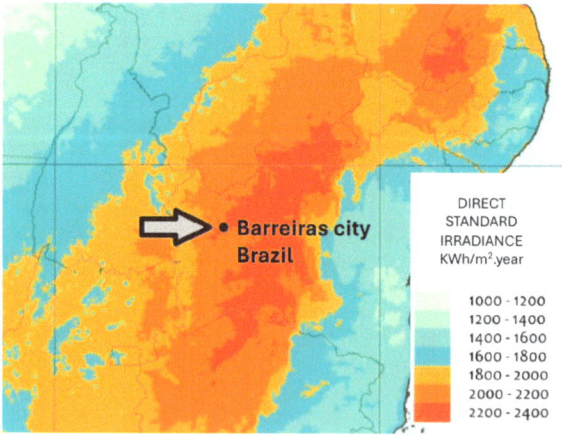

Figure 4. Average annual irradiation in Barreiras' City, Brazil. Source: [57].

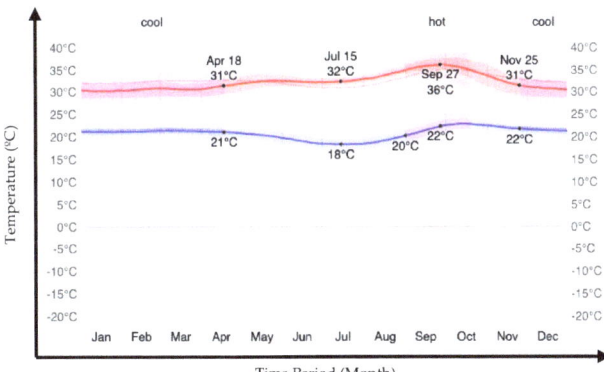

Figure 5. The average temperature highs and lows in Barreiras City. Source: [57].

After verifying the geographical conditions of the region of Barreiras City, it was defined that for this installation, the evaluation criterion to be maximised was the installation cost. Therefore, both decision support methods should select alternatives with lower fees. The other criteria were determined considering the coherence ratio, whose value must be less than 10%. Therefore, if the weight for the installation cost is 100, the other criteria have weights of 75. When applying the expert method for determining the PV set, a proposal was obtained, as shown in Figures 6 and 7.

Figure 6. Comparison of the alternatives selected by the MCDSS for photovoltaic set definition concerning the global range of criteria for the case study of Barreiras City.

AHP	TOPSIS
PV modules	
PV Module selected: TEST MOD285W_15 Quantity: 6 Installed power: 1710.0W Payback: 0.92 years Cost: USD 585.69 Efficiency: 15.0% Surface: 11.4 m^2	PV Module selected: TEST MOD285W_15 Quantity: 6 Installed power: 1710.0W Payback: 0.92 years Cost: USD 585.69 Efficiency: 15.0% Surface: 11.4 m^2
PV Inversor	
PV Inversor selected: TEST 2KW_96 Quantity: 1 Installed power: 2000W Payback: 1.75 years Cost: USD 698.79 Efficiency: 96.0%	PV Inversor selected: TEST 2KW_96 Quantity: 1 Installed power: 2000W Payback: 1.75 years Cost: USD 698.79 Efficiency: 96.0%
Global Information	
Power output: 3322 KWh.year Average annual demand: 4200 KWh.year Availability demand: 1200 KWh.year Energy balance: 322 KWh.year Overall method performance Energy efficiency rate: 0.0% Payback time rate: 100.0% Investment cost rate: 100.0% System payback time: 2.67 years System cost: USD 1 284.50 System Efficiency: 14.4% Net Present Value: USD 10,338.27 Internal Rate of Return: 49.0% Energy savings over 25 years: USD 28,289.03	Power output: 3322 KWh.year Average annual demand: 4200 KWh.year Availability demand: 1200 KWh.year Energy balance: 322 KWh.year Overall method performance Energy efficiency rate: 0.0% Payback time rate: 100.0% Investment cost rate: 100.0% System payback time: 2.67 years System cost: USD 1 284.50 System Efficiency: 14.4% Net Present Value: USD 10,338.27 Internal Rate of Return: 49.0% Energy savings over 25 years: USD 28,289.03

Figure 7. Analysis of the alternatives selected by the MCDSS for photovoltaic set definition of the City of Barreiras.

After examining the proposals generated by both methods, it became evident that the selected photovoltaic equipment was identical. As anticipated, both methods prioritised equipment with the lowest cost, aligning with the user's requirements. Given these case study findings, it is impossible to determine the method that demonstrates the most suitable performance because both methods choose the same PV set for a micro-generation.

3.2. Case Study of Curitiba City, Brazil

The second city to be analysed is Curitiba of Paraná state in Brazil. According to Pereira et al. (2017), the estimated average daily irradiation for the country's Southern region is 4.53 kWh/m^2·day. The Southern region presents an average daily irradiation 17.48% lower than the Northeast region. Curitiba has the following coordinates: latitude: -25.401; longitude: -49.249; altitude: 935 m; and GMT -3. Figure 8 presents the annual irradiance map of Brazil's south and highlights Curitiba city in Parana. Figure 9 demonstrates the average high and low temperatures.

Due to the first case study prioritising installation cost, the weight of the investment payback time was maximised for the case study in Curitiba. Therefore, the MCDSS for photovoltaic set definition tended to have a balanced value between efficiency and cost for determining the system to be installed. The weight assigned to "payback time" was 100%, and for the other criteria, the weight was 75%. The proposal generated by the MCDSS can be seen in Figures 10 and 11.

Figure 8. Average annual irradiation in Curitiba city, Brazil. Source: [57].

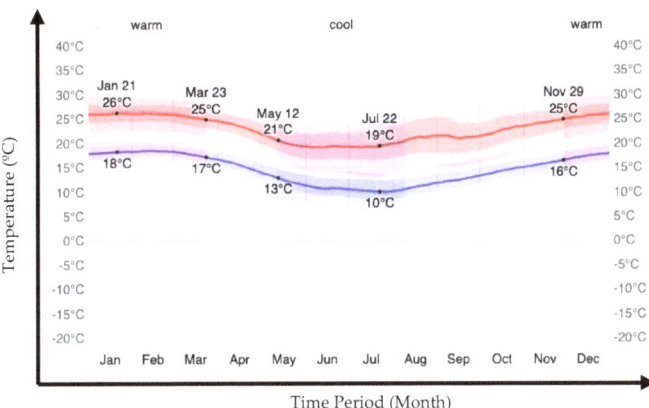

Figure 9. Average high and low temperature in Curitiba city, Brazil. Source: [57].

As observed in Figures 10 and 11, the methods selected divergent alternatives. For the selection of photovoltaic modules, the AHP method sought the equipment with the shortest payback time among the options, as desired by the user. This photovoltaic module model had the lowest cost among the possible options. On the other hand, the TOPSIS method selected a photovoltaic module model that was quite similar but had slightly higher efficiency than the one AHP selected. The methods used to determine inverters had completely divergent responses. The AHP method selected an inverter model with the shortest payback time possible, like when choosing photovoltaic modules. However, the TOPSIS method selected the most efficient inverter model among the available options, ignoring models with shorter payback times and lower costs. Upon analysing the system, it was possible to verify that the photovoltaic system selected by the AHP method minimised the investment payback time and selected the cheapest possible system within the range offered by the alternatives. The TOPSIS method determined a slightly more efficient system than the proposal provided by AHP. Still, it did not achieve a satisfactory result for the payback time criterion as required by the user.

Figure 10. Comparison of the alternatives selected by the MCDSS for photovoltaic set definition concerning the global range of criteria for the Curitiba case study.

Upon analysing the systems proposed by the decision methods, it is possible to verify that despite the evaluation graphs of the selected alternatives being completely different, the photovoltaic systems determined by AHP and TOPSIS are similar due to the restricted range of options for choosing the inverters. The annual power generated by the systems is 3036 kWh/year for the installation selected by the AHP method and 3056 kWh/year for the system chosen by the TOPSIS method, generating a positive energy balance of 36.0 kWh and 56.0 kWh, respectively. For the analysis of the maximised criterion, the investment payback time, the AHP method selected a system with a payback time value of 2.76 years. On the other hand, the TOPSIS method selected photovoltaic component alternatives so that the payback time was 2.95 years. When analysing the different criteria for efficiency, the TOPSIS method selected alternatives whose overall efficiency was higher than the proposal of the AHP method, reaching a global efficiency value of 14.8% compared to the 14.4% chosen by the AHP method. For the installation cost criterion, the AHP method selected an installation that was 6.1% cheaper than the system proposed by the TOPSIS method, whose total cost was USD 1284.49.

When analysing the economic viability, the system proposed by the AHP method obtained a better IRR value, reaching 52.0%. The NPV value was also higher for the system determined by the AHP method, which was USD 9336.15. Analysing the amount saved on electricity at the end of the photovoltaic system's life, the installation proposed by the TOPSIS method presented a higher value compared to the system proposed by the AHP method, where the resulting value was USD 26,021.92, 0.7% higher than the value determined by the photovoltaic installation by the AHP method.

AHP	TOPSIS
PV modules	
PV Module selected: TEST MOD285W_15 Quantity: 6 Installed power: 1710.0W Payback: 1.01 years Cost: USD 585.69 Efficiency: 15.0% Surface: 11.4 m²	PV Module selected: TEST_mod286,9W_15,1 Quantity: 6 Installed power: 1721.4W Payback: 1.02 years Cost: USD 595.00 Efficiency: 15.1% Surface: 11.4 m²
PV Inversor	
PV Inversor selected: TEST 2KW_96 Quantity: 1 Installed power: 2000W Payback: 1.75 years Cost: USD 698.79 Efficiency: 96.0%	PV Inversor selected: TEST 2KW_98 Quantity: 1 Installed power: 2000W Payback: 1.93 years Cost: USD 772.35 Efficiency: 98.0%
Global Information	
Power output: 3036 KWh.year Average annual demand: 4200 KWh.year Availability demand: 1200 KWh.year Energy balance: 36 KWh.year Overall method performance Energy efficiency rate: 0.0% Payback time rate: 100.0% Investment cost rate: 100.0% System payback time: 2.76 years System cost: USD 1 284.49 System Efficiency: 14.4% Net Present Value: USD 9336.15 Internal Rate of Return: 52.0% Energy savings over 25 years: USD 25,849.61	Power output: 3056 KWh.year Average annual demand: 4200 KWh.year Availability demand: 1200 KWh.year Energy balance: 56 KWh.year Overall method performance Energy efficiency rate: 11.0% Payback time rate: 77.0% Investment cost rate: 84.0% System payback time: 2.95 years System cost: USD 1 367.35 System Efficiency: 14.8% Net Present Value: USD 9324.03 Internal Rate of Return: 49.0% Energy savings over 25 years: USD 26,021.92

Figure 11. Analysis of the alternatives selected by the MCDSS for photovoltaic set definition of Curitiba City.

4. Conclusions

This research presents a multi-criteria decision support system (MCDSS) designed to optimise the selection of photovoltaic (PV) sets for microgrid installations. By integrating two robust multi-criteria decision-making (MCDM) methods, AHP and TOPSIS, the MCDSS provides a comprehensive framework for evaluating PV sets based on efficiency, cost, and return on investment. Applying this system in case studies from Barreiras and Curitiba demonstrates its effectiveness, yielding global efficiencies of 14.4% and 14.8% and internal rates of return (IRR) of 56.0% and 52.0%, respectively.

The findings highlight significant analytical, methodological, and managerial contributions. Analytically, the study offers a detailed assessment model for PV set selection, addressing the critical factors impacting energy generation. Methodologically, it showcases the integration of AHP and TOPSIS in renewable energy applications, enhancing decision-making processes. Managerially, the MCDSS serves as a practical tool for decision-makers, improving the feasibility and attractiveness of microgeneration projects.

Challenges like low energy conversion efficiency and shading effects remain despite technological advancements and reduced costs. The proposed MCDSS addresses these issues, facilitating more efficient and accessible solar energy generation. This research underscores the potential of MCDSSs to support the broader adoption of renewable energy sources, contributing to a sustainable energy future.

Implementing this system can reduce the complexity of selecting the most appropriate PV components, making it easier for experts and non-experts to make informed decisions. The MCDSS ensures that the selected PV sets are tailored to maximise energy output and economic viability by considering various factors such as climatic conditions, geographic location, and specific installation requirements. Additionally, the research highlights the importance of considering local environmental factors and specific installation conditions in the selection process. By incorporating these variables into the MCDSS, the system can provide more accurate and context-sensitive recommendations, ultimately leading to better performance and higher satisfaction for end-users.

Therefore, the MCDSS is a method for assessing and selecting PV sets based on efficiency, cost, and return on investment. Methodologically, it integrates multiple MCDM techniques, demonstrating their applicability in renewable energy. Managerially, it offers a practical tool for decision-makers in the energy sector to enhance the feasibility and attractiveness of microgeneration projects. The MCDSS can potentially improve the efficiency and accessibility of solar energy generation, promoting the adoption of renewable energy sources and supporting a transition to a sustainable energy infrastructure.

5. Future Works

Future research could expand the applicability of the MCDSS to other renewable energy sources, such as wind or hydropower, and explore the integration of additional decision-making criteria. Further validation of the system in diverse geographical locations and varying climatic conditions would also strengthen its utility and robustness. Moreover, incorporating real-time data and advanced forecasting techniques could enhance the system's predictive capabilities, providing even more precise and dynamic recommendations.

Author Contributions: Conceptualisation, G.Z. and A.L.S.; Methodology, G.Z.; Software, G.Z.; Validation, G.Z., A.L.S. and O.C.J.; Formal Analysis, A.L.S. and O.C.J.; Writing—Original Draft Preparation, A.L.S.; Writing—Review and Editing, A.L.S. and O.C.J.; Visualization, G.Z., A.L.S. and O.C.J.; Supervision, A.L.S. and O.C.J.; Funding Acquisition, A.L.S. All authors have read and agreed to the published version of the manuscript.

Funding: This research was funded by NHS Sistemas Eletrônicos, grant number TA01/2018 and the APC was supported by the National Council for Scientific and Technological Development (CNPq), grant number 302406/2023.

Data Availability Statement: There are no data available online that we can share with other researchers.

Acknowledgments: The authors thank the Pontifical Catholic University of Parana (PUCPR) for all its support during the project development.

Conflicts of Interest: The authors declare no conflicts of interest.

References

1. Ang, T.-Z.; Salem, M.; Kamarol, M.; Das, H.S.; Nazari, M.A.; Prabaharan, N. A Comprehensive Study of Renewable Energy Sources: Classifications, Challenges and Suggestions. *Energy Strategy Rev.* **2022**, *43*, 100939. [CrossRef]
2. Bayrak, F.; Ertürk, G.; Oztop, H.F. Effects of Partial Shading on Energy and Exergy Efficiencies for Photovoltaic Panels. *J. Clean. Prod.* **2017**, *164*, 58–69. [CrossRef]
3. Kumar Sahu, B. A Study on Global Solar PV Energy Developments and Policies with Special Focus on the Top Ten Solar PV Power Producing Countries. *Renew. Sustain. Energy Rev.* **2015**, *43*, 621–634. [CrossRef]
4. Hirsch, A.; Parag, Y.; Guerrero, J. Microgrids: A Review of Technologies, Key Drivers, and Outstanding Issues. *Renew. Sustain. Energy Rev.* **2018**, *90*, 402–411. [CrossRef]
5. Yue, X.; Di, G.; Yu, Y.; Wang, W.; Shi, H. Analysis of the Combination of Natural Language Processing and Search Engine Technology. *Procedia Eng.* **2012**, *29*, 1636–1639. [CrossRef]
6. Bošnjaković, M.; Santa, R.; Crnac, Z.; Bošnjaković, T. Environmental Impact of PV Power Systems. *Sustainability* **2023**, *15*, 11888. [CrossRef]
7. Almadhhachi, M.; Seres, I.; Farkas, I. Sunflower Solar Tree vs. Flat PV Module: A Comprehensive Analysis of Performance, Efficiency, and Land Savings in Urban Solar Integration. *Results Eng.* **2024**, *21*, 101742. [CrossRef]
8. Allouhi, A.; Rehman, S.; Buker, M.S.; Said, Z. Recent Technical Approaches for Improving Energy Efficiency and Sustainability of PV and PV-T Systems: A Comprehensive Review. *Sustain. Energy Technol. Assess.* **2023**, *56*, 103026. [CrossRef]
9. Su, X.; Luo, C.; Chen, X.; Nie, T.; Yu, Y.; Zou, W.; Wu, Y. Study on Impact of Photovoltaic Power Tracking Modes on Photovoltaic-Photothermal Performance of PV-PCM-Trombe Wall System. *Energy Build.* **2023**, *301*, 113714. [CrossRef]
10. Han, Z.; Liu, K.; Li, G.; Zhao, X.; Shittu, S. Electrical and Thermal Performance Comparison between PVT-ST and PV-ST Systems. *Energy* **2021**, *237*, 121589. [CrossRef]
11. Bouakkaz, A.; Mena, A.J.G.; Haddad, S.; Ferrari, M.L. Efficient Energy Scheduling Considering Cost Reduction and Energy Saving in Hybrid Energy System with Energy Storage. *J. Energy Storage* **2021**, *33*, 101887. [CrossRef]

12. Kuznetsov, P.; Yuferev, L.; Voronin, D.; Panchenko, V.A.; Jasiński, M.; Najafi, A.; Leonowicz, Z.; Bolshev, V.; Martirano, L. Methods Improving Energy Efficiency of Photovoltaic Systems Operating under Partial Shading. *Appl. Sci.* **2021**, *11*, 10696. [CrossRef]
13. Yanine, F.F.; Sauma, E.E. Review of Grid-Tie Micro-Generation Systems without Energy Storage: Towards a New Approach to Sustainable Hybrid Energy Systems Linked to Energy Efficiency. *Renew. Sustain. Energy Rev.* **2013**, *26*, 60–95. [CrossRef]
14. Gheorghiu, C.; Scripcariu, M.; Tanasiev, G.N.; Gheorghe, S.; Duong, M.Q. A Novel Methodology for Developing an Advanced Energy-Management System. *Energies* **2024**, *17*, 1605. [CrossRef]
15. Ceccon, W.F.; Freire, R.Z.; Szejka, A.L.; Junior, O.C. Intelligent Electric Power Management System for Economic Maximization in a Residential Prosumer Unit. *IEEE Access* **2021**, *9*, 48713–48731. [CrossRef]
16. Collotta, M.; Pau, G. An Innovative Approach for Forecasting of Energy Requirements to Improve a Smart Home Management System Based on BLE. *IEEE Trans. Green Commun. Netw.* **2017**, *1*, 112–120. [CrossRef]
17. Alhousni, F.K.; Ismail, F.B.; Okonkwo, P.C.; Mohamed, H.; Okonkwo, B.O.; Al-Shahri, O.A. A Review of PV Solar Energy System Operations and Applications in Dhofar Oman. *AIMS Energy* **2022**, *10*, 858–884. [CrossRef]
18. Nawaz, I.; Tiwari, G.N. Embodied Energy Analysis of Photovoltaic (PV) System Based on Macro- and Micro-Level. *Energy Policy* **2006**, *34*, 3144–3152. [CrossRef]
19. Dwivedi, P.; Sudhakar, K.; Soni, A.; Solomin, E.; Kirpichnikova, I. Advanced Cooling Techniques of P.V. Modules: A State of Art. *Case Stud. Therm. Eng.* **2020**, *21*, 100674. [CrossRef]
20. Shaik, F.; Lingala, S.S.; Veeraboina, P. Effect of Various Parameters on the Performance of Solar PV Power Plant: A Review and the Experimental Study. *Sustain. Energy Res.* **2023**, *10*, 6. [CrossRef]
21. Tiwari, G.N.; Tiwari, A. *Shyam Handbook of Solar Energy: Theory, Analysis and Applications*; Energy Systems in Electrical Engineering; Springer: Singapore, 2016; ISBN 978-981-10-0805-4.
22. Zabihi, A.; Parhamfar, M.; Sarathbabu Duvvuri, S.S.S.R.; Abtahi, M. Increase Power Output and Radiation in Photovoltaic Systems by Installing Mirrors. *Meas. Sens.* **2024**, *31*, 100946. [CrossRef]
23. Hameiri, Z. Photovoltaics Literature Survey (No. 171). *Prog. Photovolt. Res. Appl.* **2022**, *30*, 116–120. [CrossRef]
24. Lewis, N.S. Research Opportunities to Advance Solar Energy Utilization. *Science* **2016**, *351*, aad1920. [CrossRef] [PubMed]
25. Sasidharan, N.; Singh, J.G. A Novel Single-Stage Single-Phase Reconfigurable Inverter Topology for a Solar Powered Hybrid AC/DC Home. *IEEE Trans. Ind. Electron.* **2017**, *64*, 2820–2828. [CrossRef]
26. Wu, J.-C.; Chou, C.-W. A Solar Power Generation System With a Seven-Level Inverter. *IEEE Trans. Power Electron.* **2014**, *29*, 3454–3462. [CrossRef]
27. Xuewei, P.; Rathore, A.K.; Prasanna, U.R. Novel Soft-Switching Snubberless Naturally Clamped Current-Fed Full-Bridge Front-End-Converter-Based Bidirectional Inverter for Renewables, Microgrid, and UPS Applications. *IEEE Trans. Ind. Appl.* **2014**, *50*, 4132–4141. [CrossRef]
28. Wu, T.-F.; Kuo, C.-L.; Sun, K.-H.; Chen, Y.-K.; Chang, Y.-R.; Lee, Y.-D. Integration and Operation of a Single-Phase Bidirectional Inverter with Two Buck/Boost MPPTs for DC-Distribution Applications. *IEEE Trans. Power Electron.* **2013**, *28*, 5098–5106. [CrossRef]
29. Choi, W.-Y.; Lee, C.-G. Photovoltaic Panel Integrated Power Conditioning System Using a High-Efficiency Step-up DC-DC Converter. *Renew. Energy* **2012**, *41*, 227–234. [CrossRef]
30. Arshadi, S.A.; Poorali, B.; Adib, E.; Farzanehfard, H. High Step-Up DC–AC Inverter Suitable for AC Module Applications. *IEEE Trans. Ind. Electron.* **2016**, *63*, 832–839. [CrossRef]
31. Zhao, Z.; Lee, W.C.; Shin, Y.; Song, K.-B. An Optimal Power Scheduling Method for Demand Response in Home Energy Management System. *IEEE Trans. Smart Grid* **2013**, *4*, 1391–1400. [CrossRef]
32. Cha, W.-J.; Kwon, J.-M.; Kwon, B.-H. Highly Efficient Step-up Dc–Dc Converter for Photovoltaic Micro-Inverter. *Sol. Energy* **2016**, *135*, 14–21. [CrossRef]
33. Jathar, L.D.; Ganesan, S.; Awasarmol, U.; Nikam, K.; Shahapurkar, K.; Soudagar, M.E.M.; Fayaz, H.; El-Shafay, A.S.; Kalam, M.A.; Bouadila, S.; et al. Comprehensive Review of Environmental Factors Influencing the Performance of Photovoltaic Panels: Concern over Emissions at Various Phases throughout the Lifecycle. *Environ. Pollut.* **2023**, *326*, 121474. [CrossRef] [PubMed]
34. Taherdoost, H.; Madanchian, M. Multi-Criteria Decision Making (MCDM) Methods and Concepts. *Encyclopedia* **2023**, *3*, 77–87. [CrossRef]
35. Brans, J.-P.; De Smet, Y. PROMETHEE Methods. In *Multiple Criteria Decision Analysis*; Greco, S., Ehrgott, M., Figueira, J.R., Eds.; International Series in Operations Research & Management Science; Springer: New York, NY, USA, 2016; Volume 233, pp. 187–219, ISBN 978-1-4939-3093-7.
36. Figueira, J.R.; Mousseau, V.; Roy, B. ELECTRE Methods. In *Multiple Criteria Decision Analysis*; Greco, S., Ehrgott, M., Figueira, J.R., Eds.; International Series in Operations Research & Management Science; Springer: New York, NY, USA, 2016; Volume 233, pp. 155–185, ISBN 978-1-4939-3093-7.
37. Chakraborty, S. TOPSIS and Modified TOPSIS: A Comparative Analysis. *Decis. Anal. J.* **2022**, *2*, 100021. [CrossRef]
38. González-Prida, V.; Barberá, L.; Viveros, P.; Crespo, A. Dynamic Analytic Hierarchy Process: AHP Method Adapted to a Changing Environment. *IFAC Proc. Vol.* **2012**, *45*, 25–29. [CrossRef]

39. Uzun, B.; Almasri, A.; Uzun Ozsahin, D. Preference Ranking Organization Method for Enrichment Evaluation (Promethee). In *Application of Multi-Criteria Decision Analysis in Environmental and Civil Engineering*; Uzun Ozsahin, D., Gökçekuş, H., Uzun, B., LaMoreaux, J., Eds.; Professional Practice in Earth Sciences; Springer International Publishing: Cham, Switzerland, 2021; pp. 37–41, ISBN 978-3-030-64764-3.
40. Hashemi, S.S.; Hajiagha, S.H.R.; Zavadskas, E.K.; Mahdiraji, H.A. Multi-criteria Group Decision Making with ELECTRE III Method Based on Interval-Valued Intuitionistic Fuzzy Information. *Appl. Math. Model.* **2016**, *40*, 1554–1564. [CrossRef]
41. Madanchian, M.; Taherdoost, H. A Comprehensive Guide to the TOPSIS Method for Multi-Criteria Decision Making. *Sustain. Social. Dev.* **2023**, *1*, 2220. [CrossRef]
42. Saaty, R.W. The Analytic Hierarchy Process—What It Is and How It Is Used. *Math. Model.* **1987**, *9*, 161–176. [CrossRef]
43. Yuen, K.K.F. Analytic Hierarchy Prioritization Process in the AHP Application Development: A Prioritization Operator Selection Approach. *Appl. Soft Comput.* **2010**, *10*, 975–989. [CrossRef]
44. U-Dominic, C.M.; Ujam, J.C.; Igbokwe, N. Applications of Analytical Hierarchy Process (AHP) and Knowledge Management (KM) Concepts in Defect Identification: A Case of Cable Manufacturing. *Asian J. Adv. Res. Rep.* **2021**, *15*, 9–21. [CrossRef]
45. Liao, Y.; Deschamps, F.; de Loures, E.F.R.; Ramos, L.F.P. Past, Present and Future of Industry 4.0—A Systematic Literature Review and Research Agenda Proposal. *Int. J. Prod. Res.* **2017**, *55*, 3609–3629. [CrossRef]
46. Ogonowski, P. Integrated AHP and TOPSIS Method in the Comparative Analysis of the Internet Activities. *Procedia Comput. Sci.* **2022**, *207*, 4409–4418. [CrossRef]
47. Anthony Jnr, B. Validating the Usability Attributes of AHP-Software Risk Prioritization Model Using Partial Least Square-Structural Equation Modeling. *J. Sci. Technol. Policy Manag.* **2019**, *10*, 404–430. [CrossRef]
48. Maputi, E.S.; Arora, R. Gear Concept Selection Procedure Using Fuzzy QFD, AHP and Tacit Knowledge. *Cogent Eng.* **2020**, *7*, 1802816. [CrossRef]
49. Farhan, U.H.; Tolouei-Rad, M.; Osseiran, A. Use of AHP in Decision-Making for Machine Tool Configurations. *J. Manuf. Technol. Manag.* **2016**, *27*, 874–888. [CrossRef]
50. Saeidi, R.; Noorollahi, Y.; Aghaz, J.; Chang, S. FUZZY-TOPSIS Method for Defining Optimal Parameters and Finding Suitable Sites for PV Power Plants. *Energy* **2023**, *282*, 128556. [CrossRef]
51. Instituto Nacional de Meteorologia—INMET. Available online: https://portal.inmet.gov.br/ (accessed on 11 June 2024).
52. Karki, R. Reliability of Renewable Power Systems. In *Encyclopedia of Sustainable Technologies*; Elsevier: Amsterdam, The Netherlands, 2017; pp. 217–230, ISBN 978-0-12-804792-7.
53. Renesola_Módulos Fotovoltaicos, Sistema Distribuído, Grande Central Elétrica de Superfície. Available online: https://pt.renesola-energy.com/ (accessed on 10 June 2024).
54. UPSolar. Available online: http://upsolar.com/ (accessed on 10 June 2024).
55. Canadian Solar. Available online: https://www.csisolar.com/br/module/ (accessed on 10 June 2024).
56. SCHUTEN. Available online: https://www.schutten-solar.com/product/139.html#c_portalResFile_relatedlist-16009603568217740 (accessed on 10 June 2024).
57. Weather Spark The Weather Year Round Anywhere on Earth—Weather Spark. Available online: https://weatherspark.com/ (accessed on 13 May 2024).
58. Boxwell, M. *Solar Electricity Handbook—2019 Edition: A Simple, Practical Guide to Solar Energy—Designing and Installing Solar Photovoltaic Systems*, 2019th ed.; Greenstream Publishing: Coventry, UK, 2019; ISBN 978-1-907670-71-8.

Disclaimer/Publisher's Note: The statements, opinions and data contained in all publications are solely those of the individual author(s) and contributor(s) and not of MDPI and/or the editor(s). MDPI and/or the editor(s) disclaim responsibility for any injury to people or property resulting from any ideas, methods, instructions or products referred to in the content.

Article

Maximizing the Average Environmental Benefit of a Fleet of Drones under a Periodic Schedule of Tasks

Vladimir Kats [1] and Eugene Levner [2],*

[1] Institute for Industrial Mathematics, Ben Gurion University, Beer-Sheva 8424902, Israel; vkats782@gmail.com or katzlu@bgu.ac.il
[2] School of Computer Science, Holon Institute of Technology, Holon 5810201, Israel
* Correspondence: levner@hit.ac.il

Abstract: Unmanned aerial vehicles (UAVs, drones) are not just a technological achievement based on modern ideas of artificial intelligence; they also provide a sustainable solution for green technologies in logistics, transport, and material handling. In particular, using battery-powered UAVs to transport products can significantly decrease energy and fuel expenses, reduce environmental pollution, and improve the efficiency of clean technologies through improved energy-saving efficiency. We consider the problem of maximizing the average environmental benefit of a fleet of drones given a periodic schedule of tasks performed by the fleet of vehicles. To solve the problem efficiently, we formulate it as an optimization problem on an infinite periodic graph and reduce it to a special type of parametric assignment problem. We exactly solve the problem under consideration in $O(n^3)$ time, where n is the number of flights performed by UAVs.

Keywords: sustainable scheduling; fleet of drones; maximizing the environmental benefit; polynomial-time algorithm

Citation: Kats, V.; Levner, E. Maximizing the Average Environmental Benefit of a Fleet of Drones under a Periodic Schedule of Tasks. *Algorithms* **2024**, *17*, 283. https://doi.org/10.3390/a17070283

Academic Editors: Alexandre Dolgui, David Lemoine, María I. Restrepo and Frank Werner

Received: 7 May 2024
Revised: 24 June 2024
Accepted: 24 June 2024
Published: 28 June 2024

Copyright: © 2024 by the authors. Licensee MDPI, Basel, Switzerland. This article is an open access article distributed under the terms and conditions of the Creative Commons Attribution (CC BY) license (https://creativecommons.org/licenses/by/4.0/).

1. Introduction

Transport by road and air is one of the largest contributors to the highest greenhouse gas emissions and fuel consumption in the logistics industry. In recent years, due to rising carbon dioxide emissions and fuel costs, the issue of sustainable daily scheduling of transport operations aimed at reducing environmental pollution has attracted increasing interest and concern from large logistics companies. In such a situation, unmanned aerial vehicles (UAVs, drones) are not just a technological advancement based on modern ideas of artificial intelligence but actually provide a sustainable solution to green technologies in logistics, transport, and material handling. In this light, the ability of UAVs to carry out sustainable autonomous deliveries efficiently and effectively has been researched and explored by large logistics companies (e.g., DHL Express, UPS), e-commerce retailers, and companies (e.g., Walmart, Google) [1,2].

The environmental benefits of UAVs are universal and intertwined with economic and social benefits; their environmental friendliness has systematically improved in recent years as drone delivery technologies (e.g., batteries, autonomous navigation, obstacle avoidance, and detection algorithms) have been greatly improved. Because drones are much smaller than trucks and airplanes, drones generally cost less and consume less energy and fuel per unit distance traveled. Furthermore, most delivery drones consume electricity, which can be generated from clean energy sources such as solar or wind, so they emit fewer harmful emissions per unit of energy consumed compared to traditional trucks and airplanes while also increasing the efficiency of clean technologies.

We observe that the environmental benefits of UAVs are mainly driven by the overall benefits and profits of modern digital and artificial intelligence-based technologies. They were comprehensively studied and classified by Dolgui and Ivanov [3,4]. Here, we select and highlight three main factors that directly lead to environmental benefits and economic profits:

- Using battery-powered UAVs in the air instead of trucks on the road can significantly reduce energy and fuel expenses;
- It reduces environmental pollution, carbon dioxide emissions, and other negative impacts of transport processes on the environment;
- It improves the efficiency of clean technologies by increasing energy-saving efficiency.

A broader and more detailed categorization of the relevant environmental benefits of UAVs is beyond the scope of this article. The interested reader is referred to the available comprehensive surveys and studies in this area cited therein [1,2,5–7].

It is known that scheduling and routing of vehicles subject to external, in particular, environmental constraints, is a complex combinatorial problem that, generally, is NP-hard, meaning it cannot be solved optimally for large instance sizes in reasonable (polynomial) computational time [8,9]. In this regard, a practical alternative would be either to obtain efficient exact algorithms for practically important special cases of the problem or to develop fast and sufficiently effective approximation algorithms. Increased theoretical and practical interest in this problem and its applications has been noted, for example, in a number of reviews [1,2,5–7]. For a detailed description of various problem formulations, models, and corresponding algorithms for the general drone fleet assignment problem, we refer the interested reader to the surveys [10–15], which provide excellent reviews of work in this area.

In what follows, we limit our attention to graph models for maximizing the average UAV fleet profit and solve this optimization problem in strongly polynomial time, reducing it to a special type of parametric assignment problem. In addition to the results presented in the above-mentioned reviews and the works cited there, the main contributions of this paper are as follows:

(i) We present and explore a new, environmentally oriented problem of finding the optimal number of vehicles that maximizes the average profit of a UAV fleet; (ii) the maximum-profit problem for a UAV fleet is formulated as a graph-theoretic problem and reduced to a parametric assignment problem; (iii) a new efficient algorithm for the parametric assignment problem has been developed, which continues and extends the well-known polynomial algorithms of Ford and Fulkerson, Karzanov and Livshits, and Orlin for robotics and aircraft flight scheduling; (iv) the parametric assignment problem under study is exactly solved in strongly polynomial time using a Newton-type algorithm; and finally; (v) a method is introduced to speed up the Newton-type algorithm by a factor of n, which exactly solves the original UAV fleet scheduling problem in $O(n^3)$ time, where n is the given number of flights.

The rest of the article is organized as follows: In the next section, we describe previous work. In Section 3, we describe the problem under study. In Section 4, we reformulate it as a graph-theoretic problem of maximizing the average total weight of a chain cover on an infinite graph; then we re-construct the infinite graph into an equivalent finite graph; as a result, the problem under consideration is reduced to the problem of covering the nodes of the last graph with a set of cycles that maximizes the average total weight. Section 5 reformulates the cycle-covering problem as a bi-matrix assignment problem and reduces the latter problem to a particular type of fractional assignment problem (FAP). Section 6 reduces FAP to a parametric assignment problem, and Section 7 solves it using Newton's method. Section 8 improves the complexity of the latter algorithm. Section 9 concludes the paper.

2. Previous Work

Since we realize that the general problem under study is very complex (NP-hard in fact) and large in size, making it difficult to solve exactly, the challenge is to decompose it into smaller and simpler sub-problems that can be solved efficiently and thus provide the "building blocks" for solving the overall problem. We are interested in finding a special case that, on the one hand, makes the problem solvable and, on the other hand, gives good upper/lower bounds on the objective functions of the general optimization problem.

The special case studied in this paper is an extension of the problem of minimizing the number of vehicles (airplanes, drones, robots, cars, etc.) needed to meet a fixed, periodically repeating schedule of tasks. This optimization problem has a long history in operations research. A non-periodic, finite-horizon version of the problem, concerned with minimizing the number of tankers to meet a fixed schedule, was solved in 1954 by Dantzig and Fulkerson [16]. A few years later, Ford and Fulkerson [17] reduced that problem to finding a chain cover of minimum cardinality for finitely partially ordered sets. Using an infinite periodic graph model and a chain covering, Karzanov and Livshits [18] elegantly reduced the periodic minimum-size vehicle problem to an assignment problem solvable in polynomial time. Kats [19] has modified and slightly simplified the Karzanov–Livshits algorithm. Orlin [20] proposed a chain-covering algorithm for the periodic case, where a finite number of tasks must be executed periodically over an infinite horizon to efficiently solve the problem as a finite network flow problem. Kats and Levner [21,22] proposed a periodic graph model that solved a similar scheduling problem with non-Euclidean distances. Orlin [23] has solved the more general problem of minimizing the average fleet cost per day of flying subject to a fixed number of aircraft; however, this optimization problem is different from the problem in this study, and besides this, it involves a solution technique induced from dynamic minimum-cost network flows that is substantially different from the technique presented here. Campbell and Hardin [24] considered the problem of minimizing the number of vehicles required to make periodic deliveries to a set of customers under the assumption that each delivery requires the use of a vehicle for a full day; they thoroughly examined the problem structure, evaluated its complexity, and presented an algorithm that optimally solved the problem for some special cases. Extensive reviews of UAV fleet size optimization techniques and industrial applications are presented, for example, in [12–15].

In this paper, we present and explore a more general case of the vehicle scheduling problem; namely, our goal is to find the optimal number of vehicles that maximizes the average environmental fleet benefit per vehicle and, thereby, the UAV fleet's environmental efficiency. This problem is a continuation and extension of the models studied in [16–23]. Note that the optimal number of vehicles in the latter problem may be strictly greater than the minimum number of vehicles required to meet a given periodic schedule. We propose a new fast algorithm, the logic and main stages of which are presented in Figure 1.

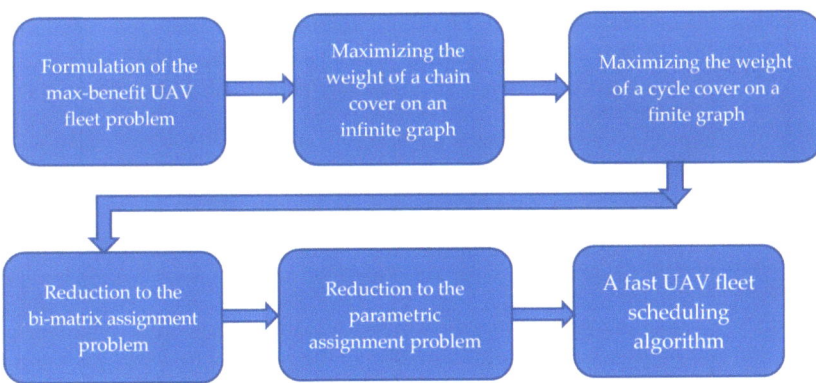

Figure 1. Schematic diagram of the proposed fast algorithm.

3. Description of the Problem

Let $J_1, \ldots, J_n$ be a set of n tasks (e.g., flights) that must be carried out periodically by a fleet of drones, and let p denote a given period length. Associated with task J_i are non-negative real numbers a_i and b_i such that $a_i < p$ and $b_i < p$, where a_i and b_i are the start and finish times of task J_i in the time interval $[0, p)$, respectively. If $a_i < b_i$, then the kth iteration (or instance) of task J_i is executed in the time interval $[a_i + kp, b_i + kp)$. If $a_i > b_i$, then the kth iteration of task J_i is performed in the time interval $[a_i + kp, b_i + (k+1)p)$, for $k = 0, 1, 2, \ldots$. Thus, the times $a_i, b_i, i = 1, \ldots, n$, define a predetermined periodic schedule for all tasks.

Any task can be conducted by any autonomous vehicle, and any vehicle can carry out any task. We use this assumption to simplify the presentation of our algorithm, though, in fact, the proposed general graph approach can be extended to handle multiple aircraft types and efficiently solve other combinatorial problems. There is a known setup time r_{ij} between the sequential processing of instances of task J_i and task J_j by the same vehicle. The setup time r_{ij} is the required delay between the arrival of flight J_i and the departure of flight J_j, assuming the same aircraft is used for both flights. It is allowed that the arrival site s for flight J_i may differ from the departure site t for flight J_j; in this case, the setup time r_{ij} will include the deadhead time from s to t.

Unlike the known models mentioned above, this study takes into account not only the size of the fleet but also the environmental *benefit* (profit) accrued from using the UAV fleet, which depends on the fleet size and the assignment of tasks performed by the vehicles. Suppose that profit e_{ij} is accrued from the use of a UAV when performing task J_j following task J_i; this quantity is known in advance, while the number of vehicles and the assignment of tasks to vehicles are the decision variables that need to be found.

Let K be the (unknown) number of vehicles required to meet a periodic fixed schedule, and let E be the total environmental profit obtained by all vehicles over period p. Then our problem to be solved is the following:

Problem 1. *Assign tasks to vehicles so as to maximize the ratio.*

$$E/K = \frac{\text{Total environmental benefit accrued from the use of the UAV fleet over period } p}{\text{Number of vehicles required to meet a fixed schedule of tasks}},$$

That is, to maximize the average benefit obtained by the fleet of vehicles over the period for a given task schedule, which is defined by the known times $\{a_i, b_i, i = 1, \ldots, n\}$.

Remark 1. *In the verbal formulation of Problem **1** above, we do not reveal the explicit dependence of the total environmental benefit on the distribution of vehicles among tasks. This will be explained and formalized below in Problems **4** and **FAP** in the following sections.*

Remark 2. *The reader may notice that the problem under consideration in its current formulation resembles the well-known vehicle allocation problem. The latter problem, in its various forms, is known to be NP-hard (see, for example, [8,20,25,26]). However, in this paper, we will prove that the problem under study can be solved in polynomial time; this is because this problem has a special structure that greatly reduces the problem's complexity.*

4. Reduction to Graph Problems

Consider an infinite weighted periodic graph G_∞, which is constructed as follows: $G_\infty = (N_\infty, A_\infty)$, where N_∞ is an infinite set of nodes and A_∞ is an infinite set of arcs. In this graph, node $i_k \in N_\infty$ represents the kth iteration of task J_i. A directed arc $(i_k, j_l) \in A_\infty$ leads from node i_k to node j_l if the vehicle is able to carry out the lth iteration of task J_j after it has completed the kth iteration of task J_i. The weight of the arc (i_k, j_l) represents the profit e_{ij} collected by the vehicle from serving the task J_j following the task J_i. Let us formulate all profits e_{ij} in the form of the $n \times n$ matrix $E = \|e_{ij}\|$.

Consider a periodic directed chain in graph G_∞. Note that the period of such a chain can span several periods, p, as defined in the previous section. The chain determines the schedule of an individual vehicle visiting a sequence of tasks, and the sum of its arc weights e_{ij} determines the profit earned by that vehicle during that period. The set of directed chains in G_∞ covering all nodes determines the total number of required vehicles, their schedule, and the total environmental benefit obtained. Thus, the original allocation Problem **1** is reduced to the following graph-theoretic problem on the infinite graph G_∞:

Problem 2. *Find a periodic infinite chain cover of graph G_∞ that maximizes the following average environmental benefit (profit) obtained by the UAV fleet:*

$$E/K = \frac{\text{Total environmental profit obtained by the UAV fleet in period } p}{\text{Number of vehicles required}} = \frac{\text{Sum of arc weights } e_{ij} \text{ in chain cover in period } p}{\text{Number of directed chains covering nodes}}$$

The next step is to transform the infinite graph G_∞ into an equivalent finite graph. Due to the periodicity of the graph G_∞, we can roll it up into the so-called finite *generating graph*, $G_{gen} = (N_{gen}, A_{gen})$, defined as follows: node $i \in N_{gen}$ represents all periodic implementations of task J_i; in other words, all nodes $i_k \in N_\infty$, $0 \leq k < \infty$, of the infinite graph G_∞ are "packed" into one node i of the graph G_{gen}. Similarly, all arcs $(i_k, j_l) \in A_\infty$ are "packed" into one arc $(i, j) \in A_{gen}$. Thus, every infinite, periodically repeated arc chain in graph G_∞ can be transformed into a corresponding directed cycle in graph G_{gen}. Knowing the generating graph G_{gen}, we can transform Problem **2** of covering graph G_∞ with chains into the following Problem **3** of covering the nodes of the graph G_{gen} with cycles. Let c denote a set of such cycles.

Problem 3. *Find a covering of the nodes of the graph G_{gen} with a set of cycles c so as to maximize the ratio.*

$$E/K = \frac{\sum_{(i,j) \in c} e_{ij}}{\text{Number of required vehicles}}$$

Next, we associate two weights with each arc $(i, j) \in A_{gen}$. The first weight is the profit e_{ij} introduced above. The second weight, denoted k_{ij}, is needed to calculate the required number of vehicles. It is defined similarly to the model in [20]; namely, k_{ij} is the number of periods p that must exist between an arbitrary departure iteration $k(i)$ of a flight J_i and the departure iteration $l(j)$ of the flight J_j that is closest to J_i in the graph G_∞, provided that the two flights are operated by the same aircraft; it is possible that $j = i$. Then,

$$k_{ij} = l(j) - k(i). \tag{1}$$

For the reader's convenience, consider the definition of the weight k_{ij} in more detail. Let $k(i)$ be an arbitrary integer, and the symbol $k(i)$ denotes that the flight J_i occurs during the $k(i)$-th period. Further, suppose that in graph G_∞, there are arcs from the node representing the flight J_i to all other nodes representing iterations (repetitions) of the flight J_j; it is clear that then, in our notation, the numbers $\{k(j)\}$ will denote the numbers showing in which periods those repetitions of J_j occur. Among these numbers, $k(j)$, choose the minimum one—this number is denoted as $l(j)$. Then, as stated above, $k_{ij} = l(j) - k(i)$. In other words, after completing the $k(i)$th iteration of task J_i, the vehicle does not have enough time to arrive and carry out the $(l(j) - 1)$th iteration of task J_j but has time to successfully perform the $l(j)$th iteration of task J_j.

Remark 3. *Since the process under consideration is periodic, the values k_{ij} are valid for all task iterations. As we will show shortly, the sum of k_{ij} over all cycles in any cycle covered in the graph G_{gen} is equal to the number of vehicles required to meet a given schedule.*

Remark 4. *Formally, the main property of the parameter $l(j)$ can be presented as follows: Let d_i denote the duration of the flight, J_i, that is,*

$$d_i = b_i - a_i, \text{ if } a_i < b_i \text{ and}$$

$$d_i = b_i + p - a_i, \text{ if } a_i > b_i.$$

Then, the following inequalities hold:

$$a_j + (l(j) - 1) \cdot p < a_i + k(i) \cdot p + d_i + r_{ij} \leq a_j + l(j) \cdot p.$$

Thus, we introduce the $n \times n$ matrix $\mathbf{K} = \|k_{ij}\|$ with the entries k_{ij} just described. If the arc (i, j) does not exist in the graph G_{gen}, then we set $e_{ij} = 0$ and $k_{ij} = \infty$. To obtain this matrix, we need $O(n^2)$ time.

Consider a small example to illustrate the above definition of k_{ij} in Equation (1). Assume that we have three tasks: J_1, J_2, J_3; $p = 10$, $a(J_1) = a_1 = 5$, $b(J_1) = b_1 = 8$; $a(J_2) = a_2 = 9$, $b(J_2) = b_2 = 2$; $a(J_3) = a_3 = 4$, $b(J_3) = b_3 = 9$; $r_{12} = 2$, $r_{13} = 1$, $r_{21} = 1$, $r_{23} = 3$. Let us consider, for example, the 12*th* iteration of these tasks, i.e., set $k(1) = 12$, $k(2) = 12$, and $k(3) = 12$; then the task J_1 will be executed in the time interval [125, 128], the task J_2—in the time interval [129, 132], and the task J_3 in the time interval [124, 129]. Therefore, the nearest iteration of task J_2 that can be performed by the same vehicle, which has performed the 12th iteration of J_1, will be the 13th iteration. Therefore, the nearest iteration of task J_3, which can be performed by the same vehicle following the 12th iteration of J_1, will also be the 13th iteration. Hence, $k_{12} = k_{13} = 13 - 12 = 1$. Similarly, we obtain that $k_{23} = 14 - 12 = 2$; $k_{21} = 1$.

At this point, let us recall a remarkable property of the weights k_{ij} in the periodic minimum-size vehicle problem, discovered by Karzanov and Livshits [18] in 1978 and independently by Orlin [20] in 1982, that establishes a direct connection between the *minimum number* of vehicles required and the *minimum-weight cycle cover* of the graph G_{gen}, the arc weights of which are the weights k_{ij} defined by Equation (1). Denote by c an arbitrary cycle cover of the generating graph G_{gen}, and S the set of all possible cycle covers of the graph G_{gen}.

The Karzanov–Livshits–Orlin Theorem. A *minimum-weight* cycle cover, having the total weight $\min_{c \in S} \sum_{(i,j) \in c} k_{ij}$, provides the *minimum number* of vehicles K_{min} required to perform a given task schedule: $K_{min} = \min_{c \in S} \sum_{(i,j) \in c} k_{ij}$.

For our further analysis, we need to extend the above claim to formulate it for the bi-matrix optimization Problem 3:

Proposition 1. *Let c be an arbitrary cycle cover of the generating graph G_{gen} with two arc weights, e_{ij} and k_{ij}, where k_{ij} is the weight defined by Equation (1). Then, the total weight $\sum_{(i,j) \in c} k_{ij}$ of the cycle cover is equal to the number of vehicles K required to carry out all the tasks in the considered cycle cover c in Problem 3: $K = \sum_{(i,j) \in c} k_{ij}$.*

Proof. Let σ be a simple cycle entering the cycle cover c of the generating graph G_{gen} with two arc weights, and let $s = \sum_{(i,j) \in \sigma} k_{ij}$. Consider the periodic graph G_∞ that corresponds to the initial Problem 2, which has generated the generating graph G_{gen}. Recall that each node $i \in \sigma$ corresponds to an infinite number of nodes i_k in graph G_∞, $0 \leq k < \infty$. As proven in [20], a cycle σ can be unpacked into exactly s chains in graph G_∞ such that no node in one chain is linked to a node in another chain. From the description of Problem 2 and the definition of the cycle weight, it follows that each chain corresponds to one vehicle performing the tasks of the chain, and then the value $\sum_{(i,j) \in \sigma} k_{ij}$ is equal to the number of vehicles required to carry out all the tasks of the cycle σ. To complete the proof, it suffices to notice that the graph G_{gen} can be partitioned into a set c composed of a finite number of simple cycles, and therefore, the total number of chains $\sum_{(i,j) \in c} k_{ij}$ corresponding to all simple cycles in partition c is equal to the number of vehicles required, which proves the claim.

From Proposition 1, it follows that Problem 3 reduces to the following Problem 4. □

Problem 4. *Find a cycle cover of the graph G_{gen} with a set of cycles c, so as to maximize the ratio $E/K = \sum_{(i,j) \in c} e_{ij} / \sum_{(i,j) \in c} k_{ij}$.*

The question remains: how to efficiently solve the resulting cycle-covering problem for the graph G_{gen}? We will answer this question in the following sections:

The illustrative example. For the reader's convenience, consider a numerical example. It is adapted from the work of Orlin [20], who studied the problem of minimizing the number of aircraft to operate a fixed daily repeating set of flights; we generalize Orlin's example for the problem of maximizing the average fleet profit. While the latter numerical example was used in [20] to schedule daily aircraft flights, it is extended here to also serve to illustrate all the steps of the proposed algorithm for maximizing the average benefit of a drone fleet.

4.1. Model of the Fixed Daily Repeating Set of Drone Flights

Three daily flights are shown in Table 1.

Table 1. Daily required flights.

Flight No.	Departure	Arrival
1	Honolulu, 1:00 p.m.	Washington, DC, 11:00 p.m.
2	New York, 3:00 p.m.	Tokyo, 4:00 a.m.
3	London, 1:00 p.m.	Paris, 2:00 p.m.

It is also necessary to take into account the "deadhead" time, that is, the time that a given aircraft takes after completing a flight to reach the departure location of the next scheduled flight. The deadhead times are given in Table 2.

Table 2. The deadhead flight times are in hours.

From \ To	Honolulu	London	New York
Paris	15	1	7
Tokyo	8	12	13
Washington	10	7	1

In the notation introduced above, the input data from Tables 1 and 2 are given in Table 3. Tasks J_1, J_2, and J_3 represent flights 1, 2, and 3, respectively.

Table 3. Input data.

Flight No.	Departure	Arrival		Setup Times r_{ij}		
i	a_i	b_i	i \ j	1	2	3
1	13	23	1	10	1	7
2	15	4	2	8	13	12
3	13	14	3	15	7	1

We consider a daily repeating schedule of flights; therefore, the period length p is 24 h.

4.2. Reduction to a Problem on a Periodic Graph

Let the profits be given by the following matrix E:

$$E = \begin{pmatrix} 300 & 900 & 600 \\ 600 & 600 & 1200 \\ 900 & 300 & 300 \end{pmatrix}$$

Using the flight schedule given in Table 3, it is possible to plot graph G_∞. A fragment of graph G_∞ drawn for three consecutive periods, starting with period 1, is presented in Figure 2.

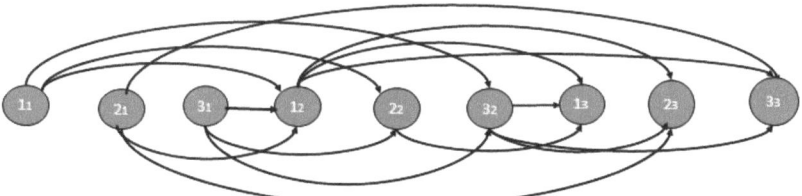

Figure 2. A 3-period fragment of the graph G_∞.

The nodes in Figure 2 depict the daily flights denoted 1, 2, 3 and repeated for three sequential periods indexed by 1, 2, and 3; node i_k depicts flight i ($i = 1, 2, 3$) during period k ($k = 1, 2, 3$). For simplicity of notation, Figure 2 shows only the arcs (i_k, j_l) between the nearest iterations k and l of tasks J_i and J_j. Each arc (i_k, j_l) in G_∞ has the associated weight $e(i, j)$. However, the weights are not shown in Figure 2 in order not to overload it. At this point, our initial fleet assignment problem is equivalent to finding the optimal number of infinite periodic disjoint paths covering all nodes and having a maximum average profit per path per period.

4.3. Construction of the Generating Graph

According to the above description, the finite graph G_{gen} can be portrayed as follows (see Figure 3):

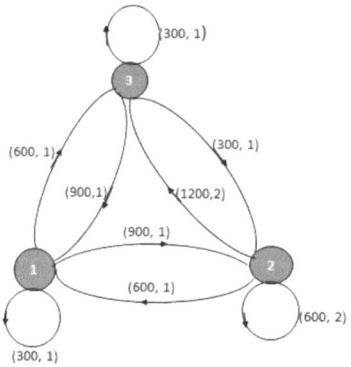

Figure 3. Generating graph G_{gen}.

Each arc is double-weighted, and the weight of arc (i, j) has the form (e_{ij}, k_{ij}), where the number k_{ij} is determined by arc (i_k, j_l) in Figure 2, $k_{ij} = l - k$ ($i, j = 1, 2, 3$). Note that the generating network for the airplane scheduling example presented in [20] is different from the graph G_{gen}; namely, the arcs of the graph G_{gen} are double-weighted, whereas in the Orlin graph, the weights on arcs (i, j) are specified by a single number.

4.4. Calculation of the Second Weight k_{ij}

According to the definition of the second weight k_{ij} and the data in Table 1, we see that flights 1 and 3 can be repeated every period (every day) by the same aircraft (the arc from node 1_1 to node 1_2 and the arc from node 3_1 to node 3_2 in Figure 2); therefore, $k_{11} = k_{33} = 1$. Flight 2 can be repeated by the same vehicle every two days; therefore, $k_{22} = 2$. Further, if an aircraft starts its flight no. 2 at 15:00 in the first period (node 2_1 in Figure 2), then it can start the nearest flight no. 3 only after 13 + 12 = 25 h, i.e., on the third day at 13:00 (node 3_3 in Figure 2); hence, $k_{23} = 3 - 1 = 2$. Similarly, we compute all other values k_{ij} shown in Figure 3 and the following matrix K:

$$K = \begin{pmatrix} 1 & 1 & 1 \\ 1 & 2 & 2 \\ 1 & 1 & 1 \end{pmatrix}$$

The illustrative numerical example will be continued and completed in Section 7.

5. Reduction to the Fractional Assignment Problem

In this section, we reformulate Problem 4 as a fractional assignment problem. Recall that an *assignment* can be stated in the form of an $n \times n$ matrix A whose entries, denoted a_{ij}, are 0 or 1, and $a_{ij} = 1$ occurs in each row and each column of the matrix A exactly once.

Consider Problem 4, defined in the previous section, and the corresponding cycle cover of the graph G_{gen}.

Proposition 2. *The set of all cycles in the cycle cover $c = (C_1, C_2, \ldots, C_q)$ of the graph G_{gen}, where q is the number of cycles in c, can be considered as an $n \times n$ assignment A in the matrix form defined as follows:*

$$a_{ij} = 1 \text{ if and only if the arc } (i,j) \text{ from } G_{gen} \text{ belongs to } c, \text{ and } a_{ij} = 0 \text{ otherwise.} \quad (2)$$

Indeed, from the definition of the cycle cover, it follows that the matrix A contains n rows and n columns, its elements are 1 or 0, and each $a_{ij} = 1$ occurs exactly once for each row i and each column j ($i, j = 1, \ldots, n$), which proves the claim.

Given a profit matrix E, a weight matrix K, and an arbitrary assignment matrix A, the profit and weight values corresponding to the assignment A are defined, respectively, as follows:

$$E(A) = \sum_{(i,j) \in A} e_{ij} a_{ij} \text{ and } K(A) = \sum_{(i,j) \in A} k_{ij} a_{ij}.$$

In the above expression and wherever necessary, the notation $(i,j) \in A$ denotes all pairs of indices i, j corresponding to entries $a_{ij} = 1$ of the assignment matrix A. For ease of notation, in the expressions $E(A)$ and $K(A)$ below, we will omit the symbol a_{ij}. In what follows, in accordance with (2), instead of maximizing $P = \sum_{(i,j) \in c} e_{ij} / \sum_{(i,j) \in c} k_{ij}$ over all cycle covers of the graph G_{gen} (Problem 4), we will focus on finding the *optimal assignment* that maximizes $P = E(A)/K(A) = \sum_{(i,j) \in A} e_{ij} / \sum_{(i,j) \in A} k_{ij}$.

Let us denote by $\mathbf{C}$ the set of all assignments A in the form of $n \times n$ matrices. Now Problem 4 in Section 2 reduces to the following fractional assignment Problem 5 (FAP):

Problem 5 (FAP). *Given two $n \times n$ matrices E and K, find the optimal assignment A^*, common to the matrices E and K, that is, the one that maximizes the average fleet profit per vehicle $P = E(A)/K(A)$:*

$$P^* = E(A^*)/K(A^*) = \max_{A \in \mathbf{C}} E(A)/K(A) = \max_{A \in \mathbf{C}} \sum_{(i,j) \in A} e_{ij} / \sum_{(i,j) \in A} k_{ij}.$$

The following statement shows that the elements of matrix K in the considered problem are the small positive integers not exceeding 3; in fact, this is an important property that reduces the complexity of the problem by a factor of n.

Proposition 3. *If the arc $(i, j) \in G_{gen}$, then, for any element k_{ij} of matrix K, it holds that $k_{ij} \leq 3$.*

Proof. Consider the $k(i)$th iteration of task J_i that starts at time $a_i + k(i) \cdot p$, and let $l(j)$ be the nearest iteration of task J_j that the vehicle can perform after the $k(i)$th iteration of task J_i. Consider two cases: $a_i < b_i$ and $a_i > b_i$.

(i) $a_i < b_i$.

In this case, the $k(i)$th iteration of task J_i ends at time $b_i + k(i) \cdot p$. Then, the nearest iteration of task J_j satisfies the following inequalities:

$$a_j + [l(j) - 1] \cdot p < b_i + k(i) \cdot p + r_{ij} \leq a_j + l(j) \cdot p,$$

or

$$a_j + [l(j) - k(i) - 1] \cdot p < b_i + r_{ij} \leq a_j + [l(j) - k(i)] \cdot p.$$

(ii) $a_i > b_i$.

In this case, the $k(i)$th iteration of task J_i ends at time $b_i + [k(i) + 1] \cdot p$. Then, the nearest iteration of task J_j satisfies the following inequalities:

$$a_j + [l(j) - 1] \cdot p < b_i + [k(i) + 1] \cdot p + r_{ij} \leq a_j + l(j) \cdot p,$$

or

$$a_j + [l(j) - k(i) - 1] \cdot p < b_i + p + r_{ij} \leq a_j + [l(j) - k(i)] \cdot p.$$

From the definition of $k_{ij} = l(j) - k(i)$ in Section 2, it immediately follows that each element k_{ij} is an integer satisfying the following relations:

$$a_j + (k_{ij} - 1) \cdot p < b_i + r_{ij} \leq a_j + k_{ij} \cdot p, \text{ if } a_i < b_i$$

and

$$a_j + (k_{ij} - 1) \cdot p < b_i + p + r_{ij} \leq a_j + k_{ij} \cdot p, \text{ if } a_i > b_i.$$

This means that, due to the given time constraints, the element k_{ij} is equal to the minimum number of periods p that the vehicle must skip before it can start task J_j after it has started task J_i. Since each task (flight) J_j is to be executed in every period p, the vehicle must skip k_{ij} instances of task J_j in the skipped periods.

It is natural to assume that all the setup times are $r_{ij} < p$; then, from the definition of k_{ij}, we derive that the largest value of k_{ij} can appear only in the following inequalities:

$$a_j + (k_{ij} - 1) \cdot p < b_i + p + r_{ij} \leq a_j + k_{ij} \cdot p. \tag{3}$$

Suppose that $b_i > a_j$ and $p > r_{ij} > p - (b_i - a_j)$. Then, on the one hand, we have that

$$b_i + p + r_{ij} > b_i + p + p - (b_i - a_j) = a_j + 2p, \tag{4}$$

and, on the other hand, $b_i < a_j + p$; then we have that

$$b_i + p + r_{ij} \leq (a_j + p) + p + p = a_j + 3p. \tag{5}$$

Comparing inequalities (3)–(5), we find that, in this case, $k_{ij} = 3$. Q.E.D. □

6. Reduction to the Parametric Assignment Problem

In this section, we reduce the fractional assignment problem **FAP** with the objective function P defined above to a parametric assignment problem. Let us introduce a parameter λ that, for each assignment A from the set **C** of all assignments, satisfies the following inequality:

$$\sum_{(i,j) \in A} e_{ij} / \sum_{(i,j) \in A} k_{ij} \leq \lambda, \text{ for all } A \in \mathbf{C}. \tag{6}$$

Since the sum $\sum_{(i,j)\in A} k_{ij}$ is positive in any assignment A, inequalities (6) can be rewritten as follows:

$$\sum_{(i,j)\in A} e_{ij} \leq \lambda \sum_{(i,j)\in A} k_{ij}$$

or

$$0 \leq \lambda \sum_{(i,j)\in A} k_{ij} - \sum_{(i,j)\in A} e_{ij}$$

and, finally,

$$0 \leq \sum_{(i,j)\in A} (\lambda\, k_{ij} - e_{ij}) \text{ for all } A \in \mathbf{C}. \tag{7}$$

Thus, problem **FAP** of finding the maximum average profit P^* presented in the previous section takes the following form:

To find the minimum λ that satisfies (6), or, equivalently, to find the minimum λ that satisfies (7).

Consider the matrix $\mathbf{W}(\lambda) = \lambda \cdot \mathbf{K} - \mathbf{E}$ with entries $w_{ij} = (\lambda \cdot k_{ij} - e_{ij})$, called *arc costs*, or simply *costs*. Consider some fixed value of λ. Let $A^*(\lambda)$ denote the assignment with the minimum cost across all the assignments $A \in \mathbf{C}$, defined as follows:

$$\sum_{(i,j)\in A^*(\lambda)} (\lambda \cdot k_{ij} - e_{ij}) = \min_{A \in \mathbf{C}} \sum_{(i,j)\in A} (\lambda \cdot k_{ij} - e_{ij}), \tag{8}$$

and denote the latter function, called the *minimum-cost function*, by $L(\lambda)$:

$$L(\lambda) = \sum_{(i,j)\in A^*(\lambda)} (\lambda \cdot k_{ij} - e_{ij}). \tag{9}$$

Proposition 4 below states that the assignment problem of finding the maximum average fleet profit P^*, defined in problem **FAP**, can be reduced to the following parametric minimum-cost assignment problem **PAP**:

Problem 6 (PAP). *Find the value of the parameter $\lambda = \lambda^*$ for which the minimum-cost function $L(\lambda)$ is equal to zero:*

$$L(\lambda) = \sum_{(i,j)\in A^*(\lambda)} (\lambda \cdot k_{ij} - e_{ij}) = 0, \tag{10}$$

and, further, together with the optimal value of the parameter λ^*, find the corresponding minimum-cost assignment $A^*(\lambda^*)$ for the matrix $\mathbf{W}(\lambda^*)$; for the simplicity of notation, we denote the latter assignment by Φ^*: $\Phi^* = A^*(\lambda^*)$.

Proposition 4. *Let λ^* be the optimal solution to the problem **PAP**, and $\Phi^* = A^*(\lambda^*)$ be the corresponding minimum-cost assignment for the matrix $\mathbf{W}(\lambda^*)$. Then,*

$$\lambda^* = P^* = \sum_{(i,j)\in A^*} e_{ij} / \sum_{(i,j)\in A^*} k_{ij} = \max_{A \in \mathbf{C}} \sum_{(i,j)\in A} e_{ij} / \sum_{(i,j)\in A} k_{ij},$$

and $\Phi^* = A^*$,

*that is, in meaningful terms, (i) the value of $\lambda = \lambda^*$ defined by expression (10) is equal to the optimal profit value P^*, which we are looking for, and (ii) the assignment Φ^*, which is optimal for the problem **PAP**, coincides with the optimal assignment A^* for the maximum average fleet profit in the problem **FAP**.*

Proof. From Equation (10), we have:

$$L(\lambda^*) = \sum_{(i,j)\in A^*(\lambda^*)} (\lambda^* \cdot k_{ij} - e_{ij}) = 0. \tag{11}$$

In addition, from (8), we have:

$$\sum_{(i,j)\in A^*(\lambda^*)} (\lambda^* \cdot k_{ij} - e_{ij}) = \min_{A \in \mathbf{C}} \sum_{(i,j)\in A} (\lambda^* \cdot k_{ij} - e_{ij}).$$

Then,

$$\sum_{(i,j)\in A} (\lambda^* \cdot k_{ij} - e_{ij}) \geq 0 \text{ for all } A \in \mathbf{C}. \tag{12}$$

Thus, from (11), we obtain that

$$\lambda^* = \sum_{(i,j) \in A^*(\lambda^*)} e_{ij} / \sum_{(i,j) \in A^*(\lambda^*)} k_{ij},$$

and from (12), we have

$$\lambda^* \geq \sum_{(i,j) \in A} e_{ij} / \sum_{(i,j) \in A} k_{ij} \text{ for all } A \in \mathbf{C},$$

that is, $\lambda^* = P^*$ and $\Phi^* = A^*$, which completes the proof. □

The following claim is an extension of Proposition 4 that formulates a way of how we can optimally and efficiently solve the optimization problem PAP:

Corollary 1. *Let λ^* be the optimal parameter value, i.e., one such that*

$$L(\lambda^*) = \sum_{(i,j) \in A^*(\lambda)} (\lambda \cdot k_{ij} - e_{ij}) = 0.$$

Then, the parameter λ^* represents the maximum average profit per vehicle in the problem under study, and $K(A^*) = \sum_{(i,j) \in A^*} k_{ij}$ is equal to the optimal number of required vehicles, where $A^* = A^*(\lambda^*)$.

In the following sections, we propose two strongly polynomial time algorithms for the parametric assignment problem under consideration, which in turn optimally solve the problem of maximizing the average profit of a fleet of identical vehicles.

7. A Newton-Type Algorithm for the Parametric Assignment Problem

Consider the cost value $w(A, \lambda) = \sum_{(i,j) \in A} (\lambda \cdot k_{ij} - e_{ij})$ of an arbitrary assignment A, whose costs are the elements of the matrix $W(\lambda)$. This value is a linear function $w(A, \lambda) = (d_A \lambda - f_A)$ of the parameter λ, where $d_A = \sum_{(i,j) \in A} k_{ij}$ is the slope and $f_A = \sum_{(i,j) \in A} e_{ij}$. In the UAV model considered, each $k_{ij} \leq 3$, so $d_A \leq 3n$. Let A be a collection of q cycles—$A = (C_1, C_2, \ldots, C_q)$. Consider an arbitrary cycle $C \in (C_1, C_2, \ldots, C_q)$. The sum of the elements k_{ij} over the cycle C is not less than one; $\sum_{(i,j) \in C} k_{ij} \geq 1$. Indeed, if $C = \{i_1, i_2 = j(i_1), i_3 = j(i_2), \ldots, i_s = j(i_{s-1}), i_1 = j(i_s)\}$, then after task J_{i1}, the vehicle performs task J_{i2}, and after task J_{is}, the vehicle again performs task J_{i1}, but not at the same iteration as at the previous one. Two iterations of task J_{i1}, carried out by the same vehicle, are separated by a time interval equal to $\sum_{(i,j) \in C} k_{ij} \geq 1$ period. Therefore, $1 \leq d_A \leq 3n$.

There is a set of linear functions corresponding to different assignments A of the matrix $W(\lambda)$, each of which has the form:

$$\sum_{(i,j) \in A} (\lambda \cdot k_{ij} - e_{ij}), A \in \mathbf{C}.$$

According to (8) and (9), $L(\lambda)$ is a lower bound for the costs of all assignments $A \in \mathbf{C}$; it is an increasing concave piecewise linear function of the parameter λ with slope $\sum_{(i,j) \in A^*(\lambda)} k_{ij}$. Since $1 \leq \sum_{(i,j) \in A^*(\lambda)} k_{ij} \leq 3n$, the number of pieces in $L(\lambda)$ does not exceed $3n$.

Let us select some arbitrary value, $\lambda = \lambda'$. Determine the corresponding minimum-cost assignment $A' = A^*(\lambda')$ and the corresponding cost as follows:

$$L(\lambda') = \sum_{(i,j) \in A'} (\lambda' k_{ij} - e_{ij}). \tag{13}$$

Consider the function $d_{A'} \lambda - f_{A'} = \sum_{(i,j) \in A'} (\lambda \cdot k_{ij} - e_{ij})$. Let us select a starting value λ' such that it is so small that $L(\lambda') < 0$, then $\lambda' < \sum_{(i,j) \in A'} e_{ij} / \sum_{(i,j) \in A'} k_{ij} \leq \lambda^*$. The first inequality follows from (13); the second inequality follows from (12). Now we can set a new value of λ' that is equal to $\sum_{(i,j) \in A'} e_{ij} / \sum_{(i,j) \in A'} k_{ij}$. Then, determine the minimum-cost assignment for the updated $\lambda = \lambda'$. This procedure must be continued until the optimal solution λ^* of the problem **PAP** is found. The following Algorithm 1 implements the described idea.

Algorithm 1. Implementation of the described idea.

Initialization
Step 1. Solve the standard assignment problem for the known matrix K (using a standard assignment algorithm). Denote by I the obtained optimal (minimum-cost) assignment for this matrix.
Step 2. Calculate the average profit λ_0 received for the obtained assignment I:
$$\lambda_0 = \sum\nolimits_{(i,j) \in I} e_{ij} / \sum\nolimits_{(i,j) \in I} k_{ij}.$$
(Note that at this stage, $\lambda_0 \leq \lambda^*$, where λ^* is the maximum average profit that we are looking for).
Step 3. Set $i = 0$.
Iterative procedure
Step 4. Find the minimum-cost assignment $A^*(\lambda_i)$ for the matrix $W(\lambda_i)$.
Step 5. Calculate the average profit λ_{i+1} of the assignment $A^*(\lambda_i)$:
$$\lambda_{i+1} = \sum\nolimits_{(i,j) \in A^*(\lambda i)} e_{ij} / \sum\nolimits_{(i,j) \in A^*(\lambda i)} k_{ij}.$$
Step 6. If $\lambda_{i+1} > \lambda_i$ then {set $i = i + 1$; go to Step 4},
else go to step 7.
Solution
Step 7. Set the maximum average profit per vehicle: $P^* = \lambda^* = \lambda_i$.
Set the optimal assignment $\Phi^* = A^*(\lambda_i)$
Determine the optimal number of vehicles needed to meet the obtained schedule:
$$K = \sum\nolimits_{(i,j) \in \Phi^*} k_{ij}.$$
End.

The proposed algorithm is a discrete version of Newton's optimization method adapted to solving Equation (10).

7.1. Complexity of Algorithm 1

In Algorithm 1, in the iterative procedure (Steps 4–6 above), the slope of the minimum-cost function $L(\lambda)$ in (9), $\sum_{(i,j) \in A^*(\lambda i)} k_{ij}$, decreases, i.e.,

$$\sum\nolimits_{(i,j) \in A^*(\lambda i)} k_{ij} > \sum\nolimits_{(i,j) \in A^*(\lambda i+1)} k_{ij}.$$

Therefore, steps 4–6 return at most $O(n)$ times. Each pass of the iterative procedure solves the assignment problem once. The complexity of solving the assignment problem is $O(n^3)$, which is repeated at most $O(n)$ times. Thus, the overall complexity of Algorithm 1 is $O(n^4)$.

7.2. The Illustrative Example (Continued)

7.2.1. Reduction to the Fractional FAP and Parametric PAP Problems

Problem FAP. Given two $n \times n$ matrices E and K, defined in the previous step, find the *optimal* assignment A^*, common to the matrices E and K, that is, the one that maximizes the average fleet profit per vehicle $P = E(A)/K(A)$:

$$P^* = E(A^*)/K(A^*) = \max\nolimits_{A \in C} E(A)/K(A) = \max\nolimits_{A \in C} \sum\nolimits_{(i,j) \in A} e_{ij} / \sum\nolimits_{(i,j) \in A} k_{ij}.$$

To solve this problem, we reduce it to the following parametric assignment problem:
Problem PAP. Find the value of the parameter $\lambda = \lambda^*$ for which the minimum-cost function $L(\lambda)$ is equal to zero: $L(\lambda) = \sum_{(i,j) \in A^*(\lambda)} (\lambda \cdot k_{ij} - e_{ij}) = 0$, and find the corresponding minimum-cost assignment $A^*(\lambda^*)$ for the matrix $W(\lambda^*)$.

7.2.2. Solution of the Parametric Assignment Problem by the Newton-Type Algorithm

Let us solve the standard minimum-weight assignment problem with the matrix K. We can see that assignment $I = \{C_1 = [(1, 2), (2, 1)]; C_2 = (3, 3)\}$ is optimal for this standard single-matrix problem, $\sum_{(i,j) \in I} k_{ij} = k_{1,2} + k_{2,1} + k_{3,3} = 3$. This is the minimum number of vehicles required to meet the given flight schedule.

Calculate the average profit received with the assignment I:

$$\lambda_0 = (900 + 600 + 300)/(1 + 1 + 1) = 600.$$

The value λ_0 can be taken as the lower bound of the desired maximum average profit P^*, $600 \leq P^*$.

Consider the following matrix $W(\lambda_0 = 600)$:

$$W(600) = \begin{pmatrix} 600 \cdot 1 - 300 & 600 \cdot 1 - 900 & 600 \cdot 1 - 600 \\ 600 \cdot 1 - 600 & 600 \cdot 2 - 600 & 600 \cdot 2 - 1200 \\ 600 \cdot 1 - 900 & 600 \cdot 1 - 300 & 600 \cdot 1 - 300 \end{pmatrix} = \begin{pmatrix} 300 & -300 & 0 \\ 0 & 600 & 0 \\ -300 & 300 & 300 \end{pmatrix}$$

The optimal assignment $A^*(\lambda_0 = 600)$ of the matrix $W(\lambda_0 = 600)$ is as follows:

$$A^*(\lambda_0 = 600) = \{C = [(1, 2), (2, 3), (3, 1)]\}.$$

The cost of the assignment $A^*(\lambda_0 = 600)$ at point $\lambda_0 = 600$ is negative; $w(A^*, \lambda_0) = -300 + 0 + (-300) = -600$. Therefore, $\lambda_0 = 600$ is not an optimal solution to the **PAP** problem considered. This means that the average profit λ_1 obtained with the assignment $A^*(\lambda_0)$ is greater than λ_0: $\lambda_1 = (900 + 1200 + 900)/(1 + 2 + 1) = 750$.

Now, in a similar way, consider the following matrix $W(\lambda_1 = 750)$:

$$W(750) = \begin{pmatrix} 750 \cdot 1 - 300 & 750 \cdot 1 - 900 & 750 \cdot 1 - 600 \\ 750 \cdot 1 - 600 & 750 \cdot 2 - 600 & 750 \cdot 2 - 1200 \\ 750 \cdot 1 - 900 & 750 \cdot 1 - 300 & 750 \cdot 1 - 300 \end{pmatrix} = \begin{pmatrix} 450 & -150 & 150 \\ 150 & 900 & 300 \\ -150 & 450 & 450 \end{pmatrix}$$

The optimal assignment $A^*(\lambda_1 = 750)$ of the matrix $W(\lambda_1 = 750)$ is the same as $A^*(\lambda_0 = 600)$. The cost of the assignment $A^*(\lambda_1 = 750)$ at the point $\lambda_1 = 750$ is zero; $w(A^*, \lambda_1) = -150 + 300 + (-150) = 0$. Thus, $\lambda^* = \lambda_1 = 750$ is the optimal solution to our PAP problem, and according to Proposition 4, the maximum average profit per aircraft is $P^* = \lambda^* = 750$.

7.2.3. Solution of the Original Vehicle Fleet Optimization Problem

The optimal assignment $A^*(\lambda_1 = 750)$ consists of only one cycle $C = [(1, 2), (2, 3), (3, 1)]$. It corresponds to the following optimal sequence of flights:

Flight 1 from Honolulu to Washington, DC, then deadheading flight to New York, then

Flight 2 from New York to Tokyo, then a deadheading flight to London,

Flight 3 from London to Paris, then a deadheading flight to Honolulu.

The considered circular route C takes four days; $\sum_{(i,j)\in C} k_{ij} = k_{1,2} + k_{2,3} + k_{3,1} = 4$. This schedule requires four aircraft, each repeating the same sequence of flights as the previous one, lagging behind it in time by a day. This is the optimal number of aircraft in the considered example. Note that in this illustrative example, the optimal number of vehicles is four, and the minimum number of vehicles required to meet a given flight schedule is three; the optimal average fuel efficiency obtained in this example (i.e., for four vehicles) is 20% better than the corresponding fuel efficiency for the minimum number of vehicles required; $(750 - 600)/750 = 0.2$.

7.2.4. Discussion

The Newton-type algorithm proposed in this section is relatively simple and easy to program. The question arises whether an algorithm of similar or even better complexity can be obtained for the problem under study if one exploits the existing polynomial algorithms for the general fractional assignment problem. However, all polynomial algorithms for the general fractional assignment problem known to us (see, e.g., [26–30]) have a total running time similar to or worse than $O(n^4)$, even in the case where the coefficients of the linear function in the denominator of the fractional objective are restricted to the values {0, 1}.

However, unlike these studies, we found another way to speed up the solution time of the Newton-type algorithm. In the next section, we present an improved algorithm that can solve the parametric assignment problem under study in $O(n^3)$ time and, hence, can optimally solve the original max-benefit UAV fleet problem in $O(n^3)$ time.

8. A Faster Parametric Assignment Algorithm

8.1. Comparison of Two Parametric Assignment Problems

Reducing the original aircraft profit maximization Problem **1** to the special-type parametric assignment problem **PAP** formulated in Section 6 opens an opportunity to exploit another solution algorithm that is faster than the Newton-type algorithm proposed in the previous section. For this purpose, we adapt and use, after appropriate adaptation, a fast and elegant parametric assignment algorithm developed more than a decade ago by Elizabeth Gassner and Bettina Klinz [31].

Although the parametric assignment problem solved by Gassner and Klinz is similar to the assignment problem described above and denoted PAP, the two problems are quite different and cannot be solved by simply changing the sign of the objective function. Actually, we should make the necessary changes to the Gassner–Klinz algorithm (GKA) to make the adapted version of GKA applicable to solve the PAP in question. We begin by comparing two related parametric assignment problems, focusing on their differences (see Table 4). Note that the significant difference between the two studies is that the present work is motivated and focused on the practical aircraft fleet assignment problem, while the problem in [31] is rooted in and limited to an application in the max-plus algebra.

Table 4. Comparison of two assignment problems.

	Gassner and Klinz [31]	Problem PAP in This Paper
Problem formulation	Given a bipartite graph G and parametric arc costs $c_\lambda(i,j) = (c_{ij} - \lambda \cdot b_{ij})$, find the *minimum of objective function* $z(\lambda) = \{\sum_{(i,j) \in A} c_\lambda(i,j): A$ is an assignment in $G\}$, for all $\lambda \in R$ together with the corresponding optimal assignments.	Given a matrix W with parametric entry costs $w_\lambda(i, j) = (\lambda \cdot k_{ij} - e_{ij})$ and the *minimum cost function* $L(\lambda) = \sum_{(i,j) \in A^*(\lambda)} (\lambda \cdot k_{ij} - e_{ij})$, find a *parameter value* $\lambda = \lambda^*$ for which the $L(\lambda) = 0$ and the optimal assignment $A^*(\lambda^*)$ (see Figure 4)
Parametric arc costs	$c_\lambda(i,j) = (c_{ijj} - \lambda \cdot b_{ij})$, where $b_{ij} = 0, 1$	$w_\lambda(i,j) = (\lambda \cdot k_{ij} - e_{ij})$, where $k_{ij} = 0, 1, 2, 3$
Decision to be found	To solve the problem for all λ in $(-\infty, +\infty)$ and to find all the assignments.	To find a single value λ^* and a single assignment, for which $L(\lambda) = 0$
Practical application	To solve the problem of computing the characteristic max-polynomial of a matrix in the max-plus algebra.	To solve the problem of maximizing the average profit for a fleet of vehicles.

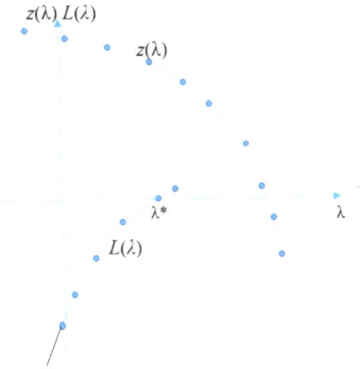

Figure 4. Graph of two objective functions, $z(\lambda)$ of the Gassner–Klinz problem and $L(\lambda)$ of the average fleet profit maximization problem.

8.2. A Brief Review of the Gassner–Klinz Algorithm and Its Adaptation

The GKA algorithm aims to solve the parametric assignment problem described in Table 4 for *all possible* values of parameter λ; its worst-case complexity is $O(n^3)$. That is, the same as that for the standard (non-parametric) linear assignment problem. In contrast to the Newton-type Algorithm 1, the GKA does not solve each of the $O(n)$ assignment problems appearing at critical points but rather solves an assignment problem only once and then transforms the obtained assignment into a new one with certain local operations so that the minimum-cost assignments for all the values of λ are found in $O(nm + n^2 \log n)$ time, where m and n are the number of arcs and the number of nodes, respectively, in an underlying bipartite graph described below. We will follow the same idea of the GKA and adapt it, adding necessary changes, in order to take into account that the objective functions in the two problems are different (see Table 4).

Since the two optimization problems in Table 4 are very close, it suffices to replace $c_\lambda(i, j) = (c_{ij} - \lambda \cdot b_{ij})$ in the Gassner–Klinz problem by $c'_\lambda(i,j) = (c'_{ij} - \lambda \cdot b'_{ij}) = (-e_{ij} - \lambda \cdot (-k_{ij}))$ and then use the existing algorithm GKA. In this case, the slope of the parametric objective function in the derived problem (which, obviously, in this case, will be our PAP) will be positive and will decrease with the growth of parameter λ until $L(\lambda)$ becomes zero, whereas the slope of the objective function in the original Gassner–Klinz problem is negative and its absolute value increases when the parameter increases to infinity (see Figure 4). Another observation is that in the original Gassner–Klinz problem, $b_{ij} \in \{0, 1\}$, whereas b'_{ij} are to be $\{0, -1, -2, -3\}$; however, this difference can be easily overcome, and it does not influence the algorithm complexity. Finally, the starting point and the stopping rule are different in the GKA and in the modified algorithm. Indeed, when solving the PAP problem, one does not need to solve the assignment problems at all the critical points for all possible $\lambda \in (-\infty, +\infty)$; rather, the modified algorithm starts with a known lower bound of the parameter and stops as soon as the cost $L(\lambda)$ of a current assignment becomes zero.

Below, for the reader's convenience, we review the proposed modification of the GKA and, in order to give a more complete picture, describe the steps of the adapted algorithm. For easier comparison, in this subsection, we borrow graph-theoretic terminology from [31] to describe the modified algorithm.

Consider the parametric assignment problem as a minimum-cost matching problem in a bipartite graph $G = (U, V, W)$, where the vertices U and V correspond, respectively, to the rows and columns of the matrix $W(\lambda)$, $|U| = |V| = n$, $|W| = m$. Arc $(i, j) \in W$ only if arc (i, j) exists in the graph G_{gen}. Arcs lead from set U to set V. The parametric cost of arcs $(i, j) \in W$ is $w(i, j) = (\lambda \cdot k_{ij} - e_{ij})$, where $i \in U$ and $j \in V$, i.e., the element of the matrix $w_{ij} \in W(\lambda)$ is equal to the cost of the arc (i, j), $w(i, j) = w_{ij}$.

Let $A^*(\lambda')$ be a minimum-cost assignment in graph G for $\lambda = \lambda'$. Exactly as in [31], we associate with the graph G and assignment $A = A^*(\lambda')$ a residual graph $N(A) = (U, V, W^*)$ constructed as follows: All the arcs $(i, j) \in A$, where $i \in U$ and $j \in V$, are replaced by *backward arcs* (j, i) of cost $w(j, i) = -w(i, j) = (-\lambda \cdot k_{ij} + e_{ij})$.

Note that it is at this point that we make changes that need to be made because the coefficients k_{ij} in our objective function have the opposite sign compared with the corresponding b_{ij} in the GKA.

The remaining arcs, called *forward arcs*, as well as their costs, remain the same as in graph G. Graph $N(A)$ has no cycles with a negative cost for $\lambda = \lambda'$. Let us increase parameter λ and let λ_c be the minimum value of λ such that in the residual graph $N(A)$, there is a cycle C with zero cost, $w(C, \lambda_c) = 0$, and $w(C, \lambda) < 0$ when $\lambda > \lambda_c$. Value λ_c and cycle C are the *critical point* and *critical cycle*, respectively. The assignment A remains a minimum-cost assignment in the interval $\lambda \in [\lambda', \lambda_c]$. Then, in the interval $\lambda \in [\lambda_c, \lambda'_c]$, where λ'_c is a critical point next to the critical point λ_c, the minimum-cost assignment changes to $A' = (A \setminus C') \cup (C' \setminus A)$, where C' is a subset of the arcs obtained from the C by replacing all the backward arcs with the corresponding forward arcs; the cost of A' changes to $w(A', \lambda) = w(A, \lambda) + w(C, \lambda)$. It is worth noticing at this stage that the following essential property is valid: when the parameter λ increases, the objective function of our problem also increases, while the objective function in the Gassner–Klinz problem decreases (see Figure 4). At point $\lambda = \lambda_c$, the costs of assignments A and A' are equal; $w(A, \lambda_c) = w(A', \lambda_c)$. By changing the cost and the direction of all the arcs in cycle C to opposite ones in the residual graph $N(A)$, one obtains the residual graph $N(A')$.

The following question is crucial: Starting with the minimum-weight assignment A for $\lambda = \lambda'$, how can one determine the critical point λ_c? Recall that in the residual graph $N(A)$, for $\lambda = \lambda'$, there are no cycles with a negative cost, and that when the parameter λ increases, some cycle C with a zero cost appears only at the point $\lambda = \lambda_c$, $w(C, \lambda_c) = 0$. To determine this cycle, we follow the approach proposed in [31] and also use the parametric shortest path algorithm of Karp and Orlin [32] and its improved version in [33].

Let us take some vertex s as the source vertex in the graph $N(A)$ and build a shortest path tree $T(\lambda) = T(\lambda')$ for $\lambda = \lambda'$. As λ increases from λ' to λ_c, the tree $T(\lambda)$ is transformed; namely, some arcs are replaced by others. The values of λ at which the tree changes are called breakpoints. Let us denote these breakpoints in ascending order as $\mu_1, \mu_2,$ and μ_l. Denote $T_r = T(\lambda)$, $\lambda \in [\mu_r, \mu_{r+1}]$, where $r = 0, 1, 2, \ldots, l - 1$. Tree $T_{l-1} = T(\lambda)$, where $\lambda \in [\mu_{l-1}, \mu_l]$, is the last constructed tree. Since in our problem of fleet assignment $\mu_l \neq \infty$, it follows that a zero-weight cycle C appears in $N(M)$ at $\lambda = \mu_l$, and at $\lambda > \mu_l$, the weight of the cycle C becomes negative. This means that μ_l is a critical point, and $\lambda_c = \mu_l$. At each breakpoint, the slope of any path can only decrease. Since at each breakpoint, at least one path to a vertex changes, the number of breakpoints is limited to $O(n^2)$. Thus, it turns out that transforming the current assignment into a new one at a critical point is simpler than solving the assignment problem anew.

The steps of the modified GKA adapted for solving our **PAP** problem are the following Algorithm 2:

Algorithm 2. The modified GKA adapted for solving our **PAP** problem.

Step 1. *Initialization*
1.1. Solve the initial standard assignment problem for the known matrix K. Denote by I the obtained optimal (minimum-cost) assignment.
1.2. Calculate the average profit λ_0 achieved with the obtained assignment I:
$$\lambda_0 = \sum_{(i,j) \in I} e_{ij} / \sum_{(i,j) \in I} k_{ij}.$$
//This step is different from the corresponding initialization step in the original GKA.
1.3. Find the minimum-cost assignment $A = A^*(\lambda_0)$ in the graph G for $\lambda = \lambda_0$.
1.4. Construct the residual graph $N(A)$.
Step 2. *Finding the nearest critical point.*
//In this step, we take into account that in the objective function, the term $b'_{ij} = -k_{ij}$ is of the opposite sign compared to the Gassner–Klinz assignment problem.
2.1. Apply the parametric shortest path algorithm to find the nearest critical point λ_c and the critical cycle C for which $w(C, \lambda_c) = 0$.
2.2. Calculate the cost of the assignment A at the point $\lambda = \lambda_c$:
$$w(A, \lambda_c) = \lambda_c \sum_{(i,j) \in A} k_{ij} - \sum_{(i,j) \in A} e_{ij}.$$
//When we increase the values of parameter λ from one critical point to the next, we stop and go to Step 3.1 at the moment when we find (for the first time) a current assignment A such that $w(A, \lambda_c) \geq 0$. According to Proposition 4 in Section 4, this assignment A maximizes the average fleet profit per vehicle.
2.3. If $w(A, \lambda_c) \geq 0$, go to Step 3.
2.4. Create the new minimum-cost assignment $A' = (A \setminus C') \cup (C' \setminus A)$.
//C' is a subset of arcs obtained from C by replacing all the backward arcs with the corresponding forward arcs.
2.5. Convert graph $N(A)$ to graph $N(A')$; set $N(A) := N(A')$ and $A := A'$.
2.6. Return to Step 2.1.
Step 3. *Solution of the vehicle scheduling problem*
//This step is absent in the GKA because the max-benefit UAV fleet problem was not a subject studied by Gassner and Klinz.
//Let us denote by A^* the optimal assignment, which maximizes the average fleet profit per vehicle; $\sum_{(i,j) \in A^*} k_{ij}$ expresses the corresponding optimal number of the required vehicles.
3.1. Set the assignment that maximizes the average fleet profit per vehicle: $A^* = A$. Calculate the maximal average profit $P^* = \lambda^* = \sum_{(i,j) \in A^*} e_{ij} / \sum_{(i,j) \in A^*} k_{ij}$.
3.2. Calculate the optimal number of vehicles, which is $\sum_{(i,j) \in A^*} k_{ij}$, to meet the given vehicle schedule.
End.

Evidently, the adapted version of GKA has the same complexity as the original GKA, and hence, the original max-benefit UAV fleet problem is solved in $O(n^3)$ time.

9. Conclusions

In this article, we consider the problem of scheduling/assigning periodically repeated flights performed by a fleet of UAVs/drones. We extend the known scheduling/assignment problem for minimizing the number of aircraft to a more general problem of maximizing the average drone fleet profit per vehicle.

The main contribution of the present study is two-fold. First, we formulate and optimally solve a new bi-matrix average fleet profit maximization model using profit and capacity matrices, which is a special case of airline fleet assignment problems widely used in the airline industry. Secondly, the aircraft fleet profit optimization problem is reduced to a special type of parametric assignment problem. Moreover, we find a way to speed up the solution time of a Newton-type algorithm and provide an improved algorithm that solves the initial aircraft assignment problem in question in $O(n^3)$ time. Such a noticeable improvement in the worst-case algorithm complexity (by a factor of n) allows us to optimally solve the profit maximization problem for significantly larger fleets of UAVs than any previously known exact algorithm.

In addition to the above, the special case problem solved in this study clearly not only has its own merits but can also serve as a "building block" for solving more complex problems. For example, it can be used as a "warm start" for solving a mathematical programming-based model using branch-and-bound strategies.

A challenging open question for further research is to find other solvable cases of the general max-profit fleet assignment/scheduling problem. We believe that the proposed graph approach to problem analysis and algorithm design can be extended and applied to efficiently solve other combinatorial periodic assignment/scheduling problems, such as minimizing fuel consumption and CO_2 emissions, planning periodic maintenance checks and recovery operations for unexpected disruptions, dynamic scheduling of periodic and sporadic tasks in real time for large-size fleets, and others.

Author Contributions: Conceptualization, V.K. and E.L.; formal analysis, E.L.; investigation, V.K. and E.L.; methodology, E.L.; validation, V.K. and E.L.; visualization, V.K.; writing—original draft preparation, V.K. and E.L.; writing—review and editing, E.L. All authors have read and agreed to the published version of the manuscript.

Funding: This research received no external funding.

Data Availability Statement: The original contributions presented in the study are included in the article, further inquiries can be directed to the corresponding author.

Conflicts of Interest: The authors declare no conflicts of interest.

References

1. Engesser, V.; Rombaut, E.; Vanhaverbeke, L.; Lebeau, P. Autonomous Delivery Solutions for Last-Mile Logistics Operations: A Literature Review and Research Agenda. *Sustainability* **2023**, *15*, 2774. [CrossRef]
2. Rejeb, A.; Rejeb, K.; Simske, S.J.; Treiblmaier, H. Drones for supply chain management and logistics: A review and research agenda. *Int. J. Logist. Res. Appl.* **2021**, *26*, 708–731. [CrossRef]
3. Dolgui, A.; Ivanov, D. Ripple effect and supply chain disruption management: New trends and research directions. *Int. J. Prod. Res.* **2021**, *59*, 102–109. [CrossRef]
4. Dolgui, A.; Ivanov, D. 5G in digital supply chain and operations management: Fostering flexibility, end-to-end connectivity and real-time visibility through internet-of-everything. *Int. J. Prod. Res.* **2021**, *60*, 442–451. [CrossRef]
5. Shakhatreh, H.; Sawalmeh, A.H.; Al-Fuqaha, A.; Dou, Z.; Almaita, E.; Khalil, I.; Othman, N.S.; Khreishah, A.; Guizani, M. Unmanned Aerial Vehicles (UAVs): A Survey on Civil Applications and Key Research Challenges. *IEEE Access* **2019**, *7*, 48572–48634. [CrossRef]
6. Manfreda, S.; McCabe, M.F.; Miller, P.E.; Lucas, R.; Madrigal, V.P.; Mallinis, G.; Ben Dor, E.; Helman, D.; Estes, L.; Ciraolo, G.; et al. On the Use of Unmanned Aerial Systems for Environmental Monitoring. *Remote Sens.* **2018**, *10*, 641. [CrossRef]
7. Maffezzoli, F.; Ardolino, M.; Bacchetti, A.; Perona, M.; Renga, F. Agriculture 4.0: A systematic literature review on the paradigm, technologies and benefits. *Futures* **2022**, *142*, 102998. [CrossRef]

8. Garey, M.; Graham, R.; Johnson, D. Some NP-complete geometric problems. In Proceedings of the 8th Annual ACM Symposium on Theory of Computing, Hershey, PA, USA, 3–5 May 1976; pp. 10–22.
9. Psaraftis, H.N.; Wen, M.; Kontovas, C.A. Dynamic vehicle routing problems: Three decades and counting. *Networks* **2015**, *67*, 3–31. [CrossRef]
10. Rave, A.; Fontaine, P.; Kuhn, H. Drone location and vehicle fleet planning with trucks and aerial drones. *Eur. J. Oper. Res.* **2023**, *308*, 113–130. [CrossRef]
11. Zhang, K.; Lu, L.; Lei, C.; Zhu, H.; Ouyang, Y. Dynamic operations and pricing of electric unmanned aerial vehicle systems and power networks. *Transp. Res. Part C Emerg. Technol.* **2018**, *92*, 472–485. [CrossRef]
12. Balac, M.; Vetrella, A.R.; Rothfeld, R.; Schmid, B. Demand Estimation for Aerial Vehicles in Urban Settings. *IEEE Intell. Transp. Syst. Mag.* **2019**, *11*, 105–116. [CrossRef]
13. Otto, A.; Agatz, N.; Campbell, J.; Golden, B.; Pesch, E. Optimization approaches for civil applications of unmanned aerial vehicles (UAVs) or aerial drones: A survey. *Networks* **2018**, *72*, 411–458. [CrossRef]
14. Attenni, G.; Arrigoni, V.; Bartolini, N.; Maselli, G. Drone-Based Delivery Systems: A Survey on Route Planning. *IEEE Access* **2023**, *11*, 123476–123504. [CrossRef]
15. She, R.F. Design of Freight Logistics Services in the Era of Autonomous Transportation. Doctoral Dissertation, University of Illinois at Urbana-Champaign, Champaign, IL, USA, 2023.
16. Dantzig, G.B.; Fulkerson, D.R. Minimizing the number of tankers to meet a fixed schedule. *Nav. Res. Logist. Q.* **1954**, *1*, 217–222. [CrossRef]
17. Ford, L.R.; Fulkerson, D.R. *Flows in Networks*; Princeton University Press: Princeton, NJ, USA, 1962.
18. Karzanov, A.V.; Livshits, E.M. Minimal quantity of operators for serving a homogeneous linear technological process. *Autom. Remote Control* **1978**, *39 Pt 2*, 538–542.
19. Kats, V.B. An exact optimal cyclic scheduling algorithm for multi-operator service of a production line. *Autom. Remote Control* **1982**, *43 Pt 2*, 538–542.
20. Orlin, J.B. Minimizing the Number of Vehicles to Meet a Fixed Periodic Schedule: An Application of Periodic Posets. *Oper. Res.* **1982**, *30*, 760–776. [CrossRef]
21. Kats, V.; Levner, E. Minimizing the number of robots to meet a given cyclic schedule. *Ann. Oper. Res.* **1997**, *69*, 209–226. [CrossRef]
22. Kats, V.; Levner, E. Minimizing the number of vehicles in periodic scheduling: The non-Euclidean case. *Eur. J. Oper. Res.* **1998**, *107*, 371–377. [CrossRef]
23. Orlin, J.B. Minimum Convex Cost Dynamic Network Flows. *Math. Oper. Res.* **1984**, *9*, 190–207. [CrossRef]
24. Campbell, A.M.; Hardin, J.R. Vehicle minimization for periodic deliveries. *Eur. J. Oper. Res.* **2005**, *165*, 668–684. [CrossRef]
25. Kochenberger, G.A.; Glover, F.; Alidaee, B.; Rego, C. A unified modeling and solution framework for combinatorial optimization problems. *OR Spectr.* **2004**, *26*, 237–250. [CrossRef]
26. Kabadi, S.N.; Punnen, A.P. A strongly polynomial simplex method for the linear fractional assignment problem. *Oper. Res. Lett.* **2008**, *36*, 402–407. [CrossRef]
27. Megiddo, N. Combinatorial Optimization with Rational Objective Functions. *Math. Oper. Res.* **1979**, *4*, 414–424. [CrossRef]
28. Gallo, G.; Grigoriadis, M.D.; Tarjan, R.E. A Fast Parametric Maximum Flow Algorithm and Applications. *SIAM J. Comput.* **1989**, *18*, 30–55. [CrossRef]
29. Shigeno, M.; Saruwatari, Y.; Matsui, T. An algorithm for fractional assignment problems. *Discret. Appl. Math.* **1995**, *56*, 333–343. [CrossRef]
30. Radzik, T. Newton's method for fractional combinatorial optimization. In Proceedings of the 33rd Annual Symposium on Foundations of Computer Science, Pittsburgh, PA, USA, 24–27 October 1992; pp. 659–669.
31. Gassner, E.; Klinz, B. A fast parametric assignment algorithm with applications in max-algebra. *Networks* **2009**, *55*, 61–77. [CrossRef]
32. Karp, R.M.; Orlin, J.B. Parametric shortest path algorithms with an application to cyclic staffing. *Discret. Appl. Math.* **1981**, *3*, 37–45. [CrossRef]
33. Young, N.E.; Tarjant, R.E.; Orlin, J.B. Faster parametric shortest path and minimum-balance algorithms. *Networks* **1991**, *21*, 205–221. [CrossRef]

Disclaimer/Publisher's Note: The statements, opinions and data contained in all publications are solely those of the individual author(s) and contributor(s) and not of MDPI and/or the editor(s). MDPI and/or the editor(s) disclaim responsibility for any injury to people or property resulting from any ideas, methods, instructions or products referred to in the content.

Article

The Parallel Machine Scheduling Problem with Different Speeds and Release Times in the Ore Hauling Operation

Luis Tarazona-Torres, Ciro Amaya *, Alvaro Paipilla, Camilo Gomez and David Alvarez-Martinez

Industrial Engineering Department, University of Los Andes, Cra 1 N18A12, Bogota 111711, Colombia; le.tarazona@uniandes.edu.co (L.T.-T.); a.paipilla@uniandes.edu.co (A.P.); gomez.ch@uniandes.edu.co (C.G.); d.alvarezm@uniandes.edu.co (D.A.-M.)
* Correspondence: ca.amaya@uniandes.edu.co

Abstract: Ore hauling operations are crucial within the mining industry as they supply essential minerals to production plants. Conducted with sophisticated and high-cost operational equipment, these operations demand meticulous planning to ensure that production targets are met while optimizing equipment utilization. In this study, we present an algorithm to determine the minimum amount of hauling equipment required to meet the ore transport target. To achieve this, a mathematical model has been developed, considering it as a parallel machine scheduling problem with different speeds and release times, focusing on minimizing both the completion time and the costs associated with equipment use. Additionally, another algorithm was developed to allow the tactical evaluation of these two variables. These procedures and the model contribute significantly to decision-makers by providing a systematic approach to resource allocation, ensuring that loading and hauling equipment are utilized to their fullest potentials while adhering to budgetary constraints and operational schedules. This approach optimizes resource usage and improves operational efficiency, facilitating continuous improvement in mining operations.

Keywords: parallel machine scheduling problem; ore hauling equipment; mathematical model; mining industry

Citation: Tarazona-Torres, L.; Amaya, C.; Paipilla, A.; Gomez, C.; Alvarez-Martinez, D. The Parallel Machine Scheduling Problem with Different Speeds and Release Times in the Ore Hauling Operation. *Algorithms* **2024**, *17*, 348. https://doi.org/10.3390/a17080348

Academic Editors: Alexandre Dolgui, David Lemoine, María I. Restrepo and Frank Werner

Received: 2 May 2024
Revised: 24 July 2024
Accepted: 30 July 2024
Published: 8 August 2024

Copyright: © 2024 by the authors. Licensee MDPI, Basel, Switzerland. This article is an open access article distributed under the terms and conditions of the Creative Commons Attribution (CC BY) license (https://creativecommons.org/licenses/by/4.0/).

1. Introduction

One of the most essential activities in mining operations is ore hauling; this process involves moving fragmented rock from the blasting site using loading and hauling equipment [1]. The ore rocks are then transported to the crushing process to reduce their size before being sent to the recovery plant, where valuable metals such as copper, gold, molybdenum, and aluminum, among others, are extracted [2–4]. Figure 1 illustrates the schematic of the described process. Poor planning of ore hauling operations can decrease productivity levels, affect the achievement of production targets within the established timelines, and consequently impact operational costs. Several factors must be considered to effectively plan ore hauling operations, such as the amount of available loading and hauling equipment and their scheduled maintenance [5]. It is also essential to account for the established production targets, working hours, and topographic levels. Other important aspects include the ore grade, the number of available loading ramps for loading operations, and the environmental impact [6].

Mining companies have a defined amount of loading and hauling equipment allocated based on the production targets set for a specific period. It is crucial to determine the necessary amount of this equipment to efficiently transport ore rocks to control associated costs, which can be substantial depending on the time required to meet these targets [7]. Knowing the minimum amount of equipment needed optimizes operations and facilitates tactical analysis. This analysis enables better decision-making in the face of contingencies, ensuring the achievement of production targets at the lowest possible cost.

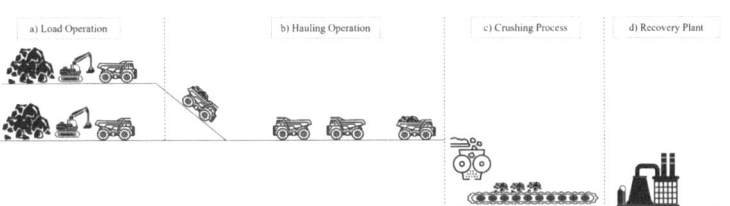

Figure 1. Schematic of the ore hauling operation.

As shown in Figure 1, the ore hauling process involves assigning hauling equipment to loading equipment. These do not necessarily operate at the same loading speed because some equipment have different loading capacities. The loading is performed simultaneously, and is described as a system of parallel machines with different speeds. Since the number of hauling equipment is finite, they are used as many times as necessary to meet the production target. However, they are unavailable while transporting the ore to the crushing process, having a "release time" before they are available again to be reloaded. Thus, this scenario can be adapted to a problem of parallel machines with different speeds and release times.

The novelty of this work lies in incorporating different speeds and release times into the mathematical model for parallel machine scheduling in mineral hauling operations (PMSPOHO). These features allow for a more realistic and accurate representation of operational conditions in the mining environment. The speed of the loading equipment plays a crucial role in this model. Variations in loading speeds can significantly impact the efficiency of the ore hauling operation. By considering different loading speeds, the model can more precisely allocate resources to match the dynamic nature of mining operations. This ensures that faster-loading equipment is utilized to its maximum potential while slower equipment is assigned tasks that better suit its capabilities, optimizing the overall workflow.

Incorporating the speed of the loading equipment into the scheduling algorithm maximizes equipment use and minimizes idle time for the hauling equipment. This enhances operational efficiency by reducing delays and ensuring a continuous flow of materials. The developed mathematical model addresses these critical variables, optimizing the allocation of hauling equipment, maximizing their use, and reducing idle time. This approach ensures greater operational efficiency by aligning equipment capabilities with the demands of the mining process. The strategic allocation of resources, guided by the speed and availability of each loading machine, contributes to a more streamlined and cost-effective operation, highlighting the importance of these variables in achieving optimal performance.

The mathematical model contributes significantly to several vital aspects. It facilitates more efficient planning and scheduling of hauling operations, allowing for dynamic adjustments based on changing conditions. Additionally, it enables a comparative analysis between costs and completion times, optimizing economic and productivity decisions. By reducing downtime and improving resource utilization, the model effectively addresses the logistical and financial challenges in mining operations and adapts to various operational scenarios, increasing its applicability and relevance in the sector. The remainder of this paper is structured as follows: Section 2 presents the related work. Section 3 details the methodology. Computational experiments and results analysis are discussed in Section 4. Finally, conclusions drawn from the study are presented in Section 5.

2. Related Works

Table 1 presents an overview of related works addressing the problem. It details the characteristics considered in our area of interest, such as release times (r_i) and different speeds (Q_m). The objective functions used are also analyzed, such as completion time (C_{max}) and costs (k), among others. Additionally, the solution methods employed are examined and categorized as exact or approximate, along with the number of machines utilized and the approaches adopted in each instance. This comparison allows for a visualization of the various methodologies and techniques implemented in the literature, highlighting their differences and similarities concerning the current analysis.

The characteristic r_i has yet to be sufficiently explored, particularly in mining research where the availability of hauling equipment is crucial, as shown by [8,9]. In contrast, studying Q_m has garnered more academic attention, though the focus largely remains on identical machines. Regarding the objective function, studies have generally centered on minimizing variables such as k and C_{max} in isolation. Meza [2] exemplifies a more complex integration, which incorporates a time and cost analysis of loading and hauling equipment through a simulation model. Hong and Lin [10] focused on minimizing maximum lateness (L_{max}), while Koryagin and Voronov [11] and Oliskevych et al. [12] considered meeting P as essential for maintaining operational continuity in production plants.

In comparison, our work significantly expands the level of analysis by including both Q_m and r_i, allowing us to model the production environments more realistically, especially in ore hauling operations. This is particularly relevant in configurations where the number of machines exceeds five, a scenario in which many studies prefer approximate methods due to their computational efficiency. Additionally, our approach includes an iterative study that enables tactical-level analysis to define the optimal utilization of equipment, complemented by robust analytical support for decision-making to maximize operational effectiveness. Our approach also incorporates a complexity analysis that has yet to be explored [10,13,14]. Thus, our work addresses a significant gap in the literature and provides critical insights that facilitate strategic decisions and enhance operational effectiveness in the mining industry.

Table 1. Related works on the parallel machine scheduling problem.

Reference	Characteristics		Objective Function			Methods		Num. Machines		Complexity Analysis	Approaches
	Q_m	r_i	C_{max}	k	Other	Exact	Approximate	$m \leq 5$	$m \geq 6$		
[2]	x		x	x			x		x		FIFO simulation model
[15]			x			x		x			Branch-and-price algorithm with single server
[16]			x			x	x	x	x		MIP formulation and hybrid heuristic algorithm with single server
[17]			x			x	x	x			MIP formulation and Tabu-Search with single server
[18]			x			x		x			MIP formulation with non-identical job sizes
[19]	x			x		x		x			MIP formulation
[20]	x			x		x		x			MILP formulation
[21]	x			x		x	x	x	x		MILP formulation and Insertion Heuristic under time-of-use tariffs
[22]	x			x		x		x			MILP formulation under time-of-use tariffs
[8]		x	x			x	x	x	x		MILP formulation and GA algorithm
[11]	x				P	x	x				Heuristic algorithm
[23]			x			x		x			MIP formulation with setup time and single server
[10]			x		L_{max}		x	x		x	Dynamic constructive algorithms
[24]			x			x	x				Constraint programming model under unavailabilityconstraints and modify LPT
[13]			x			x	x	x		x	MIP formulation and Tabu-Search

Table 1. Cont.

Reference	Characteristics		Objective Function			Methods		Num. Machines		Complexity Analysis	Approaches
	Q_m	r_i	C_{max}	k	Other	Exact	Approximate	$m \leq 5$	$m \geq 6$		
[25]				x		x			x		MIP formulation
[14]			x			x		x	x	x	MIP formulation with independent jobs
[26]	x		x			x		x			MIP formulation with function constrain
[12]	x			P	x			x			MIP formulation
[27]			x				x	x			Monte Carlo simulation model
[9]		x	x				x	x			VNS and ACO algorithms
[28]	x		x			x	x		x		MIP and TSP algorithm
[29]			x			x		x			Constraint programming model
[30]				x		x	x	x			MIP formulation and MOBSO algorithm
[31]	x			x		x	x	x			MILP formulation with time-of-use and SPT, MDPC, MDEC
[32]	x		x			x	x		x		MIP formulation and GA–GWO hybrid algorithm
Our paper	x	x	x	x		x		x	x	x	Iterative MIP formulation

Considering related studies on the optimization of the ore hauling operation, it was found that Meza [2] developed a model for the application of simulation concepts of a surface mining operation loading and hauling system, considering the type of loading and hauling equipment, arrival time, waiting time, positioning time, loading time, going time, setting time, unloading time, and return time, in addition to the number of trips as a production target, and considering a FIFO system for loading and unloading. On the other hand, Vasquez et al. [3] performed an integer programming model to minimize the total working time of a low-profile loader fleet in an underground mine, in addition to developing a polynomial time optimal algorithm integrated into the decision-making process, obtaining results quite close to the optimal total time. Eivazy and Askari-Nasab [33] developed a multi-destination mixed integer linear programming (MILP) model to minimize operations costs in surface mining; in the model, they considered stockpiles and mixing piles in addition to horizontal direction loading systems and ramp decision-making. Anjomshoa et al. [34] developed a simulation and mixed integer programming model (MIP) to optimize overtaking bays, sizing, and scheduling hauling equipment fleet in underground mining.

Moreover, Gligoric [35] developed an investigation on the overtaking bays for hauling equipment in underground mining, in which they sought to optimize the necessary amount of bays and the optimal location to minimize waiting times. Gonen et al. [36] conducted a study for underground mining where they evaluated annual production capacities with different hauling systems, considering unit hauling costs and mine depth. Eivazy and Askari-Nasab [37] presented a methodology based on production scheduling hierarchies for surface mining for the medium term, developing an MILP to minimize operating costs; the scheduling included stockpiles, processing plants, and dumps, as well as a selection of routes and ramps. Tom-Socarras [38] generated a tool for cost management based on a decision tree for material transportation in surface mining. Uribe [39] developed a study that analyzed the functionality and performance of semi-automatic operation in loading and hauling equipment used in underground mining. Więcek [40] proposed a suitable method for controlling the loading and transporting of ore in a mine with a piles and chambers system. Wiest [41] developed a scheduling model for surface mining, focusing on cost reduction.

Solomon [42] modeled ore loading and hauling systems in surface mining, developing a model that considered the excavation face, routes, equipment, and ore destinations. Gaspar and Jhasmin [43] analyzed utilization and availability indicators for ore hauling cost optimization. Li et al. [44], in their research for underground mining, developed a bee swarm algorithm to maximize the total revenue during a planning period; in addition, they created a genetic algorithm for the planning for hauling equipment dispatching to minimize the waiting time of this equipment. Elijah [45] developed a mathematical model for calculating the arrival and service rate of different amounts of hauling equipment involved in material transportation. Huisa [46] improved the use of loading and hauling equipment to reduce the cost of these operations.

Choi et al. [47] developed an intelligent non-supervisory system to predict the performance of the hauling equipment system in surface mining using a combination of different optimization models. Li et al. [48] focused on a mathematical model for rescheduling operations considering the requirements of production spaces, operating environment, and production equipment wear, while seeking to obtain the maximum planning completion rate and the lowest ore grade fluctuation. Abolghasemian et al. [49] presented a multi-objective optimization in the surface mine system, seeking the maximum amount of extraction and minimizing the transportation time, considering the storage capacity, transportation equipment, and budget. Shamsi et al. [50] performed an IP with operational restrictions to schedule the transportation system in surface mining, considering the best net present value as an objective. Parichehreh et al. [51] addressed the energy-efficient unrelated parallel machine scheduling problem, incorporating job deterioration and the learning effects of operators, providing valuable insights into multi-objective optimization for complex production environments.

Our study introduces a novel and significant approach to optimizing ore loading and hauling operations by modeling a tactical problem using a scheduling model typically employed for operational decisions. This model accounts for parallel machines with different speeds, adding greater realism. Specifically, the nature of the problem is reflected in the dynamic availability of loading equipment, represented through dynamic release times, where jobs are not known in advance but are revealed as they are executed. This approach allows for deeper and more detailed analyses that are better suited to the complexities of mining production environments. Implementing this model can be integrated into tactical and operational strategies to make them more efficient and effective, supporting decision-making in mining companies by significantly improving operational efficiency, reducing costs, and increasing productivity. Furthermore, this study will contribute to both theoretical development and practical application in mining engineering, enhancing essential operations in the sector.

3. Methodology

This section outlines the methodology employed in this study. It is structured as follows: Section 3.1 defines the problem and sets the context for the research. Section 3.2 details the modeling assumptions and presents the mathematical formulation of the problem, including the objective functions and constraints. Section 3.3 describes the algorithms used for determining and evaluating the optimal amount of ore hauling equipment. This includes the procedure for determining the minimum amount of hauling equipment and the evaluation of the cost–time trade-offs. The following subsections systematically address the research objectives and provide a comprehensive understanding of the applied methods.

3.1. Problem Definition

Due to the critical importance of ore hauling for production, this research aims to determine the minimum amount of hauling equipment necessary to minimize both the costs associated with equipment usage and the completion time of the production target within a defined time horizon. Ore hauling operations are pivotal for continuously supplying essential minerals to production plants. However, technical decisions regarding the required equipment are often made based on experience and under time pressure. While these decisions may be quick, they might only sometimes be optimal, potentially leading to increased costs or delays that impact plant production.

This research addresses the inefficiency and potential sub-optimality of traditional decision-making processes in determining the minimum amount of hauling equipment needed to realize the production target. This can result in either overestimating or underestimating hauling equipment, leading to unnecessary expenses or bottlenecks during ore transport. By developing a mathematical model that considers the parallel machine scheduling problem with different speeds and release times, we aim to provide a systematic and data-driven approach to optimizing equipment allocation.

A detailed analysis of how costs relate to completion time could reveal valuable scenarios, enabling more informed and appropriate decisions in the event of any contingency in the transportation operation. This model will allow decision-makers to balance the trade-offs between equipment costs and operational efficiency, ensuring that the right amount of equipment is deployed to meet production targets without incurring unnecessary expenses.

The problem can be conceptualized as a parallel machine scheduling problem with different speeds and release times. While the primary focus is a tactical decision to determine the minimum amount of hauling equipment and analyze costs related to completion time, an adaptation to this scheduling problem under an integer programming model is executed. According to the notation established by Graham [52], an operations scheduling problem is defined by three fields ($\alpha|\beta|\gamma$): α represents the system configuration, β the constraints and characteristics of the system, and γ the objective function. Using this framework and following the nomenclature described by Pinedo and Hadavi [53], the system configuration corresponds to parallel machines with different speeds (Q_m), where these machines are the loading equipment with varying processing times. A significant system characteristic includes the release times (r_i) incorporated within the hauling time. The objective function aims to minimize both costs and completion time. Figure 2 illustrates the schedule of the ore hauling operation conceptualized as the problem previously mentioned.

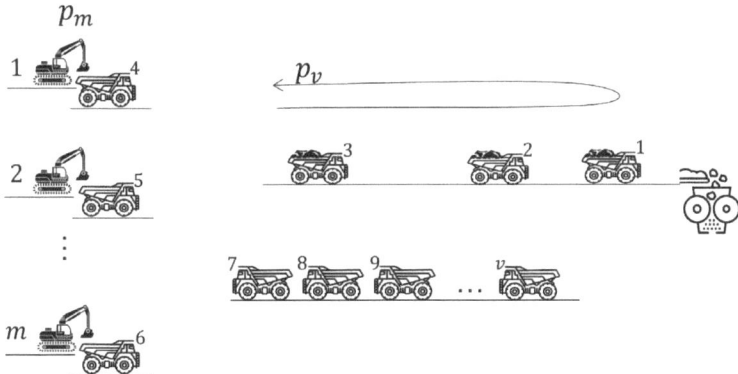

Figure 2. Schedule considering ore hauling operation.

3.2. Modeling

Model assumptions. The assumptions of the model are as follows, based on the work presented by Meza [2]:

- Only one ore unloading point was considered.
- The refueling time is negligible.
- The loading and hauling equipment is available at all times.
- The ore unloading waiting time is insignificant.

Notation. Table 2 provides the notation for the model proposed, showing the type and definition, respectively.

Table 2. Notation for the model proposed.

Var	Type	Definition
$\mathcal{M}$	Set	Set of loading equipment $\mathcal{M} = \{1, 2, \ldots, m\}$.
$\mathcal{V}$	Set	Set of hauling equipment $\mathcal{V} = \{1, 2, \ldots, v\}$.
$\mathcal{T}$	Set	Set of units of time: $\mathcal{T} = \{1, 2, \ldots, h\}$.
p_j^l	Parameter	Loading time for loading equipment j.
p_i^h	Parameter	Hauling time for hauling equipment i.
P	Parameter	The production target is the total amount of trips to be made.
h	Parameter	Time horizon to complete the production target.
k_j^l	Parameter	Cost associated with use loading equipment.
k_i^h	Parameter	Cost associated with use hauling equipment.
x_{ijt}	Variable	Principal decision variable, takes the value of 1 if the hauling equipment i is using the loading equipment j at time t, 0 otherwise.
y_{jt}	Variable	The auxiliary decision variable takes the value of 1 if loading equipment j is using at time t, 0, otherwise.
z_{it}	Variable	The auxiliary decision variable takes the value of 1 if hauling equipment i is using at time t, 0, otherwise.
C_{max}	Variable	Completion time of the production target
k	Variable	Costs associated with equipment usage

Objective function. The first objective function (Equation (1)) seeks to minimize k associated to use equipment. The second objective function (Equation (2)) seeks to minimize C_{max} of all trips.

$$\min k \quad (1)$$

$$\min C_{max} \quad (2)$$

Constraints. With respect to constraints, the set of constraints in Equation (3) ensures the assignment of only one hauling vehicle i to one loading vehicle j at time t. The set of constraints in Equation (4) ensures only one loading equipment j per hauling equipment i at time t.

$$\sum_{i \in V} x_{ijt} \leq 1 \quad \forall j \in \mathcal{M}, t \in \mathcal{T} \quad (3)$$

$$\sum_{j \in M} x_{ijt} \leq 1 \quad \forall i \in \mathcal{V}, t \in \mathcal{T} \quad (4)$$

The set of constraints in Equations (5) and (6) ensures that the loading and hauling equipment are used for the required duration when assigned.

$$\sum_{\tau=t+1}^{t+p_j^l} y_{j\tau} \geq (p_j^l - 1) \cdot x_{ijt} \quad \forall i \in \mathcal{V}, j \in \mathcal{M}, t \in \mathcal{T} \setminus (t \leq h - p_j^l) \quad (5)$$

$$\sum_{\tau=t+1}^{t+p_j^l+p_i^h} z_{i\tau} \geq (p_i^h + p_j^l - 1) \cdot x_{ijt} \quad \forall i \in \mathcal{V}, j \in \mathcal{M}, t \in \mathcal{T} \setminus (t \leq h - p_i^h - p_j^l) \quad (6)$$

The set of constraints in Equations (7) and (8) ensures that loading and hauling equipment are not double-booked and are used only when available.

$$x_{ijt} \leq 1 - y_{jt} \quad \forall i \in \mathcal{V}, j \in \mathcal{M}, t \in \mathcal{T} \quad (7)$$

$$x_{ijt} \leq 1 - z_{it} \quad \forall i \in \mathcal{V}, j \in \mathcal{M}, t \in \mathcal{T} \quad (8)$$

The set of constraints in Equation (9) ensures C_{max}.

$$C_{max} \geq t \cdot x_{ijt} + p_i^h + p_j^l \quad \forall i \in \mathcal{V}, j \in \mathcal{M}, t \in \mathcal{T} \qquad (9)$$

The set of constraints in Equation (10) ensures that P is met.

$$\sum_i^V \sum_j^M \sum_t^T x_{ijt} \geq P \quad \forall i \in \mathcal{V}, j \in \mathcal{M}, t \in \mathcal{T} \qquad (10)$$

Equation (11) calculates k.

$$k = \sum_i^V \sum_t^T k_i^h \cdot z_{it} + \sum_j^M \sum_t^T k_j^l \cdot y_{jt} \quad \forall i \in \mathcal{V}, j \in \mathcal{M}, t \in \mathcal{T} \qquad (11)$$

The set of constraints in Equations (12) and (13) ensures the nature of the variables.

$$x_{ijt}, y_{jt}, z_{it} \in \{0, 1\} \quad \forall i \in \mathcal{V}, j \in \mathcal{M}, t \in \mathcal{T} \qquad (12)$$

$$C_{max}, k \geq 0 \qquad (13)$$

The proposed model can be used in tactical and operational decision-making processes, as it accurately specifies both decisions. However, the complexity of this mixed-integer linear programming model in terms of the amount of integer variables is $i \cdot j \cdot t + j \cdot t + i \cdot j$, and it has two more continuous variables. If we analyze the number of constraints, we find a total of $7 \cdot i \cdot j \cdot t + j \cdot t + i \cdot j$. The fact that the model relies on binary vectors (to indicate truck start times and activity periods) inherently increases complexity but also opens the possibility for (i) the inclusion of valid inequalities to discard solutions that do not fit the structure of the problem or (ii) decomposition techniques, such as using combinatorial Benders' cuts, or adopting a rolling horizon framework [54], to leverage divide and conquer strategies; these are both part of ongoing research. One could consider reducing the periods, but this would prevent using these models in control schemes such as those provided by a digital twin, a technique widespread in mining operations management [55].

3.3. Algorithms for Determining and Evaluating the Optimal Amount of Ore Hauling Equipment

To incorporate the dual objectives of the model of minimizing both the completion time and cost, an iterative approach was utilized in which models are created using only one objective function. As shown in Algorithms 1 and 2, the iterative process allows for the exploration of the trade-off between completion time and costs, providing a set of solutions that balance both objectives.

Considering the tactical-level analysis, the following procedure was proposed to determine the optimal amount of hauling equipment, as detailed in Algorithm 1. The algorithm starts by defining the input data, which include $\mathcal{M}$, $\mathcal{V}$, $\mathcal{T}$, p_i^h, p_j^l, h, and P. Then, defining the output data, which include the minimum number of hauling equipment (v_{opt}), and the hauling equipment' assignment to loading equipment ($Schedule$) including C_{max}.

Then, assign v to the magnitude of $\mathcal{V}$, the total number of hauling equipment available (line 1). The variable $Continue$ is set to true to initiate the loop (line 2). As long as it remains true, a model is created (considering Equations (2)–(13) of PMSPOHO model, input data and v), and a $Result$ that minimizes the C_{max} is obtained (lines 3–5). A feasibility evaluation is conducted, where if the $Result$ is feasible, v is reduced by one unit (attempting to solve the problem with fewer hauling equipment) (lines 6–8). If it is not feasible, v_{opt} is increased by one unit, and the loop terminates (lines 9–13). This algorithm returns v_{opt} and $Schedule$ (line 14).

Algorithm 1 Optimal hauling equipment determinator.

Input: $\mathcal{M}, \mathcal{V}, \mathcal{T}, p_i^h, p_j^l, h, P$;
Output: v_{opt}: minimum hauling equipment, *Schedule*: hauling equipment' assignment to loading equipment including the C_{max}.
1: $v \leftarrow |\mathcal{V}|$
2: *Continue* $\leftarrow$ **true**
3: **while** *Continue* **do**
4:     *model* $\leftarrow$ Createmodel(*Equations*(2)–(13), Input, v)
5:     *Result* $\leftarrow$ Solve(*model*, Minimize)
6:     **if** IsFeasible(*Result*) **then**
7:         $v \leftarrow v - 1$
8:         *Result*, *Schedule*
9:     **else**
10:         $v_{opt} \leftarrow v + 1$
11:         *Continue* $\leftarrow$ **false**
12:     **end if**
13: **end while**
14: **return** v_{opt}, *Schedule*

The following procedure was proposed for an analysis of the relationship between k and C_{max}, detailed in Algorithm 2. This pseudocode allows for observing the behavior of k as C_{max} is incremented. The algorithm starts by defining the input data, which includes the same factors as in Algorithm 1: k_i^h, k_j^l, and v. Then, defining the output data includes a list of costs and a list of termination times (C_{max}). Define v (line 1). The $model_{lb}$ is created (considering Equations (2)–(13) of PMSPOHO model and input data) (line 2), and a $Result_{lb}$ from the minimization of $C_{max_{lb}}$ is obtained (line 3), extracting this result (line 4). A $model_{ub}$ is created (considering Equations (1), (3)–(13) of PMSPOHO model and input data) (line 5), and a $Result_{ub}$ from the minimization of k is obtained (line 6), extracting $C_{max_{ub}}$ for this result (line 7).

Algorithm 2 Progressive cost–time evaluator

Input: $\mathcal{M}, \mathcal{V}, \mathcal{T}, p_i^h, p_j^l, k_i^h, k_j^l, h, P$, and v;
Output: ListPair(C_{max}, k): List of cost respect to C_{max}.
1: Define v
2: $model_{lb} \leftarrow$ Createmodel(*Equations*(2)–(13), Input)
3: $Result_{lb} \leftarrow$ Solve($model_{lb}$, Minimize)
4: $C_{max_{lb}} \leftarrow$ ExtractCmax($Result_{lb}$)
5: $model_{ub} \leftarrow$ Createmodel(*Equations* (1), (3)–(13), Input)
6: $Result_{ub} \leftarrow$ Solve($model_{ub}$, Minimize)
7: $C_{max_{ub}} \leftarrow$ ExtractCmax($Result_{ub}$)
8: **for** $C_{max_{ref}}$ in $C_{max_{lb}}$ to $C_{max_{ub}}$ **do**
9:     $model_{ref} \leftarrow$ Createmodel(*Equations* (1), (3)–(8), (10)–(13), Input)
10:     $Result_{ref} \leftarrow$ Solve($model_{ref}$, Minimize)
11:     Cost $\leftarrow$ ExtractCost($Result_{ref}$)
12:     ListPair(C_{max}, k) $\leftarrow$ AddToList($C_{max_{ref}}$, Cost)
13: **end for**
14: **return** C_{max}, k

A progressive evaluation is carried out that iterates $C_{max_{ref}}$ by 1 from $C_{max_{lb}}$ to $C_{max_{ub}}$ (line 8). For each value, a $model_{ref}$ is created (considering Equations (1), (3)–(8), and (10)–(13) of PMSPOHO model and input data) (line 9). $Result_{ref}$ is obtained by minimizing k for each iteration (line 10); k is extracted and added to a list (Cost) for each corresponding $C_{max_{ref}}$ (lines 11–12). This algorithm returns the list of pairs ($C_{max_{ref}}, k$) (lines 14), providing a detailed evaluation of how k varies about changes in $C_{max_{ref}}$. In the algorithm, $C_{max_{ref}}$ serves as an intermediate reference value to iteratively evaluate the trade-off between minimizing C_{max} and k. This iterative evaluation provides insights into the cost–time trade-offs in the model.

4. Computational Experiments and Results Analysis

This section presents the computational experiments to evaluate the performance of the proposed PMSPOHO model and algorithms. All experiments were conducted on a computer with a Windows 11 operating system, 12th Gen Intel(R) Core(TM) i5-12450H, 2.50 GHz processor, and 8 GB RAM. The Python 3.11 programming language was used for the development. The Gurobi 10.0.1 commercial optimizer and CBC free optimizer were used with a search time limit of 3600 s and a GAP of 0.01.

Based on actual data provided in the studies by Meza [2], Vásquez [3], and Anchiraico and Rojas [4], which include the numbers of loading and hauling equipment, loading times, hauling times, time horizons, and production targets, 34 experimental instances were generated. These instances are designed to simulate real-world scenarios, enabling a robust evaluation of our proposed methodologies under various conditions. This approach ensures that our experimental setup is based on realistic operational parameters, enhancing the applicability and relevance of our findings. It is important to note that a direct comparison with the authors' studies above was not conducted, as their research methodologies differ significantly from our proposed approach.

4.1. Tuning the Values for the Optimizer Parameters

Gurobi Optimizer version 10.0.1 features an extensive range of parameters designed to fine-tune the optimizer performance. Given the vast array of options among possible configurations, identifying the optimal combination of parameters that enhance the overall model performance poses a significant challenge. The TuningAPI from Gurobi offers a valuable tool for exploring various parameter settings that can improve model performance in specific cases [56].

Considering the procedure indicated by Cuellar-Usaquén et al. [57], a sample of seven instances was created to identify the appropriate parameter settings for our model using TuningAPI. This sample includes those instances where the computation time obtained by the PMSPOHO model using the default parameters (PMSPOHO-D) exceeds the meantime of its respective class by two standard deviations.

Table 3 shows the results of Gurobi parameter tuning across seven different problem instances. Each table row represents an instance, with columns indicating the specific Gurobi parameters adjusted for that instance. The parameters include Symmetry, DegenMove, Heuristics, GomoryPasses, PreDepRow, MIPFocus, Method, CutPasses, and BranchDir.

Table 3. Parameters configurations found for the mathematical model.

Summary				Value Parameters										
Inst	v	m	P	Symmetry	DegenMoves	Heuristics	GomoryPasses	PreDepRow	MIPFocus	Method	CutPasses	BranchDir	Tc-D	Tc-T	Variation
1	3	2	20	2									0.8	0.79	1.25%
2	6	2	20		2								1.22	1.15	5.74%
3	8	4	81			0	1	1					69.59	55.03	20.92%
4	12	4	81						2				46.54	44.4	4.60%
5	15	4	81							0			32.53	31.64	2.74%
6	8	4	90				1					1	139.22	120.68	13.32%
7	20	4	100								1		81.62	79.9	2.11%

The third instance stands out significantly because it shows the highest variation (20.92%) between the default computational time (Tc-D) and the tuned computational time (Tc-T), indicating a significant improvement in performance with the adjusted parameters. In this instance, the parameters Heuristics, GomoryPasses, and PreDepRow were adjusted, resulting in a substantial reduction in computation time from 69.59 to 55.03 time units. This adjustment reduced the overall calculation time and optimized the use of computational resources, making the process more efficient and effective. The considerable difference between Tc-D and Tc-T underscores the importance of customization and fine-tuning model parameters to achieve maximum efficiency in solving complex mathematical problems.

In this instance, the adjusted parameter Heuristics emerges as a key player in accelerating the solving process. By increasing the use of heuristic methods, which are solving strategies that employ simple and fast rules to generate satisfactory solutions quickly, the model explored and evaluated potential solutions more efficiently. This approach significantly reduced the time required to reach a feasible solution, demonstrating its practicality and effectiveness. Applying heuristics is a valuable tool, particularly in scenarios where speed is critical and some precision can be sacrificed for improved resolution speed.

GomoryPasses, another adjusted parameter, controls the amount of Gomory cut passes. These passes are optimization techniques that strengthen the model linear relaxation, leading to faster convergence. Adjusting the amount of these passes can significantly impact the solution efficiency, balancing the need to improve the solution with the additional time required for each cut. PreDepRow, which handles the preprocessing of dependent rows, also fundamentally improved efficiency by reducing problem size and enhancing numerical stability. Effective preprocessing can simplify the model by eliminating redundancies and reducing overall complexity. In the third instance, adjusting PreDepRow significantly reduced computational time, noting the importance of proper model management. These adjustments underscore the importance of tuning parameters to enhance the efficiency solver, enabling faster and more accurate results.

4.2. Benchmarking Results for Optimizers

Table 4 presents the benchmarking results of optimizers across 34 instances. The instances were organized considering the production target, as an increase in computational time (Tc) was noted as this target increased. The results were compared between the default model (PMSPOHO-D), the tuned model (PMSPOHO-T), and the model with the free optimizer (PMSPOHO-CBC). The critical parameters for comparison were Tc and GAP, which measure the complexity model and the efficiency solver. In this study, the GAP value is provided directly by the Gurobi optimizer as part of its solution output.

The tuned model (PMSPOHO-T) consistently handles lower computational times than the other models. This indicates that parameter tuning has significantly improved the solver efficiency. The GAP, which is the difference between the best-known solution and the best lower bound found by the solver, is 0.00% for both PMSPOHO-D and PMSPOHO-T, indicating that the solutions found are optimal. However, PMSPOHO-CBC shows a higher GAP in several instances, reflecting lower precision and highlighting the limitations of a commercial optimizer.

PMSPOHO-T stands out with the best results in terms of Tc, solving instances faster while maintaining solution precision. This starkly contrasts with the model with the free optimizer (PMSPOHO-CBC), which shows a higher GAP in many cases, thereby highlighting its limitations. It also demonstrates that the problem's complexity is NP-Hard, meaning that as instances increase, optimal results could be obtained after significantly longer times, making a free optimizer an inefficient option for field applications.

Figure 3 compares the computational time (Tc) and C_{max} for the PMSPOHO-D, PMSPOHO-T, and PMSPOHO-CBC optimizers for instance 34. PMSPOHO-D and PMSPOHO-T achieve the same C_{max} of 183, but PMSPOHO-T is more efficient in terms of computational time, with 671.8 compared to 798.8 for PMSPOHO-D. On the other hand, PMSPOHO-CBC shows the worst performance, with a C_{max} of 229 and a computational time of 3600. This indicates that PMSPOHO-T is the most efficient among the three evaluated optimizers, achieving a good balance between computational time and C_{max}.

Table 4. Benchmarking results for optimizers per instances.

				PMSPOHO-D			PMSPOHO-T			PMSPOHO-CBC		
Instance	P	v	m	C_{max}	Tc	GAP	C_{max}	Tc	GAP	C_{max}	Tc	GAP
1	20	20	2	29	14.52	0.00%	29	9.73	0.00%	30	3600	4.58%
2	20	16	2	29	9.51	0.00%	29	5.92	0.00%	30	3600	4.64%
3	20	10	2	29	3.82	0.00%	29	2.91	0.00%	31	3600	5.21%
4	20	8	2	29	2.51	0.00%	29	1.85	0.00%	30	3600	4.82%
5	20	6	2	31	1.6	0.00%	31	1.58	0.00%	32	3600	3.77%
6	20	5	2	34	1.41	0.00%	34	1.03	0.00%	35	3600	2.36%
7	20	4	2	40	1.13	0.00%	40	1.01	0.00%	41	3600	2.56%
8	20	3	2	51	0.9	0.00%	51	1.82	0.00%	51	1846	0.00%
9	81	20	4	55	28.25	0.00%	55	26.74	0.00%	60	3600	8.52%
10	81	16	4	55	18.34	0.00%	55	18.61	0.00%	60	3600	8.20%
11	81	10	4	64	49.23	0.00%	64	46.08	0.00%	68	3600	6.45%
12	81	8	4	78	69.59	0.00%	78	50.86	0.00%	82	3600	5.50%
13	81	6	4	100	66.54	0.00%	100	63.01	0.00%	106	3600	5.72%
14	81	4	4	147	76.29	0.00%	147	59.78	0.00%	152	3600	3.27%
15	81	20	6	38	42.12	0.00%	38	42.26	0.00%	42	3600	10.25%
16	81	16	6	42	318.67	0.00%	42	130.11	0.00%	46	3600	9.86%
17	81	10	6	63	94.3	0.00%	63	76.82	0.00%	70	3600	10.52%
18	81	8	6	77	100.46	0.00%	77	100.13	0.00%	85	3600	10.73%
19	81	6	6	98	145.77	0.00%	98	90.32	0.00%	110	3600	12.72%
20	90	5	3	130	42.98	0.00%	130	26.41	0.00%	163	3600	25.32%
21	90	4	3	161	83.77	0.00%	161	40.36	0.00%	202	3600	25.47%
22	90	3	3	212	44.52	0.00%	212	30.78	0.00%	259	3600	22.23%
23	200	19	4	125	1784.21	0.00%	125	1627.21	0.00%	161	3600	29.03%
24	200	18	4	125	1693.64	0.00%	125	1437.64	0.00%	161	3600	28.53%
25	200	17	4	125	1634.63	0.00%	125	1463.63	0.00%	161	3600	28.93%
26	200	16	4	125	1640.24	0.00%	125	1400.24	0.00%	161	3600	28.73%
27	200	15	4	125	1584.04	0.00%	125	1437.04	0.00%	164	3600	31.45%
28	200	14	4	125	1554.43	0.00%	125	1291.43	0.00%	159	3600	27.32%
29	200	13	4	125	1532.23	0.00%	125	1349.23	0.00%	161	3600	29.05%
30	200	12	4	151	1524.64	0.00%	151	1372.64	0.00%	194	3600	28.63%
31	200	11	4	151	1279.45	0.00%	151	1019.45	0.00%	189	3600	25.43%
32	200	10	4	151	1017.6	0.00%	151	746.6	0.00%	186	3600	23.23%
33	200	9	4	166	865.6	0.00%	166	615.6	0.00%	203	3600	22.01%
34	200	8	4	183	798.8	0.00%	183	671.8	0.00%	229	3600	24.93%

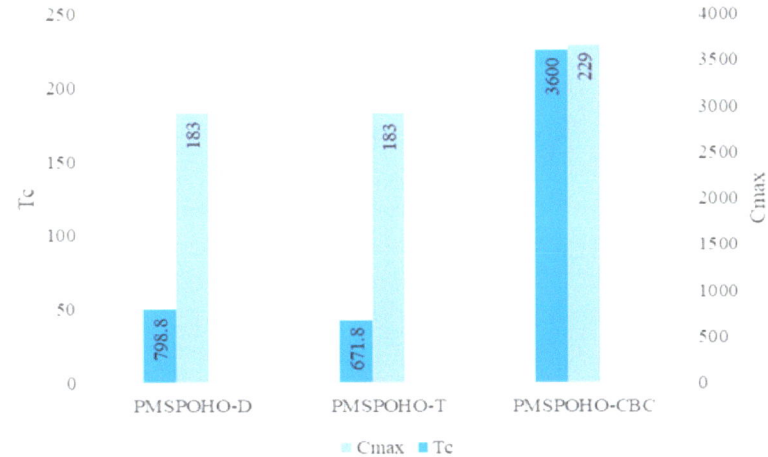

Figure 3. Comparison of computational time and C_{max} for instance 34.

4.3. Tactical Approach Insights

Table 5 shows the efficiency of the applied algorithms. Algorithm 1 calculates the minimum number of hauling equipment, resulting in eight equipment. On the other hand, Algorithm 2 performs a k-C_{max} evaluation, allowing for a more appropriate analysis between these two variables. This improves tactical decision-making by showing how varying C_{max} impacts k and vice-versa. Minimizing C_{max} results in significantly reduced values (between 33 and 49), although an increase in k enables planners to balance temporal efficiency and operational costs. Algorithm 2 provides a more comprehensive and balanced perspective for tactical decision-making and is supported by Algorithm 1, which defines the number of resources needed to meet the production target.

Table 5. Results of optimizing the proposed algorithms.

			Minimize k			Minimize C_{max}		
v	m	P	C_{maxub}	k	Tc	C_{maxlb}	k	Tc
19	4	200	51	2350	151.46	33	6998	54.97
18	4	200	51	2350	219.68	33	6648	46.31
17	4	200	51	2350	117.08	33	6298	38.57
16	4	200	51	2350	99.44	33	5948	33.81
15	4	200	51	2350	125.16	33	5598	31.16
14	4	200	51	2350	162.80	33	5248	26.78
13	4	200	51	2350	75.34	34	4898	24.63
12	4	200	51	2350	58.55	35	4548	20.73
11	4	200	51	2350	111.22	37	4198	21.40
10	4	200	51	2350	103.30	40	3848	32.76
9	4	200	50	2350	44.62	44	3498	19.40
8	4	200	51	2350	76.94	49	3148	15.93

As completion times shorten, costs rise disproportionately, indicating a trade-off between time and cost efficiency in ore hauling operations. The steeper curves at lower completion times imply significant cost increases for faster operations, while the flatter slopes at higher times suggest a minimum cost threshold. The broader range of completion times with more hauling equipment means that, although additional equipment can speed up operations, it also incurs higher costs, highlighting the importance of balancing budgetary limitations with operational urgency in scheduling mining operations.

Figure 4 shows the relationship between costs and completion time for different numbers of hauling equipment. There is a marked cost decrease with only a slight increase in completion time. A tactical approach to determining the minimum amount of hauling equipment needed to meet production targets should consider not only cost and completion time but also the slope of each line, which supports the application of the algorithms proposed in this paper. For instance, moving from nine to eight hauling units marginally increases completion time while significantly reducing cost. This suggests that operating with eight hauling units could be an effective tactical decision if the additional time does not compromise other priorities of the ore hauling operation.

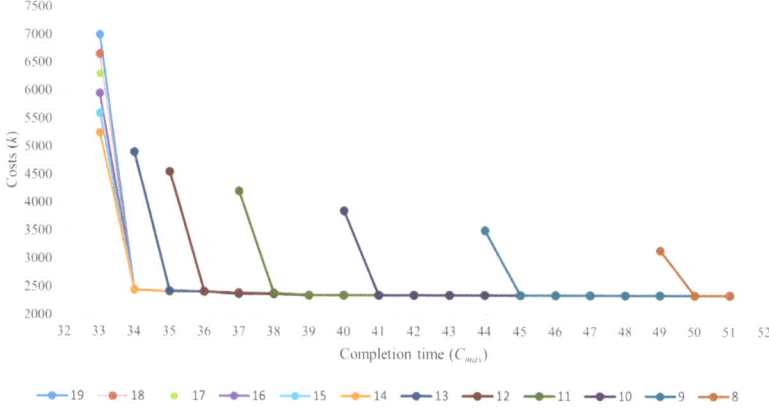

Figure 4. Costs k vs. completion time C_{max} for the instances proposed in Table 5.

Decision-makers must weigh the cost increase associated with using more equipment against reducing hauling time. Beyond a certain point, adding more hauling units diminishes the benefit of lowering completion time but incurs substantially higher costs. Pinpointing the moment when the additional cost no longer justifies the decrease in hauling time is critical for optimizing operations and managing resources efficiently.

4.4. Operational Approach Insights

Figure 5 shows the schedule, for instance 34, which considers eight hauling and four loading equipment. This visualizes the ore loading program for a mining operation during the first 50 trips of the production target. It is interesting to see how the allocation is organized to ensure that the minimum necessary amount of hauling equipment is kept in constant motion, indicating a careful assessment of loading times and intervals between tasks. This strategy ensures that no loading equipment remains idle and that the hauling equipment is effectively distributed to meet the production target.

By minimizing the amount of hauling equipment, the operation can become more cost-effective and improve logistics by reducing congestion and potential bottlenecks in the ore hauling operation. This balanced approach between efficiency and effectiveness in scheduling is crucial for a successful operation that adapts to the dynamic and often unpredictable demands of mining.

Figure 5. Schedule for instance 34 considering minimize completion time C_{max}.

Table 6 provides a detailed distribution of loading and hauling equipment utilization in a mining operation, highlighting the allocation and usage of these resources in production. It is observed that loading equipment two and three are the most utilized, with utilization percentages of 32% and 30%, respectively, indicating high demand and frequent use. In contrast, loading vehicle four is the least utilized, operating at only 12% utilization. This suggests that resources are not being fully optimized, particularly considering that loading vehicle four might be the most costly to operate, as less frequently used equipment typically requires regular maintenance and occupies valuable space that could be better utilized.

The under-utilization of the costly loading equipment fourraises significant cost management and operational efficiency considerations. The high cost of this equipment may be due to specialized features that necessitate more sophisticated maintenance or a higher initial investment. However, its sub-optimal utilization implies that this investment needs to yield the expected returns, which is critical in operations aiming to maximize efficiency and profitability. This situation underscores the urgent need to reassess task distribution and resource allocation to ensure that all loading equipment are utilized in a manner that justifies their cost, thereby optimizing the entire operation and reducing potential resource wastage.

The results demonstrate that the proposed model is efficient in terms of computational time and that the proposed algorithms are useful tactical tools for more effective decision-making regarding the allocation of hauling equipment necessary to achieve the targets set in ore transport operations. However, it is essential to acknowledge that analyzing more significant instances as a mathematical model could complicate the time required to obtain results, even with the optimizer parameters finely tuned. Therefore, it will be essential to extend the solution search periods and develop approximate methods to reduce these times and attain practical and executable solutions.

Table 6. Loading and hauling equipment utilization.

Hauling Equipment	Loading Equipment				Total	Utilization
	1	2	3	4		
0	3	2	1	0	6	12%
1	3	2	1	1	7	14%
2	1	1	3	0	5	10%
3	1	1	2	2	6	12%
4	1	4	2	0	7	14%
5	2	2	3	0	7	14%
6	1	1	2	2	6	12%
7	1	3	1	1	6	12%
Total	13	16	15	6	50	
Utilization	26%	32%	30%	12%		

5. Conclusions

The proposed model demonstrates significant efficiency in terms of computational time, effectively balancing cost and completion time in ore hauling operations. Applying the two algorithms provided tactical tools that enhance decision-making regarding the allocation of hauling equipment. The model efficiency is evident in the computational results, showing that parameter tuning can significantly improve solver performance. The tuned model consistently handled lower computational times than default settings, highlighting the importance of careful parameter adjustments. Furthermore, incorporating dynamic release times and different speeds of hauling equipment in the model adds a layer of realism, ensuring that the scheduling reflects actual operational conditions. This aspect further optimizes the allocation process, making the model computationally robust.

Despite the results, the model has limitations. A primary limitation is its scalability. As the size of the instances increases, the time required to obtain results can become prohibitive, even with optimized parameters. This issue is inherent in mathematical models dealing with complex, NP-hard problems. Additionally, the reliance of the model on exact optimization methods may only sometimes be practical for real-time decision-making in dynamic environments where quick responses are essential.

Future work should focus on extending solution search periods and developing approximate methods to address these limitations. These methods, including heuristic or metaheuristic approaches, can reduce computational times and provide near-optimal practical and executable solutions in real-world scenarios. Additionally, integrating machine learning techniques to predict and dynamically adjust parameters could enhance the model's performance and adaptability [58].

Author Contributions: Conceptualization, L.T.-T., C.A., and D.A.-M.; methodology, L.T.-T. and C.A.; software, L.T.-T. and C.G.; formal analysis, L.T.-T. and A.P.; investigation, L.T.-T. and A.P.; data curation, L.T.-T.; writing—original draft preparation, L.T.-T.; writing—review and editing, L.T.-T., C.A., and D.A.-M.; visualization, L.T.-T.; supervision, C.A. and D.A.-M.; project administration, L.T.-T. All authors have read and agreed to the published version of the manuscript.

Funding: The APC was funded by University of Los Andes.

Institutional Review Board Statement: Not applicable.

Informed Consent Statement: Not applicable.

Data Availability Statement: The data presented in this study are available on: https://github.com/LuisTarazonaTorres/Parallel-Machine-Scheduling-problem---Hualing-Equipment.git (accessed on 29 July 2024).

Acknowledgments: The authors greatly acknowledge all the participants who contributed to the conduct of this study.

Conflicts of Interest: The authors declare no conflicts of interest.

References

1. Rout, M.; Parida, C.K. Optimization of Blasting Parameters in Opencast Mines. Ph.D. Thesis, National Institute of Technology Rourkela, Odisha, India, 2007.
2. Meza Castro, J.E. Desarrollo de un Modelo para la Aplicación de Simulación a un Sistema de Carguío y Acarreo de Desmonte en una Operación Minera a Tajo Abierto. Bachelor's Thesis, Pontifical Catholic University of Peru, San Miguel, Peru, 2011.
3. Vasquez, O.C.; Sepúlveda, J.M.; Córdova, F. Modeling and optimization of vehicle operations in underground copper mining. *Rem Rev. Esc. De Minas* **2011**, *64*, 365–371. [CrossRef]
4. Anchiraico, A.; Rojas, K. Optimización del Sistema de Acarreo y Transporte en Labores de Preparación de las Zonas de Profundización Mediante la Metodología Six Sigma Operada por la E.C.M. Zicsa en la Unidad Minera Inmaculada. Bachelor's Thesis, Universidad Peruana de Ciencias Aplicadas, Santiago de Surco, Peru, 2023.
5. Soofastaei, A.; Karimpour, E.; Knights, P.; Kizil, M. *Energy-Efficient Loading and Hauling Operations*; Springer: Cham, Switzerland, 2018; pp. 121–146. [CrossRef]
6. Choi, Y.; Baek, J.; Park, S. Review of GIS-based applications for mining: Planning, operation, and environmental management. *Appl. Sci.* **2020**, *10*, 2266. [CrossRef]
7. Owolabi, A. Loading and haulage equipment selection for optimum production in a granite quarry. *Int. J. Min. Sci.* **2019**, *5*, 35–40.
8. Marte Collado, J.M. Programación de la Producción en Máquinas Paralelas Sujeto a Adelantos, Retrasos y Fechas límite. Master's Thesis, Universitat Politècnica de València, Valencia, Spain, 2017.
9. Salazar-Hornig, E.; Soto-Gavilán, G. Minimización del makespan para el problema de máquinas paralelas no relacionadas con tiempos de setup dependientes de la secuencia mediante un algoritmo híbrido VNS/ACO. *Rev. Ing. Univ. De Medellín* **2021**, *20*, 171–184. [CrossRef]
10. Hong, H.C.; Lin, B.M. Parallel dedicated machine scheduling with conflict graphs. *Comput. Ind. Eng.* **2018**, *124*, 316–321. [CrossRef]
11. Koryagin, M.; Voronov, A. Improving the organization of the shovel-truck systems in open-pit coal mines. *Transp. Probl.* **2017**, *12*, 113–122. [CrossRef]
12. Oliskevych, M.; Kovalyshyn, S.; Magats, M.; Shevchuk, V.; Sukach, O. The optimization of trucks fleet schedule in view of their interaction and restrictions of the European agreement of work of crews. *Transp. Probl.* **2020**, *15*, 157–170. [CrossRef]
13. Wu, L.; Wang, S. Exact and heuristic methods to solve the parallel machine scheduling problem with multi-processor tasks. *Int. J. Prod. Econ.* **2018**, *201*, 26–40. [CrossRef]
14. Elidrissi, A.; Benmansour, R.; Benbrahim, M.; Duvivier, D. Mathematical formulations for the parallel machine scheduling problem with a single server. *Int. J. Prod. Res.* **2021**, *59*, 6166–6184. [CrossRef]
15. Gan, H.S.; Wirth, A.; Abdekhodaee, A. A branch-and-price algorithm for the general case of scheduling parallel machines with a single server. *Comput. Oper. Res.* **2012**, *39*, 2242–2247. [CrossRef]
16. Kim, M.Y.; Lee, Y.H. MIP models and hybrid algorithm for minimizing the makespan of parallel machines scheduling problem with a single server. *Comput. Oper. Res.* **2012**, *39*, 2457–2468. [CrossRef]
17. Hasani, K.; Kravchenko, S.A.; Werner, F. Minimising interference for scheduling two parallel machines with a single server. *Int. J. Prod. Res.* **2014**, *52*, 7148–7158. [CrossRef]
18. Kosch, S.; Beck, J.C. A new mip model for parallel-batch scheduling with non-identical job sizes. In Proceedings of the Integration of AI and OR Techniques in Constraint Programming: 11th International Conference (CPAIOR 2014), Cork, Ireland, 19–23 May 2014; Proceedings 11; Springer: Berlin/Heidelberg, Germany, 2014; pp. 55–70.
19. Sharma, A.; Zhao, F.; Sutherland, J.W. Econological scheduling of a manufacturing enterprise operating under a time-of-use electricity tariff. *J. Clean. Prod.* **2015**, *108*, 256–270. [CrossRef]
20. Bajany, D.; Xia, X.; Zhang, L. A MILP Model for Truck-shovel scheduling to minimize fuel consumption. *Energy Procedia* **2017**, *105*, 2739–2745. [CrossRef]
21. Che, A.; Zhang, S.; Wu, X. Energy-conscious unrelated parallel machine scheduling under time-of-use electricity tariffs. *J. Clean. Prod.* **2017**, *156*, 688–697. [CrossRef]
22. Cheng, J.; Chu, F.; Zhou, M. An improved model for parallel machine scheduling under time-of-use electricity price. *IEEE Trans. Autom. Sci. Eng.* **2017**, *15*, 896–899. [CrossRef]
23. Elidrissi, A.; Benmansour, R.; Benbrahim, M.; Duvivier, D. MIP formulations for identical parallel machine scheduling problem with single server. In Proceedings of the 2018 4th International Conference on Optimization and Applications (ICOA), Mohammedia, Morocco, 26–27 April 2018; IEEE: Piscataway, NJ, USA, 2018; pp. 1–6.
24. Kaabi, J.; Harrath, Y. Scheduling on uniform parallel machines with periodic unavailability constraints. *Int. J. Prod. Res.* **2019**, *57*, 216–227. [CrossRef]
25. Quiroz Silva, E.E. Programación por Objetivos para el Dimensionamiento y la Asignación de Una Flota de Camiones en una Empresa Minera. *Interfases* **2021**, 87–112. [CrossRef]
26. Hsu, C.L.; Liao, J.R. Two parallel-machine scheduling problems with function constraint. *Discret. Dyn. Nat. Soc.* **2020**, *2020*, 1–6. [CrossRef]

27. Tapia, E.; Salazar Araya, A.; Saavedra, N.; Nehring, M.; Mora, J. An analysis of full truck versus full bucket strategies in open pit mining loading and hauling operations. *Int. J. Min. Reclam. Environ.* **2021**, *35*, 1–11. [CrossRef]
28. Tigreros Cardenas, I.D. Propuesta Para la Programación de Producción en Máquinas Paralelas con Tiempos de Alistamiento en una Empresa del Sector Agroindustrial. 2021. Available online: https://repositorio.uceva.edu.co/bitstream/handle/20.500.12993/2744/T00031983.pdf?sequence=1&isAllowed=y (accessed on 29 July 2024).
29. Yunusoglu, P.; Topaloglu Yildiz, S. Constraint programming approach for multi-resource-constrained unrelated parallel machine scheduling problem with sequence-dependent setup times. *Int. J. Prod. Res.* **2022**, *60*, 2212–2229. [CrossRef]
30. Ma, X.; Fu, Y.; Gao, K.; Zhu, L.; Sadollah, A. A multi-objective scheduling and routing problem for home health care services via brain storm optimization. *Complex Syst. Model. Simul.* **2023**, *3*, 32–46. [CrossRef]
31. Feng, L.; Chen, G.; Zhou, S.; Zhou, X.; Jin, M. An Energy-Efficient Unrelated Parallel Machine Scheduling Problem with Batch Processing and Time-of-Use Electricity Prices. *Mathematics* **2024**, *12*, 376. [CrossRef]
32. Hu, B.; Xiong, Z.; Sun, A.; Yuan, Y. Scheduling of Container Transportation Vehicles in Surface Coal Mines Based on the GA–GWO Hybrid Algorithm. *Appl. Sci.* **2024**, *14*, 3986. [CrossRef]
33. Eivazy, H.; Askari-Nasab, H. A mixed integer linear programming model for short-term open pit mine production scheduling. *Min. Technol.* **2012**, *121*, 97–108. [CrossRef]
34. Anjomshoa, H.; Albrecht, A.; Lee, D.; Pudney, P. Efficient vehicle haulage in underground mines. *Min. Technol.* **2012**, *121*, 83–90. [CrossRef]
35. Gligoric, Z. Optimization of Haulage System in An Underground Small Scale Mine Using Fuzzy Sets. Systems Design. p. 63. Available online: https://www.researchgate.net/publication/287397565_Optimization_of_haulage_system_in_an_underground_small_scale_mine_using_fuzzy_sets (accessed on 29 July 2024).
36. Gonen, A.; Malli, T.; Kose, H. Selection of ore transport system for a metalliferous underground mine/Dobór systemu transportu rud w kopalni podziemnej rud metalu. *Arch. Min. Sci.* **2012**, *57*, 779–785. [CrossRef]
37. Eivazy, H.; Askari-Nasab, H. A hierarchical open-pit mine production scheduling optimisation model. *Int. J. Min. Miner. Eng.* **2012**, *4*, 89–115. [CrossRef]
38. Tom Socarras, J.N. Árbol de Decisión para la Gestión y Control de Costo de Transporte Interior Mina. Bachelor's Thesis, University of Chile, Santiago, Chile, 2014.
39. Uribe Neira, P.A. Análisis de la Funcionalidad y Desempeño de la Operación Semiautónoma en Equipos de Carga; Acarreo y Descarga en Minería Subterránea Load Haul-Dump Vehicle (LHD). Bachelor's Thesis, University of Chile, Santiago, Chile, 2014.
40. Więcek, D.; Burduk, A.; Kuric, I. The use of ANN in improving efficiency and ensuring the stability of the copper ore mining process. *Acta Montan. Slovaca* **2019**, *24*, 1–14.
41. Wiest Goyeneche, J.R. Modelo de Programación de Operaciones en una Mina a Cielo Abierto: Aplicación en Organización Corona. Master's Thesis, Universidad de La Sabana, Chía, Colombia, 2019.
42. Solomon, L.; Ortiz, A. Conceptual model of open pit ore loading and transport systems. *Univ. Cienc. Y Tecnol.* **2020**, *24*, 41–50.
43. Gaspar, S.; Jhasmin, C. Mejora de la Productividad en Equipos de Acarreo y Transporte de Mineral y Desmonte en la Veta Gavia–Nivel 100, Unidad Minera Huarón. Bachelor's Thesis, Universidad Continental, Los Olivos, Peru, 2020.
44. Li, N.; Feng, S.; Ye, H.; Wang, Q.; Jia, M.; Wang, L.; Zhao, S.; Chen, D. Dispatch Optimization Model for Haulage Equipment between Stopes Based on Mine Short-Term Resource Planning. *Metals* **2021**, *11*, 1848. [CrossRef]
45. Elijah, K.; Joseph, G.; Samuel, M.; Mauti, D. Optimisation of shovel-truck haulage system in an open pit using queuing approach. *Arab. J. Geosci.* **2021**, *14*, 973. [CrossRef]
46. Huisa Supho, A. Optimización de Equipos de Carguío y Acarreo en el Tramo Botaderos-Trituradora Thyssen Krupp, para el Incremento de Producción en una Empresa Cementera. Bachelor's Thesis Universidad Tecnológica Del Perú, Lima, Peru, 2021.
47. Choi, Y.; Nguyen, H.; Bui, X.N.; Nguyen-Thoi, T. Optimization of haulage-truck system performance for ore production in open-pit mines using big data and machine learning-based methods. *Resour. Policy* **2022**, *75*, 102522. [CrossRef]
48. Li, N.; Feng, S.; Lei, T.; Ye, H.; Wang, Q.; Wang, L.; Jia, M. Rescheduling Plan Optimization of Underground Mine Haulage Equipment Based on Random Breakdown Simulation. *Sustainability* **2022**, *14*, 3448. [CrossRef]
49. Abolghasemian, M.; Kanafi, A.G.; Daneshmand-Mehr, M. Simulation-based multiobjective optimization of open-pit mine haulage system: A modified-NBI method and meta modeling approach. *Complexity* **2022**, *2022*, 3540736. [CrossRef]
50. Shamsi, M.; Pourrahimian, Y.; Rahmanpour, M. Optimisation of open-pit mine production scheduling considering optimum transportation system between truck haulage and semi-mobile in-pit crushing and conveying. *Int. J. Min. Reclam. Environ.* **2022**, *36*, 142–158. [CrossRef]
51. Parichehreh, M.; Gholizadeh, H.; Fathollahi-Fard, A.; Wong, K. An energy-efficient unrelated parallel machine scheduling problem with learning effect of operators and deterioration of jobs. *Int. J. Environ. Sci. Technol.* **2024**, 1–26. [CrossRef]
52. Graham, R.L.; Lawler, E.L.; Lenstra, J.K.; Kan, A.R. Optimization and approximation in deterministic sequencing and scheduling: a survey. In *Annals of Discrete Mathematics*; Elsevier: Amsterdam, The Netherlands, 1979; Volume 5, pp. 287–326.
53. Pinedo, M.; Hadavi, K. Scheduling: Theory, algorithms and systems development. In *Proceedings of the Operations Research Proceedings 1991: Papers of the 20th Annual Meeting/Vorträge der 20. Jahrestagung*; Springer: Berlin/Heidelberg, Germany, 1992; pp. 35–42.
54. Yu, K.; Yang, J. MILP model and a rolling horizon algorithm for crane scheduling in a hybrid storage container terminal. *Math. Probl. Eng.* **2019**, *2019*, 4739376. [CrossRef]

55. Tarazona-Torres, L.E.; Amaya-Guio, C.A.; Álvarez-Martínez, D. Asynchronous Team for Flow Shop Scheduling Problem: A Case Study. In Proceedings of the 4th South American International Conference on Industrial Engineering and Operations Management, Lima, Peru, 9–11 May 2023.
56. Gurobi Optimization, LLC. *Gurobi Optimizer Parameters Version 10.0.2*; Gurobi Optimization, LLC.: Beaverton, OR, USA, 2024.
57. Cuellar-Usaquén, D.; Palacio, A.; Ospina, E.; Botero, M.; Álvarez-Martínez, D. Modeling and solving the endpoint cutting problem. *Int. Trans. Oper. Res.* **2023**, *30*, 800–830. [CrossRef]
58. Hou, Y.; Wang, H.; Huang, X. A Q-learning-based multi-objective evolutionary algorithm for integrated green production and distribution scheduling problems. *Eng. Appl. Artif. Intell.* **2024**, *127*, 107434. [CrossRef]

Disclaimer/Publisher's Note: The statements, opinions and data contained in all publications are solely those of the individual author(s) and contributor(s) and not of MDPI and/or the editor(s). MDPI and/or the editor(s) disclaim responsibility for any injury to people or property resulting from any ideas, methods, instructions or products referred to in the content.

Article

An Algorithm for Part Input Sequencing of Flexible Manufacturing Systems with Machine Disruption

Yumin He [1,*], Alexandre Dolgui [2] and Milton Smith [3]

1. School of Economics and Management, Beihang University, Beijing 100191, China
2. IMT Atlantique, LS2N-CNRS, 44307 Nantes, France
3. Department of Industrial Engineering, Texas Technology University, Lubbock, TX 79409, USA
* Correspondence: heyumin@buaa.edu.cn; Tel.: +86-010-18514218907

Abstract: Because disruption happens unpredictably and generates serious impact in supply chain and production environments in the real world, it is important to develop approaches to handle disruption. This paper investigates disruption handling in part input sequencing of flexible manufacturing systems (FMSs). An algorithm is proposed for FMS part input sequencing to handle machine breakage. Evaluation is performed for the proposed algorithm by simulation experiments and result analyses. Finally, conclusions are summarized with managerial implications discussed and further research works suggested.

Keywords: disruption handling; machine breakage; part input sequencing; FMS scheduling; dynamic scheduling; reactive scheduling

Citation: He, Y.; Dolgui, A.; Smith, M. An Algorithm for Part Input Sequencing of Flexible Manufacturing Systems with Machine Disruption. *Algorithms* **2024**, *17*, 470.
https://doi.org/10.3390/a17100470

Academic Editor: Roberto Montemanni

Received: 5 June 2024
Revised: 18 September 2024
Accepted: 24 September 2024
Published: 21 October 2024

Copyright: © 2024 by the authors. Licensee MDPI, Basel, Switzerland. This article is an open access article distributed under the terms and conditions of the Creative Commons Attribution (CC BY) license (https://creativecommons.org/licenses/by/4.0/).

1. Introduction

Disruption events occur unpredictably in supply chain (SC) and production environments. Unexpected events in real-world manufacturing environments include resource-related events and operation-related events [1]. Disruption happens in various fields in supply chain and production environments. Supply disruption, production disruption, and transportation disruption are examples of disruption forms [2]. With the increase in SC activities and global business activities, the impact of disruption could be substantial [3]. Because of the uncertainty in disruption event occurrence and the seriousness of disruption impact, disruption handling is an important issue. Manufacturing systems should be flexible so as to absorb disturbance on a short horizon [1].

Flexible manufacturing systems (FMSs) produce a middle volume and a wide variety of part types [4,5]. The systems aim to achieve efficiency of mass production systems and flexibility of job shops. FMSs possess not only computer numerical control machines but also automated material handling devices. These devices include automated guided vehicles, rail-guided vehicles, robots, and so forth. Researchers categorize different types of FMSs mainly as flexible flow systems and general flexible machining systems [6]. It is very complicated to manage FMS production. An FMS with capacity constraint may not produce orders in time, resulting in some parts having to be sent to a job shop [7].

Supply chain engineering is a very important issue in the area of production research. Because of the serious impact of disruption in supply chains and in production systems, research efforts are placed on disruption handling in supply chains and in production systems. The mitigation of disruption risk can be made proactive or reactive. Therefore, there are two types of disruption handling approaches for production scheduling, that is, proactive scheduling and reactive scheduling [8]. Proactive scheduling takes into account unexpected disruption to build protection when schedules are generated. Reactive scheduling adjusts schedules when unexpected disruption events happen. Dynamic systems can be managed by applying advanced information technology such as Radio Frequency Identification (RFID). Therefore, the application of advanced information technology makes it possible to obtain and process information to handle disruption reactively. This paper applies reactive scheduling to handle machine disruption in FMS part input sequencing. The paper proposes an algorithm to provide a solution for part input sequencing of FMSs with machine breakage.

The remainder of the paper is described in the following. Section 2 presents related works. In Section 3, an algorithm for part input sequencing of FMSs to handle machine breakage is proposed. Evaluation with the analyses of the results of the proposed algorithm is described in Section 4. Conclusions, managerial implications, and further works are summarized finally in Section 5.

2. Related Works

Disruption handling in supply chain environments has been investigated by researchers. For example, selection of part suppliers and schedule of customer orders over a planning horizon were studied under disruption risk in supply chains with a solution approach proposed to optimize the expected cost and customer service level [9]. A mixed-integer programming (MIP)-based approach was developed for decision- making to simultaneously select part suppliers and schedule production and delivery in an SC with disruption risk [10]. The adjustment in order activity in a four-echelon SC for recovery from disruption was investigated with dynamic order-up-to policies developed to obtain the benefits of the dynamic policies incorporated by a metaheuristic parameter search [3]. A two-period modeling approach and a multi-period modeling approach with mixed-integer programming were developed with supply chain disruption risk, requiring a very short computational time to obtain proven optimal solutions for reasonably sized problems [11]. Production ordering dynamics in the situation of disruption were suggested after studying production ordering behavior in a supply chain under disruption risk [12]. Integration of lot sizing and supplier selection under disruption risk with lead time uncertainty was studied with reliability and the price of suppliers considered and polyhedral-budgeted uncertainty sets applied to obtain a lot size for minimizing total cost [13]. A novel quantitative approach was developed for SC viability under ripple effect with the two conflicting objectives of cost and customer service level considered to obtain very high computation efficiency [14].

Disruption handling in production systems has been studied. For example, the lot-sizing and sequencing problem was investigated for production lines considering random machine breakage with an optimal approach developed based on the decomposition of the problem [15]. A model and a solution approach were developed for production inventory management in an imperfect production environment with numerical examples demonstrated for real-time disruption recovery [16]. The continuous flow problem with processing capacity disruption was studied with schedule robustness considered and a method developed for schedule robustness analysis based on attainable sets [8]. A flexible production inventory model was proposed to manage production and inventory with the consideration of disruptions of demand and production, for a manufacturer to decrease losses [17]. A model was formulated by applying genetic algorithm as well as pattern search to handle production disruption for an imperfect production inventory system with multiple products and a single stage [18]. A heuristic-based column generation approach was proposed for production planning to mitigate disruption from demand uncertainty for flexible manufacturing systems with good numerical results [19].

Scheduling in flexible manufacturing environments with disruption has been investigated by researchers. The following provides a brief summary. In particular, flexible job shop (FJS) scheduling considering machine disruption is summarized. In early research, reactive scheduling policies were proposed, such as when-to-schedule, how-to-schedule, and so forth, for handling machine breakage and processing time variation in a flexible manufacturing system [20]. A genetic hybrid control architecture ORCA was proposed for an FMS, which could provide the ability to switch between a hierarchy and heterarchy architecture when an unexpected event occurs [21]. A game model was developed for the flexible job shop scheduling problem subject to machine breakdown with two objectives of robustness and stability considered in their game procedure in rescheduling [22]. Evolutionary algorithms were applied to the FJS scheduling problem for improving makespan and stability with a comparison of the two proposed algorithms on example problems [23]. A hybrid approach was proposed for the FJS scheduling problem in dynamic environments for scheduling and rescheduling in disruption and experiments were performed for evaluation with the result of the competitiveness of the approach obtained [24]. Scheduling/rescheduling of flexible job shops were considered for machine recovery with an improved Jaya algorithm developed to minimize makespan in scheduling and to minimize both instability and makespan in rescheduling, generating the improved Jaya algorithm better than NSGAII and ISFLA in the non-dominated results [25]. Production scheduling and maintenance planning were considered in a flexible job shop in the situation of machine deterioration and a real-time system was proposed, which used a hybrid GA, an integrated model, and hybrid rescheduling policies [26]. A hybrid deep Q-network was built for dynamic FJS scheduling and for training to face disruption and experiments were performed to compare the method to scheduling rules, demonstrating the superiority of the proposed method [27]. A hierarchical-based deep reinforcement learning method was proposed for FJS scheduling and rescheduling and comparisons were made between the method and scheduling rules and other dynamic methods, demonstrating the superiority of the proposed method [28]. A flexible job shop scheduling method was proposed to consider machine breakdown and other dynamic events and to apply their dynamic event response strategy and their multi-objective model and to apply a multi-objective particle swam arithmetic optimization [29]. Even though disruption handling in FJS scheduling and in FMS scheduling has been investigated by researchers, the investigation of disruption handling in FMS part input sequencing is not seen. This paper investigates disruption handling in FMS part input sequencing. An algorithm for part input sequencing of FMSs with machine breakage is proposed.

3. Proposed Algorithm

The application of segment set functions to FMS scheduling problems has been conducted. For example, the functions have been utilized for developing the simultaneous part input sequencing and robot scheduling algorithm to simultaneously sequence and input parts and to schedule a robot in FMSs [5]. The functions are utilized here in developing the proposed algorithm. The functions are described by discrete mathematics. Discrete mathematics involves algorithm, logic, Boolean algebras, and so forth [30].

Segment set functions include the concepts of sets, domains, ranges, parts, and so forth. The functions consist of pair-wise elements of domains and ranges. For a simple set function, the 1st element of the function is a part in a set. The 2nd element of the function is an integer number representing the range of the function. For a transform function, the 1st element of the function is also a part in a set. The 2nd element of the function is the range of the function. The domain of the function is in multiple regions. The range of the function has segment values corresponding to different sets of parts. For a weight function, the 1st element of the function is similarly a part in a set. The 2nd element of the function is the range of the function. Different weights are assigned to the function to correspond to different sets of parts. For an overall function, the 1st element of the function is similarly a part in a set. The 2nd element of the function is similarly the range of the function. The range of the function has segment values corresponding to different sets.

A set of parts in the preprocess area of an FMS at time t are denoted as $A_x(t)$, $A_x(t) = \{b_{hi} | g_{b_{hi}x}(t) = 1\}$, where x is a part set indicator, b_{hi} is part h of order i, i is an order index, $i = 1, 2, \cdots$, h is an part index, $h = 1, 2, \cdots r_i$, r_i is the production requirement for order i; $g_{b_{hi}x}(t)$ is the part set status, $g_{b_{hi}x}(t) = \begin{cases} 1, & \text{part } b_{hi} \text{ is in set } A_x(t); \\ 0, & \text{otherwise}. \end{cases}$

$A_x(t)$ is classified as the other two sets of $A_a(t)$ and $A_b(t)$. Subset $A_a(t)$ is a balanced set. Subset $A_b(t)$ is an unbalanced set.

$$A_a(t) = \left\{ b_{hi} \big| b_{hi} \in A_x(t) \wedge g_{b_{hi}a}(t) = 1 \wedge M_{b_{hi}1} = \hat{j} \right\}, \tag{1}$$

$$A_b(t) = \left\{ b_{hi} \big| b_{hi} \in A_x(t) \wedge g_{b_{hi}b}(t) = 1 \wedge M_{b_{hi}1} \neq \hat{j} \right\}, \tag{2}$$

$A_a(t)$ and $A_b(t)$ are classified as other four sets, $A_u(t)$, $A_v(t)$, $A_m(t)$, and $A_n(t)$. Among those, $A_u(t)$ and $A_v(t)$ are subsets of $A_a(t)$.

$$A_u(t) = \left\{ b_{hi} \big| b_{hi} \in A_a(t) \wedge g_{b_{hi}u}(t) = 1 \wedge M_{b_{hi}1} = \hat{j} \wedge M_{b_{hi}2} = \tilde{j} \right\}, \tag{3}$$

$$A_v(t) = \left\{ b_{hi} \big| b_{hi} \in A_a(t) \wedge g_{b_{hi}v}(t) = 1 \wedge M_{b_{hi}1} = \hat{j} \wedge M_{b_{hi}2} \neq \tilde{j} \right\}, \tag{4}$$

$A_m(t)$ and $A_n(t)$ are subsets of $A_b(t)$.

$$A_m(t) = \left\{ b_{hi} \big| b_{hi} \in A_b(t) \wedge g_{b_{hi}m}(t) = 1 \wedge M_{b_{hi}1} \neq \hat{j} \wedge M_{b_{hi}1} = \tilde{j} \right\}. \tag{5}$$

$$A_n(t) = \left\{ b_{hi} \big| b_{hi} \in A_b(t) \wedge g_{b_{hi}n}(t) = 1 \wedge M_{b_{hi}1} \neq \hat{j} \wedge M_{b_{hi}1} \neq \tilde{j} \right\}. \tag{6}$$

The symbols in the above equations are explained in the following. $g_{b_{hi}q}(t)$ indicates the status of a part set, $g_{b_{hi}q}(t) = \begin{cases} 1, & \text{part } b_{hi} \text{ is in set } A_q(t); \\ 0, & \text{otherwise.} \end{cases}$ $M_{b_{hi}k}$ expresses the machine for k of part b_{hi}, k is an operation index. $\hat{j}$ expresses the machine that has the minimum of $\eta_j(t)$. $\tilde{j}$ expresses the machine that has the second minimum of $\eta_j(t)$. j is a machine indicator. $\eta_j(t)$ expresses the workload of machine j. For the above sets, the segment set functions can be obtained. A detailed description of these segment set functions is provided in [5].

An algorithm is proposed by applying the segment set functions to part input sequencing of FMSs for handling machine breakage. The proposed algorithm is segment set-based. It also applies the earliest due date scheduling rule for machine scheduling. Its aim is to achieve part input sequencing of FMSs to handle a machine breakage. It is simply called the machine disruption handling algorithm (MDH Algorithm, Algorithm 1). The proposed algorithm is depicted as follows. Additional symbols utilized in the algorithm are listed in Table 1.

Algorithm 1: Machine Disruption Handling Algorithm

Step 1. Initialize $t = t_0$, $\rho(t) = 0$, $\delta(t) = 0$, $m_r(t) = 0$, $m_j(t) = 1$, $j \in J$.
Step 2. Check the current t, If $t \geq T$, Stop.
Step 3. Check the current status of part b_{hi}. If part b_{hi} finishes processing, $\delta(t) = 1$, then $t = c_{hi}$. If $\delta(t) = 0$, go to Step 10.
Step 4. Obtain machine status. $m_j(t)$, $j \in J$. If $\forall j \in J$, $m_j(t) \vee m_r(t) = 0$, then identify and remove broken machine. Remove parts from broken machine.
$BM(t) = \left\{ j \big| j \in J \vee m_j(t) = 0 \right\}$, $t = t_p$, $m_r(t) = 1$.
Step 5. Place parts in preprocess area in $A_x(t)$, $A_x(t) = \left\{ b_{hi} \big| g_{b_{hi}x}(t) = 1 \right\}$. Update parts at $BM(t)$ in set $A_e(t)$, $A_e(t) = \left\{ b_{hi} \big| g_{b_{hi}e}(t) = 1 \right\}$. Update parts in $A_x(t)$ for not processing at $BM(t)$ in set $A_o(t)$, $A_o(t) = \left\{ b_{hi} \big| b_{hi} \in A_x(t) \wedge g_{b_{hi}o}(t) = 1 \right\}$. Update parts in set $A_x(t)$ for processing at $BM(t)$ in set $A_c(t)$, $A_c(t) = \left\{ b_{hi} \big| b_{hi} \in A_x(t) \wedge g_{b_{hi}c}(t) = 1 \right\}$.
Step 6. If $(m_r(t) \neq 0) \wedge (A_o(t) \neq \phi)$, then $A_y(t) = \left\{ b_{hi} \big| b_{hi} \in A_o(t) \right\}$, go to **Step 7**, else if $(m_r(t) = 0) \wedge (A_e(t) \neq \phi)$, then $A_y(t) = \left\{ b_{hi} \big| b_{hi} \in A_e(t) \right\}$, go to **Step 7**, else if $(m_r(t) = 0) \wedge (A_c(t) \neq \phi) \vee (m_r(t) = 0) \wedge (A_o(t) \neq \phi)$, then $A_y(t) = \left\{ b_{hi} \big| \{ b_{hi} \in A_c(t) \} \cup \{ b_{hi} \in A_o(t) \} \right\}$.

Algorithm 1. Cont.

Step 7. Obtain workload in the FMS at time t. Obtain the least workload machine, $\tilde{j} = \left\{ j | j \in J \wedge \eta_j(t) = \min\limits_{j \in J} \eta_j(t) \right\}$. Also, obtain the 2nd least workload machine $\tilde{\tilde{j}} = \left\{ j | j \in J \wedge \eta_j(t) = \min\limits_{j \in J, j \neq \tilde{j}} \eta_j(t) \right\}$. $A_x(t) = A_y(t)$. Apply Equation (1) to (6) to obtain subsets $A_q(t)$ for $q = a, b$, also for $q = u, v, m, n$. $g_{b_{hi}q}(t) = 1$, for $q = x, a, b$, also for $q = u, v, m, n$.

Step 8. Obtain segment set functions by equations in [5]. Obtain the simple set functions λ_q of set set $A_q(t)$ by Equation (13) for $q = x, a, b$, also for $q = u, v, m, n$. Obtain the transform function $\overline{\lambda}$ by Equations (14) and (19). Assign weights ξ_q for $q = u, v, m, n$. $\xi_u = -5K$ for $A_u(t)$, $\xi_v = -3K$ for $A_v(t)$, $\xi_m = -K$ for $A_m(t)$, $\xi_n = 0$ for $A_n(t)$. $K = 0.5S$. Obtain the weight function $\widetilde{\lambda}$ applying Equations (15) and (18). Obtain the overall function $\hat{\lambda}$ by Equations (16), (17) and (20).

Step 9. Obtain the minimal value of $\hat{\lambda}$, $\hat{\lambda}(t) = \min\limits_{b_{hi} \in A_x(t)} \left\{ \hat{\lambda}_q(t, b_{hi}), q = u, v, m, n \right\}$. Obtain the input part $b^* = \left\{ b_{hi} | b_{hi} \in A_x(t) \wedge a_{hi} = \min\limits_{b_{hi} \in A_x(t)} \left\{ a_{hi} | \hat{\lambda}_q(t, b_{hi}) = \hat{\lambda}(t), q = u, v, m, n \right\} \right\}$, $\delta(t) = 0$. $u(t) = m_{hi1} + t$, $t = u(t)$.

Step 10. If $\rho(t) = 1$, $u(t) = f_{b_{hi}k}(t)$, $t = u.(t)$. Obtain $m_{b_{hi}k}(t)$, $g = m_{b_{hi}k}(t)$, $\rho(t) = 0$, Obtain machine queue set $A_g(t) = \left\{ b_{hi} | g_{b_{hi}g}(t) = 1 \right\}$, else go to Step 2.

Step 11. Identify the part to be processed in the following. $p^* = \left\{ b_{hi} | b_{hi} \in A_g(t) \wedge a_{hi} = \min\limits_{b_{hi} \in A_{\backslash g}(t)} \left\{ a_{hi} | d_{hi} = \min\limits_{b_{hi} \in A_g(t)} d_{hi} \right\} \right\}$, $g_{b_{hi}g}(t) = 0$, go to Step 2.

Table 1. Additional symbols utilized in Algorithm 1.

Notation	Explanation
	Indices and Sets
g	Machine queue set indicator
J	Machine set, $J = \{1, 2, \cdots, M\}$
q	Part set indicator
	Parameters
a_{hi}	Arrival time of b_{hi}
d_{hi}	Due date of b_{hi}
K	Constant
M	Number of machines
m_{hik}	Robot move time for k of b_{hi}
S	Size of preprocess area
T	Production cycle
t_0	Initial time
ξ_q	Weight of $A_q(t)$
	Variables
$A_c(t)$	Part set for processing at $BM(t)$
$A_e(t)$	Part set needs repairing at t
$A_g(t)$	Machine queue set g at t
$A_o(t)$	Part set for not processing at $BM(t)$
$A_q(t)$	Part set q at t
$A_y(t)$	Part set y at t
b^*	Part for inputting
$BM(t)$	Broken machine at t
c_{hi}	Completion time of b_{hi}
$f_{b_{hi}k}(t)$	Completion time of k of b_{hi} at t
$g_{b_{hi}g}(t)$	$g_{b_{hi}g}(t) = \begin{cases} 1, & b_{hi} \text{ is in } A_g(t); \\ 0, & \text{otherwise.} \end{cases}$
$g_{b_{hi}q}(t)$	$g_{b_{hi}q}(t) = \begin{cases} 1, & b_{hi} \text{ is in } A_q(t); \\ 0, & \text{otherwise.} \end{cases}$
$m_{b_{hi}k}(t)$	Machine finishing k of b_{hi} at t

Table 1. Cont.

Notation	Explanation
$m_j(t)$	Machine operating status if it is available at t $$m_j(t) = \begin{cases} 1, & \text{machine } j \text{ is available at } t; \\ 0, & \text{otherwise.} \end{cases}$$
$m_r(t)$	Machine repair status if a broken machine is repairing at t $$m_r(t) = \begin{cases} 1, & \text{a brokrn machine is repairing at } t; \\ 0, & \text{otherwise.} \end{cases}$$
p^*	Part for processing
t_p	Machine broken time
$\delta(t)$	Part processing status when a part finishes its processing at t $$\delta(t) = \begin{cases} 1, & \text{a part finishes its processing at } t; \\ 0, & \text{otherwise.} \end{cases}$$
$\overline{\lambda}$	Transform function
$\tilde{\lambda}$	Weight function
$\hat{\lambda}$	Overall function
λ_q	Simple set function for $A_q(t)$
$\check{\lambda}(t)$	Minimal value of $\hat{\lambda}$
$\hat{\lambda}(t, b_{hi})$	Range of $\hat{\lambda}$ for b_{hi} at t
$\mu(t)$	Temporary completion time
$\rho(t)$	Part operation status when a part finishes an operation at t $$\rho(t) = \begin{cases} 1, & \text{a part finishs an operation at } t; \\ 0, & \text{otherwise.} \end{cases}$$

The proposed MDH Algorithm (Algorithm 1) is a dynamic algorithm. It utilizes the information of the dynamic workload to make an input decision. The dynamic workload is described in [5]. When a part completes operations, Algorithm 1 then inputs a part dynamically. The proposed algorithm identifies a broken machine on an FMS shop floor. It also identifies part processing at a broken machine. The algorithm handles machine breakage according to a different part processing status at a broken machine to identify parts for inputting. Advanced information technology like RFID can be applied for the implementation of a shop floor monitoring system. The shop floor monitoring system collects and processes dynamic information on an FMS shop floor. The proposed algorithm runs with the shop floor monitoring system that applies RFID to identify and handle machine breakage.

4. Evaluation with Result Analyses

The evaluation of the proposed algorithm is based on a simulation. It is difficult to simulate machine breakage and repair in flexible manufacturing systems in real-world production environments. Therefore, the proposed Algorithm 1 is evaluated by simulation experiments and statistical analyses in the situation with no machine breakage. The proposed algorithm is compared to an FMS part input sequencing algorithm, the state-dependent part input algorithm (SPI algorithm) in the literature [31]. The compared algorithm, the SPI algorithm (Algorithm A1), is provided in Appendix A.

The simulation model of the FMS and the simulation experiment settings are the same as those in [5,31]. One of the FMS scenarios in the numerical study in [31] does not obtain the best or the worst results among the four scenarios studied. This scenario was used for numerical study in [5]. This scenario is also utilized here for evaluating the proposed algorithm. The data used for evaluation are provided in Appendix B. Due dates for parts are $d_{hi} = 7500 + U(0, 6500)$. The adjustable constant is 7500 s. The uniformly distributed random variable is in the range of 0 to 6500 s. The parameters are set according to preliminary experiments so that the FMS generates approximately thirty percent of tardy parts.

Two approaches are compared using common random number technique for each pair of approaches so as to decrease variance. Ten independent simulation runs are performed with terminating simulation used. The simulation time per run for each approach is 200,000 s or 3333 min. There are more than 1000 parts produced during this simulation time. The system is in a steady state.

The performance measures used for evaluating the proposed algorithm include TP, MF, and RU. TP represents total parts produced, that is, the total number of parts produced in a production cycle. MF represents mean flowtime, that is, the total flowtime divided by the total parts produced. RU represents robot utilization, that is, the sum of the total time of robot moves divided by a production cycle.

The simulation data of TP, MF, and RU are analyzed. Averages of the performance measures TP, MF, and RU of Algorithm 1 from 10 independent simulation runs are displayed in Table 2. Averages of the performance measures TP, MF, and RU of Algorithm A1 from 10 independent simulation runs are also displayed in Table 2. The absolute improvement of Algorithm 1 versus Algorithm A1 is computed. The relative improvement of Algorithm 1 versus Algorithm A1 is also computed. The following equations are utilized for computing the absolute improvement and the relative improvement.

$$\omega = \left(\sum_{r=1}^{10}(\psi_r - \varphi_r)\right)/10, \tag{7}$$

$$\varpi = \left(\sum_{r=1}^{10}(\psi_r - \varphi_r)/\varphi_r\right) * 10, \tag{8}$$

where ω is absolute improvement. ϖ is relative improvement (%). r is simulation run index. ψ_r is the performance measure of approach ψ in simulation run r. φ_r is the performance measure of approach φ in simulation run r. The absolute improvement and relative improvement of Algorithm 1 versus Algorithm A1 for all performance measures TP, MF, and RU are also in Table 2.

Table 2. Comparison of Algorithm 1 to Algorithm A1.

Measure	TP (Parts)	MF (Minutes)	RU (%)
Algorithm 1	1254.9	86.38	71.03
Algorithm A1	1251.8	87.36	70.87
ω	3.1	0.98	0.16
ϖ (%)	0.25	1.12	0.23
Test statistic	1.4 *	2.44 *	1.17

Note: A bold number indicates the improvement of a performance measure. * indicates significant improvement of a performance measure.

It can be seen from the table that the averages of TP, MF, and RU by the proposed Algorithm 1 are 1254.9 parts, 86.4 min, and 71.03%, respectively. The averages of TP, MF, and RU by the comparative Algorithm A1 are 1251.8 parts, 87.4 min, and 70.87%, respectively. Algorithm 1 has better performance than Algorithm A1 for all performance measures of TP, MF, and RU as shown in the table. In the table, the absolute improvements ω of TP, MF, and RU by Algorithm 1 versus Algorithm A1 are 3.1 parts, 0.98 min, and 0.16%, respectively. The relative improvements ϖ of TP, MF, and RU for Algorithm 1 versus Algorithm A1 are 0.25 parts, 1.12 min, and 0.23%, respectively. The absolute and relative improvements in the table display the improvements of all the performance measures: TP, MF, and RU. The values in the table display that all performance measures obtained by Algorithm 1 are better than those obtained by Algorithm A1.

Significance tests are applied. The paired t-tests are conducted. The significance level is 0.1. The t-test statistic has the critical value of 1.37 at a significance level of 0.1. The test statistics obtained for the relative improvements by Algorithm 1 are 1.4, 2.44, and 1.17 for TP, MF, and RU, respectively, as illustrated in Table 2. The results show that TP and MF are improved significantly. Because MF improves, parts are produced faster with more parts produced. That TP and MF are significantly improved indicates a significant production increase. The results indicate that production is significantly increased by Algorithm 1 in comparison to Algorithm A1.

In summary, the comparative results show significant production increase by Algorithm 1 compared to Algorithm A1. All performance measures of TP, MF, and RU obtained by Algorithm 1 show improvements in comparison to the comparative Algorithm A1. The comparative results indicate that the performance of Algorithm 1 is improved compared to Algorithm A1. That is, Algorithm 1 is superior to Algorithm A1 from the literature in the situation with no machine breakage.

5. Conclusions and Future Work

Disruption happens in the real world in supply chain and production environments. This paper studies disruption handling of machine breakage in FMS part input sequencing. The MDH Algorithm is proposed for part input sequencing of FMSs with machine breakage. The proposed algorithm is based on reactive scheduling. Because of the difficulty in simulating FMS machine breakage and repair in real-world production environments, the proposed algorithm is evaluated in a situation with no machine breakage. The proposed algorithm is compared to an existing FMS part input sequencing algorithm from the literature, the state-dependent part input algorithm. The comparative results indicate that the proposed MDH Algorithm improves the performance significantly, generating the significant increase in total parts produced and mean flowtime decrease in the situation with no machine breakage. The evaluation results indicate the superiority of the MDH Algorithm in comparison to the state-dependent part input algorithm in terms of total parts produced, mean flowtime, and robot utilization in the situation with no machine breakage.

This paper contributes an applicable and effective algorithm for part input sequencing of FMSs to handle machine breakage. Managerial implications include the following. The proposed algorithm provides an applicable approach to the managers of FMSs to make FMS part input sequencing decisions for handling machine breakage. Disruption usually happens unpredictably in the real world. Real-time decision making applying advanced information technology such as RFID makes it possible to detect and handle disruption reactively and quickly. The proposed algorithm makes it possible to realize real-time decision making for part input sequencing of FMSs with machine breakage.

There are more random factors that affect FMS part input sequencing such as high-tech devices added on an FMS shop floor and rushed orders arriving at an FMS. Suggestions for future research could be to develop more effective algorithms to handle more situations of disruption in FMS part input sequencing. Additional suggestions for future research could be the development of decision support systems for part input sequencing of FMSs to handle machine disruption.

Author Contributions: Conceptualization, Y.H. and A.D.; formal analysis, Y.H.; investigation, Y.H.; methodology, Y.H., A.D. and M.S.; writing—original draft, Y.H.; writing—review and editing, Y.H., A.D. and M.S. All authors have read and agreed to the published version of the manuscript.

Funding: The second author's research was funded by the French National Research Agency (ANR), project ANR-21-CE10-0019.

Data Availability Statement: Data used in the performance evaluation in this study are from the previous studies. They are cited and are also provided in the Sections A and B in this paper. Additional supportive data can be made available from Yumin He upon reasonable request.

Acknowledgments: The efforts of the Academic Editor and the reviewers are appreciated. The comments and suggestions helped to improve our paper.

Conflicts of Interest: The authors declare no conflicts of interest.

Appendix A

Algorithm A1: State-Dependent Part Input Algorithm

Step 1. Form part set $M(t)$ from waiting parts in the preprocess area of an FMS at time t.

Step 2. Partition the parts in $M(t)$ into subsets of balanced set $X(t)$ and unbalanced set $Y(t)$. $X(t)$ possesses the parts having their first operation at the least loaded machine to help balance workload. $Y(t)$ possesses the parts not having the first operation at the least loaded machine. $X(t)$ and $Y(t)$ are further divided into another two subsets individually so that $M(t) = \cup_q G_q(t), q = \beta, \gamma, \mu, \nu$. $X(t) = G_\beta(t) \cup G_\gamma(t)$. $Y(t) = G_\mu(t) \cup G_\nu(t)$.

Step 3. Obtain the following simple set functions, λ_e for $M(t)$, λ_s for balanced set, and λ_p for unbalanced set,
$\lambda_e : M(t) \to I$. $\lambda_e = \{(\alpha_i, \lambda_e(t, \alpha_i)) \mid \alpha_i \in M(t), \lambda_e(t, \alpha_i) \in I\}$. $\lambda_s : X(t) \to I$. $\lambda_s = \{(\alpha_i, \lambda_s(t, \alpha_i)) \mid \alpha_i \in X(t), \lambda_s(t, \alpha_i) \in I\}$. $\lambda_p : Y(t) \to I$. $\lambda_p = \{(\alpha_i, \lambda_p(t, \alpha_i)) \mid \alpha_i \in Y(t), \lambda_p(t, \alpha_i) \in I\}$. Obtain the simple set functions $\lambda_q, q = \beta, \gamma, \mu, \nu$ for the subsets of balanced and unbalanced sets $G_q(t), q = \beta, \gamma, \mu, \nu$. $\lambda_\beta : G_\beta(t) \to I$. $\lambda_\beta = \{(\alpha_i, \lambda_\beta(t, \alpha_i)) \mid \alpha_i \in G_\beta(t), \lambda_\beta(t, \alpha_i) \in I\}$. $\lambda_\gamma : G_\gamma(t) \to I$. $\lambda_\gamma = \{(\alpha_i, \lambda_\gamma(t, \alpha_i)) \mid \alpha_i \in G_\gamma(t), \lambda_\gamma(t, \alpha_i) \in I\}$. $\lambda_\mu : G_\mu(t) \to I$. $\lambda_\mu = \{(\alpha_i, \lambda_\mu(t, \alpha_i)) \mid \alpha_i \in G_\mu(t), \lambda_\mu(t, \alpha_i) \in I\}$. $\lambda_\nu : G_\nu(t) \to I$. $\lambda_\nu = \{(\alpha_i, \lambda_\nu(t, \alpha_i)) \mid \alpha_i \in G_\nu(t), \lambda_\nu(t, \alpha_i) \in I\}$.

Step 4. Obtain the segment set function, $\lambda' : M(t) \to I$.
$\lambda' = \{\{(\alpha_i, \lambda_q(t, \alpha_i)) \mid \alpha_i \in G_q(t), \lambda_q(t, \alpha_i) \in I\}, q = \beta, \gamma, \mu, \nu\}$. Obtain the transform function that is also a segment set function, $\overline{\lambda} : M(t) \to I$. $\overline{\lambda} = \{\{(\alpha_i, \overline{\lambda}_q(t, \alpha_i)) \mid \alpha_i \in G_q(t), \overline{\lambda}_q(t, \alpha_i) \in I\}, q = \beta, \gamma, \mu, \nu\}$. $\overline{\lambda}_\beta(t, \alpha_i) = \lambda_s(t, \alpha_i) + \lambda_\beta(t, \alpha_i), \alpha_i \in G_\beta(t)$; $\overline{\lambda}_\gamma(t, \alpha_i) = \lambda_s(t, \alpha_i), \alpha_i \in G_\gamma(t)$; $\overline{\lambda}_\mu(t, \alpha_i) = \lambda_\mu(t, \alpha_i), \alpha_i \in G_\mu(t)$; $\overline{\lambda}_\nu(t, \alpha_i) = 0, \alpha_i \in G_\nu(t)$.

Step 5. Assign weights $\xi_q, q = \beta, \gamma, \mu, \nu$, $\xi_\beta = -5K$ for $G_\beta(t)$, $\xi_\gamma = -3K$ for $G_\gamma(t)$, $\xi_\mu = -K$ for $G_\mu(t)$, $\xi_\nu = 0$ for $G_\nu(t)$. $K = 0.5S$. $\hat{\lambda}_s(t, \alpha_i) < \hat{\lambda}_p(t, \alpha_i)$ is satisfied as explained in [31].

Step 6. Obtain the weight function,
$\widetilde{\lambda} : M(t) \to I$. $\widetilde{\lambda} = \{\{(\alpha_i, \widetilde{\lambda}_q(t, \alpha_i)) \mid \alpha_i \in G_q(t), \widetilde{\lambda}_q(t, \alpha_i) \in I\}, q = \beta, \gamma, \mu, \nu\}$. $\widetilde{\lambda}_q(t, \alpha_i) = \overline{\lambda}_q(t, \alpha_i) + \xi_q, q = \beta, \gamma, \mu, \nu$. Obtain the overall function,
$\hat{\lambda} : M(t) \to I$. $\hat{\lambda} = \{\{(\alpha_i, \hat{\lambda}_q(t, \alpha_i)) \mid \alpha_i \in G_q(t), \hat{\lambda}_q(t, \alpha_i) \in I\}, q = \beta, \gamma, \mu, \nu\}$. $\hat{\lambda}_\beta(t, \alpha_i) = \lambda_e(t, \alpha_i) + \lambda_s(t, \alpha_i) + \lambda_\beta(t, \alpha_i) + \xi_\beta, \alpha_i \in G_\beta(t)$; $\hat{\lambda}_\gamma(t, \alpha_i) = \lambda_e(t, \alpha_i) + \lambda_s(t, \alpha_i) + \xi_\gamma, \alpha_i \in G_\gamma(t)$; $\hat{\lambda}_\mu(t, \alpha_i) = \lambda_e(t, \alpha_i) + \lambda_\mu(t, \alpha_i) + \xi_\mu, \alpha_i \in G_\mu(t)$; $\hat{\lambda}_\nu(t, \alpha_i) = \lambda_e(t, \alpha_i) + \xi_\nu, \alpha_i \in G_\nu(t)$.

Step 7. Identify the minimal value of $\hat{\lambda}$, $\hat{\lambda}(t) = \min_{\alpha_i \in M(t)} \{\hat{\lambda}_q(t, \alpha_i), q = \beta, \gamma, \mu, \nu\}$. Then, input the part corresponding to the minimal element in the range of the overall function and arriving the earliest.

Table A1. Symbols in state-dependent part input algorithm.

Notation	Explanation
	Indices
α_i	Part in order $i, i = 1, 2, \cdots$
q	Part set indicator
	Parameters
K	Constant
S	Size of preprocess area
ξ_q	Weight of $G_q(t)$
	Variables
$G_q(t)$	Part set q at t
$M(t)$	Set of parts in preprocess area at t
$X(t)$	Balanced set of parts at t
$Y(t)$	Unbalanced set of parts at t
λ_e	Simple set function for $M(t)$
λ_p	Simple set function for $Y(t)$
λ_q	Simple set function for $G_q(t)$
λ_s	Simple set function for $X(t)$
λ'	Segment set function
$\overline{\lambda}$	Transform function

Table A1. *Cont.*

Notation	Explanation
$\widetilde{\lambda}$	Weight function
$\hat{\lambda}$	Overall function
$\hat{\lambda}(t)$	Minimal value of $\hat{\lambda}$
$\lambda_e(t, \alpha_i)$	Range of λ_e for $M(t)$ at t
$\lambda_p(t, \alpha_i)$	Range of λ_p for $Y(t)$ at t
$\lambda_q(t, \alpha_i)$	Range of λ_q for $G_q(t)$ at t
$\overline{\lambda}_q(t, \alpha_i)$	Range of $\overline{\lambda}$ for $G_q(t)$ at t
$\widetilde{\lambda}_q(t, \alpha_i)$	Range of $\widetilde{\lambda}$ for $G_q(t)$ at t
$\hat{\lambda}_q(t, \alpha_i)$	Range of $\hat{\lambda}$ for $G_q(t)$ at t
$\lambda_s(t, \alpha_i)$	Range of λ_s for $X(t)$ at t

Appendix B Data Used in Evaluation

Table A2. Production information.

Part Type	Prod. Req.	Part Type	Prod. Req.	Part Type	Prod. Req.
1	6%	10	8%	19	6%
2	2%	11	2%	20	4%
3	2%	12	6%	21	4%
4	2%	13	2%	22	6%
5	10%	14	4%	23	4%
6	2%	15	6%	24	2%
7	6%	16	4%	25	4%
8	2%	17	2%		
9	2%	18	2%		

Table A3. Processing times and part routes.

Type	Route	Processing Time (Seconds)
1	1 6 3 8	115 165 135 285
2	6 8 9 4 7 1 2 5 3	165 185 195 145 175 115 125 155 135
3	4 1 2 5 6	45 15 25 55 65
4	5 1 4 2 6 8	155 115 145 125 165 185
5	4 2 6 8 1	245 225 265 185 15
6	3 1 8	35 15 85
7	6 7 4 5 1 3 2	65 175 45 155 115 135 125
8	8 4 2	185 345 325
9	2 5 6 3 1 4	225 255 165 135 115 245
10	9 1 7 8	195 115 175 185
11	4 5 3 1 9 7 2 8 6	245 255 35 115 295 275 225 185 165
12	8 5 6 3 9 1 7	185 155 65 135 195 15 175
13	3 2 6 7 5	135 125 165 175 155
14	5 1 4 7 6 2	450 110 440 470 160 420
15	7 1 3 5	70 210 130 250
16	6 4 1 8 2	160 140 110 180 120
17	3 5 2 8 1	130 350 320 180 110
18	6 3 1 8 4	60 30 10 80 40
19	1 7 6 8 2 4 3	110 470 160 180 420 440 130
20	9 6 5 1 8 4 2	195 165 155 15 185 145 125
21	2 7 5 3	225 275 255 135
22	7 5 6 2 3 1	170 150 160 120 130 110
23	4 1 7 2 5	145 115 175 125 155
24	7 4 1 9	75 45 15 95
25	8 3 5 2 6 4 1 9	85 235 255 225 165 245 115 295

References

1. Proth, J.M. Scheduling: New trends in industrial environment. *Annu. Rev. Control* **2007**, *31*, 157–166. [CrossRef]
2. Ivanov, D.; Dolgui, A.; Sokolov, B.; Ivanova, M. Literature review on disruption recovery in the supply chain. *Int. J. Prod. Res.* **2017**, *55*, 6158–6174. [CrossRef]
3. Schmitt, T.G.; Kumar, S.; Stecke, K.E.; Glover, F.W.; Ehlen, M.A. Mitigating disruptions in a multi-echelon supply chain using adaptive ordering. *Omega* **2017**, *68*, 185–198. [CrossRef]
4. Stecke, K.E. Formulation and solution of nonlinear integer production planning problems for flexible manufacturing systems. *Manag. Sci.* **1983**, *29*, 273–288. [CrossRef]
5. He, Y.; Stecke, K.E. Simultaneous part Input sequencing and robot scheduling for mass customisation. *Int. J. Prod. Res.* **2022**, *60*, 2481–2496. [CrossRef]
6. Rachamadugu, R.; Stecke, K.E. Classification and review of FMS scheduling procedures. *Prod. Plan. Control* **1994**, *5*, 2–20. [CrossRef]
7. Tetzlaff, U.A.W.; Pesch, E. Optimal workload allocation between a job shop and an FMS. *IEEE Trans. Robot. Autom.* **1999**, *15*, 20–32. [CrossRef]
8. Ivanov, D.; Dolgui, A.; Sokolov, B.; Werner, F. Schedule robustness analysis with the help of attainable sets in continuous flow problem under capacity disruptions. *Int. J. Prod. Res.* **2016**, *54*, 3397–3413. [CrossRef]
9. Sawik, T. On the fair optimization of cost and customer service level in a supply chain under disruption risks. *Omega* **2015**, *53*, 58–66. [CrossRef]
10. Sawik, T. Integrated supply, production and distribution scheduling under disruption risks. *Omega* **2016**, *62*, 131–144. [CrossRef]
11. Sawik, T. Two-period vs. multi-period model for supply chain disruption management. *Int. J. Prod. Res.* **2019**, *57*, 4502–4518. [CrossRef]
12. Ivanov, D. Disruption tails and revival policies: A simulation analysis of supply chain design and production-ordering systems in the recovery and post-disruption periods. *Comput. Ind. Eng.* **2019**, *127*, 558–570. [CrossRef]
13. Thevenin, S.; Ben-Ammar, O.; Brahimi, N. Robust optimization approaches for purchase planning with supplier selection under lead time uncertainty. *Eur. J. Oper. Res.* **2022**, *303*, 1199–1215. [CrossRef]
14. Sawik, T. A stochastic optimisation approach to maintain supply chain viability under the ripple effect. *Int. J. Prod. Res.* **2023**, *61*, 2452–2469. [CrossRef]
15. Dolgui, A.; Levin, G.; Louly, M.-A. Decomposition approach for a problem of lot-sizing and sequencing under uncertainties. *Int. J. Comput. Integr. Manuf.* **2005**, *18*, 376–385. [CrossRef]
16. Paul, S.K.; Sarker, R.; Essam, D. Managing disruption in an imperfect production–inventory system. *Comput. Ind. Eng.* **2015**, *84*, 101–112. [CrossRef]
17. Xu, X.; Shang, J.; Wang, H.; Chiang, W.-C. Optimal production and inventory decisions under demand and production disruptions. *Int. J. Prod. Res.* **2016**, *54*, 287–301. [CrossRef]
18. Malik, A.I.; Sarkar, B. Disruption management in a constrained multi-product imperfect production system. *J. Manuf. Syst.* **2020**, *56*, 227–240. [CrossRef]
19. Elyasi, M.; Altan, B.; Ekici, A.; Özener, O.O.; Yanıkoğlu, I.; Dolgui, A. Production planning with flexible manufacturing systems under demand uncertainty. *Int. J. Prod. Res.* **2024**, *62*, 157–170. [CrossRef]
20. Sabuncuoglu, I.; Kizilishik, O.B. Reactive scheduling in a dynamic and stochastic FMS environment. *Int. J. Prod. Res.* **2003**, *41*, 4211–4231. [CrossRef]
21. Pach, C.; Berger, T.; Bonte, T.; Trentesaux, D. ORCA-FMS: A dynamic architecture for the optimized and reactive control of flexible manufacturing scheduling. *Comput. Ind.* **2014**, *65*, 706–720. [CrossRef]
22. Sun, D.; He, W.; Zheng, L.; Liao, X. Scheduling flexible job shop problem subject to machine breakdown with game theory. *Int. J. Prod. Res.* **2014**, *52*, 3858–3876. [CrossRef]
23. Ahmadi, E.; Zandieh, M.; Farrokh, M.; Emami, S.M. A multi objective optimization approach for flexible job shop scheduling problem under random machine breakdown by evolutionary algorithms. *Comput. Oper. Res.* **2016**, *73*, 56–66. [CrossRef]
24. Zhang, S.; Wong, T.N. Flexible job-shop scheduling/rescheduling in dynamic environment: A hybrid MAS/ACO approach. *Int. J. Prod. Res.* **2017**, *55*, 3173–3196. [CrossRef]
25. Gao, K.; Yang, F.; Li, J.; Sang, H.; Luo, J. Improved Jaya algorithm for flexible job shop rescheduling problem. *IEEE Access* **2020**, *8*, 86915–86922. [CrossRef]
26. Ghaleb, M.; Taghipour, S.; Zolfagharinia, H. Real-time integrated production-scheduling and maintenance-planning in a flexible job shop with machine deterioration and condition-based maintenance. *J. Manuf. Syst.* **2021**, *61*, 423–449. [CrossRef]
27. Li, Y.; Gu, W.; Yuan, M.; Tang, Y. Real-time data-driven dynamic scheduling for flexible job shop with insufficient transportation resources using hybrid deep Q network. *Robot. Comput. Integr. Manuf.* **2022**, *74*, 102283. [CrossRef]
28. Luo, S.; Zhang, L.; Fan, Y. Real-time scheduling for dynamic partial-no-wait multiobjective flexible job shop by deep reinforcement learning. *IEEE Trans. Autom. Sci. Eng.* **2022**, *19*, 3020–3038. [CrossRef]
29. Duan, J.; Wang, J. Robust scheduling for flexible machining job shop subject to machine breakdowns and new job arrivals considering system reusability and task recurrence. *Expert Syst. Appl.* **2022**, *203*, 117489. [CrossRef]

30. Johnsonbaugh, R. *Discrete Mathematics*; Prentice Hall: Hoboken, NJ, USA, 2004; pp. 55–111.
31. He, Y.; Rachamadugu, R.; Smith, M.L.; Stecke, K.E. Segment set-based part input sequencing in flexible manufacturing systems. *Int. J. Prod. Res.* **2015**, *53*, 5106–5117. [CrossRef]

Disclaimer/Publisher's Note: The statements, opinions and data contained in all publications are solely those of the individual author(s) and contributor(s) and not of MDPI and/or the editor(s). MDPI and/or the editor(s) disclaim responsibility for any injury to people or property resulting from any ideas, methods, instructions or products referred to in the content.

Minimum-Energy Scheduling of Flexible Job-Shop Through Optimization and Comprehensive Heuristic

Oludolapo Akanni Olanrewaju [1], Fabio Luiz Peres Krykhtine [2] and Felix Mora-Camino [1,3,*]

1. Industrial Engineering Department, Durban University of Technology, Steve Bicko Campus, Durban 4001, South Africa; oludolapoo@dut.ac.za
2. Industrial Engineering Department, Escola Politécnica, Universidade Federal do Rio de Janeiro, Rio de Janeiro 21941-853, Brazil; krykhtine@poli.ufrj.br
3. Industrial Engineering Department, Universidade Federal Fluminense, Campus de Rio das Ostras, Rio das Ostras 28895-532, Brazil
* Correspondence: felixmora@id.uff.br

Abstract: This study considers a flexible job-shop scheduling problem where energy cost savings are the primary objective and where the classical objective of the minimization of the make-span is replaced by the satisfaction of due times for each job. An original two-level mixed-integer formulation of this optimization problem is proposed, where the processed flows of material and their timing are explicitly considered. Its exact solution is discussed, and, considering its computational complexity, a comprehensive heuristic, balancing energy performance and due time constraint satisfaction, is developed to provide acceptable solutions in polynomial time to the minimum-energy flexible job-shop scheduling problem, even when considering its dynamic environment. The proposed approach is illustrated through a small-scale example.

Keywords: flexible job shop; scheduling; energy savings; make-span; two-level MILP; heuristics

1. Introduction

The improvement in energy efficiency has not played an explicitly relevant role in the operation of many manufacturing systems in the past since minimizing the make-span has often been the priority. Today, with the increasing prices of energy and the new environmental protection regulations, the energy-saving issue in workshops has become an important research field for universities backed by industrial organizations in advanced countries. The relation between industrial management styles, in particular Lean Management (LM) and its variants, and energy savings has been of recent concern [1], while new formulations of the job-shop scheduling problem, including the issue of energy, have been proposed. Further, authors such as those in [2–4] discussed the possibility of noticeably reducing energy consumption in manufacturing spaces with limited capital investment by rearranging the production process for a given demand through adequate machine selection and operation sequences. Also, in [5], it was shown that, by adjusting the power for each operation in a job-shop environment, relevant energy savings can be obtained. In the case of flexible job shops where machines can competitively perform different operations with differentiated energy costs [6], it is expected that energy-saving opportunities can be made more effective through appropriate machine allocation and the sequencing of operations in the job shop.

1.1. Literature Review

Before introducing the minimum-energy flexible job-shop scheduling problem with the due times considered in this study, an overview of previous instances of job-shop scheduling problems is presented here. The flexible job-shop scheduling problem, at first considered as a mere extension of the job-shop scheduling problem, where it is also necessary to assign machines to the operations of different jobs, has turned out to be, by its added complexity and its adequacy with current industrial practice (Industry 4.0), "a job shop scheduling problem of its own" [7]. In recent years, different reviews covering assumptions, models, and solution techniques for the flexible job-shop scheduling problem have been published [7–11]. Most of the formulations adopted have resulted in Mixed-Integer Linear Programming (MILP) optimization problems with sizes and complexity that often limit the use of exact methods. This has led to the proliferation of heuristics and meta-heuristics, notably nature-inspired ones, which proved rather effective [6,12].

In many studies, the exercise carried out when solving the scheduling problem boils down to delivering a mathematical solution without considering the conditions of its implementation. However, some authors have considered the real-life issues of their implementation by integrating them into the formulation of the scheduling problem to have more effective scheduling: the maintenance of machine condition [13], the availability of machines during production [14], and processing time uncertainties [15] are some of the covered topics. The real environment of production systems is dynamic and is subject to unexpected events such as sudden machine breakdowns, power outages, shortages of materials, the unavailability of operators, and unusual activity durations. Dynamic job-shop scheduling techniques were developed to cope with this reality [16,17]. These techniques are based on three different scheduling policies: predictive, reactive, and predictive–reactive [18]. Predictive approaches build a schedule that is maintained during execution, but when disturbances may appear, the maintenance of its feasibility has a time cost (slack times incorporated into the duration of the operations to absorb delays) and an equipment cost (spare machines to face breakdowns). The scheduling is recomputed with purely reactive approaches after each notable disturbance. Predictive–reactive approaches are a mix of the two previous approaches, where a pre-existent schedule is adapted online during its execution. These techniques increasingly involve tools from artificial intelligence (AI) [19].

When considering energy consumption in a job shop, it is composed of the processing energy consumed by machines; of the transfer energy of raw, semi-finished, or finished products within and around the job shop; of the idle energy consumed by machines during the time intervals between consecutive operations; of the set-up energy of machines to enable the processing of operations; and of the common energy consumed for maintaining acceptable operating conditions in the workshop (lighting, air conditioning, and heating). In flexible job shops, the energy-saving opportunities are not limited to those of job shops, i.e., turning off idle machines, slowing down machine speed, and producing during off-peak periods [20]; they also include the allocation of operations to more energy-efficient machines and the choice of energy-efficient means of transport between machines. This newer and more specialized area of the flexible job shop has been the subject of far fewer survey articles [4,21], even though articles on this subject are published regularly. In these studies, the classical concern has been about minimizing the make-span shifts toward the minimization of energy. Some articles consider a multi-criteria optimization problem with energy and make-span as equal objectives [22–26]; others adopt a single criterion, which can be the weighted sum of energy and make-span [27], the total energy with the make-span as a constraint [28], or the total energy and the make-span as a consequence [3]. Some publications have already addressed the problem of minimum-energy dynamic scheduling in flexible job shops using the predictive reactive approach [23,29].

1.2. The Adopted Approach to Tackle a New Instance of a Job-Shop Scheduling Problem

Considering this literature review and the adopted assumptions of the current study in Section 2, the scheduling problem treated in this study characterizes a sub-class of minimum-energy flexible job-shop scheduling problems for which, to our knowledge, until today, no specific study has been published. The specific characteristics of this problem include the following:

- Release and due time constraints are considered for each job instead of the make-span, which is an objective to be minimized. This differentiates the current problem from, for example, [3,22–28].
- Contrary to all the references consulted, the structures of the jobs are not limited to a mere sequence of activities and allow us to consider complex assembly and de-assembly operations.
- The delays and energy consumption resulting from product transfers between machines are considered. The only reference that considers transfer delays is [26]. However, transfer energy is not considered there.
- The adopted mono-criterion objective function. All the references cited in our literature review for flexible job shop scheduling consider the energy issue, except [3,28], which formulate a multi-criteria optimization problem.

The field of scheduling in industrial production workshops is all the more varied as numerous constraints specific to each realistic situation lead to problems for which different and often new resolution methods and associated algorithms must be developed. The philosophy adopted in this study to deal with a new scheduling problem, as is the case here, is the following:

- First, precisely mathematically formulate the optimization problem and analyze the feasibility of its resolution as a MILP problem using exact standard methods.
- Second, analyze the conditions for implementing a scheduling solution in a dynamic environment. This generally leads to considering the use of approximate resolution methods. At this stage, the generation of a heuristic appears interesting for several reasons: it allows us to obtain, at reduced computational cost, a feasible solution, and it supposes the identification and understanding of relatively simple decision-making mechanisms that can produce acceptable solutions. Heuristics that have been developed for scheduling problems with some common characteristics can be a source of inspiration for its design, and the resolution of their blocking points can be a start for the new heuristic. Once the heuristic has been developed, its performance must be compared with those obtained using exact methods and basic scheduling rules such as priority rules.
- Finally, in the case where it looks interesting to go beyond the performance of the solutions provided by the heuristic, in general by considering the use of metaheuristics (which are much more computation intensive in time and memory than heuristics), the generated heuristic method can be useful. It can provide a starting solution for an available metaheuristic. When a new metaheuristic has to be developed, the heuristic can also give directions for the design of new search mechanisms in the construction of more efficient solutions, or it can even be embedded in the metaheuristics.

1.3. The Objective of the Study

The objective of this study is to contribute to energy efficiency in the manufacturing industry, more particularly in high-energy-consuming integrated, flexible production plants, by developing a new approach to generate energy-efficient schedules with acceptable production delays for flexible job-shop scheduling problems. This study considers the main energy consumption sources in a flexible job shop, machine processing, and transfer of materials. Energy consumed by idle machines is not contemplated. Effectively, if idle times are small, the energy consumed by an idle machine may be negligible, while if idle times are large, the corresponding machines will certainly be shut off.

In this study, jobs are composed of a finite set of operations linked together by precedence–succession constraints without cycling, and due times are assigned to them. Flexibility here refers to the ability to assign the processing of certain operations to different machines. One important element of the solution is the concurrent assignment of the machines to the operations of the different jobs. As early as 1993, Brandimarte [30] considered a two-level approach with the decomposition of the flexible job-shop scheduling problem into routing and job-shop sub-problems to minimize the make-span of a given production plan. His work has received over 400 citations, mainly for his flexible job shop scheduling benchmark and its early use of Taboo Search [31] to solve the two sub-problems than for the proposed decomposition.

In this study, this dual view of the flexible job-shop problem is first adopted to achieve minimum energy schedules by considering the machine assignment of all the operations of a job as a decision variable. The non-consideration of the energy consumed by idle machines means that the energy consumption associated with a production program only depends on the allocation of the operations of each job to the different machines of the job shop and not the timing adopted for their execution. This leads to a formulation of a two-level optimization problem where energy costs and job shop dynamics are separated, opening the way to use exact or approximate solution approaches for this class of mathematical programming problem. This will provide nominal solutions to production plans over a finite period. However, the objectives of this study go well beyond this result. The goal is to propose a scheduling scheme that can adapt easily to cope efficiently with the following:

- Planned (scheduled maintenance, for example) or unplanned disturbances (machine or conveyor breakdown between machines, for example);
- The fast generation of energy-efficient schedules to cope with the arrival of new jobs, allowing permanent operation with the efficient energy performance of the job shop.

This goal has led to the development, in a second step of the study, an ad hoc heuristic able to produce promptly after any significant perturbation or event, an updated solution consistent with the current operational state of the job shop for this original scheduling problem.

The rest of this paper is organized as follows: first, the characteristics of the considered job shop and the adopted notations are displayed in section two; section three presents a separable formulation of a nominal minimum-energy flexible job-shop problem is introduced to ease the search for its exact solution; a heuristic based on the earliest processing time with minimum energy is introduced to generate an open-loop solution to the scheduling problem in the fourth section. Then, the extensions of this heuristic to enable it to cope with disruptions and new jobs are discussed, and the application to a small illustrative case is displayed. Finally, in the Conclusion section, additional research directions are pointed out.

2. The Considered Class of Flexible Job Shops and Their Representation

The considered class of production systems is composed of flexible machines that operate in parallel. There, different products are processed through a subset of production stages in which a machine is assigned to perform a specific operation on a given product. The final products are obtained at the end of the sequences of operations.

2.1. Basic Assumptions

The basic assumptions characterizing the considered flexible job-shop scheduling problem are introduced.

2.1.1. The Plant

The plant is composed of a set of machines, some of which may perform the same tasks. Machines have a fixed position in the workshop, and physical connections exist between some of these machines to allow the transfer of semi-processed products from one machine to the next. The transfer operations are supposedly independent of each other, and it is assumed that there is no traffic congestion in the plant. Then, for each job, the transfer times and energies are constant parameters whose values depend on the position and characteristics of the assigned machines.

2.1.2. The Production Plan

The production plan is composed of independent jobs that can be identical or different; this production plan is known in advance. Each job consists of a set of operations performed on different machines. A directed acyclical graph can represent the precedence/succession constraints between these operations. The introduction of this graph allows one to handle parallel operations within the same job. This does not prevent the repeated use of the same machine for different operations of the same job but assumes that the operations are only executed once per job. This last limitation can be easily overcome by renaming an operation each time, which must be repeated a given number of times within a job. The subset of machines that can carry out each job operation in the workshop is known. For each job of the production plan, a release time and a due time are attached. It is supposed that there are global schedules satisfying the resulting time constraints. Contrary to the Just-In-time scheduling problem, tardiness is not allowed here.

2.1.3. The Operations

The common working period starts at time 0, and its maximum time span is noted as T. All considered jobs have a known release time and a preferred due time. Machines are available for operations since time 0; in the first stage, it is assumed that no breakdowns and maintenance operations occur until time T. Non-dummy operations need only one machine to be performed, machines can only execute one operation at a given time, and pre-emption of machines by other operations is not allowed. A machine can be used more than once by a given job but in different operations. The set-up times of the machines are integrated into the processing times, which, with the transportation times between machines, are considered in this study. Some jobs may have a declared due time that induces a time constraint, which, depending on the context, may be considered hard or soft; the other jobs use T as the due time.

2.1.4. The Objectives

The main objective of this study is to propose a method to minimize the total energy needed to perform a given production plan while satisfying due time constraints for each job. The energy of interest is composed of the processing energy of the different operations on their assigned machines and of the internal logistics energy spent to transport materials from one machine to the next. Here, it is assumed implicitly that there is a unique source of energy, electricity, but this hypothesis could easily be revised.

2.2. Adopted Notations and Representation for Work Plans

The main indexes used to identify the different elements of the sets of interest are as follows:

- i: index of jobs, $i \in \{1, \ldots, n\}$ with $n = |J|$, where J is the set of jobs to be processed.
- k, h: index of operations, $k, h \in \{1, \ldots, S_i\}$ with $S_i = |O_i|$, where $O_i = \{O_{i1}, \ldots, O_{S_i}\}$ is the set of operations of job i.
- l: index of machines, $l \in \{1, \ldots, m\}$ with $m = |M|$, where M is the set of machines.

To each job i, a directed a-cyclical graph (DAG) is attached, which represents the precedence and succession constraints between its operations. The operations of each job are performed to start and finish with dummy operations of zero duration on the same dummy machines. The operations of a job i are ordered by their increasing rank in G_i. Let Γ_{ik}^{-1} and Γ_{ik} be, respectively, the set of predecessor and successor operations of O_{ik}. The depth of the DAG associated with job i has a depth dr_i, where rank 1 corresponds to the dummy starting operation and rank dr_i corresponds to the dummy closing operation. GL_{ir} is the subset of operations of job i at rank r and $O_i = \oplus_{r=1}^{r=dr_i} GL_{ir}$. Let rt_i and dt_i be, respectively, the release time and the due time of job i, $i = 1$ to n, where these due times are supposed to be inferior or equal to T. M_{ik} is the subset of machines that can perform operation O_{ik}, δ_{ikl} is the processing time of O_{ik} with its lth machine, and $\tau_{ill'}$ is the transfer time between machine l and machine l' for job i. The nominal transfer time is, in general, the transportation time of the product from one machine to the next, but it can also include other side operations (drying delays, set-up times, and inspection delays). Let pe_{ikl} be the energy necessary for machine l, $l \subset M_{ik}$, to perform O_{ik}, and let $te_{ill'}$ be the energy necessary to transfer product i from machine l to machine l' and other necessary inputs to perform O_{ik} on machine l'.

Figure 1 introduces the DAGs associated with a production plan composed of three jobs. Table 1 shows the machines that can perform the operations of these three jobs, and Figure 2 represents the different possible transfers between successive machines according to the different jobs.

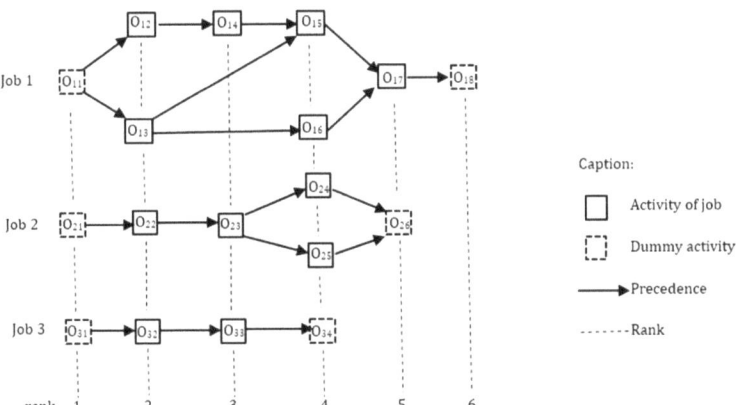

Figure 1. Graphical representation of a production plan.

Table 1. Machines available for operations in production plan.

O_{ik}	O_{11}	O_{12}	O_{13}	O_{14}	O_{15}	O_{16}	O_{17}	O_{21}	O_{22}	O_{23}	O_{24}	O_{25}	O_{26}	O_{31}	O_{32}	O_{33}	O_{34}
M_{ik}	∅	{m_1,m_2}	{m_1,m_2}	{m_3,m_4}	{m_3,m_4}	{m_5}	∅	∅	{m_6,m_7}	{m_2}	{m_3,m_4,m_5}	{m_3,m_4,m_5}	∅	∅	{m_1,m_2}	{m_6,m_7}	∅

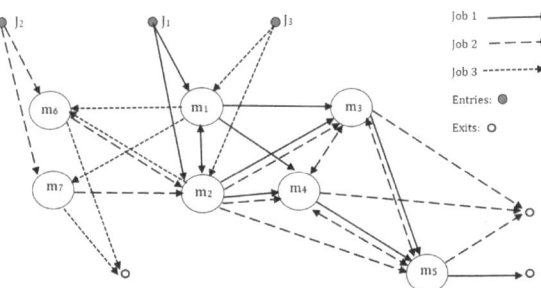

Figure 2. Transfers between machines in a flexible job shop.

The assignment of machines to the successive operations of a job build a unique path between its entry and exit nodes in the directed graph of Figure 2.

The material flow of product under transformation is supposed to be mainly composed of original products to which additional inputs can be aggregated at the level of the operations and from which waste can be retrieved. These aggregations or removals induce costs which, beyond the physical characteristics of the operations, can be related to the position of the machines into the plant. In this study, the different flows of material under processing are taken into consideration. A physical interdependence between the different jobs results from the way the set of machines is shared during the period of operation.

3. Two-Level Formulation of the Minimal-Energy Flexible Job-Shop Scheduling Problem

The flexibility of the job shop presents an additional dimension to the scheduling problem: the assignment of machines to the operations of each job. Technical and functional considerations mean that this choice is limited and multiplies with the number of operations comprising the jobs and with the presence of several machines capable of carrying out the same operations. Here, the assignment of machines to the operations of each job is identified by a decision variable, leading to a two-level formulation of the considered scheduling problem. To accomplish this, additional notations must be introduced.

3.1. Adopted Notations and Representation

Here, A is the set of possible assignments of machines to the operations of all the jobs to be processed, $A = \{A_j, j = 1, \ldots, |A|\}$, and A_{ij} is the projection of the jth assignment on the operations of job i. $A_i = \oplus_{j=1}^{|A|} A_{ij}$ is the set of all possible machine assignments for job i. The overall knowledge of the allocation of machines to the different jobs is necessary to treat the case of a specific job since these jobs may use subsets of machines concurrently. The index of the machine attached to the processing of O_{ik} in the jth machine assignment is written as l_{ikj}.

The maximum number of different assignments of machines for a job i is given by

$$n_i^A = |A_i| = \prod_{k=2}^{S_i - 1} |M_{ik}| \tag{1}$$

and the maximum number of different machine assignments for the whole production plan is given by

$$n^A = |A| = \prod_{i=1}^{n} n_i^A \tag{2}$$

These numbers can be significantly reduced considering the layout of the plant, the existing transfer system, and the operational state of the machines. In the illustrative case of Section 2.2, we have the following: $n_1^A = 16$, $n_2^A = 18$ and $n_3^A = 4$, leading to $n^A = 1152$, which is a rather large number. But if adopting the rule that, when two successive operations of the same job can be processed by the same machine, there is no change of machine from the first to the second operation, then the number of accepted machine assignments decreases to 96. In fact, this rule allows one to melt down these pairs of operations into a single one, reducing the size of the scheduling problem.

Let us introduce the processing and transfer times for a given machine assignment: d_{ikj} is the processing duration of O_{ik} by machine l_{ikj}, $i = 1$ to n, $k = 1$ to S_i, and $j = 1$ to n^A; and T_{ihkj} is the nominal transfer time of product (i,h) from machine l_{ihj} to machine l_{ikj}, $i = 1$ to n, $h = 1$ to S_i, $k \in \Gamma_{ih}$, and $j = 1$ to n^A.

When, for machine assignment j, a destination machine l_{ihj} of operation O_{ik} is busy with another operation, it is supposed that the semi-processed material of job i can wait without using energy until machine l_{ihj} becomes available.

3.2. Absolute Time Bounds

In this subsection, lower bounds for the earliest start times and upper bounds for the latest start times of the operations of each job for a given machine assignment j are introduced:

- est_{ikj} is the earliest start time of operation O_{ik} with machine assignment A_{ij} when the release time is respected.
- lst_{kjk} is the latest start time of operation O_{ik} with machine assignment A_{ij} when the due time is respected.

We have the following for job i with machine assignment A_{ij}:

$$est_{i1j} = rt_i \text{ and } est_{ikj} = est_{ik-1j} + \max_{h \in \Gamma_{ik}^{-1}} \left\{ est_{ihj} + d_{ihj} + T_{ihkj} \right\}, k = 2 \text{ to } S_i \tag{3}$$

$$lst_{iS_ij} = dt_i - d_{iS_i} \text{ and } lst_{ikj} = \min_{h \in \Gamma_{ik}} \left\{ lst_{ihj} - T_{ikhj} \right\} - d_{ikj}, k = S_i - 1 \text{ to } 1 \tag{4}$$

where rt_i and dt_i are, respectively, the release time and the due time of job i.

It can be observed that these earliest and latest start times do not consider the possible concurrent use of the machines by different jobs and the resulting additional delays, so they are, respectively, a lower bound for the earliest start time and an upper bound of the latest start times. Consistency conditions for the time data are

$$est_{ikj} \leq lst_{ikj}, \quad i = 1 \text{ to } n, \, k = 1 \text{ to } S_i, \, j = 1 \text{ to } |A_i| \quad (5)$$

$$lst_{i1j} - d_{i1j} \geq rt_i \quad \text{and} \quad est_{iS_ij} + d_{iS_ij} \leq dt_i \quad i = 1 \text{ to } n, \, j = 1 \text{ to } |A_i| \quad (6)$$

If a machine assignment j for job i does not satisfy fully relations (5) and (6), it must be eliminated from A_i.

It is also possible to compute the absolute earliest start time for each operation of each job:

$$Est_{ik} = \min_{j \in A_i}\left\{est_{ikj}\right\} \quad i = 1 \text{ to } n, \, k = 1 \text{ to } S_i \quad (7)$$

It can be observed here that the release time and the due times are not, in general, of the same nature: the release times are independent of the considered process and result from upstream logistics; the due times result from downstream logistics. Then, here, release times are hard constraints, while due times can be a production objective that may not be completely achieved. Thus, the latest starting times and due times constraints can be violated, and the resulting delays characterize a deficit in the production capacity of the job shop to process a given production plan.

3.3. Total Energy Consumed

Here, for a given machine assignment j, the energy consumption is considered composed of the energy PE_{ikj} necessary to process operations with machines l_{ikj} and the energy $TE_{ikl_{ihj}j}$ to transport processed products from a machine l_{ikj} to the successor machines l_{ihj} with h in Γ_{ik}. Then, the energy used in processing job i within machine assignment j can be written as

$$E_{ij} = \sum_{k=1}^{S_i} PE_{ikj} + \sum_{k=0}^{S_i} \sum_{h \in \Gamma_{ik}} TE_{ikl_{ihj}j} \quad i = 1 \text{ to } n, \, j = 1 \text{ to } |A| \quad (8)$$

This expression does not consider the energy consumed by idling machines. Depending on the machine and the durations of its idling periods, it may be interesting to save energy to turn them off when they are not in use rather than leaving them on. Restarting a machine can not only result in a temporary overconsumption of energy but also in a delay of its availability. In this study, it is assumed, since it is generally the case in industrial workshops, that the energy consumption of the idling machines is negligible compared to the processing and transfer energies. So, it does not seem necessary to explicitly introduce this component of the energy spent in a mathematical formulation of the scheduling problem, especially since this would lead to increased complexity resulting from the new variables and constraints to be introduced. What can be achieved—once a solution to the overall scheduling problem has been obtained that minimizes the main components of the consumed energy, whether this solution is exact or approximate—is, in a second step, to evaluate the idle periods of each machine and decide whether to turn them off or keep them on until their next use. This is the kind of problem that could be solved by an expert system using artificial intelligence techniques to exploit both the characteristics of the scheduling solution and the energy performance of each machine.

3.4. The Two-Level Minimum-Energy Scheduling Problem

The minimum-energy flexible job-shop scheduling problem formulated as an optimization problem by using the machine assignment variables x_{ij}, the precedence variables $z_{iji'j'kk'}$ and the timing variables t_{ijk} is the following:

$x_{ij} = 1$ if machine assignment j is chosen to perform job i, and $x_{ij} = 0$ otherwise;

t_{ikj}: the starting time of operation O_{ik} at machine l_{ikj};

$z_{iji'j'kk'} = 1$ if operation O_{ik} with machine l_{ikj} is decided to be realized before operation $O_{i'k'}$ using the same machine ($l_{ikj} = l_{i'k'j'}$), and $z_{iji'j'kk'} = 0$ otherwise.

The problem is formulated as a mono-criterion optimization problem, avoiding the introduction of relative weights between criteria or the exploration of a Pareto frontier involving energy and make-span. The global criterion to be minimized is expressed as

$$\min_{x,t,z} E_T = \sum_{i=1}^{n} \sum_{j=1}^{|A_i|} x_{ij} \cdot E_{ij} \qquad (9)$$

The considered constraints are

$$\sum_{j \in A_i} x_{ij} = 1 \qquad i = 1 \text{ to } n \qquad (10)$$

and for ij, such as $x_{ij} = 1$:

$$est_{i1j} \leq t_{i1j} \quad i = 1 \text{ to } n \qquad (11)$$

$$\max_{h \in \Gamma_{ik}^{-1}} \left\{ t_{ihj} + d_{ihj} + T_{ihj} \right\} \leq t_{ikj} \; i = 1 \text{ to } n, k = 2 \text{ to } S_i \qquad (12)$$

$$t_{iS_ij} + d_{iS_ij} \leq dt_i \; i = 1 \text{ to } n \qquad (13)$$

For ij and $i'j'$, such as $x_{ij} = x_{i'j'} = 1$:

$$\forall i \neq i', \forall j, j', \forall k, k' \text{ with } l_{ikj} = l_{i'k'j'} : z_{iji'j'kk'} + z_{i'j'ijk'k} = 1 \qquad (14)$$

$$\forall i \neq i', \forall j, j', \forall k, k' \text{ with } l_{ikj} \neq l_{i'k'j'} : z_{iji'j'kk'} = z_{i'j'ijk'k} = 0 \qquad (15)$$

and $\forall i \neq i', \forall j, j', \forall k, k'$ with $l_{ikj} = l_{i'k'j'}$:

$$t_{ikj} + d_{ikj} \leq t_{i'k'j'} + V\left(1 - z_{iji'j'kk'}\right) \text{ and } t_{ikj} + d_{ikj} + V \cdot z_{iji'j'kk'} \geq t_{i'k'j'} \qquad (16)$$

The significance of the different constraints are as follows: constraint (10): the choice of a unique path for each job; constraint (11): feasibility bounds for the starting time of the first operation of job i with machine assignment j; constraint (12): starting time succession constraints along a path; constraint (13): due time constraints for the different jobs, where $t_{iS_ij} + d_{iS_ij}$ is the completion time of job i along path j; constraints (14), (15), and (16): non-overlapping of operations of chosen paths on the same machine, where V is a very large number. However, in situations in which the feasible time intervals for processing on a same machine ($l_{ikj} = l_{i'k'j'}$) do not intersect, the value of the z variable is already fixed:

$$lst_{ikj} + d_{ikj} \leq est_{i'k'j'} : z_{iji'j'kk'} = 1 \qquad (17)$$

$$est_{ikj} \geq lst_{i'k'j'} + d_{i'k'j'} : z_{iji'j'kk'} = 0 \qquad (18)$$

Problem (9)–(16) is a two-level optimization problem, where the machine assignment problem, with the objective of minimizing total energy consumption, is considered at the upper level (relations (9) and (10), with only decision variable x_{ij}), while at the lower level, the satisfaction of dynamic constraints (11)–(16) lead to a feasible scheduling. Different approaches appear of interest to generate solutions for instances of this problem, which is expected to be of the NP-Complete complexity class [32]. The transformation of formulation (9)–(16) into an MILP-type formulation greatly increases the number of variables and constraints, making its exact numerical resolution difficult. In [33], a greedy heuristic was developed to provide, within the adopted formalism, a feasible sub-optimal solution for a simplified version of this problem: there, the DAGs of the jobs reduced to single chains, which were selected repeatedly according to their energy performance until the due dates were satisfied. To design exact solution algorithms, Branch and Bound strategies appear here to be of direct interest. Also, Benders decomposition-based algorithms, developed to solve general two-level optimization problems, could be particularized to this problem [34]. The above problem can also be seen as a simplified case of a bi-level MILP problem. In that last field, many exact [35,36] and approximate [37,38] methods have been proposed in the recent literature. Relevant work could improve the computational efficiency of some of these methods when applied to problems (9)–(16).

3.5. Evaluation of Solution Performance

The solution of the above problem produces the make-span:

$$MS = \max_{\forall i, \forall j \in A_i} \left\{ (t_{iS_i j} + d_{iS_i j} | x_{ij} = 1) \right\} - \min_{\forall i, \forall j \in A_i} \left\{ (t_{i1j} | x_{ij} = 1) \right\} \qquad (19)$$

In Equations (14)–(16), the decision variables x_{ij} are absent; then, by choosing for each t_{ijk} with $x_{ij} = 0$, their earlier starting time, constraints (14)–(16) are satisfied by these t_{ijk} variables. Then, in the case in which all the release time are to zero, (19) can be rewritten more simply:

$$MS = \max_{\forall i, \forall j \in A_i} \left\{ t_{iS_i j} + d_{iS_i j} \right\} \qquad (20)$$

In the general case, the make-span for machine l is given by

$$MS_l = \max_{i,k,j} \left\{ t_{ikj} | x_{ij} = 1 \text{ and } l_{ikj} = l \right\} - \min_{i,k,j} \left\{ t_{ikj} | x_{ij} = 1 \text{ and } l_{ikj} = l \right\} \qquad (21)$$

and the total processing time of machine l is given by

$$PT_l = \sum_{i=1}^{n} \sum_{j \in A_i} x_{ij} \sum_{k \in \{1, \ldots, S_i\}, \, l_{ikj} = l} d_{ikj} \qquad (22)$$

Assuming that the machines once started are shut down only when their last operation is completed, their idle time where a residual amount of energy is used is given by

$$IT_l = MS_l - PT_l \qquad (23)$$

It can be observed that the resolution of problem (9)–(16) will provide a scheduling of minimum total energy without considering the consequences for its make-span. If the jobs had no due times and the working period [0, T] was sufficiently large, the solution of problem (9)–(16) will consist of selecting each job's machine assignment of minimum energy E_{ij}. A way to introduce the make-span minimization objective can be obtained by setting, at smaller values, the due times of the different jobs or their global maximum value $\max_i \{dt_i\}$ according to the production context. Successive resolutions of the problem with decreasing due times will make it possible to highlight the influence of the make-span on the energy performance of the workshop for a given production plan J. This influence should be analyzed to enable the identification of characteristic patterns within some families of production plans, which will allow, once again by using artificial intelligence techniques such as Machine Learning [39,40], to guess correctly the feasibility of the adopted due times before embarking on the numerical resolution of the optimization problem.

4. Minimum-Energy Scheduling Heuristic with Due Times

The previous section considered a deterministic situation, and the solution of the minimum-energy flexible job-shop will provide the best schedule to follow during nominal conditions. The analysis of optimal solutions makes it possible to evaluate the performance of the job shop and identify its blocking points, eventually leading to its redesign or resizing. Then, different configurations of the job shop can be assessed through the optimal solution of the scheduling problem by considering a set of typical production plans. However, when considering the very common situation in which the workshop is subject to disturbances (delays, malfunctioning or breakdowns of machines, and unavailability of operators), to postponement of jobs, or to the arrival of new jobs to be processed in the same period, the optimal schedule is no more completely feasible. Until a new stabilized situation is established in the job shop and a new optimal schedule is established, short-term local decisions should be taken to keep the job shop in operation. In the case in which perturbations occur frequently, it will be necessary to establish a much more responsive system. Also, when the job shop is working full time, the segmentation of production into finite production plans should lead to sub-optimal schedules. Considering the limitations of this approach, an open-loop heuristic to cope, on a reactive basis with the minimum-energy flexible job-shop scheduling problem, is introduced in this section. In the first stage, the heuristic is developed to cope with a given production plan where jobs have release and due times; then, it is shown how to extend its application to the dynamic environment of workshops.

4.1. Adopted Principles to Design the Heuristic

Here, the main idea is to develop, on a moving time front line, the allocation of machines and time schedules at the earliest start time of operations in ascending rank in any of the active jobs. This greedy scheme will promptly produce a solution promoting energy savings that is feasible for the current situation of the job shop. This will allow a reactive approach to reschedule the current production plan as many times as necessary. The solution must face the dilemma of having to choose between short job processing times and minimizing the necessary energy. This is achieved as follows: on the one side, the earliest assignment of a machine to a new operation is performed, but on the other side, the choice between the available machines is limited to the more energy efficient ones. The decision to assign a machine and to schedule the starting time for an operation will be based, on one side, on the processing delays and transfer delays from its directly preceding operations and, on the other side, on the transfer energy from the preceding operations and on the processing energy of the candidate machine. The driving dimension in the heuristic is time, since this will yield feasible solutions constructed step by step in the timeline according to the earliest feasible starting time for the operations. To assess, according to energy, the transitions from one operation to a successor one, new parameters must be defined. For operations O_{ih} and O_{ik} such that $O_{ik} \in \Gamma_{ih}$, the energy cost of deciding that O_{ik} will be processed by machine l', while O_{ih} is performed by machine l_h, is the sum of the transfer energy and of the process energy $tpe_{ihkll'}$ given by $tpe_{ihkll'} = \sum_{h \in \Gamma_{ik}^{-1}} te_{il_hl'} + pe_{ikl'}$ (see Figure 3).

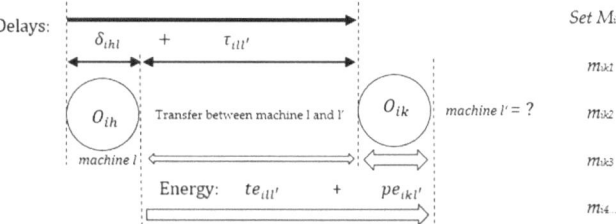

Figure 3. Delays and energy costs for machine assignment to O_{ik}.

Consider now the sets of machines $MM_{ih} = M_{ih} \times \cup_{k \in \Gamma_{ih}^{-1}} M_{ik}$, $h = 1$ to S_i and their associated energy costs. In large job shops, several machines may be identical, with almost equal transport time and energy between some pairs of machines. Pairs (l, l') with the same total transfer energy costs can be grouped into the same subset, and these subsets can be ranked by increasing energy costs. Let MM_{ih}^w be these sets, with $w_i = 1$ to W_i, where $MM_{ih} = \oplus_{w_i=1}^{w_i=W_i} MM_{ih}^w$. Here, MM_{ih}^1 is the subset of pairs with the minimum total (transportation and processing) energy costs, while $MM_{ih}^{W_i}$ is the subset of pairs with the highest energy cost.

It is important to note that the operations that can be candidates to be assigned a machine are those for which all their predecessor operations have already been assigned and scheduled. Then, the operations of each job are addressed by increasing rank in the corresponding DAG. The scheduling approach is a greedy one, so idle periods of machines may happen, but on the other side, decisions about machines will only consider their next free time up to the end of the working period, which is much easier to treat. It is important to also observe that, contrary to the approach presented in the previous section, in this case, the machine assignment to operations is performed step by step in the timeline.

4.2. Algorithm of the Scheduling Heuristic

The algorithm is composed of three stages: The first stage initializes the values of the different variables and sets, and the second stage assigns a machine and a time schedule to the earliest possible operation of any job. This stage is repeated until all the operations of all the jobs have been assigned a machine and scheduled a processing time. In the third stage, the feasibility of the obtained solution is assessed to conclude the assignment or to widen the set of machines to perform critical operations.

Adopted notations for varying quantities and sets used by the algorithm in the solution-building process include the following:

Γ_{ik}^U: the set of predecessors of operation k in job i, which have not been used to process O_{ik}. Γ_{ih}^D: the set of successor operations of operation O_{ih} in job i, which have not been processed. GL_{ir} is the subset of operations of job i at rank r. GU_{iu}: the set of operations of job i at rank u in DAG_i, which have unprocessed successor operations. GD_{iu}: the set of operations of job i at rank u in DAG_i, which are not completely processed. $nft(l)$: the next free time of machine l until the end of the working period. J_a: the set of active jobs, i.e., jobs whose activities have not been completely processed.

Figure 4 shows a flowchart of the proposed heuristic, which is described in detail afterward in Algorithm 1.

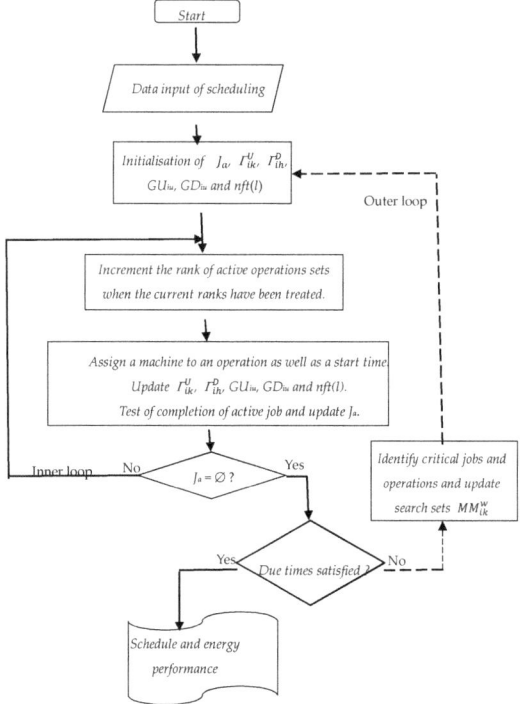

Figure 4. Flowchart of proposed heuristic.

Algorithm 1: Proposed Scheduling Algorithm

(0) Initialization of the solution process.
$i = 1$
While $i \leq n$ do
$\quad k = 1$, $t_{ik} = rt_i$, $\delta_{ik} = 0$, $w_i = 1$, $u_i = 1$, $u = 1$, $l = 1$;
$\quad$ While $u \leq dr_i$
$\quad\quad GU_{iu} = GL_{iu}$ and $GD_{iu} = GU_{iu}$
$\quad$ End While u
$\quad\quad$ While $k \leq S_i$
$\quad\quad\quad t_{ik} = Est_{ik}$ and $\quad \Gamma^D_{ik} = \Gamma_{ik}$ and $\Gamma^U_{ik} = \Gamma^D_{ik}$
$\quad\quad$ End While k
End While i
While $l \leq m$ do
$\quad nft(l) = 0$
End While l
$J_a = \{1, 2, \ldots, n\}$ is the set of active jobs.
End of initialization

(1) Inner loop: Iteration on the schedule of the next operation and selection of machine to process it.

While $J_a \neq \emptyset$ do
$\quad$ Shift of rank in the DAGs:
$\quad\quad \forall i \in J_a :$ if $GD_{iu_i} = \emptyset$, increment u_i: $u_i = u_i + 1$.
$\quad$ Select the next job, operation to be processed and machine on the time line:
$\quad\quad$ Choose (i^*, h^*, k^*, l^*) such as:

$$(i^*, h^*, k^*, l^*) = \underset{i \in J_a, O_{ih} \in GU_{iv}, 1 \leq v < u_i, O_{ik} \in GD_{iu_i}}{\operatorname{argmin}} \left\{ \max_{(l_{ih}, l) \in MM^{w_i}_{ik}} \{t_{ih} + \delta_{ihl_{ih}} + \tau_{il_{ih}l}, nfl(l)\} \right\} \quad (24)$$

$\quad$ Update the subsets of active operations:
$\quad\quad \Gamma^D_{i^*h^*} = \Gamma^D_{i^*h^*} - \{O_{i^*k^*}\}$ and if $\Gamma^D_{i^*h^*} = \emptyset : \; GU_{iu_{i^*-1}} = GU_{iu_{i^*-1}} - \{O_{i^*h^*}\}$
$\quad\quad \Gamma^U_{i^*k^*} = \Gamma^U_{i^*k^*} - \{O_{i^*h^*}\}$ and if $\Gamma^U_{i^*k^*} = \emptyset : \; GD_{iu_{i^*}} = GD_{iu_{i^*}} - \{O_{i^*k^*}\}$
$\quad$ Machine assignment and start time update:
$\quad$ The machine assigned to $O_{i^*k^*}$ is $l_{i^*k^*} = l^*$ and its earliest start time is updated to:

$$t_{i^*k^*} = \max\{t_{i^*k^*}, \max\{t_{i^*h^*} + \delta_{i^*h^*l_{i^*h^*}} + \tau_{i^*l_{i^*h^*}l}, nfl(l^*)\}\} \quad (25)$$

$\quad$ Update next free time of machine $l_{i^*k^*}$:

$$nft(l_{i^*k^*}) = t_{i^*k^*} + \delta_{i^*k^*l_{i^*k^*}} \quad (26)$$

$\quad$ Closing job i:
$\quad\quad$ If $k_{i^*} = S_{i^*}$ and $\Gamma^U_{i^*k^*} = \emptyset$, job i is completed, then: $J_a = J_a - \{i^*\}$
End While J_a

For a given production plan, the finite number of iterations is upper-bounded by the sum of the number of operations in the different DAGs, and the finite number of operations inside an iteration is majored by $n \cdot S^2 \cdot \mu$, where $S = \max_{i=1 \text{ to } n} S_i$ and $\mu = \max_{i,k} \left| MM^{\bar{w}_i}_{ik} \right|$ which is upper-bounded by m^2. Then, the time complexity of this heuristic is polynomial (P). This heuristic can therefore claim to provide, within a reduced computational time, a feasible solution, aimed at energy savings, to production plans with large dimensions (the number of jobs, the number of operations per job, and the number of machines).

4.3. Illustration of the Assignment and Scheduling Process of the Proposed Heuristic

To illustrate the core of the new assignment process represented by relation (24), Figure 5 represents a situation after seven machine assignments and scheduling of the operations of the jobs considered in Section 2.2. For the eighth iteration of the inner loop of the algorithm, the active rank of job 1 is 4, with candidate activity O_{15} for machine assignment and scheduling; for job 2, the active rank is also 4, with candidate activities O_{24} and O_{25}; and finally, for job 3, the active rank is 3, with candidate activity O_{33}.

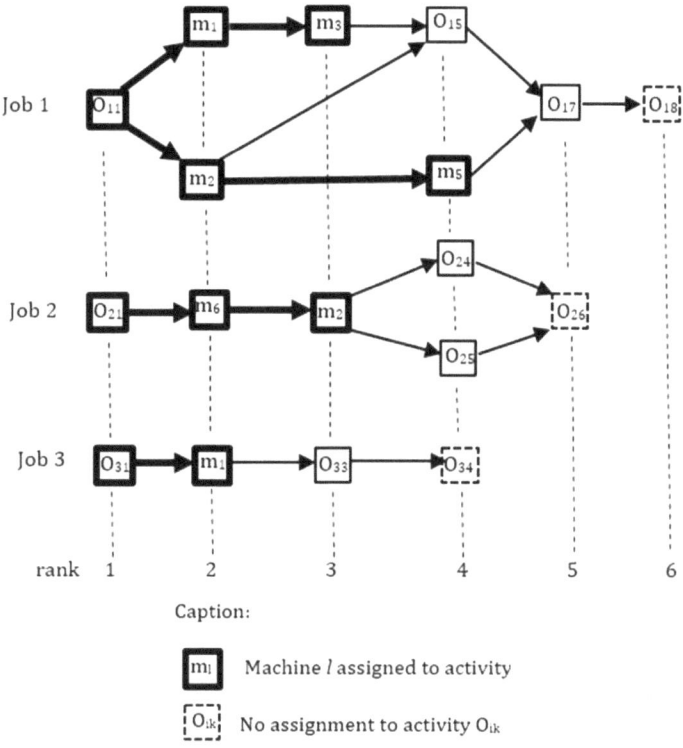

Figure 5. Current machine assignment after 7 iterations of the inner loop.

Here, only numerical values necessary to understand the selection process of Equation (24) are introduced. Table 2 gives the next free times for the seven machines; Table 3 gives the end time of already scheduled and assigned operations, and Table 4 gives the added delays and energies resulting from a machine assignment to each candidate operation in the active rank of each job.

Table 2. Current next free times for the machines in the job shop.

Machine l	1	2	3	4	5	6	7
$nft\ (l)$	0+12	0+14	0+17	0	0	0+7	0

Table 3. End time of assigned parent operations.

Operations	O_{15}	O_{24}	O_{25}	O_{33}
O_{13}	17	------	------	------
O_{14}	5	------	------	------
O_{23}	------	12	12	------
O_{32}	------	------	------	7

Table 4. Added delays/energies with machine assignment.

	O_{15}	O_{24}	O_{25}	O_{33}
m_3	8/100	12/80	10/120	------
m_4	10/80	8/140	10/100	------
m_5	------	10/100	6/140	------
m_6	------	------	------	14/60
m_7	------	------	------	12/90

Now, assuming that the sets MM_{ik} for the candidate operations are subdivided in two subsets according to the spent energy and are given by $MM^1_{15} = \{m_4\}$, $MM^2_{15} = \{m_3\}$, $MM^1_{24} = \{m_3, m_5\}$, $MM^2_{24} = \{m_4\}$, $MM^1_{33} = \{m_6\}$, and $MM^2_{33} = \{m_7\}$, the earliest start time for O_{15} is $max\{0, 17 + 10\}$; for O_{24}, it is $min\{max\{14, 12 + 8\}, max\{14, 12 + 10\}\}$; and for O_{33}, it is $max\{0, 7 + 14\}$. Then, at this stage, relation (24) produces $i^* = 3$, $k^* = 3$, $h^* = 2$, and $l^* = 3$, i.e., at this stage, operation O_{33} is scheduled at $t_{33} = 20$, and machine m_3 is assigned to process it.

The local decision rule of this heuristic, which first addresses the temporal constraints by considering the most quickly available machines to perform an operation, before making a choice based on energy consumption, seems adapted to the situation of flexible workshops where different machines can perform the same operations.

4.4. The Resulting Solution, Assessment, and Adaptation (Outer Loop of Algorithm)

The solution (written without the asterisk symbol) provides, for each job, the starting time and the assigned machine for each operation: t_{ik} and l_{ik} for $k = 2$ to $S_i - 1$, $i = 1$ to n.

The completion time of job i is $ct_i = t_{iS_i} + \delta_{iS_il_{S_i}}$ and the energy necessary to perform the jobs is given by

$$E = \sum_{i=1}^{n} E_i = \sum_{i=1}^{n} \sum_{k=2}^{S_i-1} ep_{ikl_{ik}} + \sum_{h=1}^{S_i-1} \sum_{k \in \Gamma_{ih}} te_{il_{ih}l'_{ik}} \quad (27)$$

If the following conditions are satisfied,

$$ct_i \leq dt_i \quad i = 1 \text{ to } n \quad (28)$$

the proposed solution composed of the selected machines and schedules is feasible.

When one or more conditions (28) are not satisfied, it means that some jobs are over-delayed in queues at machines corresponding to minimum-energy steps, and a new feasible solution must be found. For that, let us widen the search process to less energy-efficient machines to process critical jobs in the current solution. These critical jobs include

$$I_c = \{i \in I \text{ with } ct_{ij} > dt_i\} \quad (29)$$

Considering the succession of restrictions in the process of a job and the competition for energy efficient machines, the difference t_{ik}-Est_{ik} is expected to increase with k for a given job i. However, a large variation of this difference from an operation to the next can be interpreted as the presence of a queue to use machine l_{ik}. Then, for the operation

O_{ik}, the search for an energy-efficient machine will be relaxed by increasing the index w_i and searching in sets $MM_{ik}^{\bar{w}_i}$ of relation (24). To avoid a large degradation in the energy performance, this will be performed for the most critical operation k_{ic} of each critical job, where k_{ic} is given by

$$k_{ic} = \underset{k, 2 \leq k \leq S_i - 1}{\operatorname{argmax}} \{(t_{ik+1} - Est_{ik+1}) - (t_{ik} - Est_{ik})\} \quad i \in I_c \quad (30)$$

and the search for the next free machine to perform operation $O_{ik_{ic}}$ will be performed now over the sets

$$MM_{ik_{ic}}^{w'_i} \text{ with } w'_i = w_i + 1 \quad i \in I_c \quad (31)$$

Another solution could be, when the machines have different regimes of operation, to choose faster regimes of operation in the critical sets $MM_{ik_{ic}}^{w_i}$. The search process must be restarted until conditions (28) are met. If, after many iterations of this process, conditions (28) are not met and no progress is achieved with respect to the completion times, the current solution, which is a feasible one with respect to all the other constraints, should be adopted, and the current completion times should be considered as new due times.

4.5. Dynamic Scheduling with Heuristic

What can be accomplished to face a dynamic workshop environment with the objective of preserving the energy efficiency of the computed schedule depends on the nature and the magnitude of the disruption:

4.5.1. Small Delays

To cope with small delays that are observed or expected in the processing of operations, once a scheduling solution is obtained, it should be of interest to compute from it the current time margins (total, free, and certain margins) and to check if the delay can be absorbed by the margin of interest. If this is not sufficient, some machines operating, or operating a late operation, may be speed up, but in general, at an increase of energy cost.

4.5.2. Programmed Unavailability of Machines

To cope with programmed unavailability of machines (maintenance of condition, for example), the production plan can include a dummy job whose unique activity is the maintenance of the machine with release and due times corresponding to the planned maintenance period.

4.5.3. Sudden Breakdown of Machines

To cope with a sudden breakdown of a machine that is or is not in operation, first estimates of its reparability and, if repairable, its repair time, must be performed. Then, if the resulting delay until repair cannot be absorbed by time margins and, if other machines able to perform the directly impacted operations are not available, a complete rescheduling must be computed with the new expected situation during the work period.

4.5.4. Modification of the Production Plan

To cope with a new arriving order with jobs during the current working period, one option could be to use the idle slots of the machines in the current schedule, but with the risk of choosing the less energy efficient ones that have been bypassed by the current optimal schedule. Another option, often the only feasible one, is to compute a new solution for problem (9)–(16) where the current state of the jobs is updated to their current state of completion: the remaining operations of jobs partially processed, the release times of operations currently under processing, and the next free time for a machine under operation or under maintenance or repair. The rationale of the proposed heuristic is that the scheduling up to the release date of the new jobs remains unchanged, avoiding disruptions in the job shop operations. In the case of a continuum of new job arrivals, the rationale of the proposed heuristic, the earliest start time, should limit the accumulation of late jobs. The responsiveness of this last solution will depend not only on the calculation time of the new schedule but mostly on the time necessary to update the input data of the problem.

5. Evaluation of the Proposed Scheduling Heuristic

The purpose of this section is to comprehensively assess the behavior of the proposed heuristic by comparing it with priority rules for flexible job shop problems. The operation of the proposed heuristic was described in detail in Section 4.3 through an example. Several benchmarks are available in the literature [41] to compare heuristics for flexible job-shop problems, particularly minimizing the make-span of production plans. However, in these benchmarks, due times for jobs, as well as costs and delays associated with transfers between machines, are not considered in general. Since the operation of the proposed heuristic is totally deterministic, it seemed to us that instead of carrying out a cumbersome statistical evaluation, as should be performed with complex metaheuristic involving random processes, it seemed more judicious to us to explain why this heuristic produces better results than priority rules of the same class, i.e., greedy deterministic constructive ones, where the schedule solution is constructed step by step from scratch through deterministic processes according to a local evaluation of a criterion [42].

5.1. Priority Rules for Flexible Job Shop Scheduling

Simple priority rules were developed first for jobs processed by a single machine and then for jobs composed of a string of operations to be processed on given machines in a job shop; a survey classifying tens of them is given in [43]. When the objective is to minimize the make-span of a production plan, one of the more intuitive priority rules is the Shortest Processing Time (SPT) algorithm, which prioritizes operations based on their processing times, with the shortest operations being handled first. Since the focus in this study is on minimizing total energy, a new basic rule, a counterpart of SPT, can be introduced: the Smaller Processing Energy (SPE), whose algorithm prioritizes tasks based on their processing energy, with the more energy-efficient tasks being selected first. However, when considering flexible job shop scheduling, this is not sufficient, since some operations can be processed concurrently on different machines. Then, in this case, a priority rule must address two sub problems [44]: machine assignment and job sequencing. In the schedule of a flexible job shop, when an operation of a job is planned to finish to be processed on a machine at some scheduled time, the schedule must provide two pieces of information:

- Which machine will process the next operation of that job?
- What will be the next operation of a job processed by that machine?

The successive answers to the first question can describe the processing of the jobs according to the schedule. In contrast, the successive answers to the second question can describe the load plan of each machine according to this same schedule. The answer to the second question results from the choice of an operation among the ones waiting at that machine. If the queue of operations at that time is empty, the machine becomes idle until new operations are assigned to it. Simple priority rules will tackle these two decision problems in sequence and not simultaneously, contrarily with what is achieved in the heuristic proposed in this study with relation to (24). Then, in the case of a flexible job shop, a priority rule will have first to assign, for each operation, a machine, and then schedule each operation on its assigned machine. It is important to observe that assigning each operation a priori to a machine according to its processing time or processing energy for this operation would result in priority rules that are much simpler to implement, but this could generate additional delays since it would be necessary to wait for the machine previously assigned to an operation to become free, while other machines may be available earlier. Then, two on-line priority rules, which can be seen as extensions of SPT and SPE to the flexible case of job shop scheduling, are considered for comparison with the proposed heuristic:

- One focusing on processing time, named TTE (indicating Time–Time–Energy according to the nature of the criterion considered at each stage of the priority rule), where the machine is able to process earlier that operation is assigned to it and where the operation to be next processed among the waiting operations of a machine is chosen according to SPT. When different machines have the same fastest processing time for an operation, the one with the smallest processing energy will be assigned to it, and in case of equal energy performance, a random choice will be made among them. If different queuing operations at the same machine have the same processing time, the FIFO rule is applied.
- One focusing on processing energy, named ETT (for Energy–Time–Time), where a machine is able to process with the minimum energy that operation is assigned to it, while the operation to be next processed among the waiting operations of a machine is also chosen according to SPT. In the case of machines with equal processing energy performance, the one with the shortest processing time will be assigned to it, and in the case of an equal processing time, a random choice will be made among these waiting operations. If different queuing operations at the same machine have the same processing time, the FIFO rule is also applied.

5.2. Comparison of Performances Between the Heuristic and the Priority Rules

Figure 6 displays a local situation where several operations, represented by black dots, are candidates to be assigned to different machines according to the proposed heuristic (called HET), the ETT, and the TTE heuristics. There, the abscissa and the ordinate inform, respectively, for each candidate solution, its additional energy cost (δe) and resulting delay (δd). According to the description of the three different decision processes, the heuristic selects a local solution that has intermediate performance in terms of additional energy and delay ($\delta e_{ETT} \leq \delta e_H \leq \delta e_{TTE}$ and $\delta d_{TTE} \leq \delta d_H \leq \delta d_{ETT}$).

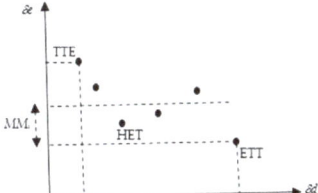

Figure 6. Example of local decision space.

To illustrate the propagation of this property, let us consider a small flexible job shop, displayed in Figure 7, with three machines (m_1, m_2, and m_3) with two jobs (J_1 and J_2), composed of two operations (O_{11} and O_{12}) and (O_{21} and O_{22}). The operations O_{11} and O_{21} can be performed either with machine m_1 or with machine m_2, while operations O_{12} and O_{22} are performed with machine m_3. The processing and transfer costs (delays and energies) are given by d/e in the figure.

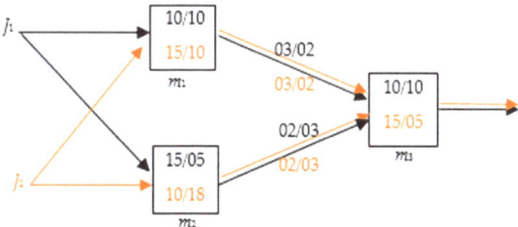

Figure 7. Small flexible job shop (job 1 in black; job 2 in orange).

The application of the heuristic and the two priority rules leads to the schedules displayed in Figure 8, with the performances displayed in Table 5.

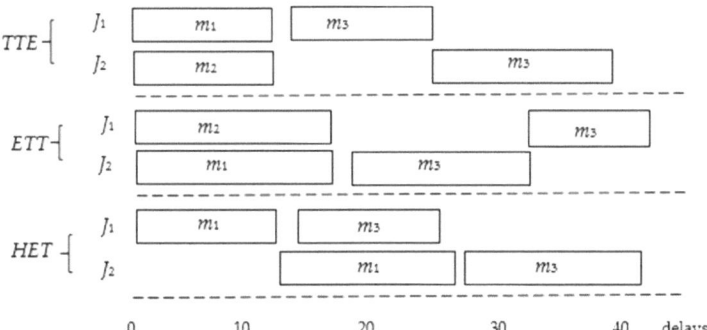

Figure 8. GANTT diagrams of the different heuristics.

Table 5. Comparison of performances between heuristic and priority rules.

Heuristic	TTE	ETT	HET
Make-span	38	43	42
Energy	48	35	40

Given the above, it appears that the proposed heuristic produces performances that are midway between minimizing the make-span and minimizing the processing and transfer of energy. This result appears to be favored by two conditions: on the one hand, the existence of an inverse relationship between time and energy required on two machines capable of carrying out the same operation (the faster machine expending more energy), and, on the other hand, if the structure of the production plan induces between the machines of the job shop, a rank in accordance with the solution building process of the heuristic.

5.3. Illustration of Resulting Scheduling in a Flexible Job Shop

The number of jobs n and the number of machines m are equal to 7, and the job shop is organized into three rows of machines to process raw material (job 1 and job 2), semi-raw material (job 3, job 4, and job 5), and semi-finished products (job 6 and job 7). The machines of the job shop and the possible connections between them are represented in Figure 9. There, jobs 1 and 2 have three operations; jobs 3, 4, and 5 have two operations; and jobs 6 and 7 have one operation. To these operations, a dummy initial and a dummy final operation are added for each job. For job 1, operation O_{12} can be performed by machines 1 and 2, operation O_{13} can be performed by machines 3 or 4, and operation O_{14} can be performed by machine 6. For job 2, operation O_{22} can be performed by machines 1 and 2, operation O_{23} can be performed by machines 3 or 4, and operation O_{24} can be performed by machine 7. For job 3, operation O_{32} can be performed by machine 4, and operation O_{33} can be performed by machines 6 or 7. For job 4, operation O_{42} can be performed by machine 3, and operation O_{43} can be performed by machines 6 or 7. For job 5, operation O_{52} can be performed by machine 5, and operation O_{53} can be performed by machine 6 or 7. For job 6, operation O_{62} can be performed by machine 6. For job 7, operation O_{72} can be performed by machine 7. This shows that there is flexibility in the assignment of machines to some operations of each job.

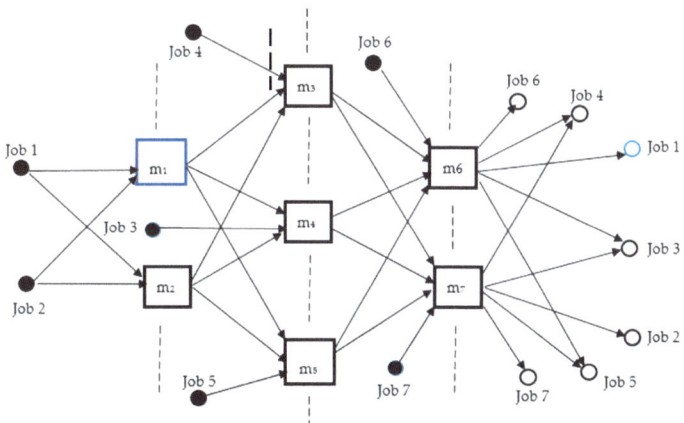

Figure 9. The considered job shop.

The following tables provide data on the operations' processing times and energy per machine (Table 6), the transportation delays and energy between machines (Table 7), and finally, the release and due times (Table 8).

Table 6. Processing delays/energy per jobs and machines.

Machines	m_1	m_2	m_3	m_4	m_5	m_6	m_7
Job 1	8/50	12/40	15/70	15/60	---	10/50	---
Job 2	10/55	7/40	---	15/70	15/55	---	8/60
Job 3	---	---	---	8/30	---	15/30	15/25
Job 4	---	---	15/50	---	---	10/40	8/45
Job 5	---	---	---	---	10/60	6/60	10/50
Job 6	---	---	---	---	---	12/50	---
Job 7	---	---	---	---	---	---	15/55

Table 7. Transportation delays and energy.

Delay/Energy	m_1	m_2	m_3	m_4	m_5	m_6	m_7
m_1	---	---	5/5	5/5	8/10	---	---
m_2	---	---	8/10	5/5	5/5	---	---
m_3	---	---	---	---	---	5/15	8/10
m_4	---	---	---	---	---	5/5	5/5
m_5	---	---	---	---	---	8/10	5/5
m_6, m_7	---	---	---	---	---	---	---

Table 8. Release and due times per jobs.

Jobs	Job 1	Job 2	Job 3	Job 4	Job 5	Job 6	Job 7
Release time	0	15	10	0	10	15	20
Due time	65	65	55	55	55	45	45

Here, only the delays and energy consumption resulting from the transfer of products between machines are considered; they are also supposed to be independent of the type of product that is transported.

The due times were chosen so that the jobs requiring only final machining (jobs 6 and 7) are cleared first to free up space in the job shop for the remaining activities of the other jobs. This is repeated with jobs 3, 4, and 5 concerning jobs 1 and 2.

5.4. Comparison of Results of the Heuristic Concerning the Priority Rules

The results obtained with the proposed heuristic in Section 4 are compared with the results of the priority rules TTE and ETT. When due times are not considered, the range of values for the necessary energy is [725, 785]. The heuristic presented in Section 4 provides a solution after 18 iterations; the obtained scheduling is displayed in Figure 10.

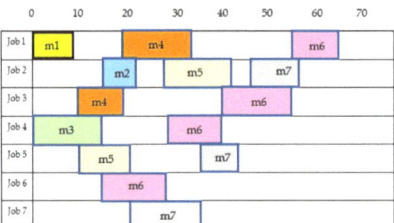

Figure 10. Gantt diagram of HET heuristic solution.

This solution has a total energy cost of 725 with a make-span of 65, while the due times are respected for each job.

Figures 11 and 12 present the corresponding Gantt diagrams, and Table 9 presents a comparison of their performances.

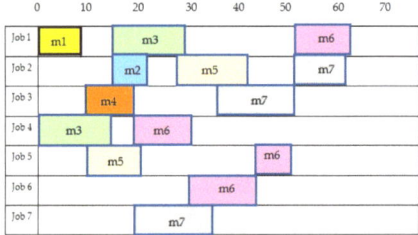

Figure 11. Gantt diagram of TTE solution.

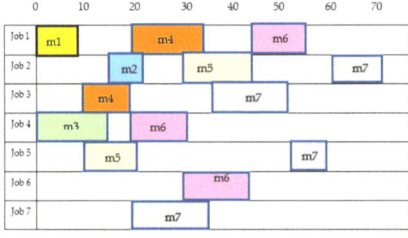

Figure 12. Gantt diagram of ETT solution.

Table 9. Performances of heuristic HET and priority rules TTE and ETT.

	Energy Cost	Make-Span
HET	725	65
TTE	745	62
ETT	725	70

In the considered case study, the proposed heuristic reaches the optimal performance concerning total energy, while due time constraints are satisfied for all the jobs. The TTE priority rule reduces the make-span of the considered production plan (from 65 to 62), but this is achieved at the expense of an increase in the energy cost, which is 33.3% of the total energy variation range [785,725]. Finally, the ETT priority rule achieves the same energy performance as the heuristic, but the two jobs do not comply with their due dates.

6. Conclusions

This study addressed the problem of minimizing the energy spent in a flexible production workshop with the operation of its machines and its internal logistics. The hypotheses retained led to the formulation of a particular scheduling problem that fits well with operational practice in this field. There, the operation of the flexible job shop is considered not as a mere juxtaposition of tasks but as a set of coordinated production flows that can be assigned to different machines. The field of application of this study goes well beyond the scheduling in industrial job shops and, among others, can also cover the operation of intermodal transport terminals. This is particularly important in the case of airport operations when considering the ground handling activities for aircraft at arrival and departure. There, due time constraints have an essential role in guaranteeing the punctuality of departure flights, while the energy consumption and the emissions of the numerous ground handling vehicles must be minimized as much as possible [45].

The optimization problem considered in this study was formulated as a mono-criterion optimization problem, avoiding the introduction of relative weights or the exploration of a Pareto frontier involving energy and make-span. At the same time, the consideration of release and due times allows the integration of a flexible job shop into more global processes of Industry 4.0. Its two-level structure is the result of having adopted as decision variables, besides the scheduling variables of the operations, the assignment of machines to the different operations of the jobs. This two-level structure offers opportunities to use known optimization approaches to obtain exact solutions for real-size instances of this problem. However, considering its computational complexity and the requirements to generate efficient schedules in the dynamic environment of flexible job shops, an ad hoc heuristic was designed.

With this heuristic, the machine assignments to operations are not generated a priori for each job but are constructed step by step according to the information available about the downstream operational state of the job shop. The solution generated by this heuristic derives from a permanent trade-off between energy and delays, where the subsets of candidate machines to perform an operation can be enlarged to include less energy-efficient machines that operate faster, satisfying the due time constraints for each job. This heuristic was applied with success to a small-size case study, where it outperformed two basic scheduling rules. Given the results obtained so far, it seems interesting to evaluate the performance of this heuristic when applied to higher-dimensional problems targeting other application domains.

The present research can be completed following different directions:

- Enlarging the scope of the problem by considering other sources of energy consumption (idle machines, for example).

- Enhancing the efficiency of the heuristic—for example, by integrating priority rules, such as the critical ratio (between the time remaining until the due date and the work time remaining), to better cope with the due date constraints [46].

To further examine the quality of the solutions provided to the minimum-energy flexible job-shop scheduling problem, this study can be a basis for the development of metaheuristics, such as those described in [47,48]. This will allow the use of artificial intelligence techniques to cope more globally with the search for an efficient solution.

Author Contributions: Conceptualization, O.A.O., F.L.P.K. and F.M.-C.; methodology, O.A.O., F.L.P.K. and F.M.-C.; validation, O.A.O., F.L.P.K. and F.M.-C.; investigation, O.A.O., F.L.P.K. and F.M.-C.; writing—original draft preparation, O.A.O. and F.M.-C.; writing—review and editing, F.M.-C.; visualization, O.A.O. and F.L.P.K.; supervision and project administration, F.L.P.K.; funding acquisition, O.A.O. All authors have read and agreed to the published version of the manuscript.

Funding: This research received no external funding.

Data Availability Statement: The original contributions presented in the study are included in the article; further inquiries can be directed to the corresponding author.

Acknowledgments: The corresponding author acknowledges the special logistics support of Durban University of Technology during this research.

Conflicts of Interest: The authors declare no conflicts of interest.

References

1. Shaardan Nur, A.; Roslin Eida, N.; Ahamat, M. Lean Management Concept in Energy Efficiency Improvement in Non-domestic. *Int. J. Appl. Eng. Res.* **2017**, *12*, 15242–15251.
2. Zhang, L.; Li, X.; Gao, L.; Zhang, G. Dynamic rescheduling in FMS that is simultaneously considering energy consumption and schedule efficiency. *Int. J. Adv. Manuf. Technol.* **2016**, *87*, 1387–1399. [CrossRef]
3. Meng, L.; Zhang, C.; Shao, X.; Ren, Y. MILP models for energy-aware flexible job shop scheduling problem. *J. Clean. Prod.* **2018**, *210*, 710–723. [CrossRef]
4. Gahm, C.; Denz, F.; Dirr, M.; Tuma, A. Energy-efficient, scheduling in manufacturing companies: A review and research framework. *Eur. J. Oper. Res.* **2015**, *248*, 744–757. [CrossRef]
5. Tang, D.; Dai, M. Energy-efficient approach to minimizing the energy consumption in an extended job-shop scheduling problem. *Chin. J. Mech. Eng.* **2015**, *28*, 1048–1055. [CrossRef]
6. Xie, J.; Gao, L.; Peng, K.; Li, X.; Li, H. Review on flexible job shop scheduling. *IET Collab. Intell. Manuf.* **2019**, *1*, 67–77. [CrossRef]
7. Dauzière-Pérès, S.; Ding, J.; Shen, L.; Tamssaouet, K. The flexible job shop scheduling problem: A review. *Eur. J. Oper. Res.* **2024**, *314*, 409–432. [CrossRef]
8. Fattahi, P.; Mehraba, M.S.; Jolai, F. Mathematical modeling and heuristic approaches to flexible job shop scheduling problems. *J. Intell. Manuf.* **2007**, *18*, 331–342. [CrossRef]
9. Demir, Y.; Kursat Islayen, S. Evaluation of mathematical models for flexible job-shop scheduling. *Appl. Math. Model.* **2013**, *37*, 977–988. [CrossRef]
10. Chaudhry, I.A.; Khan, A.A. A research survey: Review of flexible job shop scheduling techniques. *Int. Trans. Oper. Res.* **2016**, *23*, 551–591. [CrossRef]
11. Coelho, P.; Pinto, A.; Moniz, S.; Silva, C. Thirty years of flexible job-shop scheduling: A bibliometric study. *Procedia Comput. Sci.* **2021**, *180*, 787–796. [CrossRef]
12. Pezzella, F.; Morganti, G.; Ciaschetti, G. A genetic algorithm for the flexible job-shop scheduling problem. *Comput. Oper. Res.* **2008**, *35*, 3202–3212. [CrossRef]
13. Zheng, Y.; Lian, L.; Mesghouni, K. Comparative study of heuristics algorithms in solving flexible job shop scheduling problem with condition based maintenance. *J. Ind. Eng. Manag.* **2014**, *7*, 518–531.
14. Perroux, T.; Arbaoui, T.; Merghem-Boulahia, L. A mathematical model for the flexible job-shop scheduling problem with availability constraints. *IFAC Pap.* **2023**, *56*, 5388–5393. [CrossRef]
15. Shen, X.N.; Han, Y.; Fu, J.Z. Robustness measures and robust scheduling for multi-objective stochastic flexible job shop scheduling problems. *Soft Comput.* **2017**, *21*, 6531–6554. [CrossRef]

16. Elgendy, A.E.; Hussein, M.; Elhakeem, A. Optimising dynamic flexible job shop problem based on genetic algorithm. *Int. J. Curr. Eng. Technol.* **2017**, *7*, 368–373.
17. Mohan, J.; Lanka, K.; Rao, A.N. A review of dynamic job shop scheduling techniques. *Procedia Manuf.* **2019**, *30*, 34–39. [CrossRef]
18. Echsler Minguillon, F.; Stricker, N. Robust predictive-reactive scheduling and its effect on machine disturbance mitigation. *CIRP Ann.-Manuf. Technol.* **2020**, *69*, 401–404. [CrossRef]
19. Zhou, T.; Zhu, H.; Tang, D.; Liu, C.; Cai, Q.; Shi, W.; Gui, Y. Reinforcement learning for online optimization of job-shop scheduling in smart manufacturing factory. *Adv. Mech. Eng.* **2022**, *14*, 1–19. [CrossRef]
20. Wu, X.; Sun, Y. A green scheduling algorithm for flexible job shop with energy-saving measures. *J. Clean. Prod.* **2018**, *172*, 3249–3264. [CrossRef]
21. Gao, K.; Huang, Y.; Sadollah, A.; Wang, L. A review of energy-efficient scheduling in intelligent production systems. *Complex Intell. Syst.* **2020**, *6*, 237–249. [CrossRef]
22. He, Y.; Li, Y.; Wu, T.; Sutherland, J.W. An energy-responsive optimization method for machine tool selection and operation sequence in flexible machining shops. *J. Clean. Prod.* **2014**, *87*, 245–254. [CrossRef]
23. May, G.; Stah, B.; Taisch, M.; Prabhu, V. Multi-objective genetic algorithm for energy-efficient job shop scheduling. *Int. J. Prod. Res.* **2015**, *53*, 7071–7089. [CrossRef]
24. Liu, Y.; Dong, H.; Lohs, N.; Petrovic, S. A multi-objective genetic algorithm for optimisation of energy consumption and shop floor production performance. *Int. J. Prod. Econ.* **2016**, *179*, 259–272. [CrossRef]
25. Mokhta, H.; Hasani, A. An energy-efficient multi-objective optimization for flexible job-shop scheduling problem. *Comput. Chem. Eng.* **2017**, *104*, 339–352. [CrossRef]
26. Zhang, Z.; Wu, L.; Peng, T.; Jia, S. An Improved Scheduling Approach for \Minimizing Total Energy Consumption and Makespan in Flexible Job Shop Environment. *Sustainability* **2019**, *11*, 179. [CrossRef]
27. Salido, M.A.; Escamilla, J.; Barber, F.; Giret, A.; Tang, D.; Dai, M. Energy efficiency, robustness, and makespan optimality in job-shop scheduling problems. *AI EDAM* **2016**, *30*, 300–321. [CrossRef]
28. Rakovitis, N.; Li, D.; Zhang, N.; Li, J.; Zhang LAnd Xiao, X. Novel approach to energy-efficient flexible job-shop scheduling problems. *Energy* **2022**, *238*, 121773. [CrossRef]
29. Nouiri, M.; Bekar, A.; Trentesaux, D. Towards energy efficient scheduling and rescheduling for dynamic flexible job shop problem. *IFAC Pap.* **2018**, *51*, 1275–1280. [CrossRef]
30. Brandimarte, P. Routing and scheduling in a flexible job shop by tabu search. *Ann. Oper. Res.* **1993**, *41*, 157–183. [CrossRef]
31. Gendreau, M. An Introduction to Tabu Search. In *Handbook of Metaheuristics. International Series in Operations Research & Management Science*; Glover, F., Kochenberger, G.A., Eds.; Springer: Boston, MA, USA, 2003; Volume 57.
32. Lenstra, J.K.; Rinnooy Kan AH, G.; Brucker, P. Complexity of machine scheduling problems. In *Annals of Discrete Mathematics*; Elsevier: Amsterdam, The Netherlands, 1977; Volume 1, pp. 343–362.
33. Olanrewaju, O.A.; Kabuya, K.; Ramirez, L.; Mora-Camino, F. A Model-Based Heuristic for Minimum Energy Scheduling of Flexible Job-Shop Programs. In Proceedings of the IEEE CoDIT 2024 Conference, Valetta, Malta, 1–4 July 2024.
34. Rahmaniani, R.; Crainic, T.G.; Gendreau, M.; Rei, W. The Benders decomposition algorithm: A literature review. *Eur. J. Oper. Res.* **2017**, *259*, 801–817. [CrossRef]
35. Kalashnikov, V.A.; Dempe, S.; Pérez-Valdés, G.; Kalashnykova, N.; Camacho-Vallejo, J.C. Bilevel programming and applications. *Math. Probl. Eng.* **2015**, *2015*, 310301. [CrossRef]
36. Dempe, S.; Zemkoho, A. Springer Optimization and Its Applications. In *Bilevel optimization Advances and New Challenges*; Pardalos, P.M., Thai, M.T., Eds.; Springer: Berlin/Heidelberg, Germany, 2020; Volume 161.
37. Angelo, J.S.; Barbosa HJ, C. A study on the use of heuristics to solve a bilevel programming problem. *Int. Trans. Oper. Res.* **2015**, *22*, 861–882. [CrossRef]
38. Camacho-Vallejo, J.F.; Corpus, C.; Villegas, J.G. Metaheuristics for bilevel optimization: A comprehensive review. *Comput. Oper. Res.* **2024**, *161*, 106410. [CrossRef]
39. Bishop, C.M. *Pattern Recognition and Machine Learning*; Springer: Berlin/Heidelberg, Germany, 2006; ISBN 978-0-387-31073-2.
40. Aytug, H.; Bhattacharyya, S.; Koehler, G.J.; Snowdon, J.L. A review of machine learning in scheduling. *IEEE Trans. Eng. Manag.* **1994**, *41*, 165–171. [CrossRef]
41. Behnke, D.; Geiger, M.J. *Test Instances for Job Shop Scheduling Problems with Work Centers*; Research Report RR-12-01-01; Helmut Schmit University: Hamburg, Germany, 2012.
42. Araujo KA, G.; Birgin, E.G.; Ronconi, D.P. Models, constructive heuristics, and benchmark instances for the flexible job shop scheduling problem with sequencing flexibility and position-based learning effect. *arXiv* **2024**, arXiv:2403.16766.
43. Haupt, R. A survey of priority rule-based scheduling. *OR Spektrum* **1989**, *11*, 3–16. [CrossRef]
44. Demir, Y.; Yilmaz, H. An efficient priority rule for flexible job shop scheduling problem. *J. Eng. Res. Appl. Sci.* **2021**, *10*, 1906–1918.
45. Alonso Tabares, D.; Olanrewaju, O.A.; Krykhtine, F.P.; Felix Mora-Camino, F. Characterizing Airport Ground Handling as a Multi Flexible Flow Shop. In Proceedings of the XXI SITRAER Conference-SBPTA, Fortaleza, Brazil, 16–18 October 2024.
46. Lödding, H.; Piontek, A. The Surprising Effectiveness of Earliest Operation Due-date Sequencing. *Prod. Plan. Control.* **2017**, *28*, 459–471. [CrossRef]

47. Abdolrazzagh-Nezhad, A.; Abdullah, S. A Review on Metaheuristic Approaches for Job-Shop Scheduling Problems. *Data Sci. J. Comput. Appl. Inform.* **2024**, *8*, 45–63. [CrossRef]
48. Fuladi, S.K.; Kim, C.-S. Dynamic Events in the Flexible Job-Shop Scheduling Problem: Rescheduling with a Hybrid Metaheuristic Algorithm. *Algorithms* **2024**, *17*, 142. [CrossRef]

Disclaimer/Publisher's Note: The statements, opinions and data contained in all publications are solely those of the individual author(s) and contributor(s) and not of MDPI and/or the editor(s). MDPI and/or the editor(s) disclaim responsibility for any injury to people or property resulting from any ideas, methods, instructions or products referred to in the content.

MDPI AG
Grosspeteranlage 5
4052 Basel
Switzerland
Tel.: +41 61 683 77 34

Algorithms Editorial Office
E-mail: algorithms@mdpi.com
www.mdpi.com/journal/algorithms

Disclaimer/Publisher's Note: The title and front matter of this reprint are at the discretion of the Guest Editors. The publisher is not responsible for their content or any associated concerns. The statements, opinions and data contained in all individual articles are solely those of the individual Editors and contributors and not of MDPI. MDPI disclaims responsibility for any injury to people or property resulting from any ideas, methods, instructions or products referred to in the content.

www.ingramcontent.com/pod-product-compliance
Lightning Source LLC
LaVergne TN
LVHW072337090526
838202LV00019B/2433